ARMIES AFLOAT

ARMIES AFLOAT

How the Development of Amphibious Operations in Europe Helped Win World War II

John M. Curatola

UNIVERSITY PRESS OF KANSAS

Published by the University Press of Kansas (Lawrence, Kansas 66045), which was
organized by the Kansas Board of Regents and is operated and funded by Emporia
State University, Fort Hays State University, Kansas State University, Pittsburg State
University, the University of Kansas, and Wichita State University.

Library of Congress Cataloging-in-Publication Data

Names: Curatola, John M., 1965– author.
Title: Armies afloat : how the Development of Amphibious Operations in
    Europe Helped Win World War II / John M. Curatola.
Other titles: How US amphibious units in Europe helped win World War II
Description: Lawrence : University Press of Kansas, [2025] | Series: Modern
    war studies | Includes bibliographical references and index.
Identifiers: LCCN 2024031921 (print) | LCCN 2024031922 (ebook) |
    ISBN 9780700638611 (cloth) | ISBN 9780700638628 (ebook)
Subjects: LCSH: World War, 1939–1945—Amphibious operations. | World War,
    1939–1945—Campaigns—Mediterranean Region. | World War,
    1939–1945—Campaigns—Europe. | Amphibious warfare—History—20th
    century. | World War, 1939-1945—Naval operations, American. | World
    War, 1939–1945—Campaigns—Atlantic Ocean. | BISAC: HISTORY / Wars &
    Conflicts / World War II / General
Classification: LCC D784.52.U6 C87 2025 (print) | LCC D784.52.U6 (ebook)
    | DDC 940.54/21—dc23/eng/20241122
LC record available at https://lccn.loc.gov/2024031921.
LC ebook record available at https://lccn.loc.gov/2024031922.

British Library Cataloguing-in-Publication Data is available.

Authorised Representative Details: Easy Access System Europe

Mustamäe tee 50, 10621 Tallinn, Estonia | gpsr.requests@easproject.com

This book is dedicated to the memory of Colonel Kenneth D. Tollefson,
USAF, 1939–2017
Friend, Mentor, American

Contents

List of Illustrations   ix

Introduction   1

1. Join the Army's Navy: Early Amphibious Development   14

2. Hit-or-Miss Affair: Operation Torch, November 1942   49

3. Training as Soon as Possible: FAITC and LANCRAB,
   Spring 1943   87

4. "Can't Get the Air Force to Do a Goddam Thing": Operation
   Husky, July 1943   110

5. As Much as Could Be Expected: Salerno, September 1943   141

6. The Anzio Highway: Central Italy, January 1944   169

7. The Friendly Invasion Before D-Day: Operation Overlord,
   1943–1944   198

8. Faultless on a Large Scale: Operation Anvil/Dragoon,
   August 1944   244

Conclusion   268

Notes   281

Bibliography   335

Index   349

Illustrations

British Landing Craft Assault (LCA) vessel   3

Major Hal Shook in his P-47 Thunderbolt   4

USS *Thompson* during a refueling operation   7

Japanese Type 14 landing craft   22

US Navy Landing Ship Tanks (LSTs) on Normandy Beach   25

Admiral Kent Hewitt during the Torch Campaign   29

Army DUKW vehicle   39

Landing craft crew training at Camp Bradford   42

Landing craft crew training with wooden mock-up at Camp Carrabelle   47

Trek of the Western Naval Task Force   55

Map of Port Lyautey landings conducted by Truscott's "Goal Post"   57

SS *Contessa*   61

US Army P-40 fighters depart USS *Chenago* for Port Lyautey Airfield   63

American troops coming ashore at Fedhala   68

Major General George Patton preparing for landing near Fedhala   69

Safi port facility (Task Force Blackstone's area of operations)   71

USS *Bernadou* deliberately run aground in Safi Harbor   72

Eastern Task Force scheme of maneuver for the capture of Algiers   80

US truck offloads on a British Landing Craft Medium (LCM) east of Algiers   83

Excerpt from Services of Supply report on Operations in North Africa   85

US soldier naval vessel debarkation method   92

Beach organization schematic from a 5th Army Invasion
   Training Center   100

LST (landing ship tank) carrying an LCT (Landing Craft Tank)   102

Landing Craft Infantry (LCI-222)   104

US Navy landing craft pier side at a North African port for
   Husky Landing   106

Map of the final plan for the invasion of Sicily   111

L-4 Grasshopper aircraft on the LST (landing ship tank)
   906 flight deck   121

USS *Brooklyn* after providing NSFS to Joss Force troops   122

Map of the American landings on 10 July 1943   123

Axis aircraft attacking the invasion flotilla at Sicily   126

Western Task Force LST offloads onto a pontoon at the
   Gela Beaches   129

45th ID supplies and equipment coming ashore near Scoglitti   133

LST 314 being waved ashore by a Beach Group signal man   136

Map of major allied units' movements into southern Italy   143

Lieutenant General Mark Clark and Admiral Kent Hewitt
   surveying maps   146

Map of beach landing plans for 9 September   153

US soldiers pinned down by enemy fire at Salerno   159

Map of counterattacks against VI Corps   164

Map of planned assault for Operation Shingle   174

American armor ashore at the port of Anzio   184

Army troops come ashore from the USS *LCI-38* near Anzio   187

DUKW amphibious trucks bring cargo ashore at Anzio   189

Map of VI Corps offense of 1 February 1944 at Anzio   193

English girl by a sign announcing the evacuation of
   Slapton Sands village   207

Map of American convoy movement from western UK ports   213

US troops coming ashore at Slapton Sands   214

Map of the fire support schematic for V Corps on D-Day   217

Map of US Army Air Force Operations for D-Day   229

Diagram of radio nets established at the Army level   234

CTF 122 tonnage ashore during the Normandy campaign 237

Graphic of Mulberry A plan at Omaha Beach 239

Map of planned action for the three-division assault of Anvil/
Dragoon 249

Fire support and transportation area overlays for the 15 August
assault 257

Army shore party and navy beach master's together during
Dragoon 259

LSTs being loaded in Bagnoli Italy in preparation for the
Dragoon D-Day 260

Convoy movement of the Dragoon fleet from various
Mediterranean ports 262

Map of 9th Army Plunder crossing sites for the Rhine River 270

Introduction

Nineteen-year-old Harold Baumgarten, an assistant Browning Automatic Rifle (BAR) operator, came ashore with the first wave on Normandy Beach, 6 June 1944. Assigned to A Company, 1st Battalion, 116th Infantry Regiment, 29th Infantry Division, he was one of the first men to land at Omaha Beach. After arriving in the United Kingdom months earlier, he along with other new joins were sent south by troop train to Plymouth. Shortly after arrival the battalion commander informed the men, "2 out of 3 of you are not going back the states as this unit will be the spearhead for the second front." The new joins quickly assessed the stark reality that lay before them, with some requesting a transfer. But Harold stayed.

Given the planned amphibious assault, his unit was tactically reconfigured for the planned ship-to-shore movement. Because the British-made Landing Craft Assault (LCA) vessel could carry only thirty men, Baumgarten and his fellow soldiers were reorganized into individual boat teams. Given this restructuring the troops lived, ate, and trained as a boat team and not in the standard platoon or squad organizations. Each boat team was reconfigured as a small, combined arms element with a mix of combat engineers, mortar men, machine-gunners, and riflemen. Training on the moors, the troops used landing craft mockups to learn how to debark from the LCAs, provide a hasty defensive perimeter, and attack defensive positions. Training was incessant, and the drills eventually became rote, with the men instinctively trusting their fellow boat teammates to correctly execute their tactical tasks.

For more intense and realistic training the regiment participated in exercises at the newly established American Amphibious Training Center (ATC) at Woolacombe. Located near the Taw Estuary, the facility was eerily similar to that of the Normandy coastline and specifically chosen for this feature. Training at Woolacombe included actual embarkation aboard a vessel, debarkation/ship-to-shore movement, and amphibious assault ashore. Participating in a series of exercises that

1

spring, Harold and his unit conducted live-fire assaults that were so realistic that some men died. Despite these training deaths, years later he recalled, "the exercise[s were] like a picnic compared to D-Day."

On 3 June he and the regiment moved to the Port of Weymouth and boarded the SS *Empire Javelin*. Days later on 5 June at 1700 the ship began steaming out of the harbor and headed east along with the rest of the naval flotilla. Escorted by PT boats and minesweepers, *Empire Javelin* eventually made its way offshore and anchored ten miles off the Dog Green Sector of Omaha Beach (depicted in the opening scene of *Saving Private Ryan*). Eating what might be his last meal, Baumgarten donned his gear, grabbed two bandoliers of .30-caliber ammunition, six clips of BAR ammunition, and prepared himself for the coming assault.

In the early morning darkness at 0330 Harold and his boat team began the process of debarking from *Empire Javelin* and into their assigned landing craft. High sea states (the general surface conditions of a large body of water) combined with a howling wind made the process much more difficult. Once the landing craft was lowered into the churning sea, Harold remembers that it threw the men in the LCA around "like matchsticks."[1] Packed into the tiny craft the men were cold-soaked as sea spray and waves spilled over the gunwales and pooled on the boat's deck. For the next three hours the cold, wet, and seasick men floated in the English Channel awaiting their fates ashore. For most of them, making landfall would provide no reprieve, as conditions would only worsen.

While Harold's team made it ashore, many were not as lucky. Boats were being hit by enemy fire, blown up by mines, or capsized by waves. Reflective of Mother Nature's power and German fires, less than 200 men from the battalion of over 700 made it ashore. Making it to the beach was itself a victory, but many men came off the landing craft carrying over 100 pounds of equipment and were soon swamped by the incoming surf. Countless drowned within yards of dry land without having been hit by enemy fire. Despite making it ashore and clearing the surf, the danger did not abate; twenty-eight of thirty men in Harold's LCA were killed before reaching the shingle (a rocky crest on the beachfront).

As Harold's boat team moved ashore, Major Hal Shook, a P-47 Thunderbolt pilot with 9th Air Force, 404th Fighter Group, 506th Fighter Squadron, flew over the invasion fleet. Stationed at Winkton, England, just off the coast and north of the Isle of Wight, Shook was a 23-year-old squadron commander in charge of sixteen aircraft. Despite his youth, he already had the reputation of being "the best pilot in any

A British Landing Craft Assault (LCA), the type of vessel the 116th Infantry used for movement ashore to the Dog Green Sector of Omaha Beach. (Imperial War Museum photo)

man's air force."[2] His unit's P-47s were a proven design. Nicknamed the "Jug" because of its milk-bottle profile and inelegant lines, the P-47 airframe was surprisingly nimble and powerful and proved an excellent close air support platform. With eight .50-caliber machine guns and hard points on the wings, it carried a formidable array of ordnance. Its R-2800 air-cooled radial engine produced 2,000 horsepower; the plane could sustain heavy damage yet remain airworthy.

Providing cover for the surface fleet as it crossed the channel, Shook's squadron assisted in protecting ship-to-shore movement and troops who made it ashore. In addition to this role, he and his squadron conducted battlefield air interdiction (BAI), hitting German troops and equipment inland. The need for such missions became apparent as previous amphibious assaults were often hampered by Axis aircraft hitting landing craft and other vessels or by enemy armor rolling toward invasion beaches. Given these missions, Hal sortied three times on D-Day, starting at 0500, and remained airborne for over eight hours. Seeing through breaks in the clouds above the assault force he was

Major Hal Shook of the 404th Fighter Group in the cockpit of his P-47 Thunderbolt. Able to withstand enemy fire and carry a large amount of ordnance, the aircraft was an excellent close air support platform. (American Air Museum in Britain photo)

amazed at the magnitude of the operation unfolding beneath him, marveling at the number of ships sailing off the Normandy coast.

Hal's first sortie of the day included leading a formation of aircraft to strike targets in and around Saint-Lô just south of the landing beaches. After this first mission he returned to base and swapped aircraft. He took off again, flew past the invasion beaches, and hit a railyard packed with gear and material while destroying the facility's roundhouse. However, during this second mission he also noticed a collection of German armor nearby. Sending twelve of his sixteen aircraft back to base, he and three other P-47s remained on station, with the four hitting enemy armor, personnel carriers, and staff cars.

Flying low at an airspeed of 300-plus knots, while also trying to avoid colliding with Normandy's hedgerows and man-made structures, he noticed an active antiaircraft gun and immediately turned to silence the weapon. However, in the process the German crew found their mark, and Hal's Thunderbolt took a direct hit on the right wing. The enemy rounds forced the plane's ammunition access door to open, caused the landing gear on that side to drop, and created a four-foot hole in the wing. The resulting drag from the damage flipped the plane violently to the right and almost into the ground at high speed.

Fortunately, Hal's instinctive reflexes took over; with both hands he grabbed the stick, yanked it to the left rear, causing the plane into a climbing left turn, kicking in rudder to counter the roll. As a result of these actions, Hal found himself slowed to 150 knots, at low altitude, over enemy territory. For a few moments he thought he was going in. Able to recover, the limped home and flew more sorties the next day, hitting targets in and around Saint-Lô. Before the war was over Hal would fly over 100 such missions, knocking out more tanks and guns and hitting enemy airfields in support of ground operations.[3]

In addition to Harold's and Hal's efforts, out in the English Channel Irvin Klimas was a sailor aboard the destroyer USS *Thompson* (DD-627). During D-Day his ship provided naval surface fire support (NSFS) to assault units going ashore. Having trained for weeks at many locations throughout the United Kingdom prior to D-Day, *Thompson*'s crew practiced hitting stationary targets, conducting antiaircraft drills, and participating in multiple landing exercises in southern England. On 5 June, *Thompson* along with other ships of Task Group 124.7 escorted Convoy O-1 to the Amphibious Objective Area (AOA) on the Normandy coast.[4] Screening for the larger fleet, *Thompson* arrived off French shores around 0300. That same morning the US Army Air Forces (USAAF) sent heavy and medium bombers over the Normandy beachline, attempting to soften up German defenses. While many of these air strikes hit long and failed to destroy enemy defenses, Irvin viewed this aerial bombardment from safely offshore. The *Thompson* was assigned a location just east of Pointe du Hoc (Point de la Percée) providing support to a special detachment of inbound Army Rangers. The Rangers were given the impossible mission of scaling Pointe du Hoc's near-vertical cliff face and destroy any guns atop the location. Set between the two American landing beaches (Omaha and Utah), artillery at this location could easily range the inbound assault forces. *Thompson*'s mission was to take out targets at Pointe du Hoc, keep the enemy pinned down, and allow the Rangers to scale the cliff's face.[5]

After arriving in the AOA, they commenced firing at 0530. Because of the earlier USAAF bombing and other fire-support actions, smoke obscured many of the targets. Despite this limitation, the ship hit communication towers, gun emplacements, and other installations. Given the naval guns' flat trajectories, the ship's armament had a limited ability for plunging fires. As a result, gunners used proximity-fused shells that detonated about 50 feet above the target. While not hitting the objectives directly, a detonating shell in the vicinity of the target was enough to neutralize the position. With H-Hour set for 0630, the ship ceased fire to avoid hitting the Rangers as they made it ashore. Once the Rangers scaled the cliff and secured the area, *Thompson* and its crew communicated with naval gunfire spotting teams ashore as they called for fire support.[6] Later that day the ship hit three German early-warning Wurzburg radars, toppling the dish arrays and blinding the Germans as to inbound Allied aircraft. At times sailing as close to 1,000 yards off the shoreline with only a few feet of water beneath its keel, *Thompson*'s main mounts also hit targets ashore while its smaller 40mm guns worked with shore-party teams to take out smaller gun nests.[7]

For much of the first day Irvin Klimas was in the plotting room below deck and saw the battle largely from the map board in front of him. However, he did have the opportunity to make his way topside and observed the invasion firsthand. In one such visit he reported seeing an amphibious ship unloading trucks at Omaha Beach, with German guns taking out each vehicle as it rolled ashore. With the accurate enemy fire, he observed the battleship USS *Texas* sail closer to the beachline and engage the enemy positions with its 14-inch guns. After the *Texas*'s impressive salvo, enemy fire stopped, with offload operations continuing. While decisively engaged throughout the day, *Thompson* expended most of its ammunition and had to return to port. After arriving in Weymouth Bay to restock, on 8 June Irvin and crew set sail again for the AOA. For the next few days combat action continued. In the following days the ship screened for Combined Task Force 122 (CTF122), with *Thompson* engaging German E-boats successfully driving off the naval intruder.[8]

These men represent the three domains of land, air, and sea that opened the door for the eventual liberation of Europe. However, unknown to any of them, they were witness to a newfound American core competency: amphibious assault. Forceable entry from the sea was a relatively new application that required detailed planning, coordination, execution. The ground assault echelon of Operation Overlord saw American forces employ naval fires from large- and small-caliber weapons while witnessing airpower engaging targets in the AOA, and providing top cover. In addition, US formations deployed with newly developed littoral craft with sufficient lift for troops and material while using doctrine garnered from previous assaults. While Overlord was certainly rife with mistakes, blunders, and some poorly executed elements, the success of the operation overall overshadowed

USS *Thompson* on 21 April 1944, during an underway refueling operation, while engaging in exercises leading up to operation Neptune. (US Navy photo)

these drawbacks. This operation reflected a significant advancement in American power projection and a combat capability unmatched by any other country. Creating this lodgment on the northwest European continent occurred only through a deliberate, coordinated, and joint effort on the part of all three services. Developing such a capability did not happen overnight or by mere happenstance.

The United States Marine Corps is hailed for the landings at Tarawa, Peleliu, and Iwo Jima, putting regiments and divisions ashore to secure islands during the Pacific War. However, the United States Army conducted larger amphibious operations, placing entire corps and even designated armies ashore to liberate entire countries and continents. From various locations—North Africa, Sicily, Italy, France, the Philippines—the army executed larger and more expansive amphibious operations, projecting combat power ashore and then pushing hundreds of miles inland. As the Marines made history with their exploits in the

Pacific, the US Army conducted all the American amphibious landings in the Mediterranean Theater of Operations (MTO) and subsequently in the European Theater of Operations (ETO). Even in the Pacific, the army acted as a floating reserve, assaulted beaches themselves, or secured the flanks of Marine forces. In the MTO/ETO effort the army alone conducted ten division-size landings.[9] Together in the Pacific and the MTO/ETO, the US Army conducted a staggering 146 amphibious assaults of various sizes.[10]

Reflective of Harold Baumgarten's experience, the opening twenty minutes of the 1998 movie *Saving Private Ryan* depicts horrific images of the D-Day assault. While the movie plot was a fictional account, with artistic liberties taken, aside from the coxswain the characters depicted in the scene were all army soldiers. The formations taken ashore that day were overwhelmingly army, with support coming from the United States Navy and Coast Guard along with the Royal Navy. This most important amphibious assault was not done by Marines but rather by soldiers. However, before the army could launch such an endeavor, it had to learn how to conduct amphibious operations against a contested shore. Along with its navy brethren it had to man, train, and equip formations capable of forceable entry. Creating this capability required a concerted, deliberate effor involving an extensive joint endeavor of air, naval, and ground forces developed over the course of four years. With hundreds of lessons garnered, the process occurred relatively quickly, with changes being implemented in months or at times even weeks.

Amphibious assault is a power-projection capability that utilizes the sea as maneuver space bypassing enemy defenses or seizing the initiative by picking the time and place along a shoreline.[11] Because of the United State's geographical location, its ability to project power by air and/or sea has been a key component of its modern history. During the twentieth century the US military fought on foreign soil, requiring the deployment of formations and equipment to overseas locations. In these conflicts forceable entry via amphibious assault provided the important link in the introduction of US formations into a theater. Gaining access to airfields, ports, and infrastructure has not only served as the objective of many amphibious landings; it often drove larger American strategies. Establishing logistical nodes after an amphibious assault also created conditions for deeper and more decisive operations.

The Marine Corps was already developing doctrine regarding amphibious assault during the interwar years (i.e., between World War I and World War II, 1918–1941). Through exercises, experimentation, and study, the Corps drafted the *Tentative Landing Manual* (TLM) in 1934. Serving as a doctrinal starting point, the TLM established a comprehensive approach to the execution of such operations and identified six basic components of an amphibious assault: command relationships, ship-to-shore movement, naval surface fire support, air support, beachhead establishment, and logistics/communications.[12] While these were sometimes addressed or classified in different ways depending on context, the functions for an amphibious assault boil down to these six essentials. This basic framework endures today, as explained below.

Command relationships. Amphibious operations are inherently joint endeavors, meaning they require at least two or more services to work together toward a common goal. Given this multiservice tasking, who was in charge? The army or the navy? What roles do each of these respective services play and in what domains (land, sea, air)? What commander has the authority to make certain decisions at a given time? While the doctrine placed the navy Commander of the Amphibious Task Force (CATF) in command while at sea, the Commander Landing Force (CLF) was usually a Marine (or a soldier) and subordinate to his navy counterpart while underway. Once the assault launched, the CLF became the "supported" command while the CATF served in the "supporting" role.[13] However, how does the USAAF fit into this structure? Additionally with all these questions, how do the various services work together during planning and execution to achieve an understanding of the roles and responsibilities while achieving a unified goal?

Ship-to-shore movement. While amphibious assault comes from the sea, how does the landing force arrive ashore? To make this movement, the assault force needs platforms capable of operating in surf zones in a littoral environment and also requires a controlled and orderly movement of men and ships ashore. To build combat power on a beach quickly, an amphibious assault force usually required debarkation from a seagoing, troop-carrying ship and then a transfer to a smaller littoral vessel capable of operating in the surf zone. Once this embarkation is completed, landing craft then move in organized, sequential assault waves and sent ashore in an orderly, controlled manner with protection while in transit.[14]

Naval surface fire support. Artillery is a key component of the battlefield and is often referred to as the "king of battle." However, in an amphibious operation, it is jokingly said that "the king can't swim!" Given this limitation, landing forces still require large-caliber weapons providing fire support to the assault. The heavy guns on naval ships can help provide that firepower until artillery has been transitioned ashore in direct support of the landing force. Until that happens, the landing force needs to rely on the support of naval fires.[15] The proximity between troops ashore and the impact of naval fires requires extensive liaison between landing forces and naval gunners. Given this dynamic environment, close coordination and communication are imperative.

Air support. With the advent of the airplane, the battlefield required more consideration of the third dimension. World War I saw the emergence of specific roles and missions for airplanes, such as close air support for troops. Because naval guns have relatively flat trajectories and are subject to tides and other hydrographic concerns, they have inherent limitations. Given those limitations, airpower can often fill in and augment organic capabilities when NSFS is limited. With inherent flexibility and an offensive nature, airplanes have the ability to hit enemy forces in defilade and respond quickly to dynamic taskings while providing significant amounts of firepower.[16]

Beachhead establishment. As amphibious forces come ashore, they need to consolidate any gains made and establish a perimeter for follow-on forces to arrive.[17] Establishment of the beachhead requires the emplacement of defensive positions while additional troops and supplies surge ashore. In essence the beachhead provides necessary breathing space for the amphibious force to grow and develop its combat power. Furthermore, this established beachhead needs to be organized and controlled to prevent chaos. Newly arrived supplies need to be received, accessed, and then placed so they can be retrieved when needed. Follow-on assault waves also need to be received, staged, and directed to their assigned locations. The same works with the evacuation of the wounded as medical personnel establish casualty collection points for return to the flotilla.[18]

Logistics and communications. An often-used axiom for modern warfare is the requirement to "shoot, move, and communicate." The ability to talk to the ships afloat, the aircraft above, the forces coming ashore, and the forces engaging in combat is an imperative. To fully command, control, and coordinate all the resources of an amphibious task force, establishment of radio/communication networks is required. Logistical support is equally important. Resupply of ammunition, food, water, fuel, and other essentials of war must come from the amphibious task force, then be sent ashore and finally organized for distribution under combat conditions. This requires designated beach/shore parties that receive and organize various classes of supplies and associated services and then support the landing force moving inland.[19]

This book addresses American amphibious development and capabilities in the ETO through the lens of these six components. As these six served as the framework for amphibious assault, they do the same here. The main questions addressed are: How did the US military develop these components in support of amphibious operations in the MTO/ETO that liberated parts of two continents? How did organizations with little interest or capability in littoral actions as late as 1940 develop a joint competency in the short span of a few years? This required not only a deliberate focus on the part of the army but also the development of joint capabilities with the navy and USAAF counterparts. Furthermore, what did these services do to create such a powerful capability? With the Marines establishing the doctrinal precepts and devising some of the material solutions for amphibious assault, the army was late in developing a littoral capability. However, starting shortly before the North Africa landings in 1942 and eventually resulting in the Operation Dragoon invasions liberating southern France in 1944, US Army, Navy, and Air Forces, along with our British allies, made significant progress in the field of amphibious assault in the ETO.

First I will focus on the development of army, navy, and USAAF amphibious assault capabilities in the MTO/ETO. The wartime division of labor saw Marines dominate the Pacific theater, with the army largely committed to actions in the MTO/ETO. Given this tasking the army had to consider subsequent land operations once it established itself ashore. I will address concerns pertaining to the initial landings and the subsequent creation and defense of beachheads. Furthermore, unlike in the Pacific theater, where most of the objectives were relatively small islands that did not require a robust campaign inland, the MTO/ETO operations almost always included a major inland component. However, I will not focus on combat operations and movements inland but instead will address them as they become relevant to the establishment and defense of a beachhead. I will address the preparation, assault, and establishment of beachheads and their relevance to the larger campaigns they supported. Addressing subsequent operations ashore will be included only as they pertain to amphibious operations. A review of subsequent operations inland is well covered by other historians and documented in the United States Army's official record of World War II (the "Green Book" series), providing detailed analysis of such inland operations.

Second I discuss American amphibious development specifically against the Axis in the MTO/ETO. This book is not intended to be a treatise on World War II amphibious development in all theaters. Fleet Admiral Chester Nimitz and General Douglas MacArthur's Pacific efforts had their own unique and specific requirements. While the Pacific theater did compete with the MTO/ETO for amphibious assets including landing craft and manpower, the development and execution of army and Marine operations in that theater is already covered voluminously by others including Allen Millet, Donald Miller, and Peter Isely and Phillip Crowl). Such considerations are beyond the scope of the analysis here.

This is not intended to be a critique of the services' combat records during the various assaults or an analysis or accounting of their performances. I focus on the services as learning organizations regarding amphibious assault and the six components. Specifically, what did the services do because of their shared amphibious experiences in the MTO/ETO? What steps did they take after the amphibious operations? How did they adjust? The growth from Torch to Husky, from Avalanche to Overlord, with a climax at Dragoon, was the result of tough lessons. This book illustrates and highlights the many lessons learned.

My review will be limited to the US armed forces. While the Allied formations were drawn from many nationalities and militaries, I address US developments and experiences exclusively. Certainly, Canada, Great Britain, and the other Allied nations had roles to play in many amphibious operations, but those nations' developments and experiences are beyond the scope of this work. How our allies developed their own methodologies and platforms will be addressed only as it pertains to the American experience.

I will also highlight planning considerations for littoral operations for those unfamiliar with the nuts-and-bolts of an amphibious assault. Additionally, I highlight the nuances and details of amphibious operations that are unique and often overlooked by casual observers. While amphibious assaults are akin to airborne assaults, each type has unique features and factors that cannot go unaddressed and require significant, deliberate, and detailed planning when conducting them.

This is more than a historical treatment of World War II. Following America's wars in Iraq and Afghanistan the US Armed Forces would be well advised to reflect on their collective past. Given the contemporary global environment, the rise of Chinese economic and military power, and the sea- and littoral-dominated geography of the Pacific, the US Army and US Navy may indeed be called upon to conduct amphibious operations in a future joint or combined action. With a fifth of the world's population living in South Asia and the potential for competing interests in that region, the study of amphibious operations is once again a growth industry. With a smaller military budget and limited amphibious platforms and capability, the US Army may indeed find itself in a similar situation in the future. Although Marines may bristle at the suggestion, our nation has a rich and successful tradition of casting aside perceived differences among the armed services and pursuing the national interest as a unified force. With this in mind, I aim to illustrate how Americans developed littoral projection in the past while providing some possible touchstones for future applications in the twenty-first century.

1

Join the Army's Navy
Early Amphibious Development

At the end of the nineteenth century the United States began flexing its growing overseas power. Emerging on a global stage, the 1898 war with Spain established US dominance in the Western Hemisphere, removed another European power from the Americas, and led to an American a foothold in the Philippines. During this time most US amphibious operations were largely ad hoc, small-scale affairs with varied results. The detailed planning, specialized equipment, and established procedures used in modern amphibious assaults were still decades away. With General Winfield Scott's successful 1847 expedition to Vera Cruz, Mexico, marginally successful operations during the Civil War, the 1871 American punitive assaults on Korea's Ganghwa Island, along with other minor actions, the United States had a limited experience outside its continental borders including in large-scale amphibious assault.

This inexperience with large-scale expeditionary warfare was on display during the Spanish–American War with the US landings near Santiago, Cuba.[1] US Navy Commander Admiral William Sampson and US Army General William Shafter were the respective commanders, but the American landings and assault ashore were poorly planned, coordinated, and executed. Despite the victory for the United States, the expeditionary operation was plagued by inadequate intelligence, ignorance of hydrography, deficient ship-to-shore platforms, disorganized logistics, limited NSFS, and a lack of communications.[2] Perhaps most important, the army and navy commanders focused on their own service-oriented missions instead of the joint task at hand.[3] A poor understanding of command relationships combined with a vague chain of command undermined a truly joint and unified effort. Despite these problems the Americans prevailed, but work remained if amphibious operations were to be a part of American military application as the nation sought to defended its growing overseas empire.

These problems did not go unnoticed. In 1903 President Theodore Roosevelt, a veteran of the war and former secretary of the navy, established the Joint Army and Navy Board to address the lack of military cooperation and to assist in the coordination of military planning. But service parochialism remained pervasive with no real progress as to joint operations and their associated problems. However, some were looking to confront the issue. In 1907 the Naval War College at Newport, Rhode Island, presented a lecture titled "The Cooperation of the Army and Navy."[4] Authored by Commander H. S. Knapp, the lesson clearly identified the nation as a maritime power requiring defense of America's newly acquired territory. In his remarks Knapp stated "these outlying possessions could not be assured by a navy alone, or by an army alone; hereafter the two services must work together."[5] He went on to argue "without a navy, the army of a maritime nation cannot safely strike offensively overseas, nor can it even assure when acting defensively in preserving the integrity of outlying possessions."[6] In modern parlance Commander Knapp was talking about joint strategic power projection.

Before the advent of airpower, projection of military might resided largely in America's naval flotilla as epitomized by the Great White Fleet. But true power projection also required use of land forces. In such an expeditionary environment the Knapp lecture specified three navy requirements for a campaign: (1) Secure the safe passage of troops; (2) protect and assist in the debarkation of troops; and (3) secure lines of communications and assist in a "tactical way" if required.[7] He identified how the navy needed to support army forces in such a joint effort. He further chastised those who maintained their separate service parochialism as "jealous, narrow-minded men."[8]

With an expanding empire in the Pacific and Caribbean it became ever more apparent that the United States required an expeditionary capability with advanced bases to support naval forces.[9] Increased Japanese military and political influence in Asia eclipsed the centuries-long Chinese hegemony in the area and put the United States and the Chrysanthemum Throne on a collision course. Japan's military successes after the Meiji Restoration, its development of a modern army and navy, along with its expansion on the Asian mainland created new tensions in the Pacific. Competing for markets, resources, and influence, the two nations shared similar political and economic goals in East Asia. Given this emerging threat, the navy's General Board and the Naval War College foresaw a future campaign requiring forward bases to support an American fleet.

Marine Commandant Charles Haywood did not yet grasp the requirement for seizing advanced naval bases as part of the Corps' mission but did see the need for a larger forward presence given the new American possessions.[10] While the idea of supporting what was referred to as "advanced base operations" was emerging, the services themselves were timid in their approaches. The military exercises in the century's first decade saw only minor advancement of the concept. With only a few thousand Marines, the Corps feared the idea of becoming a second land army. As a result, not all the Marine leadership was behind the idea. However, the second decade saw the naval services giving serious thought to the idea as a new Marine Commandant, Major General William Biddle, envisioned the creation of permanent expeditionary companies within each established barracks. Furthermore, he saw the need for an "Advance Base School" to study the defense of expeditionary lodgments.[11] While many still opposed the idea, in 1913 the Secretary of the Navy Josephus Daniels directed the Marines to conduct exercises on the islands of Culebra and Vieques near Puerto Rico to test and develop what was referred to as "advance base concepts."[12] These exercises helped stimulate thinking regarding the idea with the naval'services' interest in the advance base concept continuing to gain momentum.

Although such experiments proved useful and informative, World War I and sustained land operations soon grabbed the attention of the Marine Corps and army. With the revolutions in military affairs provided by the conflict, many other new concepts emerged. Use of armor, aircraft, indirect fire, mechanization, unrestricted submarine warfare, and other innovations paved the way for modern war and captured the imagination of military theorists. Additionally, the war further increased the importance of the United States on the global stage as an industrial, economic, and diplomatic power. While loathe to become a military power, the country was indeed becoming a major actor in world affairs despite its isolationist leanings.

While the war provided plenty of intellectual fodder regarding military innovations, the war also illustrated the challenges regarding amphibious warfare. The failure of 78,000 British, French, and Australian/New Zealand troops in the Dardanelles on the Gallipoli Peninsula provided a "good example of a bad example."[13] Intended to provide a knockout blow to the Ottoman Empire and relieve pressure on the Russian Caucasus Front, the Allied operation resulted in a bloody stalemate and an embarrassment for the First Lord of the British Admiralty, Sir Winston Churchill. Starting in April 1915 and lasting approximately eight months, Allied forces successfully landed ashore but failed to dislodge the Turkish defenders or make any significant headway. Combined with an epidemic of dysentery, the operation quickly became a fiasco as reinforcements failed to arrive and poor interservice coordination yielded little results. Through a lack of air support, inadequate NSFS, and poor logistics against a well-led and determined foe, the Allied amphibious operation bogged down.[14] Many of the reasons for the Gallipoli failure reflected those of the 1898 American experience in Cuba as coordination between the naval and ground forces remained poor.

However, this more recent event had much to teach students about amphibious assault and ship-to-shore movement. With the advent of modern weapons and their increased lethality, the results of an amphibious assault were seen as more costly—if not suicidal. Lack of efficient ship-to-shore movement platforms, beachhead organization, effective communications, and joint operations hobbled the offensive as assault forces had to rapidly build combat power ashore in the face of enemy defenses. After landing the Allied troops faced machine guns, long-range artillery, and prepared positions that precluded a successful assault from the sea.

After World War I most military planners gave little consideration to amphibious operations. If another war occurred, it would resemble the last fight, with large-scale deployment of troops and equipment to established ports for subsequent movement inland. France and England would again provide forward staging bases against a potential European foe, with the Asia-Pacific theater seen as largely a naval fight with capital ships slugging it out on the high seas. Having to fight one's way ashore was not given serious consideration.

Despite the failure of the Gallipoli expedition, not everyone was dismissive of amphibious assault. With its previous experiments regarding advance basing before the war, the Marine Corps renewed its interest in expeditionary operations. After the 1918 Armistice the Corps placed its emphasis, and institutional survival, on the development of the advance base concept. Trying to establish its niche in the American military establishment, the Corps assumed the lead in amphibious warfare development. In 1921 Marine Major Earl "Pete" Ellis, working at the behest of Marine Commandant Lieutenant General John A. Lejeune, conducted a detailed analysis of Pacific theater island chains in preparation for a possible war against Japan.[15] His efforts resulted in the publication in July 1923 of *Operations Plan 712: Advance Base Operations in Micronesia*. This document helped frame the problem of modern amphibious assault decades before their wartime execution. Working tirelessly, Ellis identified material requirements, crafted methodologies, and suggested structure and organization for expeditionary warfare campaigns in the Pacific theater. Lejeune approved Ellis's study and used it as a foundation for interwar Marine exercises, equipment procurement, and education.[16] Many of his ideas, concepts, and material requirements would indeed come to fruition as America entered the war and built an amphibious assault fleet that resembled Ellis's vision.

Without many historical examples to rely on, Marine Corps schools deliberately set out in 1933 to analyze the Gallipoli Campaign, conducting a monthlong classroom exercise. At the end of the study students identified the lessons of the failed expedition and presented their analysis to the faculty.[17] The Corps' schools also focused on future expeditionary problem sets analyzing offensive and defense operations in the Pacific under the auspices of War Plan Orange.[18] Additionally, the fleet exercises (FLEX) provided useful practical lessons for the development of amphibious warfare tactics, techniques, and procedures. The exercises, combined with the intellectual and academic efforts, allowed the Corps to compile what is perhaps its biggest contribution to the upcoming global conflict, the 1934 *Tentative Landing Manual*.

Between 1934 and 1938 the Marine Corps continued to refine its doctrine and went on to publish three editions of the Fleet Training Publication (FTP), titled *Landing Operations Doctrine (FTP-167)*.[19] As mentioned in the introduction, these seminal amphibious treatises outlined the basic principles of amphibious operations and identified six critical components: command relationships, ship-to-shore movement, naval gunfire support, aerial support, securing the beachhead, and logistics/communications.[20] These functions required significant joint operations, mutual understanding, and unity of effort between the Marine Commander of the Landing Force and Navy Commander of the Amphibious Task Force. *FTP-167* established the CLF as the supported command and the CATF as the supporting effort once troops had crossed the Line of Departure (L/D).[21] Up until crossing the L/D, both commanders were coequal in planning, but the CATF was the lead for the joint effort while troops remained embarked. The habitual relationship between the US Marine Corps and the US Navy paid dividends in the Pacific War, especially during the island-hopping campaign. (Though not without its exceptions.) However, for the ETO this kind of cohesion and mutual understanding would require the building of a new relationship between traditional rivals in the

Department of the Navy and the War Department. Each service continued to view the other with suspicion, and establishing such a relationship was a challenge, as neither service was particularly interested in amphibious warfare.

In addition to the various doctrinal publications, material solutions were also required. Marines continued practical experimentation at Culebra and other locations and developed efficient and practical ship-to-shore platforms.[22] Until this time in the United States there were no real developments in littoral craft specifically designed for amphibious assault. While the British took interest in developing such vessels, the American movement of men and material from ship to shore was done with existing navy launches and skiffs. Hardly conducive to amphibious assaults, these existing designs were heavy, slow, and often unstable in certain surf conditions. Furthermore, their screws and rudders were unprotected, leaving them prone to damage or fouling in shallow or vegetation-infested waters.[23]

Keynote to this development was the acquisition of the legendary Higgins Boat, which was the basis for US landing craft in World War II. Designing watercraft for use in the shallow waters of Louisiana's bayous in the 1920s, Andrew Higgins had gained a reputation as a builder of tough, reliable, and sturdy boats capable of operating in shallow waters. Before his relationship with the navy and Marines, many of his designs were already in service with the Coast Guard in its anti-smuggling operations during the years of Prohibition (a result of the Volstead Act), the Army Corps of Engineers, and the Biological Survey Agency.[24] Despite supporting government agencies, Higgins was not above shenanigans. An entrepreneur at heart, he sold littoral craft to the Coast Guard, then approached rum smugglers and told them of the boats he designed for the government. He then leveraged that illicit relationship to design better boats for the smugglers![25]

Perhaps his most innovative littoral design was realized by mistake while working on a new platform in 1926. An oversight in construction led to a (fortunate) distortion of the vessel's hull. The distortion forced water out of the boat's forequarters and aft. As a result, objects in the ship's line of travel were repelled by the distinct wave action' with water hyacinths and other obstacles forced away from the vessel's screws. Additionally the boat was stable, and maneuverable, and drafted only ten inches of water. Because it solved several technical and hydrological challenges, it was named *Eureka* and served as the starting point for American landing craft designs.[26]

Submitted for consideration with the navy, Higgins's design was turned down by the navy's Board of Construction and Repair (BCR) in 1928. It considered his designs "nice" but were unimpressed. Having their own shallow-water design, the BCR was uninterested in any outside proposals. Undaunted, Higgins in 1934 visited the Marine Corps at Quantico, Virginia, which showed great interest in his innovation. Under the hierarchy of the Department of the Navy, the Marines had little say in the procurement and development of watercraft. After all, it was the navy's job, not the Marines', to build ships. With limited budgets in the interwar years, navy priorities focused largely on engagements on the high seas with battleships and other oceangoing blue-water platforms. With the Marines as the lesser in an unequal relationship, and distrustful of navy bureaucracy, the Higgins–USMC relationship was simpatico and bloomed in the years preceding the war.[27]

Not only was the *Eureka* an effective littoral vessel; it was also extremely rugged and durable. In 1937 a Coast Guard designer traveled to New Orleans and watched the innovative craft be put through its paces. Within the confines of Lake Pontchartrain, the Coast Guard representative saw the ship run over sandbars and logs, up a seaplane ramp, over a five-foot container, and easily traverse hyacinth plants that covered the water's surface. Impressed, the representative reported: "While the general assessment of the boat has no particular 'eye appeal' as compared to conventional design of displacement boats, it's so called lack of beauty is more than compensated by its practical usefulness."[28] While it may have been considered ugly, it certainly was impressive and functional and met the requirement.

FLEX 5 in February 1939 was an important event in the development of ship-to-shore movement. During the exercise a number of littoral designs were evaluated at Flamingo Beach, Culebra, by the navy's Landing Boat Development Board. Competing against a BCR design, Higgins's design came out on top. But months later the BCR ordered the construction of both the Higgins and the BCR-inspired design.[29] Fatefully, in early 1940 FLEX 6 fell under the command of Marine General Holland M. Smith. In his evaluation of the two designs Smith saw little improvement in the BCR ship but was impressed with the Higgins's innovations and performance. In the end, Higgins finally triumphed over navy bureaucracy with the design finally adopted. His timing was impeccable with American participation in the war looming; coffers for military spending were just beginning to open with procurement of the *Eureka* design finally approved.

However, debarkation from the *Eureka* was still difficult as it retained a standard bow design. By 1941 Japan already occupied parts of China and also made significant advances in littoral platforms. With the United States still a noncombatant, Marine Captain Victor Krulak, posted in Asia, received permission to observe the Japanese assault on Chinese positions along the Yangtze River.[30] While watching the Japanese forces in their combat assault, he took a photograph of a Japanese Dai-Hatsu Type 14 landing craft. The vessel incorporated a bow ramp that facilitated the quick unloading of men and material. In April Higgins saw the picture and was asked about the possibilities of a ramp for the *Eureka*. Accepting the challenge and realizing the potential, he quickly modified his design. A month later in May 1941 he tested his new ramp on Lake Pontchartrain with his own employees running off the vessel onto shore with a truck rolling ashore from the platform. The new *Eureka* design with a ramp was quickly designated the Landing Craft Personnel (Ramp) or LCP(R) and was the forerunner of the Landing Craft Vehicle Personnel (LCVP).[31] Despite this design breakthrough, as late as January 1942 the building of landing craft was still placed in the eighth group of naval priorities. Facing a potential Mahanian-type fight in the Pacific, the navy shipbuilding focused on battleships, aircraft carriers, and other capital vessels in anticipation of larger-scale surface action.[32]

After America's entry into the war and the adoption of the Germany First strategy, many planners were already looking to a cross-channel invasion of the European continent. Seen as the shortest and most feasible route to Germany, the 1942 Sledgehammer cross-channel invasion plan for Europe was quickly determined as too ambitious given American losses in the Pacific, lack of sufficiently trained soldiers, and a paucity of equipment. The 1942 plan was shelved for the 1943 Round Up plan as staff officers determined the army would have almost 900,000 soldiers for the later operation. But even that operation was too ambitious given the state of American forces. Even with creative scheduling, the navy had limited ability to move troops overseas.[33] More important, the shortage of amphibious landing craft precluded its execution as estimates for the plan called anywhere from 4,000 to 8,500 platforms of various types.[34] Other estimates placed the required number of landing craft as high as 20,000.[35] With Higgins's company's expansion and exponentially larger workforce, the New Orleans plants could not have possibly built the number of landing craft required in 1943. Even if the lift platforms were available, it is doubtful that the Allies could have executed such a complex operation without the classroom of the MTO and the lessons it provided.

A Japanese Type 14 landing craft that helped inspire the modification of Higgins' Eureka design. The loading ramp on the front of the vessel made embarkation/ debarkation much easier on unprepared beaches. (US Navy photo)

The issue of landing craft and associated shipping became a serious strategic problem for the Allies. Army Chief of Staff General George C. Marshall was an early proponent of the cross-channel invasion plans. He also saw them as the most direct and expeditious path to the heart of Germany and hoped to mount the operations as soon as practicable.[36] Strategically the joint US/UK invasion also had other implications, as the Soviet Union in 1942 was reeling under Wehrmacht offensives and seemed to be on the verge of capitulation. The opening of a second front on the European mainland might provide the communist state some much needed relief. Even accepting the conservative requirement of 7,000 landing craft for the cross-channel invasion, that number of boats would not become available until mid-1943. Furthermore, even with landing craft production increasing, future Supreme Allied Commander General Dwight D. Eisenhower was informed by summer 1942 that the Allies were still woefully deficient in amphibious vessels. Not only were amphibious vessels in short supply, but the nation also had a strategic lift deficiency in transporting both troops and equipment.[37] While the Red Army held on at great sacrifice, the lack of shipping and trained troops available for the 1942 or 1943 invasion plans prevented any channel-based offensives.

Concurrently the British were also skeptical of a premature cross-channel invasion. Gun-shy given their World War I Gallipoli experience and combined with the more recent failure of the 1942 reconnaissance-in-force amphibious raid at Dieppe, the British were more cautious. Hoping to avoid another amphibious fiasco the British proposed a Mediterranean strategy of attacking the periphery of the Third Reich. Moreover, with the British Eighth Army barely holding on in North Africa, Prime Minister Winston Churchill and the Imperial General Staff loathed the idea of launching a risky and hastily arranged cross-channel assault. For the British, their vision included a Balkan or Italian thrusts entering Germany via a southern route. In addition, cross-channel operational failure might be unrecoverable. Given these considerations, and to strengthening the alliance, President Franklin D. Roosevelt acquiesced to the British alternative much to the chagrin of US military leaders.[38] Securing the UK sealine of communication in the Mediterranean was viewed as a sideshow by US planners, but it proved a valuable experience for American forces.

Foreseeing American involvement in the war, Congress passed and FDR signed the Two-Ocean Navy Act in July 1940. With this act increasing the size of the navy by 70 percent, FDR not only pushed for building the United States blue-water fleet but also advocated for the acquisition of amphibious vessels. However, larger capital ships were still the priority and amphibious platform procurement languished. Before assuming his roles as the Supreme Allied Commander, and while serving as Chief of the War Plans Division, Ike wrote: "At the time . . . he [FDR] was thinking only in terms of restoring the fleet. They were not particularly interested in landing craft for future offensives. But if we didn't start building, we would never attack."[39] Given this concern, the navy increased the priority of littoral platforms in summer 1942 equal to that of surface combatants. Shortly afterward American shipyards began a crash program.[40] In the following months over 8,000 such craft of various designs were constructed, with another 21,000 the next year.[41] Recognizing the emerging requirement for amphibious shipping, the president ordered the construction of hundreds of one of the most important vessels of the war, the Landing Ship Tank (LST), along with a host of other amphibious vessels.[42]

An oceangoing vessel, the LST was an extremely versatile platform, displacing some 4,000 tons fully loaded, and could disgorge cargo directly onto a beach with as little as three feet of water under its bow, then withdraw under its own power.[43] By the end of the war LST production alone stood at approximately 1,000 vessels. This was all part of the larger 1941 Victory Program as US expenditures for defense rose fivefold, from $5 billion to $25 billion in 1941 and peaking at $82 billion by V-J Day.[44] Of the many miracles of World War II, the American industrial capacity was a highlight, the foundation for the Allied victory in every theater of the war. So important were LSTs that even as late as 1944 the shortage of these ships for the Overlord invasions was a worry, causing Churchill to quip: "The destinies of two great empires seemed to be tied up in some god-dammed things called LSTs."[45]

Given the emerging global requirement and lack of its own attention to littoral operations, in 1941 the army adopted *FTP-167 Landing Operations Doctrine* and published it as *Field Manual 31-5, Landing Operations on Hostile Shores. FM 31-5* gave direct credit to the naval services, stating that the subject matter and the illustrations were taken from landing operations doctrine of 1938.[46] However, as prescient as the *Tentative Landing Manual* and *Landing Operations Doctrine* were, they focused on the kind of fighting representative of islands in the Pacific, not extended operations attacking large landmasses for a sustained land campaign. Reflective of this thinking, one army publication stated: "Marines were organized for attacks on limited objectives instead of extensive operations required as in the strategic offensive[s] in the Atlantic and the Southwest Pacific . . . [that] call[ed] for large ground forces capable of sustained action."[47] While it was relatively easy to isolate an enemy island from sources of support with a naval cordon or blockade, sustained land combat on a continent posed a different challenge.

During the interwar period the army paid little attention to amphibious operations and grappled with the development of armor, mechanization, artillery, and other ground-centric applications. As late as 1940 the Army War College still allocated only three lecture hours to the topic of amphibious assault.[48] Much like in had in World War I, the army envisioned sailing to a port facility, disembarking, and then organizing itself for subsequent operations inland.[49] For soldiers, the navy was a means of conveyance to a ground-based conflict on some distant continent.

However, given the emerging requirement of amphibious assault, the two services needed to work together in ways they never had before.[50] The foundations regarding specific service roles and missions were outlined as early as 1927 in a document titled "Joint Action of the

US Navy Landing Ship Tanks (LSTs) and other vessels disgorge their cargoes on Normandy Beach in June 1944. These amphibious platforms were key in power projection ashore for Allied forces with ship availability often driving Allied strategies. (US Navy photo)

Army and Navy." While this Joint Board document provided guidance on the two services' roles and mission in national defense, it offered only vague guidance regarding "costal operations and joint overseas operations." The 1927 version stated that in such environments "sea operations by the army or land operations by the navy are proper only when immediately auxiliary to the[ir] normal functions."[51] This statement was hardly reflective of the reality of modern amphibious assault, provided very little substantive guidance, and would require a rewrite of service responsibilities. Until the establishment of the wartime Joint Chiefs of Staff in January 1942, determining training requirements, grand strategy, and establishing priorities between the two services proved difficult.[52]

While *FM 31-5* specifically called out the importance of joint operations in an amphibious environment, the two military forces were hardly accustomed to working together or serving jointly for a common end.[53] When the two services did conduct interwar amphibious operations, the results were usually disappointing.[54] In late 1939, the 3rd Infantry Division (ID) conducted a joint amphibious assault of Monterrey, California. The results were poor and predictable, with the two services pointing fingers at each other regarding the lackluster performance.[55] The 1st ID also experimented with amphibious assaults in 1940 on Culebra, with other army units conducting various exercises in 1941 on the beaches of Onslow, North Carolina, and Cape Henry, Virginia. These results were equally unsatisfactory, as communications broke down and units were placed on the wrong beaches, often in a piecemeal fashion and in some cases outside the training areas.[56]

In a joint Army–Navy amphibious exercise held in January 1942 the commanding officer of the 18th Combat Team submitted a scathing report aimed at both services highlight many points of contention. In his after-action report he stated:

> The first conclusion is a broad indictment of the navy . . . naval personnel encountered did not have any concept of the problem from a tactical (army) point of view. Consequently, there have been countless disagreements. . . . The second conclusion indicts the army. It has always been the practice to start too late with nothing like the plan, then the last minute to flood all units with a staggering number of orders, memoranda, directives, etc. which cannot be absorbed in the time allotted.[57]

He went on to complain about the two chains of command (army and navy), poor shore party operations, lack of efficient naval gunfire support, and poor combat loading—even going so far as to reference the UK experience at Gallipoli. As for understanding the problems of command and control in this environment, he commented further "there has been a continued conflict of interest between the army and navy with the navy supreme since they are in control while at sea and up to the time the landing forces cross the high-water mark on the beach." In his final conclusions he even went so far as to claim amphibious operations should not be an army responsibility and that the Marine Corps should be increased in size to conduct such landings.[58] Obviously the two organizations had to come to a common and mutual understanding.

Despite this lack of joint interest and the poor results, in 1940 the Army Corps of Engineers began addressing the issues surrounding littoral operations. Supporting the Corps of Engineers effort was an army directive in June ordering the training of two divisions for amphibious warfare.[59] If the army was to execute an amphibious assault and then conduct subsequent operations ashore, it required a significant expeditionary throughput capability. In 1941 the Corps of Engineers created a research committee to determine procedural and engineering requirements in littoral environments. Through a study of recent Japanese operations in the Pacific and other international efforts, the committee established a requirement for battalions of engineers, separate from infantry formations, to support landing operations.[60] Placed in the initial assault waves and once ashore, these engineers, all under the protection of armor, conducted reconnaissance, destroyed enemy obstacles, and removed fixed positions.[61] Such a capability required the increase of two additional engineer battalions assigned to the amphibious-trained infantry divisions.[62]

In June 1941, with American involvement in the war looming and the Wehrmacht's victory over France, the Joint Chiefs of Staff saw the need for expeditionary capabilities and recommended the development of an American amphibious corps on both the Atlantic and Pacific Coasts.[63] For a brief period the combined elements of the 1st Marine Division and the 1st ID became the Amphibious Force Atlantic Fleet (AFAF), initially commanded by Marine General Holland Smith.[64] The structure was short-lived, as the divisions were eventually released for other duties as war planning became more refined. In this initial tasking, the 1st ID was supposedly trained in amphibious operations, along with the 34th ID and 1st Armored Division (AD). After Pearl Harbor and American entry in the war, these units were sent to the United Kingdom in July–August 1942 and could hardly be considered competent in amphibious warfare. With no formal instruction, once overseas these formations participated in combined exercises in Northern Ireland that tested the limits of cooperation between United States and British troops.[65]

But with the establishment of the AFAF the need for increased amphibious capabilities gained traction. In March 1942 the navy not only inherited the command but also accepted its responsibilities regarding amphibious training. Rear Admiral Noland Brainard took charge of the organization, with it falling under the direct authority of the Commander in Chief, Atlantic Fleet. With little to go on and much to learn, the command was divided into three divisions—a transport group, a landing craft group, and the landing force group (largely an army concern). By June the command was ramping up and placed under the charge of Rear Admiral Kent Hewitt. Headquartered at Hampton Roads, Virginia, Hewitt established and directed the much-needed amphibious training programs for both services.[66] In the interwar years Hewitt was already familiar with the need for amphibious assault capabilities and recognized the requirement for the army and navy to work together in planning littoral operations.[67] In creating the Amphibious Assault School, he recognized the joint nature of littoral operations and deliberately sought army personnel to serve in key positions. Within the school he created parallel command structures of "G-shops" staffed with army personnel and "N-shops" staffed with navy personnel, all working in tandem.[68]

With allowances made for army personnel in his staff, Hewitt in summer 1942 fought army bureaucracy for the requisite personnel to fill these positions. This trend of army reluctance continued. When Hewitt was finally assigned as the CATF for the Western Naval Task Force for Operation Torch, he hectored Army General George Patton to show more interest and attention to army responsibilities in the upcoming operation. Cognizant of the importance of combat loading, he formally invited army officers to observe and assist in the loading of ships bound for Africa.[69] However, the army's apparent disinterest in combat loading, transportation quartermaster, and shore party functions, in October 1942 the 9th ID at Fort Bragg established detailed requirements for loading ships with gear and equipment to include how to load landing craft. The document was then forwarded to the First Provisional Corps, Task Force A and then approved for use on 4 November. While the document came too late for Torch, the army as an institution was becoming aware of these requirements.[70]

In addition to his training contributions, Hewitt became an excellent practitioner in the art and science of amphibious assault. He served as the Naval Task Force Commander for Allied operations in North Africa, Sicily, and southern France. He was a catalyst in developing a mutual understanding between the two services in the MTO/ETO, and his contributions have been largely overlooked by military historians. However, according to navy historian Samuel Eliot Morison: "In amphibious experience he [Hewitt] was surpassed by none and equaled by few."[71]

With the growing appreciation of littoral operations, Army Ground Forces in March 1942 directed the establishment of an Engineer Amphibian Command and assigned it the task of training soldiers in boat operations and maintenance while providing instruction on shore-party duties.[72] The 1941 version of *FM 31-5* specified:

Admiral Kent Hewitt, commander of Task Force 34 during the Torch Campaign. He was a key figure in the development of US Army–Navy cooperation in the Mediterranean and European Theaters during the war. (US Navy photo)

The shore party consists of a headquarters and any or all of the following detachments from units of the landing force: medical, supply, labor, engineer, military police, chemical, and communications. These detachments, assigned to the shore party to secure effective operations at the beach during and immediately after the landing, revert to control of their respective organization commanders as soon as the situation warrants.[73]

Shore parties had the important task of organizing men and supplies and distributing them ashore and establishing communications landward, thereby providing an important link in the ship-to-shore chain. More specifically, according to the *FM 31-5*, shore parties were responsible for:

- Maintenance of liaison between beachmaster and senior troop commander ashore
- maintenance of order

- control of stragglers
- direction of traffic ashore and the work of prisoners
- selection and marking routes inland
- assignment of operating, bivouac, parking, and storage areas for the services using the beach
- prompt movement of equipment and supplies from shore
- establishment of information and message centers
- making recommendations as to landing of vehicles establishment of a supply system[74]

As a result, the army was largely responsible for the movement of forces off the beach, whereas the navy was responsible for movement to, and reception at, the landing site.

For the navy side, it established beachmasters to oversee the beach party. The beach party had specific functions such as reconnaissance and selection of landing sites, handling boat traffic and establishing movement lanes, offloading and launching of amphibious vessels, ship-to-shore communications, salvage repairs, and evacuation of casualties and prisoners of war.[75] The actual division of labor and responsibilities of these functions were something the army and the navy would have to develop over time. Early on the army assumed it had a responsibility for some navy functions. For the shore-party missions army Engineer Amphibian Command's tasks included:

> To organize, equip, train, operate and administer such engineer amphibian units as may be needed for time to time in the various theater of operations for shore-to-shore operations . . . with the function of transporting troops . . . together with equipment and supplies required for these operations . . . charged with the function of transporting troops of the combat unit which it is attached. . . . These units are further charged with control and improvement of the far shore, debarkation and movement of supplies to troops beyond the beach proper . . . and evacuation . . . from the far shore.[76]

In this mission army units planned to embark troops and equipment from a friendly shore-based location (near shore) to the enemy's (far shore) location. These operations were significantly different than the ship-to-shore missions that required direct naval support. The initial plans for Sledgehammer and Roundup were based upon such a concept of operations but eventually transitioned to a mix of both the ship-to-shore and shore-to-shore assault. Assigning this mission to the Corps of Engineers made sense, as it had familiarity with riverine crossings, possessed experience with small boat operations, and played a significant part in the development of the nation's waterways and harbor infrastructure.[77] This was an important first step for the army in addressing the organizational and material deficiencies regarding expeditionary operations.[78] Established at Camp Edwards, Massachusetts, and under the command of Colonel Daniel Noce, the Engineer Amphibious Corps established army-specific doctrine while providing important instruction to soldiers unfamiliar with littoral operations with a focus on shore-to-shore operations.[79] By 1943 the Engineer Amphibian Command (EAC) already drafted a number of tentative training guides addressing engineer functions in a littoral environment.[80]

Regarding the requirements of shore-to-shore movement, organizing a beachhead, and managing traffic throughput, the army determined it needed 48,000 men to serve in various amphibious engineering units. Predicting that the navy would assume responsibilities only up to the high-water mark, Army Ground Forces in May 1942 initially authorized the Services of Supply Branch to create eight brigades of engineers (later reduced to six) to conduct shore/beach party functions. A single engineer shore regiment consisted of three battalions operating at both the near and the far shores, then integrated with a boat regiment and service units to form an Engineer Amphibian Brigade (EAB).[81] With this structure these new engineer units would help transport troops, assist in debarkation, organize beaches, and evacuate the wounded while providing other combat service support functions.[82] Training for these units occurred at the army's newly formed Amphibious Training Center, also located at Camp Edwards.[83]

In terms of actual units, the 1st EAB established on 15 June was assigned the mission of providing shore-party and engineering duties.[84] Eventually six EABs were established and (subsequently redesignated Engineer Special Brigades (ESBs) with the 1st, 5th, and 6th EABs assigned to the MTO/ETO.[85] Initially manned with 349 officers, twenty warrants, and 6,814 enlisted men, the unit had a small boat regiment equipped with landing craft for shore-to-shore movement, a signal company, medical and quartermaster battalions, an ordnance company, a boat maintenance company, and a repair platoon for other associated vehicles.[86] A 1943 training guide specified that one ESB would be attached to each amphibious infantry division, with the mission of moving 1,500 tons of supplies per day across the beach with the expectation that even more might be required.[87] With this structure the army had taken the *Tentative Landing Manual* and *FTP-167* lessons to heart, understanding the requirements for movement, throughput, and organization in an unprepared littoral environment.

However, even though the services were now addressing the issue, the army and the navy still needed to arrive at agreement on roles and missions at the beach. 1st EAB was scheduled for stateside training that summer but under the auspices of Operation Bolero (the buildup of US forces in the United Kingdom for the invasion of Europe and the Combined Bomber Offensive) the unit deployed to the ETO in summer 1942.[88] Recognizing the importance of the mission, elements of the 1st EAB pulled out of the training cycle in July while still supporting division-level exercises at Camp Edwards.[89] Sent to the United Kingdom, the unit received additional training at the British Amphibious Training Center at Inveraray, Scotland, before being scattered around the United Kingdom. Select elements of the 1st EAB participated in the Torch landings that November as part of the Central Task Force landing at Arzew Beach in Algeria.[90] Following Torch, elements also participated in subsequent operations in Sicily (Husky), Salerno (Avalanche), and Normandy (Overlord).[91]

Manning the brigades and the EAC was a challenge. Since the littoral mission required special skill sets and abilities, the Adjutant General's office began scouring personnel records for uniquely qualified individuals. The Corps of Engineers also sent out 6,000 circulars to yacht/boat clubs and to shipyards and while placing notices in nautically themed publications looking for personnel with the requisite skills.[92] In the July 1942 issue of *Motor Boating* magazine, the army published an article in hopes of finding "men who are not afraid of going out in fog or heavy seas, who are willing and anxious to take chances for national security," with other adds imploring "join the Army's navy!"[93] While in direct competition with the navy over such expertise, this effort saw the army acquire 1,300 enlisted men along with many direct commissions for officers. But most of the 37,000 men required for this mission came from replacement training or reception centers, with most having little to no skills in littoral operations.[94] While Army General Cognitive Testing scores were important, the service took what it could get while also interviewing men with special interests or hobbies related to a maritime environment. In addition, the army had to create new job classifications (Military Occupation Specialty) for coxswains, seamen, and marine engineers.[95]

Hoping to build military expertise, the army also leveraged support from the United States Coast Guard, Geodetic Survey, and internationally from the United Kingdom.[96] Partnering with civilian entities, EAC industrialists in developing navigation aids and associated training.[97] Evinrude Motors, Manitowoc Shipbuilding Company, Higgins Industries, and other civilian companies also provided specialized technical training for army personnel.[98] Additional training came from existing military schools at Aberdeen, Maryland, and the Naval Operating Base in Toledo, Ohio, among others. In all, 1,481 personnel were trained outside the EAC, with an additional 3,368 at civilian institutions.[99]

With the growing realization of the forcible entry requirement, the Joint Staff in summer 1942 concluded that the nation lacked sufficient amphibious forces. Given the limited size of the Marine Corps and the immediate needs, the Joint Staff determined that the army had ample manpower to meet the requirement. Furthermore, given existing interservice rivalries, the army took a dim view of possibly being subordinate to Marine command while at the mercy of navy support. With concurrent operations in the ETO/MTO and the Pacific, the Joint US Strategic Committee proposed a notional division of labor. The Marine Corps' smaller organization best fit the geography of the Central Pacific, while the army's larger structure was suited for large land combat in the ETO/MTO and the Southwest Pacific.[100] With this geographic division of labor, the Marines largely departed the East Coast along with their resident expertise in amphibious operations.[101] With this proposal in place, the two services (army and Marine) were responsible for their own amphibious training. The Marines, given the relationship with the navy, had no issue training with the sister service for the Pacific theater. However, the army and navy were at an impasse over which should be the lead for the MTO/ETO.

In the dialogue regarding the lead service, the army claimed it should have control of shore-to-shore operations as envisioned in the upcoming cross-channel invasion. However, the navy took a different view. When presented to the Navy on 29 April 1942 the service rejected the proposal claiming that the cross-channel invasion was a "special situation." Two months later in June the army and navy reached an accord regarding amphibious training in the MTO/ETO. All shore-to-shore, cross-channel attack training would fall under the purview of the army, while ship-to-shore, amphibious attack would remain a navy requirement.[102] The navy would provide the landing craft and instruction for army-manned boat crews. Requirements and responsibilities of the services in other theaters of the war (Southwest Pacific, Central

Pacific) were also addressed but left unresolved at the time.[103] Despite this initial argument, landing craft would eventually be operated by naval personnel.[104]

In the interim and until the June agreement, on 22 May Army Ground Forces was officially tasked with training army tactical units in all phases of amphibious operations to include ship-to-shore and shore-to-shore movement. The Services of Supply Branch was charged with organizing, training, and supplying boats, equipment, and transport facilities. Given these directives the Army Staff also recommended the establishment of its own amphibious training centers for large-scale landings.[105] Searching for coastal training locations in the continental United States, the army required an area stretching eight to ten miles inland, large enough to allow division-size movement, and possessed an accompanying, offshore island. Additionally, the army desired a coastal strip that contained some twenty miles of assailable beaches for landings and a large sheltered body of water for boat exercises.[106]

During the discussion regarding amphibious instruction responsibilities, the army took the initiative and began to train infantry formations scheduled for deployment overseas.[107] Based on its World War I experience and on interwar doctrine, most of the army's amphibious operations focused on river/wet gap crossings or small commando-type raids.[108] While the 1st and 3rd IDs conducted amphibious training as directed in 1940, the exercises were not well received. But little progress was made, and in a 1942 evaluation by the commanding general of the 3rd ID, Major General John P. Lucas, reported that the training was "unwieldly, ineffective, and dangerous."[109] Lucas's 1942 evaluation of army amphibious capabilities found its way to Army Chief of Staff Marshall and reported that "planning, preparation, and training for amphibious operations up to that time had been so deficient that a real operation against a competent enemy could only end in disaster for American forces."[110] He argued further that

> only the army had both the means and the grasp of the problem to plan, prepare, and train the necessary ground and air forces for joint amphibious operations . . . [and that the army] be charged with the planning, preparation[,] and training of large-scale amphibious operations and that the navy and Marine Corps assist the Army only in procurement of the necessary shipping, landing craft, and special equipment[] and with technical advice and cooperation.[111]

Given the war's global scope, existing Marine Corps training programs were considered too small to satisfy the army's need for large-scale joint and combined air and ground assaults.[112] As a result, and to address the training shortfall, a study titled "XXX Plan" required that every division earmarked for amphibious employment receive specialized training.[113] Toward this end, Brigadier General Floyd Parks, the Army Ground Forces deputy chief of staff, submitted a recommendation that the army have its own training program. He suggested further that the naval services provide support in the form of ship and landing craft procurement, operation, and technical advice.[114] Navy concerns regarding army capability took a different perspective. With concerns over the lack of embarkation space and amphibious lift, the navy believed that the army should tailor the size and composition of its amphibious divisions. In this regard the navy envisioned a smaller, less capable division with a reduced lift footprint. The army rejected the idea, as it believed its combat formations should remain standard for a large-scale land campaign and subsequent operations ashore.[115] As a result the two services were already on two different pages.

As the army looked for training locations, an amphibious curriculum required development. What should be taught at the new locations? What should the curriculum include? What printed material and manuals were available for the various schools? Furthermore, who was qualified to conduct and supervise the education and training of this niche capability? To accomplish these tasks the army depended on outside help. A group of joint/combined staff officers worked alongside their army brethren to develop a new curriculum and plans for instruction. Marines, Coast Guardsmen, and British personnel assisted in developing lesson content and instruction.[116] In addition to the external help, the army did have some resident experience. While the army had few manuals regarding amphibious operations, many of the new school's faculty had been assigned previously to the 1st, 3rd, or 9th IDs and had some practical experience. Leveraging this familiarity, faculty members provided "poop sheets" with their observations and practices that also helped develop new lesson plans.[117]

Planners eventually designed a training regimen that was divided into three phases: individual and small arms courses that included embarkation and debarkation from landing craft; actual loading and unloading exercises; and a complete rehearsal of an amphibious landing that included combined arms integration.[118] Army Ground Forces further determined that it needed at least twelve divisions—eleven infantry and one armored—trained in shore-to-shore operations. In this mission Army Ground Forces was to build a capability for: "embarking troops and equipment in small boats on land, then approach to and landing in a hostile beach, the establishment of the beachhead, and the preparation and initiation of an attack inland."[119] Furthermore, army planners determined that such training should be completed by 1 February 1943.[120] While this was an ambitious and likely unrealistic goal, the staff planned to train three more infantry divisions and an additional armor division at overseas locations during this period. However, changes in amphibious training requirements forced the army to adjust its formal instruction programs.

To accomplish this mission, twelve stateside divisions were to be trained at three ATC locations: four at Camp Edwards (location of the army's Engineer Amphibian Command), six at Camp Carrabelle, Florida (later renamed Camp Gordon Johnston), and two at Fort Lewis, Washington. Excluded from this plan were the 1st, 3rd, and 9th IDs, as they had already received amphibious training (as poor as it was) or were in the process of receiving it in some form.[121] Given the extensive list of requirements governing the location of the amphibious bases, only the Carrabelle location met most of the established conditions and could execute training on a year-round basis.

Located in the Panhandle, the Florida training location was next to a small fishing and lumber village with a population of barely 1,000. The site included some twenty miles of the Gulf of Mexico coastline, 165,000 acres of inland training areas, and four different encampments that could train three regimental combat teams (RCTs) simultaneously.[122] While Brigadier General Frank Keating, the commander of ATC, initially rejected the location as undesirable (along with the Surgeon General finding it an "unhealthy environment"), wartime requirements overruled such detractions.[123] Clearing the site started on 8 June 1942, and it would take time to prepare the location for training.

In the interim, and until the Florida location was available for use, the army used the existing facility and the beaches around Camp Edwards.[124] Establishing the training center at Edwards began in June 1942, but the value of the location was limited, as ice during the winter months precluded boat training.[125] Despite this weather limitation, army planners believed the site addressed the urgent need, and they assumed designated unit training would be completed before winter. In support of the immediate requirement, the initial camp grew as the army leased Washburn Island in Waquoit Bay for amphibious training and expanded the size of the base acquiring adjacent support facilities.[126] Time was of the essence, as the first units were scheduled to arrive in July 1942.

To meet the emerging need, the mission and objectives for the amphibious training centers included:

1) Produce divisions ready for combat in shore-to-shore operations.
2) Accustom army personnel to landing craft and teach the technique of embarking and debarking personnel and equipment.
3) Train division and lower commanders and staffs in their duties in the entire chronological sequence of a shore-to-shore operation.
4) Establish a course of instruction for "commando" raids.
5) Terminate training with a full-scale division maneuver supported by aircraft.
6) Use tentative texts as a guide prepared by army ground forces and elaborate on it as information flows from practical experience.[127]

Beyond the training at Camp Edwards, the EAC also developed new amphibious technologies by creating the Developments Section in late August 1942. Among its significant contributions was improving the army's abilities in movement on and off an undeveloped beach. While tracked vehicles could easily transverse unimproved shorelines, wheeled vehicles were often stuck in littoral areas depending on surf, gradient, and type of sand. The section helped improve beach throughput and trafficability by experimenting with various types of landing matting/pads.[128] These materials could be laid as a rudimentary surface on unprepared beaches, allowing wheeled vehicles the traction often lost on soft sand.

Furthermore, the EAC researched the use of the amphibious truck for ship-to-shore movement. At Provincetown Bay, near Cape Cod, the section compared the Marines-inspired "Alligator" tracked vehicle with the DUKW (the "Duck").[129] While the Alligator design could easily traverse an unprepared beach, its inability to travel inland at increased speeds was problematic. The DUKW was a 2.5-ton, 6x6 wheeled truck chassis with a hull, propeller screw, and rudder allowing it to "swim" with 5,000 pounds of cargo. While the DUKW was slow in the water and swam at a speed of only five knots, it could transverse a beach and then deliver supplies and troops farther inland at a speed up to fifty miles per hour.[130] This capability perhaps best illustrated the nature of Marine assaults compared to those of the army. Subsequent operations ashore, where the DUKW could travel easily, was more in line with the army operating on a continent than the Marine Corps securing an island.

Separate from the army's efforts, under Hewitt's direction the Amphibious Force Atlantic Fleet also took significant steps to develop amphibious capabilities. With a growing mission, office and training space became a premium at the existing naval base, with Hewitt eventually procuring the Hotel Nansemond at Ocean View in September to house the emerging effort.[131] He not only established a staff at the Naval Operating Base at Norfolk, Virginia, but also created training programs for US Army, Navy, and Coast Guard personnel. Part of this instruction included operation of landing craft in the Chesapeake Bay area, with training centers in Little Creek, Virginia, and Solomons Island, Maryland. In addition, the Higgins company also assisted in developing training programs. Many AFAF instructors were sent to New Orleans and were schooled by Higgins representatives on landing craft fundamentals and then returned to the training bases. Simultaneously Higgins Industries held its own training program, which eventually included a six-week course that covered landing craft operations and maintenance. The capstone exercise required new coxswains to traverse Lake Pontchartrain in combat conditions without running lights while avoiding instructors canvassing the area in PT Boats.[132]

In addition to the Virginia training locations, another important facility was the Amphibious Training Base at Solomons Island. Known as the "Cradle of Invasions," this small base trained over a half-million men that subsequently participated in thirty-seven invasions in all theaters of the war.[133] The naval base at the mouth of the Patuxent River had three "assault beaches" in the Chesapeake along with multiple berths for amphibious ships. The initial mission of the facility was to support the 1943 Roundup Operation, but with that plan shelved the base became a key element in training men for Operation Torch. Additionally, at the behest of Marine General Holland Smith, the Chief of Naval Operations Admiral Ernest J. King authorized the purchase of Bloodworth Island in the Chesapeake for NSFS training—the first of its kind in the world.[134] This proved prescient when NSFS emerged as a key enabler for amphibious assault in all theaters of the war.

With these navy developments, men and equipment began arriving at the various amphibious bases at a rate of 1,000 sailors every two weeks, testing the capacity of the installations' billeting and service

An Army DUKW (Pronounced "Duck"). Able to swim to shore, the vehicle was also capable of speeds up to 50mph and could easily travel inland in support of subsequent operations. This inland capability made it a welcome alternative to the Marine Corps tracked vehicles that were much slower once ashore and had limited range. (US Army photo)

facilities.[135] Most of these new personnel had no seagoing experience or familiarity with naval operations. Men who had never seen an ocean or a shoreline now had to learn how to navigate and operate landing craft in dangerous surf conditions in various sea states. Difficult as these tasks were, the crews might have to execute under enemy fire. This made for a steep learning curve.

Though developing these amphibious skills was difficult, soldiers and sailors alike toiled in the shadows given the glamor of naval aviation, surface combatants, the Army Air Corps, and other, more visible military branches. The amphibious fleet was, and still is, looked down upon within the navy and was hardly considered a choice assignment. Indicative of this status was an account of a scofflaw sailor was telling another shipmate of his long list of various infractions of navy discipline. When his shipmate asked the scofflaw if he was getting a bad-conduct discharge, the scofflaw replied: "Hell no! I got fifteen days in the brig and orders to amphibs!" The shipmate's response was even more telling: "Gee . . . that's a lousy break." Newly minted officers also saw the assignment equally disappointing, calling such postings the "ensign disposal" school.[136]

While the United States was ill-prepared for any cross-channel invasion, at the time the army's focus was on shore-to-shore movement, not the more complex ship-to-shore operations.[137] With the development of new amphibious vessels still underway, movement ashore was done largely with small Landing Craft Personnel (LCP)–sized platforms. Hewitt's AFAF schools had also focused on the shore-to-shore mission, as the summer 1942 faculty had no idea about the upcoming Torch landings scheduled for November. After learning about Torch, its scheme of maneuver, and its nine planned separate amphibious assaults, the training program at Little Creek changed focus from shore-to-shore movement to emphasizing ship-to-shore operations. With less than two months and without any formal request or order, the schoolhouse adjusted its entire training focus to the more complex operation for the troops soon to enter combat overseas.[138]

Helping to bridge the interservice gap, many soldiers and sailors at Little Creek attended the Shore Party School in which students learned the function and requirements of naval beach parties. Hastily constructed in a potato field, a rudimentary schoolhouse was built next to the landing craft piers at Little Creek. In this curriculum personnel learned the art and science of receiving, organizing, and moving supplies and equipment off landing craft and organizing an established beachhead.[139] This was a redundancy in a way, since the army was also conducting similar training at the ATC at Camp Edwards and muddied the waters as to beachmaster and shore party responsibilities. However, the nation needed as many skilled beach personnel as possible given the growing requirements of the MTO/ETO and the Pacific. In conjunction with AFAF, army schools at Camp Pickett, Virginia, and Fort Pierce, Florida, conducted exercises and experiments with engineer troops to further advance the concept of logistics over the shore.[140] Hewitt established the Transportation Quartermaster School to help army officers understand the process of loading supplies and materials onto ships and the art of combat loading. While subject to navy oversight regarding trim and stability of the vessel, Hewitt unambiguously argued that loading transport vessels with men and equipment was an army responsibility.[141]

To underscore Hewitt's emphasis on joint interoperability, when 2nd AD leadership showed little interest in the pre-Torch August landing exercises and failed to attend a recent training evolution, the admiral acted. Dismayed at the lack of senior army leadership participation,

Hewitt wrote Patton of the importance of "experience[ing the] operation of landing craft and of learning, at first hand, some of the lessons
which are fundamental to the amphibious officer" and that "valuable
lessons" could be learned from observation.[142] With this he aggres-
sively tried to educate army officers on the importance of naval logistics, embarkation, and deployment. His efforts eventually paid off, as
army officers attending the Engineer School at Fort Belvoir, Virginia,
after 1943 received additional training in assaulting fortified positions,
with most sent to the United Kingdom in preparation for Overlord.[143]

In helping to create a joint mindset, Hewitt also developed the General Staff School focused on joint amphibious operations. In trying
raise awareness of the problems in littoral assaults, the curriculum
included topics such as joint loading, ship-to-shore movement, naval
gunfire support, joint training of amphibious scouts, relations with
the navy, and amphibious tactics. These lessons were based on existing
doctrinal publications and practices.[144] Hewitt placed an army colonel
in charge of the school and had mixed representation from both services. With this curriculum Hewitt hoped to assist staff officers in
their conceptual understanding of amphibious operations and to provide a fundamental understanding.[145]

Since the two services had independent communication systems,
Hewitt also set up an amphibious signal school with navy communications personnel assigned along with Signal Corps soldiers. Collocated at Little Creek, the school trained sailors and soldiers assigned to
fire control shore parties on joint ship-to-shore communications and
use of the SCR-536 radio and associated systems.[146] Fire control parties consisted of naval personnel familiar with NSFS procedures and
methodology who could translate ground force requirements for the
ship-based gunners. This became an obvious requirement, as some terminology between the two services differed. In the case of land-based
artillery, if a round landed 200 yards over a target, the forward observer
would report "over 200." However, in the case of NSFS, the navy fire
control party would report "down 200."[147] Obviously with troops in the
area, such confusion would have severe consequences. In addition, and
to facilitate close air support, the school also developed naval air liaison
teams with a naval aviator, a radio operator, and a vehicle-mounted
SCR-193 radio. Providing communication and guidance to supporting
aircraft, one liaison team was attached to each ground regiment. All of
these were small but important advances in the coordination and communication of amphibious assault operations.[148]

In addition to the established schools, Hewitt also revised existing

Training of landing craft crews at Camp Bradford at Little Creek, Virginia. (US Navy Photo)

doctrine and Standard Operating Procedures (SOPs) to reflect emerging requirements and technological innovations. In this effort he again sought army input and participation.[149] As with other initiatives, he was frustrated by the army's lack of personnel support at the schools. He badgered Major General Thomas Handy, the Assistant Chief of Staff for Army Training, and Patton for the requisite army personnel to fill their share of faculty positions and staff assignments.[150] In the closing of yet another letter to Patton, he chastised the army: "There has been more than enough talk and too little action, I should like to see some practical results of all our efforts."[151] Taking heed, by October 1942 the army developed a notional training SOP that outlined organization of an amphibious division, its requisite equipment sets, a training curriculum, shore party functions and roles, wave scheduling, boat team organization, established quartermaster and embarkation procedures, and even included Hewitt's naval SOP.[152] While many of these initial instructions would change or morph as the war progressed, the army was finally developing service-specific amphibious procedures.

Despite the fight over amphibious training responsibilities and the initial lack of army support to navy-sponsored schoolhouses, the first unit to undergo instruction at the Edwards ATC was the 45th ID. This initial progression took place starting 15 July 1942 in echelon as individual regimental combat teams cycled through a 10-day block of instruction. The 45th rotated its subordinate units for the next few weeks until 20 August. Units attending the ATC received instruction from a British commando unit including scaling techniques, physical training, and an efficiency course. The course required men to negotiate unexpected obstacles in the woods such as enemy dummies that would spew pig blood if properly bayoneted.[153] The final exercise, conducted 17–19 August, included a shore-to-shore operation as the troops embarked from Washburn Island, crossed the six miles of the sound, and landed on Martha's Vineyard.[154] The 45th was soon tested on the shores of Sicily in Operation Torch in July 1943 and again during Operation Avalanche at Salerno weeks later.

Following the 45th, the 36th ID arrived on 22 August; much like the previous class the regiments were rotated through the training syllabus.[155] They conducted a shore-to-shore exercise, and with the 36th ID capstone exercise completed the use of Edwards as a divisional training facility ended. With the winter months approaching, and after the 36th's exercise on 1–3 October, the ATC relocated to the Camp Carrabelle location. The 36th would experience combat less than a year later as part of the initial assault against the Salerno beaches in September 1943. On 6 October the school's staff and faculty started tearing down Camp Edwards.[156] The movement of the training center did not mean the end of amphibious instruction at Camp Edwards, however. The Cape Cod base would remain the training location for the newly approved engineer brigades.

In Florida 10,000 acres of land near Carrabelle was purchased directly from landowners, with another 155,000 leased from the St. Joe Paper Company. Working the swamps of Florida, they surveyed the area in three weeks, with site clearing beginning on 8 July 1942.[157] Once finished, the camp sprawled some twenty miles along the coast and was nestled between St. George Island, Carrabelle, and Alligator Point. The outlying Dog and St. George Islands were used as staging points for shore-to-shore amphibious landings on the mainland. The base also included an airstrip, airdrop landing zones, and an aerial gunnery range, as well as bazooka, grenade, and small arms ranges.[158]

The first troops arrived at Carrabelle on 10 September, consisting largely of support, medical, quartermaster, and headquarters personnel. There was little time to spare, as the first unit to undergo training was scheduled to arrive only weeks later. However, Camp Carrabelle was still unfinished, with swamps needing to be cleared, new buildings constructed, cargo net towers built, mock landing craft outlined, and other facilities established.[159] The location was hardly a garden spot, columnist Walter Winchell referring to it as the "Alcatraz of the Army" and an unhappy soldier stationed there penned a letter home with this return address: "Hell-by-the Sea, Carrabelle, Florida."[160] In his last stop before deploying overseas future Army and Joint Chief of Staff General Omar Bradley called the post "the most miserable Army installation I had ever seen since my days at Yuma" and went on further to state: "The man who selected that site should have been court-martialed for stupidity."[161] The camp rightfully earned this reputation, as the barracks that first winter were simple tar and paper prefabricated structures, many without latrines or heaters. No chow hall existed, and soldiers ate outside.[162] Rife with snakes, ticks, and mosquitoes, the makeshift camp newspaper *Amphibian* published the following poem that described life at the post:

> The rattlesnake bites you, the horsefly stings,
> The mosquito delights you with his buzzin' wings.
> Sand burrs cause you to jig and dance
> And those who sit down get ants in their pants.
>
> The heat in the summer in one-hundred and ten
> Too hot for the devil, too hot for men.
> Come see for yourself and you can tell
> It's a hellava place, this Carrabelle.[163]

Instructors and faculty at the ATC were assigned to the 75th Composite Infantry Training Battalion. The unit had a difficult mission as Carrabelle was always short of personnel, landing craft, weapons, and other equipment sets. According to one army historian:

> The story was the same from start to finish of the Amphibious Training Center—bickering and indecision in higher headquarters; expansion of the training mission and objective without corresponding expansion of facilities; and attempts on the part of the Center to accomplish its mission with whatever means could be made available. . . . Improvisation and plain Yankee ingenuity frequently saved the day.[164]

Despite such shortcomings and detractions, the first unit training at Carrabelle was the 38th ID and began the syllabus on 23 November.

The training included urban operations at a mock German village, "Shickelgruber Haven," constructed from the remains of an abandoned timber camp.[165] The 38th's capstone exercise began on 16 December with a reconnaissance of the "hostile" beach followed by an orientation the next day with embarkation to start shortly after.[166] While the embarkation phase went well, during the landing only one battalion arrived on the correct beach (but it was out of sequence), with other elements landing at various times and places. One unit landed twenty miles from its target and "captured" the undefended town of Crawfordville![167] Unlike previous divisions that underwent such training, instructors were unsatisfied with the unit's performance during the final exercise and required a redo of the entire evolution. The morale of the division was probably at low ebb given the failure, more so as the soldiers faced spending the Christmas holiday in the swamps of Florida. The 38th repeated the exercise days later on 28–30 December, but this time with satisfactory results.[168] However, the training of division-size units at this location would also be short-lived. When the 28th ID arrived in late January 1943, it was the last division-level evolution conducted by Camp Johnston.[169]

Even before the army started its amphibious training programs, the requirement for twelve amphibiously trained divisions for shore-to-shore operations was lowered to five on 1 July 1942.[170] This reduction did not immediately affect ATCs, as the five divisions were still needed "as soon as practicable."[171] The reduction was recommended due to the limited nature of landing craft and other lighterage and the existing ambiguity regarding training responsibilities between the services regarding the "XXX Plan."[172] While division-level training was suspended after the five-division requirement, in October 1942, Army Ground Forces guidance shifted, directing ATC's focus on select battalion-level units and staffs with an emphasis on individual training in amphibious techniques.

In September 1942, as the ATC was in the initial months of operation, the Joint Chiefs of Staff finally determined that training for amphibious operations was a navy responsibility.[173] There was no question on this assignment. As the Joint Chiefs of Staff wrote: "Amphibious operations are essentially the responsibility of the Navy . . . [but] it is recognized that selected army units must be made available for training and participation in amphibious operations."[174] In November

Army G-3 Lieutenant General Leslie McNair, argued that the ATC should remain open and that army administration was preferable to the navy's. It appeared that the ATC might get a stay of execution. But in a 10 March 1943 letter Chief of Naval Operations King and Army Chief Marshall agreed that the army would discontinue its amphibious training programs except for the EABs.[175] Given this guidance Camp Carrabelle's larger mission became moot.[176] The ATC officially disbanded on 10 June 1943, with the location given to Army Service Forces as a training center. For the reminder of the war the site was used for training several amphibious truck, engineer, and boat companies as well as elements of the 4th ID.[177] However, that was not the end of the army's statewide division-level efforts.

As Allied strategic plans became clearer, Eisenhower, the new US commander in the theater, concurred with the King–Marshall agreement that amphibious training was a navy responsibility.[178] The army-centric shore-to-shore focus gave way to the joint ship-to-shore requirement for Torch.[179] Eventually the two services came to a mutual agreement that the navy would operate the landing craft and the army would conduct the shore-party functions along with navy beachmasters. While some landing craft in Torch were operated by army personnel, the navy assumed the role in subsequent operations.[180] However, regardless of the King–Marshall agreement, the two services developed joint schools at various locations overseas starting as early as 1943.

Eventually Hewitt's AFAF was renamed the Maritime Command in the ETO, and by October 1943 redesignated Amphibious Force, Europe.[181] With new guidance the army's stateside training responsibilities were reduced, as were the requirements for EABs. However, this did not relieve the service of developing its amphibious training efforts. As grand strategy developed from the various planning conferences, the need for a forceable entry capability continued to grow. With the British Mediterranean strategy (the so-called Soft Underbelly approach), multiple amphibious operations occurred on North Africa and Italian beaches before the all-important cross-channel invasion. To support these emerging requirements, training occurred at several locations overseas in newly liberated areas and in the United Kingdom. Additionally, constant training was required as new formations were added to the order of battle, with refresher exercises needed for veterans of previous assaults. As a result, and despite official guidance from earlier in the 1942 agreement, army and navy commanders began sponsoring joint amphibious training overseas.

Camp Carrabelle wooden mock-up of a landing craft with troops "embarked" and an actual movement on the Florida shore. (Camp Gordon Johnston Museum Digital Archive)

In all the services had come a long way since the Spanish–American War. But there was still much to learn regarding joint operations, command relationships, and land–sea coordination. The exigency of war and the need for a vastly larger amphibious assault capability served as a catalyst for the War and Navy Departments. The development of doctrine, curriculum, and joint training for ship-to-shore and shore-to-shore operations were important first steps. Even with the significant advances the services still had to develop a mutual understanding on the nuances of an amphibious operation. Torch would be the first real test of this emerging Army–Navy relationship and would take place in the toughest classroom possible: in combat.

2

Hit-or-Miss Affair

Operation Torch, November 1942

America's first amphibious operation again the European Axis assembled off the coast of North Africa on 7–8 November 1942. This effort followed the Marine landings on Guadalcanal in the Pacific in August and was an important first step toward Normandy and the liberation of the European mainland. Planning nine individual amphibious landings, the effort was divided into three task forces. Under Major General George Patton was the Western Task Force (WTF), conducting a trio of landings in Morocco intent on capturing the important city of Casablanca along with the introduction of land-based aircraft. Approximately 1,000 miles to the east in the Mediterranean Basin on the coast of Algeria, the Central Task Force (CTF) under the command of US Major General Lloyd R. Fredendall made multiple landings near the town of Oran. CTF's mission was to capture the city's port and local airfields while establishing a line of communication with the WTF. Concurrently, the Eastern Task Force (ETF) conducted a three-pronged effort on the shores east and west of the city of Algiers. Commanded by US Major General Charles Ryder, the ETF was the main effort during Torch, as it placed Allied troops closest to German Field Marshal Erwin Rommel's Afrika Korps and sought to capture Algiers and its robust logistical infrastructure.[1]

Some in Washington gave the overall plan a 50-50 chance of success, while Ike believed the operation was of a "quiet desperate nature" in which its success depended more on political consideration than the "wisdom of military decisions."[2] However, under a Clausewitzian framework the need for Torch was obvious. The decision to invade North Africa was part of a larger diplomatic effort to strengthen the bond between the United States and the United Kingdom, and it gave the appearance of offensive action to the larger public at a time when a cross-channel invasion was still not feasible.[3] With the Soviets reeling under Germany's Operation Barbarossa, Soviet leader Joseph Stalin pleaded for a second front to take some of the pressure off the beleaguered communist state. After a visit from Russian Foreign Minister Vyacheslav Molotov, FDR received a first-hand account of the Soviets' need of relief. As the discussion progressed, FDR acceded to the request for a second front, claiming an American offensive would occur that same year.[4] However, lacking men, ships, landing craft, and know-how, an invasion of Normandy was an impossibility. Moreover, the British were reluctant to take on such a massive amphibious effort at this stage of the war. With a focus on the Mediterranean, Churchill and his generals favored an indirect approach, with offensives planned for Southern Europe and the Balkans. In 1942 the British were the senior partner in the transatlantic alliance and the Americans the junior one. While this relationship would eventually reverse itself as American forces and capabilities grew over time. During the first few senior-level conferences UK concerns largely drove Allied strategy.

However, and more important, Torch was a crucial learning evolution for US forces unfamiliar with amphibious assault. These first landings in the MTO were not decisive or bring about the capitulation of European fascist regimes. Torch was designed to control the Straight of Gibraltar, annihilate German forces in the Western Desert, and facilitate subsequent operations against the Axis on the European continent.[5] In this effort the Allies would liberate Nazi-occupied territory in North Africa, swing Vichy French support, and then conduct operations against the European mainland from forward bases in the MTO. Not the initiation of the deathblow that George Marshall hoped for with 1942's Sledgehammer or 1943's Roundup, Torch was instead an attack on the Axis periphery. In a thought similar to Ike's quip, one official army historian articulated how "[this] momentous first step, though not timorous, was hesitant, and somewhat reluctant; like the steps of a child it was more a responsible urge for action than a decision to reach some specific destination."[6]

At the strategic level the Anglo-American alliance established an integrated command structure with representatives from both countries appointed to various staff positions. At the tactical level (corps and below) the alliance usually, but not always, established parallel structures, each nation controlling its own formations with coordination occurring laterally. During execution in the ETO army generals served as Commander Landing Force and were the supported units during these amphibious operations. The corresponding naval commanders for each task force served as the Commander of the Amphibious Task Force, designated as the supporting organization once troops moved ashore. As for its naval counterpart, the CATF for Patton's WTF was US Admiral Hewitt, fresh from his training duties at AFAF. Appointed commander of Task Force 34 (TF 34), US Atlantic Fleet, on 10 October, Hewitt continued his influential role in the development of American amphibious capabilities. Torch helped solidify the doctrinal command relations between CATF and CLF as it became the established norm for future operations.[7] However, reflecting the combined nature of the operation with the British allies, the CATF for the CTF was Royal Navy Commodore Thomas Troubridge, with his fellow countryman Admiral H. M. Burroughs in the same role with the ETF.[8]

Before any assault could occur, the lion's share of the American flotilla would have to traverse the Atlantic. While some units made the shorter journey from the United Kingdom, most of the US formations had to cross the ocean. However, arriving intact during this time was not a forgone conclusion. German U-Boats had already made their mark earlier in the war, sinking merchant marine vessels in the North Atlantic destined for the United Kingdom. If the German U-boat fleet got wind of the armada heading to North Africa, dozens of submarines could be sortied in their feared wolfpacks and intercept the inbound Allied fleet. If that occurred, the losses might be staggering. Fortunately, German naval leadership had its own disputes regarding U-boat strategy and submarine placement. U-boats in the vicinity of the invasion fleet were redirected toward another convoy heading north to the United Kingdom from Freetown and failed to respond to the larger Allied movement. As a result, the entire compliment of Torch vessels arrived without loss.[9]

While able to avoid the Kriegsmarine's U-boat fleet, adding to the complexity of the operation was Vichy French loyalties in the Amphibious Objective Areas.[10] While the United States retained diplomatic relations with the collaborationist Vichy regime under Marshal Philippe Petain, it also quietly supported an exiled Free French government under Charles de Gaulle. Key French officers in the region ran the gamut of loyalty. Petain's military commander in northwestern Africa was General Maxime Weygand, a staunch French patriot who was bitter about Nazi collaboration and German occupation. However, Admiral Francois Darlan, who held a number of positions in the Vichy government, was one of Petain's closest advisers who often stood in contrast to Weygand and supported German war efforts. Adding to the ambiguity of the situation, in the months preceding the Torch invasion American ships were permitted to deliver food supplies to French

North Africa with American officers stationed at key ports.[11] Walking the diplomatic tightrope created an uncertain environment. While the Allies prepared for an assault, it was unknown just how much resistance Vichy forces might put up. Might some locations be contested and others benign? Would some occupying units fight while others simply lay down their arms?

Unable to fully ascertain Vichy resolve, both Roosevelt and Eisenhower transmitted messages of friendship along the objective areas in an effort to persuade French forces to cooperate against the common German foe. FDR's message called for French help, with the American Psychological Warfare Bureau sending out broadcasts and leaflets reminding Frenchmen of the American friendship during World War I, asking "Souvenez-vous?" (Do you remember?).[12] Ike also transmitted a message of friendship to the Vichy forces. Attempting to convince the French formations to cooperate with the Allied troops instead of fighting them, his message played on republican tomes, declaring: "Americans . . . are striving for their own safe future as well as the restoration of the ideals, liberties, and the democracy of all those who have lived under the tricolor."[13] However, Marshal Petain was unambiguous in his rejection of FDR's message. In his response the French World War I hero, now turned Nazi collaborator, retorted: "France and her honor are at stake. [If] we are attacked[] we shall defend ourselves; this is the order I am giving."[14]

Regardless of Petain's bluster, George Marshall also put out guidance to Eisenhower regarding tactical action and engagement. He directed that no offensive action should be taken against French forces unless they interfered with unit objectives and have initiated fire. Once a defender had done so, units were permitted to return fire with the "maximum intensity and continue with the utmost vigor until the action has ceased."[15] He gave further guidance that "every precaution should be taken to avoid unnecessary damage to ships and harbor installations."[16] Similarly, even the ever-aggressive Patton expressed his desire to avoid excessive violence reminding his troops: "Remember, the French are not the Nazis or Japs."[17]

Regardless of the plan's timidity or its boldness, the ambiguous political environment, or strategic implications, amphibious training for Torch fell far short of what it should have been. Preparation for the various landing forces was a hodgepodge of exercises, with some units receiving formalized training while others received little or none. Furthermore, given the geographic location of the various divisions, such training was hardly uniform or standardized.[18] The navy was in no better condition. With an interwar focus on blue-water operations and large battleship design, the amphibious "Gator Navy" was indeed the lesser fleet in the service hierarchy. Years of neglect and unpreparedness were now fully felt. Patton was not shy about his lack of faith regarding the navy's ability to efficiently land his troops ashore, remarking that "never in history has the [US Navy] landed the [US Army] at the planned time and place. If [the navy] lands us anywhere within fifty miles of Fedhala and one week of D-Day, I'll go ahead and win."[19]

Western Task Force

Setting out from the continental United States, the task force sailors were woefully deficient in required skill sets. Given the expeditious nature of the plan and the immediacy of action, few of the boat crews, if any, had sufficient experience or training in amphibious operations.[20] On 1 June 1942 only eight ships were assigned to the AFAF. However, given the operation's priority the number of ships climbed, with new construction, transfers from the West Coast, and the conversion of several others. In as little as three months there were twenty-six transports and seven cargo ships available—more than a fourfold increase.[21] Many of the larger transport ships were as green as the crews who manned them.[22] By late October TF-34 carrying Patton's WTF set sail with twenty-six transports/cargo ships from Hampton Roads, Virginia, with 35,000 troops aboard. The 9th ID and 2nd AD trained at Fort Bragg, North Carolina, with final exercises conducted at Solomons Island and Little Creek. The 3rd ID simulated landings on the West Coast and moved to Fort Pickett, Virginia, in September to join with other elements of the WTF.[23]

The WTF was divided up into three sub task forces. Truscott's task force, code-named "Goal Post," was to seize the Port Lyautey airfield and introduce ground-based airpower to the area. A second, "Blackstone," was to secure the port facilities at Safi Morocco and unload the bulk of the WTF's armor assets. Because the navy lacked the ability to land armor on an unprepared beach, and before the introduction of the Landing Ship Tank and Landing Craft Tank, pier-side offload was the only way to debark the heaviest armored vehicles.[24] Once ashore, Blackstone's armor would move north toward Casablanca. Considered too strongly defended for a frontal amphibious assault, Casablanca was to be taken by a flanking ground attack. A third task force, "Brushwood," designated as the main effort, made a landing north of the objective Fedhala. In the middle of the two other WTF landings, the Brushwood force would come ashore, move south to Casablanca, and then capture the WTF's real prize—the town's important air and seaport facilities.[25]

To avoid congestion and prevent tipping off the enemy, the ships assigned to Torch left from various locations in North America and in sequence for the African coast. The covering surface force left from Casco Bay, Maine, the Air Group from Bermuda, with the Goal Post and Blackstone flotillas leaving from Hampton Roads on 23 October. A day later the Brushwood flotilla departed.[26] For the Goal Post flotilla, one important vessel was late in departure. In addition to the surface fleet, the WTF could also count the aircraft carrier USS *Ranger* along with four escort carriers. Ample air support for the assault included a compliment of twenty-eight Avenger torpedo bombers (TBFs), thirty-six Dauntless dive bombers (SBDs), and 108 F4F Wildcat fighters. The SS *Contessa* was an old, rusty hauling scow that had a shallow draft and would play an important role in the Goal Post mission.[27] Despite its age and dubious seaworthiness, *Contessa* drafted only 15 feet and could navigate the shallow waters of the Sebou River to deliver vital aviation supplies to Goal Post's main objective, the Port Lyautey airfield. However, once *Contessa*'s international crew learned of its new tasking, many promptly jumped ship! Put in drydock, it received hasty repairs and was fitted with a new crew of reprobates found in local jails. On 26 October, three days after the flotilla, *Contessa* started lumbering across the Atlantic.[28]

The first challenge for the American flotilla, zig-zagging across the ocean to avoid enemy torpedoes, was not the Vichy French forces but Mother Nature. The weather for the first ten days of the transatlantic journey was ideal. However, by 4 November conditions changed for the worse with rough seas and strong northwest winds. Forecasted weather for the next forty-eight hours was not much better calling for heavy seas off the Moroccan coast with a 15-foot-high surf predicted on D-Day. Given the existing sea state and projected weather, the WTF amphibious assaults were now in jeopardy.[29] As Naval Task Force Commander, Hewitt had to decide if the current plan was still feasible or if he needed an alternate course of action. After conferring with Patton, and with twenty-four hours before the landings were set to commence, Hewitt decided to deal with the weather and continue the operation as planned.[30] His gamble paid off: 7 November (D-1) was 78 degrees with overcast and a light breeze.[31]

Hours after this decision, the Safi (Blackstone) sub task force broke

Trek of the Western Naval Task Force across the Atlantic to its objective beaches on the Moroccan Coast. (CARL Digital Archive)

off from the flotilla and headed for its objective beaches followed by the Fedhala (Brushwood) element hours later.[32] The plan was for all three WTF flotillas to arrive at their respective areas simultaneously by 2400 on 7 November and then commence landing operations. The Mehedia (Goal Post) sub task force under the command of Brigadier General Lucian Truscott moved into position shortly after and waited for H-Hour on 8 November. The landing force comprised the 60th Infantry Regiment of the 9th ID, the 540th Engineer Battalion, and a combat team from the 2nd AD, totaling over 9,000 men and 65 light tanks.[33] The Goal Post objective was to capture the Port Lyautey airfield using five beaches bracketing the mouth of the Sebou River. South of the river were beaches designated Green, Yellow, and Blue. Troops landing at these locations were to assist in the attack inland while controlling a coastal road preventing Vichy reinforcements coming from the south. Troops using Green Beach landed just south of the river's mouth with the mission to capture the Kasba (an old Portuguese citadel) that marked the location of French naval shore batteries.[34] This Vichy position and the troops were a threat to the invasion force and a significant obstacle for SS *Contessa* and its press-gang crew coming upriver. North of the river two other beaches (Red and Red 2) were used by the landing force with the missions of capturing the objective airfield and securing the northern (inland) bank of the river.[35]

Shore Fire Control Parties (SFCPs) were placed with each battalion combat team along with aerial spotters available to help the naval guns.[36] However, wary of NSFS abilities and hoping to maintain the element of surprise, Truscott allowed no preparatory fires. Given this first salvo of the army's MTO/ETO assaults, the army commander was unfamiliar with how accurate naval gun crews were and had "strong doubts" regarding their accuracy. Initially, unlike Marine amphibious operations in the Pacific, army commanders forbade pre–D-Day bombardment, as they prized the element of surprise over battlefield shaping. In contrast, the Marines were heavily dependent on such support and figured that the element of surprise was not worth the cost of softening up enemy defenses.[37] Furthermore, Truscott directed that NSFS could fire on enemy positions, though for no more than three minutes without checking fire. Similarly, he did not initially allow NSFS against the Kasba and preferred to reduce its defenses through surprise by a ground assault from Green Beach. Concerned about friendly fire, the Goal Post commander directed naval crews to serve only as counterbattery fire or when specifically tasked by army liaisons.[38]

With the troop carriers in the designated transport area, men of the assault force climbed down the cargo nets into the awaiting landing craft. H-Hour was set at 0400 with the morning sun hours away. Under the cover of darkness the assault forces hoped to catch the enemy by surprise.[39] Similarly to NSFS, Marines in the Pacific went in the opposite direction and preferred operations in daylight. Citing *FM 31-5*, Marines subscribed to the idea that "landing operations at night are difficult and liable to be attended by greater confusion than during daylight."[40] However, the nocturnal movement might be moot given the messages from FDR and Eisenhower and might have compromised the element of surprise.[41] Regardless of the broadcast's effect that day, debarkation from the troop transports in the early-morning darkness took much longer than expected. The ship-to-shore method of movement required men to embark into the bobbing landing craft while laden with combat gear. Troop movement was slow and dangerous. Slippery metal-chain cargo nets thrown over the side of the transports cut hands and required soldiers to move gingerly and methodically into the waiting boats. Similarly problematic, some transports used rope nets for debarkation that often stretched and could foul themselves underwater into the landing craft screws. With the first rays of sunshine appearing over the horizon, the initial assault waves did not hit the beaches until 0540, almost two hours late. With these delays and the presidential transmission, Hewitt considered the element of surprise compromised.[42]

Landing craft formed a V formation behind their respective escort ships 1,000 yards from the transport areas to the designated control points. Once at the control point each V would then proceed to the

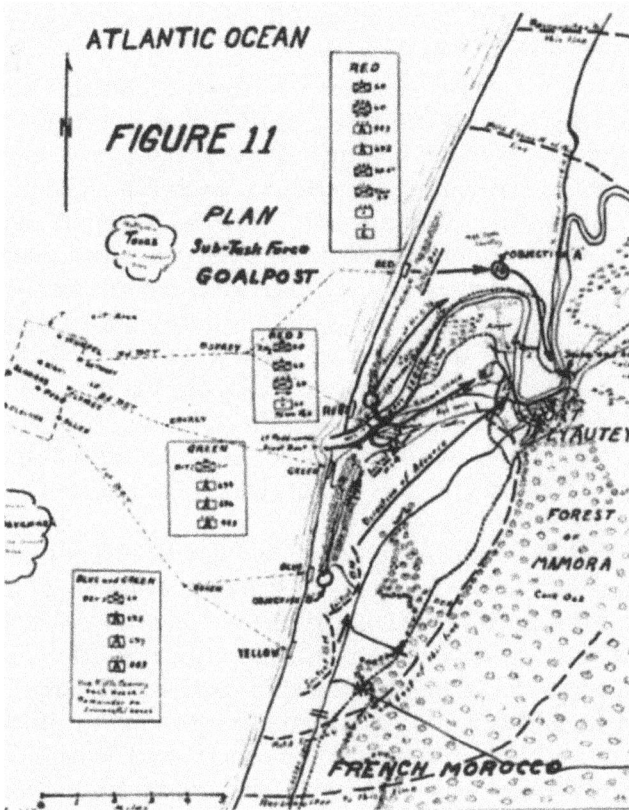

Map of the Port Lyautey landings conducted by Brigadier
General Lucian Truscott's "Goal Post" on 8 November.
Note the location of transports, fire control ships, and the
location of the landing beaches. (CARL Digital Archive)

Line of Departure some 5,000 yards from the intended color beach.
Each of the seven assault waves consisted of eighteen boats for a total of
162 landing craft.[43] Succeeding assault waves were planned at 10-minute
intervals to preclude a traffic jam in both the surf and on the beach.
Despite a 5–6-foot surf the Green Beach movement went as planned
with landing craft safely withdrawing. However, five minutes later the
morning calm broke as French batteries near the Kasba opened fire.
Army forces were instructed to use the code "batter up" when in need
of NSFS, with the affirmative response from the ship being "play ball."
With the ground forces transmitting "batter up" the US destroyer
USS *Eberle* responded "play ball" and returned fire. By 0710 general

support fires were authorized when other destroyers received the message and engaged land-based batteries.[44]

At 0630 enemy action increased as Vichy Dewoitine 520 fighter aircraft attacked the landing force, causing the aircraft carriers USS *Sangamon* and *Ranger* to launch their Wildcat fighters in pursuit. Successful in their aerial combat, American aviators claimed nine victories and chased off other Vichy aircraft.[45] At 0700 Vichy shore batteries opened fire again, placing rounds in the offshore troop transport area and causing the ships to withdraw fifteen miles farther out to sea. With this withdraw, ship-to-shore movement times increased significantly, with communications also becoming less effective.[46] NSFS engaged Vichy coastal artillery intermittently throughout the day and met with general success. With the Allied invasion underway, enemy reinforcements arrived at the Kasba, making a purely ground assault impossible. Counter to Truscott's original intent, taking the position would now require naval fires and air support.

As the Vichy aircraft began their 0630 attacks, the unit assigned to assault Blue and Yellow Beaches, 1st Battalion Landing Team (BLT), 60th Infantry, landed a mile north of the intended objective. Elements of the unit's second wave had landed before the first. Once ashore the BLT reorganized itself and continued in its mission of blocking reinforcement from the south.[47] Similarly, the 3rd Combat Team was to land at Red Beach and Red Beach 1 but experienced delays in embarkation along with confusion in assault-wave organization. Once finally formed, the landing craft headed north along the coastline, receiving enemy fire from the Vichy air attack. The unit lost two landing craft but suffered no casualties.

Despite the light from the rising sun, a morning mist prevented the battalion commander, Lieutenant Colonel John Toffey Jr., from observing the shoreline and his landing point at Red Beach. Toffey's coxswain become lost and unable to locate the designated beach. At 0600, frustrated and impatient, the commander ordered the coxswains to turn inland and make landfall. However, after checking his position the entire unit was five miles north of its intended beaches.[48] Toffey's unit spent the next few hours walking to the objective overlooking the airport. Many of the follow-on assault waves fared no better, landing at the wrong beaches; both troops and commanders became confused as to their next steps.[49]

Truscott came ashore at Blue Beach with his halftrack armored vehicle and a small staff. Despite making it to shore, he could not exercise complete command and control, as radio communications were poor and inadequate, with the surf precluding the arrival of follow-on forces. Given this limitation he circulated around the vicinity of the southern beaches (Blue and Yellow) trying to solve the most immediate issues while waiting for reinforcements.[50] Given the limitations of command and control that first day, Truscott in essence became a small unit commander largely disconnected from the larger task force that was his charge. Clearly his lack of communications reduced his combat effectiveness and jeopardized the mission.

Vichy resistance in some areas was stiff. As the 2nd Battalion Landing Team pushed forward from Green Beach to the village near the Kasba, they came under attack from Vichy infantry, armor, and artillery. Despite NSFS from USS *Savannah*, the French effectively counterattacked, pushing back the American troops that were still devoid of armor, artillery, and antitank weapons.[51] While troops were able to hold some of the adjacent ground, French airplanes and prepared positions in the objective area made Truscott's situation precarious—but not yet desperate. With limited forces ashore and problems introducing more combat power from the sea, the task force desperately needed to reinforce its beachhead positions with additional heavy weapons and troops.[52]

Follow-on assault waves proved problematic, as army beach parties were unable to manage the flow of equipment coming ashore. A rising tide swamped vehicles and supplies as beaches became littered with gear and equipment.[53] Reflecting a lack of training and only emergent doctrine, one account of the Torch shore party support stated:

> This was an unsophisticated series of beach landings by infantry battalion landing teams, each with an attached engineer shore company organized into shore parties tasked generally with carrying supplies across the beach by hand and stacking them in front of the dune line. Each company operated independently according to the judgement of its commander since no standard operating procedure existed. Manual methods . . . were tediously labor intensive and frustratingly slow. . . . Such was the cumulative delay in unloading by hand that the timetable became progressively slowed and delayed.[54]

Another observed:

> Conditions on the beaches during the night presented a scene of indescribable confusion. Surf was rising so that about half of the

landing craft were not able to retract. Exit from the beaches were possible only from tracked vehicles. Vehicles and stores were piling up so fast that the shore party could hardly keep them above the high-water mark. Elements that were supposed to land at Green Beach or later when Brown Beach might be open were landing at Blue Beach, wandering around seeking their respective units in darkness.[55]

The development of combat power stalled. A robust and effective logistical infrastructure and support for the landings failed to materialize. Had this occurred against a determined foe, the results would have been much different if not tragic.

Adding to the problem, the surf became more violent, and subsequent assault waves of landing craft broke apart and lost formation. The surf overcame many coxswains' abilities to handle their craft, with boats being overwhelmed and/or left abandoned. The transport ship USS *Henry T. Allen* alone lost fourteen of its thirty-five landing craft as they were abandoned on the beach. As night came, the rising ocean swells precluded any heavy weapons from arriving ashore. Resupply and evacuation of the wounded became too dangerous with ship-to-shore movement suspended. Truscott would have to hold on with the forces that had already landed.[56]

As a result of navigation errors, deficient seamanship, misplacement of troops ashore, and poor beach-party support, Truscott's comments were similar to the prewar observations regarding an amphibious disaster against a "competent enemy." The Goal Post commander later reported: "The combination of inexperienced land craft crews, poor navigation, and desperate hurry resulting from lateness of the hour, finally turned debarkation into a hit-or-miss affair that would have spelled disaster against a well-armed enemy intent upon resistance."[57] Indicative of these problems was the landing craft loss rate for the Goal Post landings. Of the 162 boats used in the operation, seventy were destroyed, a loss rate of 43 percent.[58]

Despite the lack of combat power ashore, the NSFS and aviation provided a significant advantage. On D+1 ships targeted Vichy armored formations and defensive positions inland with the use of navy spotter planes.[59] By afternoon more forces were able to come ashore and made their way inland. A naval air liaison party with the 2nd Battalion Landing Team helped secure the area around the Kasba by requesting air support from USS *Sangamon*. Using dive-bombing, naval aviators were already trained for such missions. Dive-bombing was seen

The SS *Contessa* was a shallow water draft scow that could navigate the Sebou River and carry aviation supplies to the Port Lyautey airfield. With her usual crew compliment jumping ship before sailing, a press gang of sorts crewed the vessel across the Atlantic and into the Moroccan interior. (Historic New Orleans Digital Collection)

as an effective method of attack against ships and ground targets, as it allowed for betting aiming while frustrating defensive antiaircraft artillery (AAA) gunners. Naval aviation was especially good at hitting the dead space that existed just beyond the first sand dunes and the higher elevations inland. Given the relatively flat trajectories of naval guns, such dead space often provided cover for defending forces just off the beach. SBD Dauntless dive-bombers were particularly adept at striking such targets. With a crew of two and with specially designed dive flaps that retarded airspeed during attack, the Dauntless would prove an invaluable airframe. The SBDs peeled off one at a time and delivered their ordnance accurately, leading to a Vichy surrender of the position.[60] Regarding close air support, a British observer used the words "splendid" and "outstanding," impressed as he was with support coming within only minutes of a request.[61]

By 0430 on 10 November, the barrier net across the Sebou River was cut by a navy boat team. This allowed the USS *Dallas*, a transport-destroyer, to make its way up the river and engage the Kasba position. With assistance from a local river pilot, and despite running aground in shallow waters, *Dallas* cleared the way for the *Contessa* and its aviation supplies.[62] While the old scow ran aground as well in the river at ebb tide, it eventually made its way to the aerodrome along with the seaplane tender USS *Barnegat*. Starting at 1107 that same day, most of the 78 P-40 Warhawk fighters left the flight deck of the transport carrier USS *Chenango* and landed at the Lyautey airfield. Given the lack of shipboard recovery capability, the P-40s were on a one-way trip.[63] Landing on the soft, pockmarked landing strip, some planes experienced landing gear damage, but the crews were met by the *Contessa* making its way up the shallow Sebou River.[64] Three days later eleven US Navy PBY Catalina patrol aircraft arrived at the airfield from the United Kingdom.[65] Despite the setbacks in the amphibious assault and subsequent land operation, by 0400 on 11 November Truscott had attained his objectives. With a formal meeting taking place near the Kasba at the mouth of the river, the Americans received Vichy General Maurice Mathinet's surrender. Graciously, Truscott explained to the Frenchman that the American forces were not looking for a surrender but rather cooperation against a common German foe.[66]

South of the Goal Post operation was the WTF's main effort. The Fedhala (Brushwood) landings focused on the city of Casablanca and its important port facilities. The 3rd ID with the 67th Armored Regiment, and an engineer battalion loaded aboard twelve transports with almost 20,000 men, 1,700 vehicles, and 15,000 tons of supplies.[67] The scheme of maneuver was to land north of Casablanca, near the town of Fedhala, conduct a subsequent operation ashore, and assault the city via ground action. Major General Johnathan Anderson planned to deploy 6,000 troops on D-Day utilizing five separate beaches designated Red, Red 2, Red 3, Blue, and Blue 2 that stretched approximately six miles. All the beaches were north of the cape that housed the accompanying town. Defending the approaches were Vichy naval shore batteries in and around the cape south of the designated beaches with accompanying guns north of Blue 2 at Pont Blondin.[68]

Very late on 7 November the troop ships arrived a few nautical miles offshore in the designated transport area.[69] With H-Hour also set for 0400 on 8 November, the plan was for scout boats to land at their respective colored beaches at 0345 ahead of the main assault.[70] Once ashore the scouts were to signal the oncoming assault waves with colored flares and infrared flashlights marking the respective landing beaches. In the early morning hours, and while the scouts were heading inland, the troop transports planned to disembarked soldiers and supplies over the side into the landing craft. After the boats were loaded, escort destroyers were to lead the assault waves to the control points.

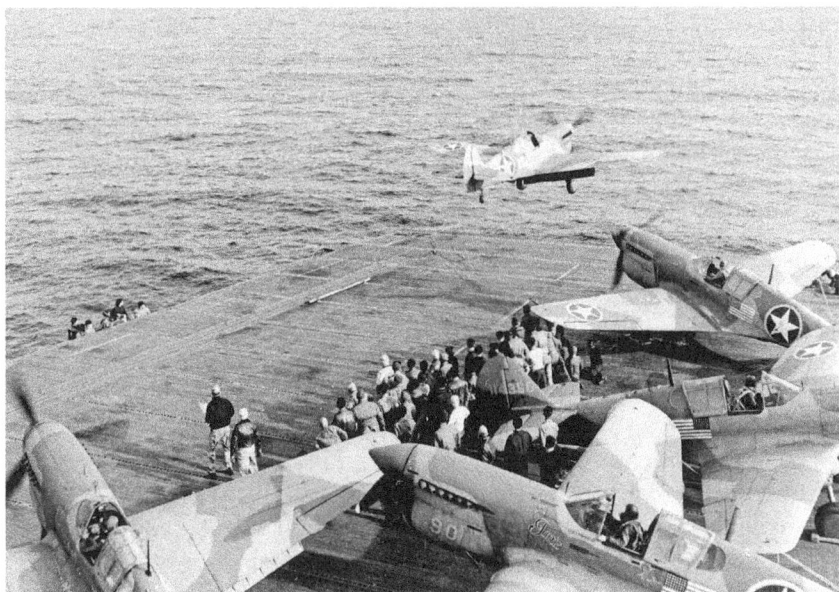

US Army P-40 fighters depart USS *Chenago* for the Port Lyautey Airfield ashore. (US Navy photo)

Converging at the L/D the landing craft were then to proceed to the assault beaches while the escort destroyers marked four boat lanes for subsequent assault waves. Once accomplished, the destroyers and the cruiser USS *Brooklyn* would then position themselves offshore for possible NSFS missions.[71]

However, the timetable for execution quickly unraveled as the unexperienced deck crews and quartermasters caused debarkation delays. Unfamiliar with davit operations, the ships crews were not efficient in lowering boats into the sea. Adding to the delay was a complicated loading sequence. Troop transports carried only thirty-four landing craft, but each BLT required approximately forty-three assault boats. Due to the shortage of shipboard landing craft, additional boats had to be moved from other ships in the Brushwood flotilla, some located miles away. Adding to the difficulty, these additional assault craft had to find their assigned troop transports under cover of darkness, many becoming lost in the night or failing in locate their designated transports. Coxswains were reduced to going from transport to transport using a megaphone to asking "Is this the *Ancon*? (or *Leonard Wood*? or any other vessels they were assigned to)." Boat crews drifted from ship to ship looking for their respective assault waves and teams. Even senior naval officers before the war understood the peril of sending one vessel to another under the cover of darkness.[72] As a result of such confusion, the landing force had an average of only thirty-two vessels per troop transport, far short of the fifty designated for the initial assault waves.[73] The poor execution of the debarkation schedule led the 3rd ID commander to report: "Failure of the ships to arrive in the transport area as scheduled completely upset the timing of the boat employment plan."[74]

But this was not the only reason for the delay, as the army shared in the fault. Given the scheme of maneuver, the nighttime staging of the initial assault would have been difficult even with experienced crews. Some 4,000 yards offshore, the USS *Leonard Wood* had all its boats in the water at 0130, well before H-Hour. However, soldiers encumbered by weapons and equipment could only slowly move down the dangerous cargo nets into the swaying and rolling landing craft.[75] One misstep by a soldier might mean falling into the ocean or breaking his neck. As a result of these delays, H-hour was moved to 0445 and then not executed until 0500. The skipper of the transport USS *Thomas Jefferson* remarked: "Overall sluggishness of Army personnel both in loading equipment in boats and in embarking themselves; the Army imposed upon transport commanders an unnecessary complicated boat employment because it wanted to get an unreasonably large number of troops ashore at Fedhala before daylight."[76] Novice sailors and inexperienced soldiers had yet to understand the intricacies of littoral operations, proving that both services still had much to learn.[77]

With the delay of H-Hour unknown to the scout boats ashore, at 0400 they began flashing their colored signals to the offshore flotilla, again compromising the element of surprise.[78] There was further confusion when Eisenhower's London radio transmission requested Vichy forces to point their searchlights skyward as a gesture of nonresistance. At H-Hour, many Vichy lights were indeed facing up, leading some Americans to hope for a peaceful landing.[79] When the first assault waves hit the shore during ebb tide at 0515, the landings were again problematic. Poor navigation, faulty compass readings, and inexperienced crews, combined with other factors, scattered units along the objective area. Disembarked from *Leonard Wood*, parts of BLT 1-7 intended to land at Red 2 came ashore almost a mile northeast on Red 3. Others from the *Leonard Wood* missed the designated beaches altogether, with many assault craft floundering in the rocky coastline between colored beaches Red and Blue.[80]

Overloaded with troops and supplies, and caught by the dangerous surf, many landing craft capsized. Equipment-laden soldiers were thrown from their boats, with several men drowning in the crashing surf.[81] Twenty-one boats of *Leonard Wood*'s initial wave aimed at the Red beaches were lost.[82] During the execution much of *Thomas Jefferson*'s landing craft were also damaged by the rocky shores or mishandled by green coxswains. Only seventeen out of the ship's thirty-three landing craft survived the initial assault, with six of the seventeen eventually requiring repairs.[83] BLT 1-30 from the USS *Charles Carroll* lost eighteen of twenty-five landing craft in the first wave and lost five more in the second, leaving only two serviceable.[84] Brushwood's best performance of the day was from USS *Joseph T. Dickman* and BLT 2-30, losing only two of twenty-seven craft in the initial wave at Blue 2. Similar to the Goal Post figures, approximately 45 percent of the landing craft fleet was expended in the Brushwood landings.[85] After the operation, a naval officer surveyed the assault beaches and counted 169 wrecked boats, some so damaged that he eventually counted only engines instead of intact hulls.[86]

This loss of landing craft was indeed high, and production of such vessels was only beginning to meet the growing need. With American industry capacity ramping up as the arsenal of democracy, such losses would require expedient production of new boats. Awaiting production of new landing craft given the Torch landing craft losses, Eisenhower lamented the shortage of such vessels. Afterward, while planning for Operation Husky and the invasion of Sicily, the Allied commander worried that the combined force might not have the lift required for the next amphibious assault. The general's aide, Captain Harry Butcher, recalled that in spring 1943 Eisenhower was so worried about the lack of landing craft that he joked that his coffin should be shaped like a landing craft, as the lack of them was "killing him with worry."[87]

As late as February 1942 Higgins received his first large order for landing craft from the Navy Bureau of Ships, requesting 508 Landing Craft Vehicle Personnel. Ever the innovator, Higgins responded quickly to the emerging need. By July 1943, six months after the Torch assaults, Higgins factories in New Orleans were producing 600 landing craft per month, an average that eventually reached over 700 by the end of the war. By that same 1943 date, the Louisiana plants had already built over 8,000 boats and would eventually build another 12,000 more over the course of the war.[88] The smaller LCVPs, Landing Craft Personnel (LCPs), Landing Craft Personnel Large (LCPL), and Landing

Craft Mechanized (LCMs) were only now coming off the production lines at increasing rates and destined for both theaters of the war.[89]

In addition to the losses, and landings on the wrong beaches, units became mixed and organizational integrity was lost. Indicative of the problem, the commanding officer of BLT 2-30 and his headquarters element landed east of the Vichy gun battery at Pont Blondin at an undesignated site, while the rest of his unit went to its correct beach at Blue 2.[90] Concurrently, BLT 2-7 planned to land at Red 3 but ended up at the beach designated Blue 3.[91] Many units adjusted and improvised, taking objectives of opportunity as opposed to assigned ones. Such initiative became a staple of the American fighting man during the war, as planned execution often fell woefully short on various D-Days in the MTO/ETO.

In addition, many landing assault waves come in at ebb tide, many landing craft becoming stranded (referred to as "drying out") on the beaches and creating obstacles for follow-on troops. Furthermore, assault waves making it ashore arrived so closely in sequence that it was impossible to halt them. As a result, a traffic jam of landing craft occurred. As more men and equipment arrived, they also became impediments and hindered naval recovery operations. Left stranded, many landing craft were battered by the surf causing further damage. Despite the training that occurred in the Chesapeake, soldiers lost discipline and rushed ashore, failing to assist in the offloading of landing craft. In the heat of execution standard procedures for the movement of supplies ashore were quickly forgotten.[92] Army shore parties struggled with vessels carrying vehicles and the unloading of supplies. This was partially the fault of embarkation personnel who threw equipment into landing craft without regard for discharge and placement. This situation would repeat itself.

Additionally, of the nine fire control parties sent ashore, only two could communicate with NSFS, even inexperienced radio operators often transmitting over each other, jamming signal traffic and delaying calls for fire.[93] Despite these miscues, the Bushwood landings were successful, landing 3,500 troops ashore during the faint morning light. Despite Ike's broadcast, once assault forces landed ashore, Vichy searchlights lowered their elevation, illuminating the assault craft for the coastal guns.[94]

American vessels targeted Vichy lights and positions shortly after 0600 as French troops opened fired from both Pont Blondin and Cape Fedhala.[95] French rounds from Port Blondin found their mark on the destroyer USS *Murphy*, hitting its engine room and killing three men.[96]

However, Allied destroyers engaged the Vichy position, destroying its guns and the accompanying stereoscopic range finder.[97] BLT 2-30, coming from beach Blue 2 along with other elements of BLT 2-7, which landed at the wrong beach, moved on the Port Blondin position and secured the garrison, establishing a defensive perimeter.[98]

Landing in the dawn light at Red Beach 2, 1st Battalion, 7th Infantry moved on the town of Fedhala, capturing a Senegalese infantry company and ten German administrators trying to flee, securing the area by 0600.[99] French gun positions at Batterie du Port near the cape faced both west and east and were located near oil tanks that Allied forces hoped to tap. Vichy 100mm guns fired across the cape at the 30th Regimental Landing Group (RLG) but were silenced by NSFS.[100] While naval gunners took pains to avoid hitting the oil tanks, one was hit. After securing the town, 1/7 moved to the Vichy gun positions on the cape and at Batterie du Port with help from naval bombardment. Teamed with four light tanks from 756th Tank Battalion, 1/7 secured the French positions by 1500.[101] The assault BLTs succeeded in obtaining their objectives, and by the end of the day the local Vichy commander met with Patton.

While the ground action was underway, at 0827 French destroyers made their way north from Casablanca and threatened the designated transport area. A Vichy naval salvo reportedly hit a landing craft near Brushwood's southernmost invasion beach (Yellow). Additionally, they successfully hit USS *Ludlow* and forced USS *Wilkes* to withdraw to the protection of nearby cruisers.[102] However, Admiral Hewitt ordered the naval covering group to shield the transports and attack the French ships. The enemy vessels came within miles of the landing beaches, but with the covering force closing in, the French ships withdrew southward. Departing, the Vichy vessels threw up a smoke screen to preclude American range-finding and engagement.

Other French vessels sailed north and engaged the covering force. The subsequent naval engagement lasted most of the day, resulting in a clear US victory. American forces assumed control of the adjacent sea space after suffering only minor hits on five ships. For the Vichy fleet, they lost four destroyers and eight submarines, with significant hits to the battleship *Jean Bart* and three others.[103] Perhaps the biggest result of the naval action was the delay of General Patton's arrival ashore. Aboard the cruiser USS *Augusta* he was scheduled to disembark at 0800, but the ensuing naval action forced the WTF commander to arrive ashore five hours later at 1320.[104]

While the fleet provided surface protection, naval aviation proved

American troops coming ashore at Fedhala. The loss of landing craft on this operation was excessive losing approximately 45 percent of the Brushwood inventory. (US Navy photo)

its worth, providing overhead defense for the assault force. French fighter aircraft did harass troops on the beach a number of times on D-Day followed by high-altitude bombers on 9 November, but they were largely ineffective. Vichy aircraft hit no ships and did not interfere with naval spotting planes. Conversely, American planes provided effective CAS, flew combat air patrols, and struck French warships and shore batteries.[105]

By late afternoon 40 percent of the 19,000 troops embarked were ashore, with many ships awaiting their turns to offload. On the established beachhead, only 16 percent of Brushwood's vehicles and 1 percent of supplies had been landed. The navy beachmaster directed all ships to unload at Red Beach or at the port facilities given the reduction of the enemy positions and the rising surf conditions. In the analysis of the operation, Admiral Hewitt stated the obvious: "The dire need of better training of boat crews was everywhere apparent."[106] While most already knew that naval personnel operating the landing craft had insufficient training before departure, the crews actions were good enough considering the enemy dispositions. In much the same sentiment as Truscott regarding the Goal Post landings, Patton's observations regarding Brushwood caused the CLF to quip: "Had the landings been opposed by Germans, we would have never gotten ashore."[107]

The Western Task Force's commanding general, Major General George Patton, prepared to land on the shores near Fedhala Morocco. (US Navy photo)

The southernmost landing of Patton's WTF occurred at the small fishing town of Safi, which housed an old phosphate port with a decidedly different execution. Since the navy's lighterage at the time could not carry the WTF's 40-ton M4 Sherman tanks to the beach, the Blackstone landings intended to capture the town's harbor and use it to unload the heavier armor.[108] Commanded by Major General Ernest Harmon of the 2nd AD, the Blackstone task force comprised 327 officers, over 6,000 troops, and 779 vehicles. The landing was a phased operation that required them to seize the Safi port facility, form a beachhead, unload the armor pier side, and establish a line of communication, and advance to the northern WTF landings near Casablanca.[109]

First the dock was secured by a commando force, then another landing force with lighter armor assets and additional infantry would seize Blue and Red Beaches, establishing the beachhead. Facing the Americans was a French force positioned at various locations around the port with one position on a 300-foot cliff overlooking the city and another strongpoint, Batterie Railleuse, with four 130mm guns. Additional defensive firepower included 75mm guns, .50-caliber antiaircraft weapons, a mobile 155mm artillery battery, and a platoon of light tanks, all of it combined with a Moroccan infantry regiment. In addition, further inland the defenders had benefit of French air support from a nearby airfield.[110]

Much like the other WTF landings, debarkation of troops from the transports in the early-morning dark to the landing craft was much slower than anticipated. Again, soldiers laden with 70–80 pounds of gear and equipment had to carefully navigate swaying cargo nets into the awaiting boats.[111] Like the Brushwood landings, additional landing craft had trouble making their way from their parent vessel to the troop transports in the darkness, causing further delays. Other complications and delays also came from poor combat loading. Despite Hewitt's calls for army participation in loading ships in Virginia Beach, vehicles and equipment of the first wave were located deep in the holds of USS *Harris*. Debarkation required an in-stream Tetris-like game, "moving embarked items and breaking open of hatch squares to access the higher priority equipment. This lack of combat loading was a serious impediment in many of the day's landings in an expeditionary environment where time and organization mattered."[112]

USS *Dorthea Dix* had similar ship-to-shore problems. After organizing only five of ten assault waves, its landing craft lost sight of the inbound escort. The frustrated assault waves returned to the transport area and did not move inland again until 0800. The embarkation of armor onto the lighters was a challenge given unexpected sea swells. Further frustrating the armor movement was the mechanical failure of one of the five lighters carrying smaller tanks to the beach.[113] Given these problems the first wave of tanks crossed the L/D thirty minutes late and without its full complement.[114]

Combat action began shortly after 0400 as an old destroyer, the USS *Bernadou*, modified and stripped of much of superstructure, steamed into the harbor carrying an American commando force. Along with USS *Cole* the ships carried troops intent on preventing the sabotage to the port facility.[115] Approaching the port's sea wall, large-caliber French guns, including from Batterie Railleuse, engaged the American vessel. American ships returned fire as the *Bernadou* made for Green Beach, located within the man-made harbor's breakwater.[116] Traveling through Vichy fire, *Bernadou*'s skipper, Lieutenant Commander Robert E. Braddy Jr., decided to forgo the planned pierside debarkation of the commandos as berthed vessels blocked his access. Instead, he gently beached the vessel and unloaded the commando troops over the side. With the ship grounded, the crew threw cargo nets over the ship's hull as Company K, 47th Infantry, 9th Division climbed down

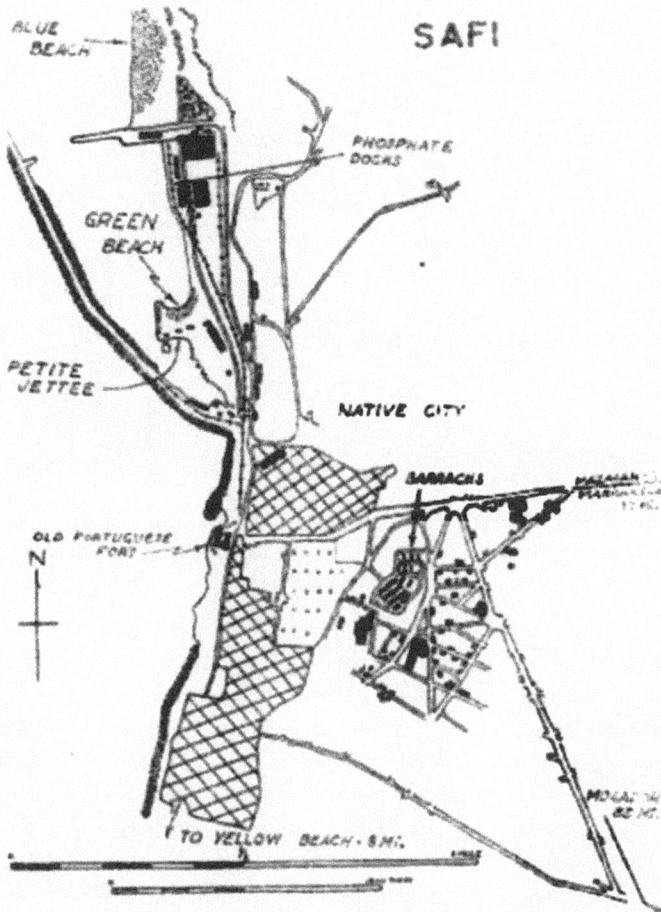

Task Force Blackstone's area of operations. The Safi port facility was used to unload the M4 Sherman tanks for subsequent land operations. (CARL Digital Archives)

at 0445.[117] After chasing away French Legionnaires, twenty minutes later three of the tank lighters arrived pierside with additional infantry troops. By the time morning light came the American troops held the port facility, major roads, and part of the town.

Additional assault waves landed at their correct Red, Blue, and Green Beaches between 0505 and 0640, just before sunrise. However,

USS *Bernadou* deliberately run aground in Safi Harbor, Morocco, with the cargo nets thrown over the sides for army commandos to disembark. Note the reduction of the ship's superstructure. (US Navy photo)

French positions were still operational and engaging American forces to the east and north.[118] NSFS with air spotters found their marks and silenced the Vichy guns. Follow-on actions cleared the Vichy forces while the Americans moved; more armor and infantry assets ashore. By 1530 General Harmon landed pierside; so did USS *Titania* and USS *Lakehurst*, commencing the WTF's heavy armor offload.[119] Simultaneously other tank and mechanized vehicles cleared out pockets of resistance that harassed America ships utilizing the port. By the time night fell the Blackstone task force established a beachhead 5,000 yards from the port, held most of the town's roads, had cut Vichy communications, and was in control of the local population.[120] Subsequent ground actions had elements of 2nd AD pushing north to the town of Mazagan toward Casablanca.

The Americans were still some fifty miles short of their objective when the French military commander in the capital city, General Charles Nogues, signaled that Vichy troops would no longer resist. With this announcement the Blackstone mission was now moot. The Safi landings were successful, with a beachhead established, the port secured, armor assets ashore, with and another American formation moving freely in Morocco.[121] Damaged occurred to only nine boats out of the 121 assigned. Of the nine damaged, eight were repaired, the other salvaged. These few loses of landing craft at Safi were significantly less than the losses experienced at the other two WTF landings.[122]

After an unauthorized air attack on the Vichy aerodrome at Marrakech, on D+1 French planes conducted a retaliatory raid over Safi. Despite a persistent fog over the beachhead, a Vichy bomb hit a pierside building housing an ammunition dump. While the explosion halted port operations for a period, the net result was negligible.[123] The Americans could no longer ignore the Vichy air threat. Shortly afterward USS *Santee* launched a strike on the Marrakech aerodrome but became sidetracked with a call for support as a still aggressive Vichy convoy of fifty trucks made its way to Safi. The American planes attacked the French column, but the results fell short. A combat command from 2AD moved out by 1413 to intercept the column. Coming in contact by 1700, the Americans subdued the French forces, with some surrendering and others withdrawing.[124]

Despite all of these problems during the assaults, ships of CTF 34 began unloading their cargo at the various ports and began building combat power ashore. To maintain the presence of American forces and assist in operational reach in-theater, the US Navy established Naval Operating Base Casablanca on 19 November. Under American command the Casablanca port was improved to handle in-stream offload with lighters and barges, with army personnel assisting.[125]

Center Task Force

As part of the trio of Torch amphibious landings, the CTF focused its operations on the northern coast of Africa at Oran. The mission of the CTF was to capture a well-constructed port and harbor for subsequent use by Allied forces, establish a permanent logistics base, and maintain the line of communication for the various Allied lodgments. This was a threefold operation with landings on beaches designated "X-Ray," "Yorker," and "Zebra." These assaults were a combined operation, as British crews operated the landing craft carrying American troops.[126] In addition to the British coxswains, Royal Navy Commodore Thomas Troubridge served as the CATF, with US Major General Lloyd Fredendall as his CLF counterpart.

The landing force included the 1st ID, 1st AD and various combat and support attachments, totaling 39,000 officers and men. None of the American formations attended the training at Camp Edwards or Camp

Carrabelle. However, the "Big Red One," as the 1st Infantry Division was known, did conduct small-scale amphibious exercises in the Caribbean with full-scale ones as Onslow Beach, North Carolina, in July 1941 and at Camp Henry, Virginia, six months later in January 1942. Arriving in the United Kingdom that August and initially billeted at Tideworth Barracks in southern England, the division conducted further amphibious training at Helensburgh, Scotland, near Glasgow.[127] Training consisted of ship-to-shore movement, loading drills, and an amphibious rehearsal. According to one battalion commander's account: "All of the Division went through endless landing exercises in which ship-to-shore movement was simulated by assembling units at a hard shore, loading on small craft, and proceeding directly to the proposed landing beach. Also, a great deal of simulating was done in regard to landing craft-a scow or a barge . . . accommodat[ing] 2, 3, 4, or 5 assault craft loads."[128] However, the actual type of landing craft used in training was different from those used during execution. With the dissimilar gear came delays on D-Day.[129] Included in the CTF troop list were elements of the 1st EAB pulled from training at Camp Edwards at the last minute and sent to the United Kingdom in August.[130] Despite its barely operational status and without its complement of landing craft, the EAB arrived at the Firth of Clyde on 17 August.[131] However, once in the United Kingdom the unit was broken up with elements distributed to various commands.[132] As a result, a fully staffed and competent shore-party function was absent from the troop list.

The 1st ID, under the command of Major General Terry de la Mesa Allen Sr., assaulted the beaches with one combat team east of Oran (Zebra Beach) seizing the city as part of a two-pronged approach. A second combat team of the 26th Infantry Regiment landed to the west near Les Andalouses Bay (Yorker Beach).[133] A third element landed farther west at Mersa Bao Zedjar (X Ray Beach) utilizing mechanized and armor assets to form a flying column and capture airfields south of Oran.[134] In addition to the amphibious assault, the operation also included the use of paratroops from the 2nd Battalion, 509th Parachute Infantry for the capture of nearby Vichy airfields, plus a commando raid to secure the important port of Oran.[135]

To secure the port in Oran a commando force, code-named "Reservist," preceded the amphibious assault. A truly joint and combined effort, the Reservist force comprised Royal Navy sailors along with US Army, Navy, and Marine personnel. The mission was to prevent Vichy sabotage or scuttling of moored ships in an attempt to frustrate Allied designs on the harbor. The plan called for the insertion of commando teams embarked from two Royal Navy cutters. After penetrating the harbor, powered launches would take the teams ashore to neutralize French defensive positions and secure the port's infrastructure.[136] Hoping that the Vichy forces might embrace the commandoes as liberators, the ships flew both American and Royal Navy ensigns. Eager to insert the commandos quietly, the ships attempted to enter the harbor stealthily and with speed under the cover of darkness.

However, Vichy troops were on the alert, aware of the Allied fleet's presence. Just before 0300 the ships approached the port's narrow, 300-foot opening; French sentries gave the alarm. Sirens wailed, shattering the early-morning calm, searchlights breaking through the darkness and illuminating the incoming vessels. The port was well protected by several fortifications and bristled with assorted heavy calibers combined with the French naval presence. Defending troops and berthed vessels opened fire on the invading ships, scoring direct hits once they breached the port's protective boom. Neither ship nor landing force succeeded in the mission with both ships sunk in the port. The action also spurred Vichy forces to do exactly what Allied planners had feared. In an act of self-sabotage by French forces, three floating drydocks and submarines along with twenty-five other vessels resident in the Oran port were put out of commission.[137] Leveraging this strategic location would now be delayed until Allied naval engineers and salvage experts could remove the wrecks.

An airborne insertion fared no better. In an operation code-named "Villain," members of the 509th Parachute Infantry Battalion (PIB) were to sortie from the United Kingdom and drop around the Vichy held airfields of La Senia and Tafaraoui. The paratroopers took off in C-47 Skytrains late on 7 November from the British airfields of St. Eval and Predanneck in Cornwall. Dealing with a shortage of maps and navigation equipment, the aircrews were expected to fly at night over 1,000 miles to their objectives.[138] Rain, fog, and thunderstorms made the mission even more difficult, as poor radio communications and faulty navigation lights made formation flying impossible. Adding to their woes, a planned navigation beacon from the British ship *Alynbank* was supposed to transmit on a frequency of 440 kilocycles but instead sent it out on 460 kilocycles.[139] As a result the navigation aid provided no directional assistance to the inbound planes. Navigation errors caused six planes to fly so disparately that one landed at Gibraltar, two in French Morocco, and three in Spanish Morocco. Many of the embarked troopers were then held by local officials.

Formation integrity had long been discarded as the planes arrived over Oran. Twelve C-47s dropped their paratroopers, but once on the ground they had to walk to the Tafaraoui airfield, arriving the next day to find the objective already secured. Some C-47s landed with troops aboard at various locations, with a few planes subsequently destroyed by Vichy artillery fire. Others were downed by Vichy fighters, and by the end of the operation only fourteen of the original thirty-nine transports remained airworthy. Moreover, by 15 November only 300 of the 556 paratroopers were accounted for. Like the Reservist operation, Villain was an abject failure, but it did mark the first use of airborne troops in conjunction with an amphibious landing; more important, it proved constructive when after-action reports provided new insights on such operations.[140]

The threefold envelopment of Oran was based on the city's considerable seaside defensive positions. Throughout the landings HMS *Rodney* engaged coastal defenses, as did other smaller vessels. An aggressive French navy sortied smaller ships that required surface action by the Royal Navy. Facing the landing force at Zebra Beach near Arzew were thirteen batteries of coastal artillery manned by a garrison of some 4,000 troops.[141] Up to 25,000 Vichy forces were also in the Oran area, which included airfields near Tafaraoui and La Senia with combat aircraft that might also thwart the American landings. Much like the landings of the WTF, there were no preparatory fires shaping the beach areas or tipping off Vichy forces as to potential locations of amphibious assaults.[142]

With use of the Royal Navy's landing craft, the British had a different methodology for guiding the landing force ashore. While the Americans used a destroyer to escort landing waves ashore, the British used submarines to help locate assault beaches. Smaller signal boats were taken near shore by a surfaced submarine and then released near the designated beach. These signal craft served as beacons for the assault waves coming ashore.[143] The weather on D-Day was conducive to amphibious assault, with a calm sea and gentle breeze. Elements of 1st AD landed to the west of Oran at X-Ray Beach organized in four parts with assault troops, shore-party units, flying columns, and a main body. While H-Hour was set at 0100 on 8 November, the first troops landed at 0143 and 0230 respectively on two colored beaches, X White and X Green. After the assault force secured the beachhead, a shore party set up assembly areas, routes of egress, traffic control points, supply dumps, communications stations, and matting for wheeled vehicles.[144] In addition each of the combat teams at the respective landing beaches received support from a battalion of the engineer shore regiment.[145] Once the flying columns came ashore they proceeded inland to seize airfields and important road junctions.[146] Following these units, the main body landed conducting subsequent operations ashore.

With no coastal defenses or enemy formations in the area, the initial landings at X Beach could be classified as an amphibious movement and not an assault. While the potential for combat existed, no exchange of fire occurred. Had Vichy forces resisted at these locations the outcome may have been very different. Despite the lack of enemy action, not all went according to plan.[147] During the initial wave local vessels interfered with the landing craft and delayed the employment of minesweepers, disrupting the initial timetable. Not unlike in the WTF's movement, landing craft mechanical and navigation errors resulted in the mislanding of the second wave landing at X-Ray Green ahead of the first.

Novel to Torch's CTF landings was the use of three converted shallow-water tankers brought from Lake Maracaibo, Venezuela. These vessels originally moved petroleum from South American refineries to Aruba and were reconfigured into prototype amphibious tankers. They could carry up to twenty light tanks, beach themselves, then unload vehicles thru clamshell doors on the ship's bow.[148] A British innovation, these ships were the prototypes for the Landing Ship Tank (LST). One of these first LSTs, the HMS *Misoa* (originally *Bachaquero*) landed at X-Ray Green at 0346 but could not make it to the shoreline. The X-Ray beaches were of low gradient with deep, soft sand that proved problematic for the new design. As a result, it grounded 360 feet from dry land, with engineers building a pontoon bridge almost up to beach. Despite this shortcoming the design was lauded as it disgorged cargo by 0830. The shallow gradient also precluded many landing craft from reaching the high-water mark, and they became mired in the surf. Given this hydrographic problem, the first tanks did not roll onto the beach until after 0800, followed by the flying columns.[149]

At Yorker Beach in the middle of the CTF area, elements of 1st ID's 26th Regimental Combat Team landed thirty minutes late, again due to the slow progress of embarking troops.[150] Twelve miles west of Oran, the landings were also unopposed, but the movement ashore again was not without its problems.[151] An unaccounted sandbar paralleled the beach, precluding movement ashore. Even shallow-draft vehicles became mired. Troops and vehicles that mistakenly disembarked on the sandbar found themselves stranded, as water between them and the shore was as deep as five feet.[152] Landing craft eventually navigated the natural obstacle, and by 0340 the transports dropped anchor only 2,000 yards from shore. With the beachhead growing, follow-on forces landed, harassed only by a short artillery barrage. Minor combat action ensued after landing and while taking the inland objectives of Bau Sfer and Mers el-Kebir, with the Yorker Beach landings succeeded in quick fashion.[153]

The main effort for the CTF resided at Zebra Beach twenty-five miles east of Oran with thirty-four transports and over twenty escorts. The landing force comprised two elements: an initial Ranger detachment followed by the main body with units primarily from 1st AD. The US Army Rangers preceded the main assault by capturing gun emplacements ashore, the port, and key locations in the town of Arzew. By 0400 the Rangers secured their objectives and signaled the main body to commence operations. Shortly thereafter the US Navy and Marines, along with Royal Navy personnel, traveled ashore to initiate port operations with the bulk of unloading occurring in the Arzew beachfront. While sporadic enemy ground action occurred, it was quickly dispatched by American troops.[154] Despite taking some fire from the French fortifications, the landings were well executed with help from a Royal Navy smokescreen. By noon Arzew was in American hands, and at the end of the day its port facility was being utilized by Allied forces.

Although initial combat action on Zebra Beach was minor in scope, the biggest obstacle to the landing was not the enemy but the wind and surf conditions.[155] As the day passed, an increasingly rough surf precluded the full landing of 1st AD's Task Force Red at Arzew as well as other landing at X and Y beaches.[156] Despite the failure of the Villian and Reservist operations, the CTF's amphibious assaults on D-Day were largely a success. The full weight of CTF combat power and equipment eventually made it to shore; over the next six days the 1st Engineer Special Brigade landed 35,000 men, 3,200 vehicles, and 13,500 tons of supplies.[157]

With the assault of the coastal area around Oran being a tactical success, the net result was a strategic victory, as the location became a major logistics hub for the Allied fleet. American forces set about improving the port and its infrastructure, with the facility designated as a formal Naval Operating Base commanded by a flag officer with a full-time staff.[158] After removing the scuttled French vessels, naval engineers quickly dredged a 20-foot-deep channel in the inner harbor to facilitate deeper-draft vessels. French port personnel assisted with tugs, salvage equipment, lighters, and other support services vital to fleet/port activities. By April 1943 Oran's port included twenty-five cranes of various capabilities, three drydocks, 4,000 US Army stevedores, and three slips accommodating vessels up to 120 feet.[159] Given this forward location and its growing logistical facilities, the Allies had an important power projection base.

Eastern Task Force

The most important Allied objective in the trio of Torch landings was Algiers. The city was the closest to the Afrika Korps and contained well-developed ports, a rail network, and adjacent airfields. Additionally, Algeria was also the seat of French governmental, administrative, and political power in the region. Its capture provided an important symbol in the Allied effort. While the strategic political implications of capturing the city were significant, so were its defenses. Algiers was protected by some 4,500 troops to the west, 3,500 to the east, tank/mechanized units within the city itself, and two adjacent airfields with fighter and bomber aircraft.[160] These defenses were augmented by coastal artillery batteries at Cape Sidi Ferruch, Pointe Pescade, and Batterie du Lazaret with thermal detectors and range finders overlooking the approaches to the city.

Unlike the WTF and CTF landings, which utilized largely US troops in the assault, landing operations around Algiers were a combined effort with British forces also used in the attack. Additionally the Royal Navy providing sealift and NSFS as British army units stormed ashore along with their Yankee counterparts. Under the command of US Major General Charles Ryder, the landing forces consisted of regimental combat teams from the US 9th and 34th IDs including brigades from the British 78th ID, as well as a combined commando brigade. In all the landing forces comprised 23,000 UK troops and 10,000 Americans.[161] Like the other task force landings, the assaults around Algiers focused on three targeted beaches. However, ETF beach names were more colorful with the designations: Apples, Beer, and Charlie. The two Apples landing beach assaults near the town of Castiglione were solely a UK operation, with the 11th Brigade representing the westernmost assault. Approximately ten miles east were the three Beer beaches used by the 168th US RCT. The Charlie assaults comprised elements from the US 39th RCT and landed east of Algeria near Cape Mantifou.[162] Additionally a commando force from 1st Ranger Battalion and the 135th Infantry Regiment was inserted by Royal Navy destroyers into the city of Algiers. Much like the CTF's Reservist operation, another special operations insertion code-named "Terminal" was to secure the

Eastern Task Force scheme of maneuver for the capture of Algiers. This operation used British landing forces combined with American. Once the city was enveloped the residing Vichy French Commander initiated a truce and called on local defenders to cease fire. (US Army map) city's important port infrastructure to prevent sabotage from Vichy personnel.[163]

Terminal was also a joint and combined effort with Royal Navy and British army personnel that included a battalion of US Army soldiers from the 34th ID aboard HMS *Broke* and HMS *Malcom*. Training for their mission in Belfast, the task force learned of its tasking only during its final movement to the port of Algiers. Approaching the harbor at 0400 and in the process of breaching a defensive barrier, HMS *Malcom* was hit by Vichy fire and forced to retire. However, at 0520 HMS *Broke* eventually made it into the port and landed the embarked American team. The landing party initially succeeded in seizing parts of the port before any sabotage could occur. However, at 0800 HMS *Broke* began taking enemy fire and by 0920 was forced to withdraw and leave the American landing party stranded. Confident they could hold out until 168th Combat Team would arrive from the adjacent Beer beach, the American commander, Lieutenant Colonel Edwin Swenson, decided to remain in place. Vichy resistance grew as armored cars and light tanks assaulted the American positions. Running out of ammunition, the Americans surrendered their position at 1230. Despite the tactical failure, the port remained undamaged and available for subsequent Allied use.[164]

Unlike the Apples landings, the operations at Charlie were mostly a US affair using an RCT from the 9th ID. Unfortunately for the 39th RCT, it received very limited amphibious training prior to its deployment to the United Kingdom. However, arriving in Ireland on 6 October and then transported to Scotland, the RCT underwent limited training at the British Amphibious Training Center at Inveraray. Coordinated by Allied Force Headquarters in the United Kingdom, troops practiced with landing craft, exercised equipment debarkation, learned waterproofing, and were then loaded into transports for the Algeria operation. Given only a few days of amphibious training and limited in scope, the 39th never conducted a full amphibious rehearsal or regimental ship-to-shore movement. Tactically they focused on infantry night assaults and exercised with only a few vehicles. Meanwhile their naval counterparts were equally untrained, with the ship crews deficient in davit and offload operations. For both sailor and soldier, there was no significant training in the functions of unloading vehicles or supplies.[165] During a short stay in the United Kingdom and while en route to Africa, the regiment conducted only a few small rehearsals in mid-October on the River Clyde.[166] Their first regiment-size landing would be in combat conditions when D-Day arrived.

Under the command of Colonel B. F. Caffey, the 39th RCT landed on four designated beaches approximately twelve miles from Algiers. Once ashore the Americans were to swing west and serve as the right pincher movement to the landings at Beer beach. With H-Hour set at 0100, the landings were made without major enemy resistance, during calm weather and sea states, and again could be classified as an amphibious movement. Despite the lack of combat action, the Charlie landings resulted in another large loss of landing craft and a poor performance in ship-to-shore movement. In a repeat of other landing force experiences, davit cranes failed, poor embarkation procedures overloaded boats, ferrous materials affected compasses, and operations in the morning dark delayed rendezvous, with vessels landing on the wrong beaches.[167] Poor seamanship and operator error hindered movement ashore, and subsequent land operations became hopelessly delayed. Only five of the sixty LCPs from four transport vessels remained serviceable after the operation.[168]

With the loss of landing craft, General Ryder placed blame squarely on the Royal Navy coxswains and went so far as to recommend US Army personnel assume these responsibilities. UK Admiral Alfred Cunningham agreed to the critique regarding poor training but rejected the idea that soldiers should assume landing craft operations. In his response he retorted that, "whatever the uniform the crews wear, they must be trained seamen with special practice in the technique of landing operations."[169] Like the decision made before regarding navy operation of landing craft, Eisenhower concurred with Cunningham. Ike also concluded that while training was indeed poor this was still a function of the navy by emphasizing "the Navy is and will be in control of landing operations until troops are ashore, when such control passes to the commanding general." However, naval personnel were not to blame for the soldiers' poor performance ashore. Army shore-party operations at Charlie were again badly executed, with equipment sets strewn on the beach, disorganized supplies and stocks ashore, and boat crews stuck unloading embarked materials themselves.[170]

The US 168th RCT scheduled to land at Beer beach had a similar pre-Torch experience. Arriving in Liverpool, the unit had limited training opportunities in the United Kingdom and practiced at the beaches of Loch Fyne. When observing the training in the United Kingdom, the 168th's commander reported diplomatically that "landing crews were somewhat confused." Hardly a ringing endorsement. In addition, the training was done with a different model of landing craft than those used in the assault, causing more confusion come D-Day.[171]

US truck offloads on a British LCM east of Algiers on 8 November 1942. While American troops were successful in landing and securing the city, the ship to shore movement was plagued by insufficient training, poor embarkation practices, and uncoordinated beach party support. (US Navy photo)

Landing near Sidi Ferruch, the unit was to assist its British counter-parts in the seizure of the Bir Touta aerodrome and then move east as a pincher movement toward Algiers.[172]

Commandos preceding the main assault at Beer seized the Fort Sidi Ferruch position, with the main landings receiving little resistance from Vichy forces. However, like in the 39th RCT, the actual landings were fraught. Boats grounded in the surf, with soldiers disembarking into water over their heads; some vessels were pushed broadside by the surf, causing further debarkation problems. Other landing craft motored on top of wading, equipment-laden soldiers. One observer noted: "We received no opposition whatsoever from the beach and if we had, in that condition of landing, it would have been a complete failure in my opinion, as troops in the wallowing boats and those in the water would have been helpless against enemy fire."[173] Like at Charlie much of the fault lay with the British coxswains' inability to locate assigned beaches and handle craft in ocean currents. The 168th moved inland as planned and worked its way toward the city, meeting sporadic enemy fire. However, on 12 November a false alarm reported an enemy am-phibious counterattack at Sidi Ferruch. When investigated, the alleged counterattack was merely ten landing craft carelessly loosed by their crews. All told, 98 out of 104 boats (94 percent) in this sector were written off or destroyed. This stood in stark contrast to the 34 percent loss rate for the WTF and 20 percent for the CTF.[174]

Some 7,000 British forces from the 11th Brigade landed on the westernmost assault beach, Apples. Planned solely as a United Kingdom operation, a reserve of 6,000 men from the 36th Brigade aboard transport vessels were stationed between Beer and Apples. The British units landed near the town of Castiglione, twenty miles west of Algiers, and proceeded inland, taking the airfield at Blida. After securing the aerodrome with Americans from Beer, elements then proceeded northeast to the town of Bir Touta and prevented reinforcement of the capital city from the south. Vichy resistance during the operation was sporadic, with some exchange of fire. Like their American counterparts at other Torch beaches, the British forces experienced significant disorder and confusion. Part of the confusion was due to an unaccounted-for strong westward current that pushed American landing craft ten miles from Beer beach to Apples and in one instance even landing west of the UK landings.[175]

Political discussions among Vichy leadership and the Allies ensued before the landings. Confusion over who had authority and control over Vichy forces muddied the waters. The chief of the French navy, Admiral Francois Darlan, a close adviser to the Vichy chief, Marshal Petain and widely viewed as a Nazi collaborator, just happened to be resident in Algiers at the time of the invasion. While Darlan's authority as a recognized commander in Algeria was in question, on 8 November he orally agreed to a controversial armistice with the Allies in the Algerian section. With this agreement, French resistance to the ETF effectively ended combat operations around the city.[176] While the special Terminal operation was overwhelmed by local defenders and surrendered, it effectively achieved its larger objective: keeping the port facility safe from sabotage. As a result, beach operations were cut short and Allied ships eventually pulled pierside to unload their cargos.[177]

The nine Torch landings met tactical objectives, and in the end the larger operation met all strategic and operational ones. However, the value of Torch went beyond the accession of North African bases and lodgments ashore. It provided a classroom for teaching hard lessons that the Allies would heed in later assaults. Even if the Americans had

Western Task Force

WESTERN TASK FORCE			LCP(L)	LCP(R) v/ramp	LCV	LCM Tank Ltr.	TOTAL All Types	%
LYAUTEY	Landing Craft used		27	21	86	27	161	
	Damaged or Destroyed		9	11	40	10	70(1)	
FEDALA	Landing Craft used		35	107	162	43	347	
	Damaged or Destroyed						137(3)	
SAFI	Landing Craft Used		10	36	53	22	121	
	Damaged or Destroyed			7	1	1	9(2)	
TOTAL for W.T.F.	Landing Craft Used		72	164	301	92	629	
	Damaged or Destroyed						216(3)	34.3%

(1) - 16 (all types) salvaged later.

(2) - 8 salvaged later.

(3) - The Navy's figures show that there were 161 lost at Fedala.

Center Task Force

No. of landing boats used	No. of boats unable to return from beaches after initial trip	Percentage of loss
223	45 (approximately)	20%

Eastern Assault Force

No. of landing boats used	No. of boats unable to return from beaches after initial trip	Percentage of loss
104	98 (approximately)	94%

Excerpt from Services of Supply report on the "Lessons Learned from Recent Amphibious Operations in North Africa" dated 12 February 1943 (Annex G). Note the Fedala and Eastern Assault Force losses. (CARL Digital Archive)

all the assets and men required for the 1942 Roundup invasion, it probably would have failed in the face of a determined foe given the lack of Allied amphibious assault experience. As it stood, the Torch landings cost almost 1,000 Americans killed in action with over 800 wounded. The nine separate operations had much to offer in terms of lessons learned and identification of deficiencies in equipment, training, and combined/joint operations.

Regarding ship-to-shore movement, the list of deficiencies was extensive. Poor combat loading on the ships often created problems during the initial assault phase when access to key equipment was difficult. The slow and cumbersome debarkation processes, inadequate lift platforms, poor davit operations, deficient navigation, and inefficient planning made for missed H-Hours or wrong beach landings. The LCPs were too lightly constructed given the surf conditions; coxswains failed to handle their crafts and deal with raging surf. With failure to appreciate the hydrography of the coastlines, LCPs were lost at an excessive rate at both the WTF and ETF landings. This was especially a concern given the lack of these platforms at this time in the war.

In addition, army shore-party and navy beach-party functions broke down, with landing sites often strewn with equipment and supplies sent adrift. Troops lost their discipline as gear was left to languish in the landing craft or in the surf. Training of the landing force was a hodge-podge affair, with some units getting sufficient practice while others received limited or no instruction on amphibious assaults. While limited in scope combined arms integration worked well, it might have been more effective had army commanders been more familiar with NSFS. Furthermore, naval aviation provided sufficient air cover for the WTF. Shortly after the North Africa landings, the Allies analyzed the operation and planned to address the myriad of problems encountered. They understood that future operations against a determined German Wehrmacht on the continent of Europe would be much deadlier.

3

Training as Soon as Possible
FAITC and LANCRAB, Spring 1943

Following Torch the Allies conducted a six-month campaign to defeat Rommel's Afrika Korps. While victory over Axis forces in Tunisia came in May 1943, in the interim the Allies had to determine next objectives. The all-important cross-channel invasion was still paramount in the minds of American planners, but such a crucial undertaking was still beyond Allied capability. A persistent U-boat threat in the Atlantic, a lack of shipping, and insufficient forces in the United Kingdom precluded the 1943 Roundup operation. The British were keen to continue the Mediterranean strategy to destabilize Mussolini and remove a part of the Axis triumvirate. Given these considerations and objectives, southern Italy appeared the only location where the Allies could reasonably engage Wehrmacht forces on the continent.[1]

With Casablanca newly liberated, in January Roosevelt and Churchill, along with their respective staffs, met to determine next steps. Without the full complement of forces and equipment for the cross-channel invasion, and most of the Allied forces in the Mediterranean theater, to keep the pressure on the Axis the British envisioned attacking the ancient island of Sicily as the next logical advance. While still having the appearance of being a sideshow to the real fight against the Germans on the main continent, offensives in the Mediterranean had major strategic benefit. By reestablishing this sea line of communication, shipping routes would be shortened by use of the Suez Canal as opposed to the Cape of Good Hope. With strategic shipping a paramount concern, American planners estimated that using the Suez Canal over the Cape route would save 1,850,000 tons of shipping in the first five months alone by economizing 225 merchant ships.[2] This move also reflected the United Kingdom's concern with this sea line of communication, as it had been a key passage to India.

On 19 January the Americans agreed to the British proposed invasion of Sicily (code-named "Husky") once the Tunisian campaign ended. Disappointed with the delay of Roundup, George Marshall did not leave the Casablanca Conference empty-handed. The Army Chief of Staff came away with an agreement from the British Imperial General Staff to revitalize planning for the cross-channel operation.[3] While the Americans were anxious to engage with Overlord, there were strategic benefits to the Sicilian operation. Diplomatically an assault of southern Italy would assist Stalin and the Soviets hanging on against the Germans' Barbarossa invasion. Politically the proposed invasion might knock out the fascist regime in Italy and materially cause the Germans to reorient formations from the Eastern Front to Southern Europe, possibly in excess of fifty-four divisions.[4] As part of a larger global alliance, the political and military benefits of undertaking Husky were clear.

Before the assault on Sicily the Americans conducted full-scale reviews of the Torch operation and the amphibious performance. Eisenhower in his first experience as Allied commander made mention of the challenges experienced during the amphibious landings. In his formal after-action report, he noted the problems with ship-to-shore movement, along with the paucity of landing craft, transport ships, and trained crews. He reported that US and UK crews were ill-prepared and pressed into use only after being "hurriedly trained."[5] This obviously reflected the WTF and ETF assaults with their excessive losses of assigned landing craft. Regarding the slow embarkation of troops at the WTF locations, he made mention of the postponement of H-Hour from 0400 to 0515 due to "delays in manning the landing craft."[6] This was certainly recognition of the clumsy and painstakingly slow process of sending troops over the sides on cargo nets. Given the size of the invasion fleet and the short preparation time allowed for embarkation, Ike also observed how this occurrence left the subordinate unit staffs little time to properly prepare or adjust the detailed landing tables and schedules.[7]

Diplomatic in his formal report, Ike focused largely on the positives, concentrating on the strategic outcomes of Torch. Additionally, in December 1942 Hewitt's AFAF compiled a detailed list of issues requiring redress. The twenty-eight-page document listed deficiencies and observations covering all nine landings. Similarly, on 16 December Allied Force Headquarters also required submission of ground-centric lessons learned. The army's compiled report was more in-depth and spanned over sixty pages. Published in January 1943, many of the army's observations overlapped with the navy's. Both reports were divided by subject and covered a variety of topics, from the micro to the macro. In reviewing the two services reports, many salient themes emerged.

The use of naval guns was key to many engagements, both ashore and afloat, and was lauded by both services. However, the AFAF made mention that had NSFS been allowed to engage the Kasba at Mehedia initially, and not restricted by Truscott, the difficult ground action might have been avoided.[8] While army commanders agreed that pre-landing fires were acceptable, there was concern about prearranged fires once troops landed. The army report suggested that, once forces were ashore, NSFS should be used only on an "on-call" basis.[9] While Hewitt wound argue for pre-assault bombardment for future landings in the MTO, the army still stuck to the belief that tactical surprise was more important than battlefield shaping.[10] This would remain an issue between the two services for the next few landings.

Ground commanders emphasized the importance of dress rehearsals with actual naval fires. The suggestion was made to familiarize army units with NSFS and its effects, as some troops reportedly froze when hearing it for the first time.[11] With a lack of artillery ashore, the army concluded that organic 81mm and 60mm mortars were efficient against prepared positions during the assault, but naval guns readily augmented organic firepower assets. Additionally, the army still encouraged use of 75mm pack howitzers during the initial assault waves.[12] Furthermore, the fleet found that destroyers were extremely effective at delivering fires ashore during initial operations and engaging targets of opportunity, especially when coordinated and controlled by spotter planes. Able to sail close to the shoreline, destroyers proved their worth as fire platforms in direct support and would soon become a staple of MTO/ETO amphibious assaults.

Despite its successful use attacking the Kasba during the Goal Post landings, the navy found that CAS bombing was not effective in destroying targets, especially when using bombs less than 1,000 pounds. Furthermore, the dust and smoke raised by the explosions obscured other possible targets. However, aircraft strafing with .50-caliber rounds was "devastating" to soft-skin targets, and the report recommended an increased use of incendiary rounds to destroy vehicles. Regarding air-ground coordination, the navy's after-action review praised Hewitt's communication-school efforts and use of jeep-mounted SCR-193 radios, helping to control naval CAS missions. Both services recommended further use of these teams and specifically stated that all commanders be "properly indoctrinated as to the desirability of . . . and limitations of air-ground liaisons."[13] The army observations mirrored that of the navy, with use of vehicle-mounted very high frequency (VHF) radios with air support parties seen as widely effective. Furthermore, ground forces also recognized the utility of strafing runs against light tanks and armored vehicles and credited air in disrupting Vichy counterattacks.[14]

Regarding embarkation and ship-to-shore movement, an endorsement to the AFAF report suggested each army group designate a senior, flag-grade Transportation Quartermaster to oversee the effective loading of ships.[15] Similarly, army observations were replete with the suggestion of combat loading of transports and the detailed planning it required on the part of the ground component. They also reflected the importance of Transportation Quartermaster representation during embarkation.[16] Such measures affected efficient ship-to-shore movement, assisted in the establishment of the beachhead, and expedited the building of combat power ashore.

While embarkation and ship loading was a significant issue, so was the failure of beach/shore party support. Similarly, both services recognized this deficiency and pointed out the lack of training, improper embarkation/debarkation methods, and inadequate equipment ashore. The AFAF recommended such parties should be integrated into a shore regiment, and further proposed that "training should begin as soon as possible . . . prior to the next amphibious operation." The report when on to state that this mission was so important that it required an "intimacy" between the two services that comes by only having a single permanent organization.[17]

Army comments were more pointed, stating beach parties were either too small, late in arrival, lacked training, or poorly led.[18] Regarding beach organization and movement, the absence of beach markers, identification panels, lights, and layout was also problematic. The report, along with other observations, commented further on the mobility problems wheeled vehicles encountered once ashore and a distinct lack of salvage and recovery capability.[19] Elements of the 1st EAB with the CTF noted an absence of centralized/unified control of movement ashore in all phases of the operation. This led to confusion as to lift priorities, landing craft schedules, and overall coordination.[20] Ground commanders were adamant that these vital functions required significant redress and required specific training for assigned units.

Like Ike's report, one of the most common observations centered on the performance of transport and landing craft crews in the ship-to-shore movement. Either poorly trained, or too few in number, davit crews caused delays even before soldiers slowly descended cargo nets into landing crafts. These poor debarkation practices, combined with coxswains' inability to find their corresponding transports, navigate the transport area, and find the correct assault beaches were glaring issues. To address part of this problem, the AFAF report recommended each crew be provided a sketch of the landing area, location of ships in the transport area, lines of departure, beaches, and other prominent features with compass bearings to and from these locations.[21] The report further recommended installation of a directional gyro, radio, and lights for each landing craft.[22]

The report also mentioned the rough surf conditions that were often too much for the fragile LCP(L)s and LCP(R)s used in the operation. Furthermore, sea states in North Africa were different from those in which the crews trained. Again, the army report mirrored that of the navy and included extensive comments on the poor performance of landing craft and coxswains. Many landing craft crews were improperly/insufficiently trained, incompetent, or simply confused in combat.[23] Counter to the earlier opinions from Ike and others, a recommendation was again made that landing craft should be operated by army personnel.[24] This suggestion was roundly rejected, with coxswain responsibilities remaining with the navy.

Related to embarkation, the navy determined that the individual soldier was overburdened with equipment, precluding quick landing craft loading.[25] Being encumbered with heavy gear only added to the perilous movement of climbing down cargo nets. So important was the topic that the navy addressed it in separate correspondence.[26] Army personnel made the same observation regarding troops moving slowly when climbing over the side and down cargo nets into awaiting landing craft.[27] Furthermore, with their full complement of equipment, troops climbing down chain cargo nets often slipped on the wet steel and their hands were easily lacerated on the net's metal burrs. The army also recognized the effect such individual loads had on solider mobility and performance once ashore.

Additionally hit with sea spray while en route to the beach, equipment-laden troops going ashore were often soaking wet, with the additional water weight increasing their physical burden. As a result, the reports recommended that the soldier's individual load be reduced to the barest necessities of combat. Observations from the Fedhala landings reported that "troops were already overloaded. So much so that many troops lost their lives in the surf at the beaches for the sole

US soldiers with their full complement climbing down a cargo net slung over the side of a naval vessel. Such debarkation methods were not only dangerous, but also time consuming. (US Navy photo)

reason that they were unable to regain their feet after being knocked over by the waves." Learning from this experience, troops going ashore during the Husky assault would carry only their weapons, ammunition, canteens, K-rations, and a small toilet kit.[28]

Related to the equipment issue, both navy and army leadership called for better individual training in amphibious techniques and troop movement/debarkation. During Torch, soldiers lacked the skills or discipline during the assault to effectively offload landing craft and supplies. In addition, many units expressed frustration as crew-served weapons and equipment were often placed in different landing craft. As a result, crews were unable to locate and employ their equipment during the initial landings. While this risked putting all the eggs into one basket, the risk was worth it. In sum, fault lay with both sides. Compounding the poor training, many units arrived just before departure, receiving little or no experience with amphibious operations.[29]

Echoing Ike's comment about a lack of time and detailed planning, army commanders made similar observations that their small units were unfamiliar with higher headquarters mission and intent. While course-of-action development was accomplished in an iterative manner, last-minute changes to landing plans and sequencing created problems for subordinate units. This was in violation of the one-third rule specifying that, for a given task, only a third of the time available should be allocated to planning with the remaining two-thirds for actual preparation. Given this time crunch, small unit leaders were left trying to plan late in the process and did not have time to effectively coordinate with other units, adjust landing craft loads, or rearrange proper unit sequencing.[30] This affected the generation of detailed unit planning documents including the serial and landing craft assignment tables. This situation also left even less time for contingency planning or adjustment for last-minute changes.[31]

Related to this topic was the disparate nature of the planning effort, as it occurred at different locations without a fully coordinated or centrally located staff. With American planning occurring in Virgina and Washington, much of the larger planning was done in the United Kingdom. As a result, the planners for this combined and joint operation were not in the same room where close coordination might have mitigated some of the problems experienced. Had that occurred, violation of the one-third rule might have been avoided.[32] This sentiment was expressed in many of the Torch after-action reports; unfortunately this same deficiency would repeat itself again during Husky.

While communications were determined to be mostly adequate, the G-6 after-action report again lamented the lack of coordinated planning, adding that frequency allocation should be done by one coordinated agency. Establishing ship-to-shore networks was slow due to the loss of equipment or lack of waterproofed radios. SCR-522 radios for VHF communication with aircraft were too few in number and were found wanting. Army SCR-511 units gave satisfactory performance, but the radio failed when exposed to saltwater; while the SCR-284 was more reliable, it was too heavy for an individual soldier and took too long to set up.[33] The same problem existed for the boat control networks, as the army SCR-541 and navy TBY radios also failed due to water fouling, short ranges, or improper operation.[34] Additionally, while calls for NSFS for the WTF and CTF were reportedly timely, the same could not said of the ETF. Multiple calls for Royal Navy support took hours to process.[35] Perhaps related to this lag in timely combined fire support, there were delays in handling the ciphers and codes for various networks. The cryptographic processes were different among different military security classifications (they all had their own special handling requirements whether British, Special British-US, Navy, Army, Joint Army–Navy, or Navy), and special amphibious systems codes, with multiple cipher procedures causing delays in transmissions.[36] Additionally, the shore fire control networks were employed only about 60 percent of the time, although the naval air liaison jeeps were largely successful throughout.[37] Like many of the previous observations, lack of training and knowledge of communications systems were problematic, with the AFAF reiterating that "communications would not have been adequate against a strong, alert, and determined enemy."[38]

In all there was agreement on ill-trained coxswains, lethargic debarkation of troops, communication issues, difficulties related to joint fires, and poor beach-party support. With all these problem areas, Torch was an important step in the army–navy relationship and an even bigger one regarding amphibious capabilities in the MTO. Although there was still much to learn and develop, the Allies met with some good luck and achieved their strategic and operational objectives. However, the next landings would be against a more determined foe.

Preparations

Shortly after Torch, on 1 December 1942, the United States Fifth Army was established by consolidating units from the WTF, I Armored Corps, II Corps formations, and XII Air Support Command (ASC). Under the command of Lieutenant General Mark Clark, its primary mission was "to prepare a well-organized, well-equipped, and mobile striking force with at least one infantry division and one armored division fully trained in amphibious operations."[39] Building on the experience gained from Torch, instruction conducted in the United Kingdom and the United States, and lessons from the North Africa campaign, Fifth Army established training programs and joint exercises in preparation for the amphibious assaults on Sicily and the Italian mainland. Much of the stateside training was displaced, reorganized, or relocated at various locations in both the continental US but more importantly overseas. In North Africa Americans coordinated with vanquished French civil and military authorities establishing new training facilities while acquiring buildings, ranges, and bivouac areas.

On 18 March 1943 Fifth Army created the "Office of the Director of

Training Centers" and managed eight different training curriculums at various locations.[40] Under the Command of Brigadier General William H. Wilbur, the training centers focused on a specific application such as amphibious invasion, airborne assault, leadership in battle, field officers planning, tank destroying, engineering, aerial observation, and even a school to develop liberated French forces. Slightly out of sequence the Fifth Army Invasion Training Center (FAITC) was set up months earlier on 14 January at Port aux Poules, Algeria (modern-day Mers El Hadjadj). With the establishment of FAITC, much of the resident instruction at the Camp Edwards ATC moved to North Africa. With the reduction of the stateside ATC's mission and capabilities, the new amphibious training center in the MTO was charged with developing doctrine, tactics, techniques, and procedures while providing instruction for future invasion operations.[41]

The FAITC location was well suited for exercises and training, as it was near Torch's CTF Zebra landing beaches. Commanded by Army Brigadier General John O'Daniel, the center included a naval contingent under Rear Admiral Andrew Bennett.[42] Having flag representation from both military departments was already significant progress from the earlier efforts at Camp Carrabelle and Camp Edwards. Training at the FAITC consisted of individual and unit-level programs. It included instruction regarding use of armor as well as joint applications with the navy and USAAF. Additionally, the FAITC provided instruction to cadre personnel on waterproofing, fording, and embarkation and debarkation procedures by "training the trainers" who would then return to their parent units.[43]

The navy also established new training locations in the region under the command of Admiral J. L. Hall. This command included the naval representation of the FAITC, but it also encompassed groups focused specifically on landing craft/supporting bases and minesweeping. While landing craft training still occurred at stateside locations, a forward school was established in the newly liberated North African ports. In February 1943, Landing Craft and Bases Northwest African Waters (LANCRAB) under Rear Admiral Richard Conolly was established near the Arzew beaches. Working directly with the FAITC, the command housed its new landing craft at ports such as Nemours, Beni-Saf, and Mostaganem among others.[44]

After commanding the WTF for Patton's landings during Torch, Hewitt again found himself tasked in the MTO. With the Allied victory in North Africa, Hewitt assumed command of the United States

Eighth Fleet (formerly Amphibious Force Northwest African Waters) and commanded Task Force 81's surface fleet and its multiple organizations. Eighth Fleet included the LANCRAB and minesweeper units, the naval personnel at FAITC, and the resident beachmaster commands in the theater. He oversaw Task Force 83, which controlled the Naval Operating Base at Oran and the facilities at Mers-el-Kébir and Arzew, Task Force 84 (conducting naval salvage operations), and finally Task Force 85 (focusing on leveraging capture ports for Allied use). As a result, many of the naval functions required to support current and future amphibious operations fell under one command.[45]

On 19 March the USS *Samuel Chase* arrived at Oran with 2,500 tons of supplies and equipment for the construction of the FAITC plus over 500 personnel to man the organization. It was followed by more vessels with additional supplies for other training locations.[46] Recommendations from both services' after-action reports were included in the center's curriculum and focused on individual and unit training in a joint littoral environment. For example, both services still considered landing under cover of darkness preferable over daytime landings despite the confusion nighttime operations often brought to navigation and debarkation.[47] As a result, instruction included night attacks as well as infiltration, demolitions, destruction of obstacles and armored vehicles, air-ground coordination, fire support, and sustainment in subsequent operations ashore.[48] The curriculum also provided instruction on shore-to-shore and ship-to-shore operations. The FAITC doctrine advocated Regiment Landing Teams (RLTs) with three battalions as the basic assault unit and further suggested the formation come ashore on the same beach and that soldiers not be separated from their equipment. Lesson plans provided specific guidance on a myriad of topics, including detailed guidance on landing wave composition, organization of landing craft, and scheduling of BLT movement.[49] The staff also revised the number of landing craft required for a division assault, subsequent wave configuration, loss rates, and turnaround times.[50] All of these were important building blocks in planning and organizing amphibious assaults.

In addition to classroom instruction, doctrinal development, and individual movement, the FAITC sponsored amphibious landing exercises. Such evolutions were as realistic as possible, with assaults carried out using live ammunition and with troops experiencing landing under fire. Combined arms exercises included the integration of armor, use of engineers to remove obstacles, and instruction in the clearing of urban areas so often adjacent to landing beaches. Construction of simulated pillboxes and defensive positions added to the reality. Troops remained under instruction for up to four months—far longer than what they received stateside or in the United Kingdom.[51]

In concert with the FAITC, the command established the Leadership and Battle Training Center on 9 May at Slissen, Algeria, that focused upon platoon-level action. The site was chosen for the terrain, similar to what existed in both Italy and France. With lessons learned from the North Africa campaign, junior officers and noncommissioned personnel learned how to train small units regarding defensive positions, tactical employment, and use of combined arms. In a three-week course, cadre personnel from the 34th and 36th IDs were given instruction and then expected to return to their parent organizations and install similar training programs.[52] This was especially useful, as both divisions lacked any combat experience and would soon face Wehrmacht forces months later on the beaches of Salerno.

Much like it did for junior officers and NCOs, the director of training established an accompanying school for field grade and staff officers. Established at Chanzy, Algeria, on 7 April, its focus was developing battalion commanders and regimental and division staff officers on the utilization of terrain and choosing favorable locations for defensive or offensive action. The curriculum included staff rides to various battlefields to illustrate applications and practical lessons. However, the course ran only two sessions due to a lack of attending students. As units prepared for the upcoming Husky and Avalanche operations, staffs could scarcely afford to have key personnel absent from their units for academic instruction.[53]

For improved use of combined arms, the Air Observation Post Center was activated on 22 March to address the scarcity of trained, in-theater personnel. Established at Sidi Bel Abbès, Algeria, the course of instruction focused on the use of aerial observers in small aircraft helping field artillery identify and then target enemy formations. Using small L-4 Grasshopper aircraft (a militarized version of the civilian Piper Cub), aerial observers had a much better perspective over the battlefield and could assist indirect fire support from both army and navy guns. These aircraft and personnel would play a key role in the upcoming Husky invasion. As US forces in North Africa began receiving more aircraft and stateside-trained observers, the school's mission fell by the wayside, with the location eventually serving as a center for assignment personnel and distribution of equipment in the theater.[54] The center's existence was a testament to the recognition of the importance of combined arms integration.

Units that underwent training at the FAITC location included the 1st, 3rd, 34th, and 36th IDs.[55] Fresh from the Torch operations, 1st and 3rd IDs were not always welcoming of the additional instruction. As part of the 1st ID, the 26th Infantry had taken part in the CTF landings in November. When assigned to the FAITC, some soldiers were chagrined to find themselves conducting training over some of the same terrain in which they had actually conducted combat operations.[56] Adding to the 26th's complaint was that some instruction provided by the FAITC faculty came from personnel who had yet to experience combat and were often at odds with their veteran students regarding methodology and application.[57] At least one battalion commander reported that the program provided little benefit. However, these 1st ID observations may have been more a reflection of its irascible and feisty commander, Lieutenant General Terry de la Mesa Allen Sr. and indicative of the unit's overall attitude rather than the actual value of the training.[58] In contrast to 1st ID, other units reported the direct opposite and lauded the training.

In late June, divisions assigned to Husky conducted an exercise code-named "Copy Book." These rehearsals included 1st ID and 2nd AD landing near Arzew, 3rd ID near the Bizerte–Tunis area, and the 82nd Airborne (AB) Division training in Oudja in northeastern Morocco.[59] The 45th Division came directly from the United States, where it had conducted training at the various Chesapeake locations. The unit made a brief stop in Arzew on 22 June so the troops could lose their sea legs and conduct its own in-theater rehearsal.[60] The 3rd ID exercise proved very successful, with some soldiers believing that it was real invasion. While Truscott's command gain confidence in the navy's ship-to-shore capabilities, other divisions had different experiences. Practicing for the landings at Gela and Scoglitti, the 1st and 45th IDs' rehearsals were limited in scope and hardly a confidence-builder. Again, as with Torch, H-Hour was missed by ninety minutes due to confusion of landing craft assembly in the rendezvous area. Additionally, many landing craft placed units on the wrong beaches, often miles from their intended locations, with troops having to reorganize themselves once ashore.[61]

Assuming that this next amphibious operation would be against a more prepared and competent enemy, such performances were disheartening to the newly appointed II Corps commander, Lieutenant General Omar Bradley. Deeply concerned given this performance,

Bradley wrote that if this was to happen on D-Day the consequences were "too grim to contemplate."[62] Given the performance of American forces in late 1942 and Bradley's observation of Copy Book, it is evident that had the planned Sledgehammer/Roundup cross-channel invasions of occurred as Marshall had hoped, the results might have been disastrous, if not irrecoverable. Even if American forces were sufficiently manned and equipped for the two proposed Normandy invasions, the execution would have fallen far short. American forces at this time were nowhere close to competently conducting these operations in either scale or scope.

The Copy Book was also narrow in scope, with only limited functions exercised and select units participating. 2nd AD and 45th ID experienced a lack of shipping that precluded full unit participation.[63] Hewitt made the same observation regarding beach- and shore-party functions during the exercise, as they were not fully exercised or practiced. The focus of the exercise was combat arms applications at the expense of logistics support. While the FAITC provided very specific guidance and doctrine for Transportation Quartermaster duties, the coordination instructions, planning timetables, wave scheduling, and organization for movement control were still concerns with few opportunities to test such operations.[64] The lack of effective debarkation, beach organization, and throughput of vehicles and supplies ashore was one of the salient complaints of the Torch landings. Designated commander of the Western Naval Task Force for the Husky landings, Hewitt worried that the rehearsals for the upcoming operation did not sufficiently test beach-party capabilities and organization.[65] The length of the Copy Book exercises and the focus on assault precluded the full employment of Engineer Special Brigades and other functions for throughput, sustainment, and beach organization. Echoing Hewitt's concern, Ike in his post-Husky assessment made specific mention of "limited time and opportunity for thorough advance training of all the shore party functions which combined naval and military elements."[66]

For the Sicily landings, the three assault divisions were each assigned a combat engineer or shore regiment to support landing-party functions. Each shore regiment consisted of multiple battalions, with some command having experience during Torch. While organization of the regiments varied, each command included a signal and ammunition ordnance along with companies, a medical battalion, a quartermaster battalion, and a military police battalion. Built from other units, the command was cobbled together, with a total compliment of 2,000 men available to assist the unloading of landing craft ashore.[67] Given

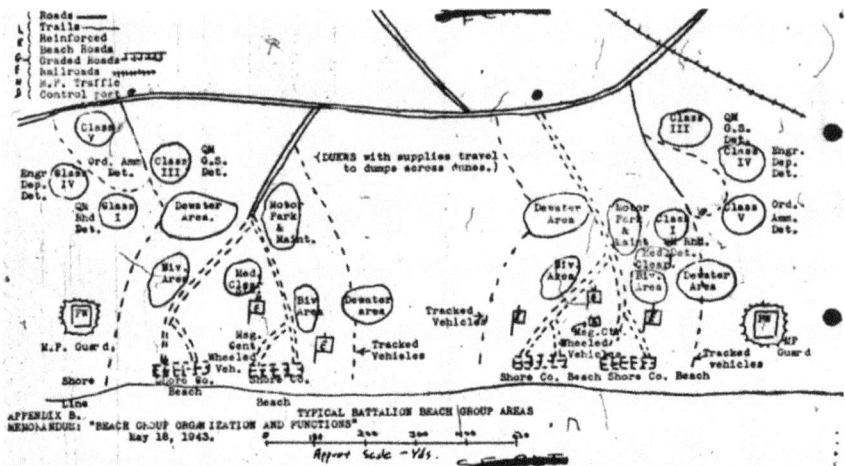

A sample beach organization schematic from a 5th Army Invasion Training Center (FAITC). Torch after action reports specifically addressed the lack of order and organization at the invasion beaches. (CARL Digital Archive)

these commands were hastily assembled from other units, no one questioned the quality of the soldiers sent from parent organizations. No commander, now or then, is willing to cut loose his best subordinates or troops to staff another organization. Such transfers usually involved the lowest quality soldiers.

Especially disconcerting about this next assault was the lack of port facilities required for sustainment and offload following the initial assault. The Husky landings focused on the southern part of the island, where no significant port facilities existed. As a result, sustainment would be sea-based via the established beachheads or through use of the small, limited piers available at Gela, Licata, and Porto Empedocle. The three separate divisions and their associated attachments planned for thirty days of sustainment without use of fixed or prepared port infrastructure.[68] This was indeed a tall order given anticipated consumption rates for food, fuel, and ammunition (designated as Supply Classes I, III, and V). This meant that whatever logistic support the landing force might receive would have to come over an unprepared beach and at the mercy of existing weather and sea conditions. This was a bold decision, as such applications had never been tried at this scale, especially in combat. When Bradley learned of the logistics plan via the beach, he anxiously described it as "mind-boggling."[69] This plan required material solutions that would mark a significant advancement in amphibious assault, addressing three of the six components in the interwar manuals (ship-to-shore movement, establishment of a beach-head, and communications and logistics).

While Bradley's concerns were legitimate given his experience, he was not familiar with emerging technology and ship design. For this next operation American forces employed new and more capable amphibious transports. Despite its low priority during the interwar years, the navy created a whole new fleet of amphibious vessels utilizing an alphabet soup of acronyms including "LCS," "LSM," "LSD," "APA," and "APD." With the navy's amphibious fleet no longer an afterthought, it was still held in lower esteem than its blue-water counterparts yet grew at a remarkable rate. More important, four basic designs stood out and became available for combat use. The Landing Ship Tank (LST), Landing Craft Tank (LCT), Landing Craft Infantry (LCI), and with more Landing Craft Vehicle and Personnel (LCVP), these innovative designs were inherently flexible and used in most theaters of the war. These platforms were a significant development in littoral operations. Their development and importance cannot be emphasized enough and is often overshadowed in the war's larger historiography.

The LST concept was inspired by the British-developed "Lake" tankers that operated in Lake Maracaibo, Venezuela. In the 1920s these shallow-draft vessels moved crude oil pumped from below the lake to offshore refineries near Aruba and Curacao. Inspired by this design, the initial use of such a platform began during Torch, in the CTF operation. A key platform that could provide bulk logistics and equipment directly to an unprepared shoreline, the LST's availability often drove Allied strategy. First floated as late as October 1942, LSTs could embark/debark troops pierside or in-stream or deliver them directly onto an unprepared beach. The use of these initial designs during Torch was widely lauded, with some already being built in early 1943.[70] While the new craft was of low speed (about ten knots), it could carry large numbers of troops and equipment, with a range over 9,000 miles. The largest beaching vessel, the LST could come ashore on gradients of 1:50 and discharge tanks over its bow ramp.[71] Carrying up to 16–19 tons of supplies and equipment, this new platform could possibly mitigate the requirement for fixed ports and infrastructure.

LSTs became the unsung heroes of the war, with the acronym derisively referred to as "Large Slow Target." But the introduction of these vessels was a proverbial game-changer. Displacing some 4,000 tons,

An LST carrying an LCT on the weather deck. These two platforms were key components in moving men and material ashore during an amphibious assault. First large-scale use of these platforms was during Operation Husky, and they became mainstays in all amphibious theaters of the war. (US Navy photo)

an LST drafted only 8–14 feet, berthed up to 150 troops, and operated with a crew of seven officers and a hundred sailors.[72] With a length of 345 feet and a beam of 54 feet, an LST could carry four to six LCVPs on davits or an LCT on its weather deck. For Husky alone thirty-six LSTs each carried six LCVPs in davits, thereby permitting each craft of this type to embark one company of infantry for the initial assault. Others could carry an LCT for increased transit of men and equipment to the shore.[73] In its holds it could carry twenty-seven medium tanks or fifteen larger ones.[74] With large clamshell doors on the bow, the ship could beach itself, open the doors, and lower a ramp, allowing for quick offload of men, vehicles, and equipment. Fixed with ballast tanks to help steady the ship, the LSTs were full seagoing vessels, and with its flat bottom the LST could navigate the shore and littoral regions with ease. However, when at sea the hull design made for a bumpy, rolling ride. Famed journalist Ernie Pyle wrote of the LST:

> The LST isn't a glorious ship to look at-it is neither sleek nor fast, nor impressively big—but it is a good ship and crews abord LSTs are proud of them. The LSTs are great rollers—the sailors say "They even roll in drydock." They have flat bottoms and consequently roll when there is no sea at all. They roll fast too. . . . The sailors say when they roll across a sandbar, the ship seems to work its way across like an inchworm proceeding forward section by section.[75]

This flexible and effective design often became a major consideration in Allied amphibious planning and strategies. This new vessel had a marked influence upon the development of the shore-to-shore technique. In fact, the need for these vessels would become a source of contention between the United States and United Kingdom during the planning for the Anzio campaign, D-Day, and follow-up assaults of southern France in August 1944.

In addition to the LST, other smaller vessels played an important role in amphibious assaults. Largely referred to as "crafts," these vessels were under 200 feet in length and therefore were not classified as "ships." Not intended to be a seagoing vessel like the LST, the Landing Craft Tank's (LCT) 117-by-32-foot hull could carry five medium tanks or four heavy ones. They were the largest of the open-deck bow-ramp vessels. Designed specifically for ship-to-shore movement and looking much like an LCVP on steroids, the vessel displaced some 300 tons when empty. Constructed in three watertight sections and capable of being transported on a larger vessel, it had a crew of one officer and ten men.[76] The bow of the vessel also had a loading ramp for quick debarkation of men and equipment. Original models were of British design, but once America entered the war newer and more capable versions became available. American LCT production began in August 1942, and in the following few months shipyards in North America built over 400 such vessels. As the middleweight of amphibious lift vessels, it could carry 150 tons of cargo with a top speed of eight to ten knots with a range over 700 miles. LCTs did much of the heavy lifting and large-scale ship-to-shore movement in the initial assault waves.[77] LCTs were also capable of being loaded in-stream and then move men or materials ashore. All told, approximately 2,000 vessels were built by the US Navy and used in a variety of capacities. With an inherently flexible design, some LCTs were modified to serve as rocket-launching platforms, utility craft, coastal minesweepers, and salvage vessels.

A third littoral craft was the Landing Craft Infantry (Large) (LCI(L)); as it moved personnel ashore and could also carry up to 200 troops or seventy-five tons of cargo at a top speed of fifteen knots. LCI(L)s were American vessels but, like the LST and LCT, had its foundations from initial British designs. Displacing 350 tons, LCI(L)s were 160 feet long with a beam of 23 feet and were manned by a crew of twenty-four.[78] Some LCI(L)s participated in the North Africa landings, but they became increasingly available in later assaults. Between Torch and Husky, over 270 LCI(L)s became available from American shipyards, with hundreds more to follow. Initially constructed in sections and transported aboard a larger vessel, LCI(L)s were fully assembled in the theater of operation. However, while they were not intended to be a seagoing platform, wartime necessity often required LCI(L)s to

LCI-222 circa 1943. This LCI(L) represents an earlier version of the
American design as it has the catwalk style landing ramps near the bow.
(US Navy photo)

traverse the oceans. Disdainfully referred to as "Lousy Crate Indeed,"
earlier versions of the vessel had two catwalk-type ramps for troop
debarkation but were removed in later types for a conventional ramp
and bow doors.[79] While LCVPs moved the initial assault waves ashore,
LCIs also helped generate combat power and became a more efficient
way of moving troops in the early phases of a landing.[80] Much like the
LST and LCT, the LCI was a very flexible vessel, with its basic hull
modified to serve as mortar, gunboat, or rocket platforms providing
fire support during an assault.

Lastly, the LCVP was an improvement on the LCP used during
Torch and could move thirty-six troops or four tons of cargo from ship
to shore. Derivative of the earlier craft, this later design had a length of
35 feet and a beam of 10 feet drafting only four feet when fully loaded.
Displacing some 18,000 pounds, it chugged along with a top speed of
nine knots depending on the sea state. With a maximum range of 150
miles and a crew of three, it was often lowered on davits from LSTs or
transports and could deliver a platoon and supplies from the platform
that brough it to the AOA.

However, at this stage of the war these designs were still unproven.
Exacerbating concerns regarding the new ships was the fact that MTO
personnel were unfamiliar with the new vessels' capabilities, with their
respective loading characteristics still a mystery.[81] While green crews

in Virginia Beach might be familiar with these new vessels, planners in the MTO were not. With this unfamiliarity 3rd ID embarkers and transportation quartermasters found their loading figures for the next operation exceeding the rated capacity of the new ships. To validate lift capabilities and test the limits of the ship, Truscott's 3rd ID conducted a science experiment in theater. He had eighteen officers, 450 troops, and ninety-four vehicles overloaded into one LST and had it sail in Lake Bizerte for forty-eight hours. Could the new design handle this much cube (length x width x height) and weight? To their great relief the ship had no problem accommodating the overload and proved the flexibility of the naval architects' design.

In concert with the introduction of amphibious platforms, the navy's stateside Landing Craft Group Unit in Little Creek established training programs for the crews operating and manning these new vessels. Staffed by inexperienced crews, with some having never actually seen an ocean before, the officers of these vessels were often as new at the ships they sailed. The first LCIs traversed the Atlantic in early 1943, with additional flotillas of the other types of landing craft following. Once in theater, Admiral Conolly included these new platforms into the training programs at Arzew and other locations.[82] Additionally, the number of amphibious platforms coming into the MTO grew exponentially. Despite having multiple locations and ports available, with so many new arrivals the American ships had to moor at every available pier, sometimes two to three ships deep.[83]

Moreover, with these new amphibious vessels and their seagoing capabilities, the army and navy could revisit the idea of shore-to-shore operations.[84] No longer were the services necessarily stuck only with the complex ship-to-shore embarkation process, with landing craft looking for troop transports in the assembly area under cover of darkness. The shore-to-shore process partially avoided the cargo-net issues and the slow movement of overburdened troops climbing down slippery chain links. More important, the beaching abilities of these vessels meant that supplies could be disgorged directly onto land without need for a port and infrastructure. However, such an expeditionary capability required a fully functional and competent beach/shore party organization. This new capability was what the Allies were betting would supply subsequent operations initially ashore on Sicily. While the logistics over the shore process was an unproved capability, Bradley's concerns were not without merit.

While the United States had a new fleet of amphibious vessels, the beaches of Sicily had an additional challenge for naval engineers: the

US Navy landing craft crammed pier side at a North African port in preparation of the July 1943 Husky landings. (US Navy photo)

shoreline was rife with "runnels." This hydrological phenomenon consisted of submerged sandbars running parallel to the beach. Just under the surface, runnels precluded LSTs and other heavier craft from reaching the shore. Offloading atop a runnel was problematic, as the surf between it and the actual beach was often deep enough to submerge any vehicle attempting to ford the expanse. To sustain the landing force over the unprepared beaches and counter the runnel issue, naval engineers built sectional pontoon bridges that were slung over the side of an LST, floated, connected, and then affixed to the vessel's bow once near the beach.[85] This allowed equipment to be offloaded in-stream via a pontoon bridge to the shoreline. For the upcoming Sicily operation ten LSTs would be outfitted with this innovate approach.[86]

Another important development for American power projection in the MTO was the navy's establishment of Advanced Amphibious Training Bases at Arzew, Tunis, Mostaganem, Tenes, Cherchel, Béni Saf, and Nemours.[87] Here coxswains learned their craft, familiarized themselves with new equipment, and trained with army units. In addition, a naval logistics support base at Bizerte provided embarkation, maintenance, and modification services to the growing amphibious fleet. With its gantry cranes, the Bizerte location could load eighteen LSTs simultaneously while also providing essential maintenance services to keep the expanding fleet seaworthy.[88] This logistical capability became even more important as LCTs arrived in theater in section pieces embarked on the decks of LSTs. The sections were offloaded, welded together at NOBs, then loaded with cargo—some of it from the LSTs that carried them across the Atlantic.[89] Augmenting these fixed facilities, the Western Naval Task Force also introduced three landing craft repair ships (*Achelous*, *Vulcan*, and *Delta*) capable of voyage repairs and modifications of landing craft in forward areas.[90] As a result, salvage and repair operations for landing craft and other vessels could be done rapidly and expeditiously, often within a few hours or days.

Concurrently, in January 1943 the navy published *Ship to Shore Movement: General Instructions for Transports, Cargo Vessels, and Landing Craft of Amphibious Forces*. The lengthy document not only outlined the performance characteristics of the current landing platforms but also included numerous chapters addressing specific functions of amphibious operations. The document provided definitions regarding roles and missions while establishing an outline for functions such as boat organization, use of control vessels, traffic control procedures, shore-party responsibilities, and communications. A two-part document, the second part was classified as restricted and addressed beach-marking procedures, salvage operations, and casualty handling and evacuation. With this document the navy was refining important doctrines that were keys to amphibious operations and planning.[91] While these definitions and publications helped outline the roles of naval personnel, this did not necessarily mean that the army was beholden to such dictates or that there would be a seamless transition between the two services. In fact, after the Husky landings, Hewitt would make specific mention that army doctrine had not kept pace with navy doctrine. In his after-action report for the Sicily operation he wrote:

It is apparent that *FM 31-5*, the only publication available to Army officers before commencement of amphibious training under navy guidance, had not kept pace with [Fleet Training Publications 155 and 167]. It is apparent also that there is a widespread misconception in the Army regarding command and responsibilities in amphibious operations. Not only is this universally experienced during the troop training period conducted by the navy, but it extends to the planning of operations and to the loading and administration of naval vessels. . . . There is a definite need for the revision of the basic documents governing joint operations.[92]

Although progress was being made, there was still much to accomplish.

For the next operation the landing forces of Seventh Army required better intelligence and information on the hydrology of the Sicilian coast than what was available during Torch. With many coxswains unfamiliar with the North African waters before the operation began, attempts were made to remedy the paucity of information regarding assault shorelines and surrounding terrain. Engineers made terrain maps of each task-force's area of operations as well as a 1:100,000 models of the entire island and forwarded them to the assault units. Additional support came from published intelligence bulletins and the dissemination of aerial photographs produced by the Northwest African Air Forces (NWAAF) Photo Reconnaissance Wing. This aerial photograph unit consisted of over 100 personnel who assembled 195,000 prints and 1,400 mosaic graphics of the island.

Despite flying over 500 missions to collect the aerial photos, Husky after-action comments were still critical. Naval forces claimed the photographic coverage was inadequate, as images regarding beach gradients and approaches were limited. Additionally, it seemed that access to the photos came only to personal with contacts and influential friends instead of via widespread dissemination.[93] In this case, access depended on personal, not institutional, relationships. Obviously, the distribution processes were less systemic and relied on individual initiatives. This problem was indicative of the air/surface rift emerging during the planning and execution of Husky.

Given these lessons and preparations, the Allies set out for their next step. The Sicily operation was yet another opportunity to develop the army's amphibious competency along with the navy's. With the new equipment, some seasoned combat veterans, and focused training efforts based on current operations, Husky would provide another tutorial for American forces. After Torch the navy made significant efforts to improve its amphibious performance through development of new platforms, doctrines, and in-theater training. Both services were moving forward, but many lessons remained in the offing.

While the US Army fought the Germans in the deserts of Tunisia, it had fought Vichy forces only during an amphibious assault. Although Italian forces would be defending the Sicilian beaches initially, on the shores of the Gela Plain on 10–11 July the US 1st ID's established lodgment would be met by Wehrmacht armor, and the Luftwaffe and Italy's Regia Aeronautica. The risks were rising even as new tactics, techniques, and procedures were developed. Facing a more determined and capable foe, the Allies had to grow combat power both onshore and then inland. Husky would provide new challenges to both services in combat and in amphibious operations.

4

"Can't Get the Air Force to Do a Goddam Thing"

Operation Husky, July 1943

After the liberation of North Africa, Sicily was the next step for the Allied forces. A continuation of the British periphery strategy, taking the island would help secure the Mediterranean Sea line of communication and possibly topple the fascist government of Benito Mussolini. However, initial planning for the operation was not a unified effort. Five separate planning centers developed courses of action with divergent visions for the operation. British Task Force 141 in Algiers was an inter-Allied, interservice force, but it was only one of several.[1] Concurrently Ike, who was to serve as overall Allied commander, created the Eastern and the Western Task Forces, which were interservice but not inter-Allied. The Eastern Task Force was composed primarily of UK troops and established its own planning cell in Cairo under the designation "Force 545." The Western Task Force (Force 343) established its own in Rabat, Morocco, mostly of US forces. In addition to these theater-based efforts, other planning cells grew out of the United States and United Kingdom, providing further proposals and courses of action. While overall responsibility for developing the plan fell to Sir Harold Alexander, Commander in Chief of Ground Forces, and his Force 141, he was still preoccupied with the Tunisian campaign up until May. As a result, with only a month before the invasion, the scheme of maneuver and course of action for the Sicilian operation had yet to be finalized.[2]

American forces were initially given only a supporting role in the Husky plan, with British and Canadian forces designated as the invasion's main effort. Landing on the southeastern tip of Sicily near Pachino and Syracuse, the British Eighth Army was to push up the eastern coast of the island toward the towns of Catania and Messina.

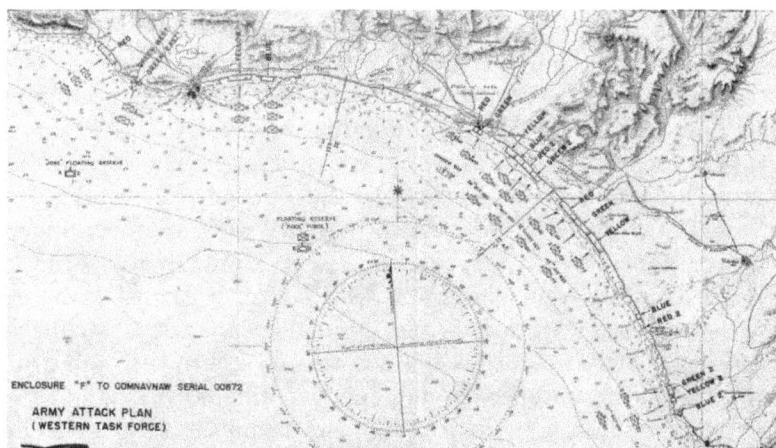

Final plan for the American invasion of Sicily. Note Joss, Dime, and Cent Forces making the amphibious assault on the southern beaches covering the UK Forces to the east. (CARL Digital Archive)

Seizing these locations would trap the Axis forces on the island in hopes of preventing them from exfiltrating at the Strait of Messina. For the Americans, they were to protect the British left flank from German and Italian formations in the western part of the island. In this secondary role, American forces engaged Axis formations in difficult, easily defensible terrain, while Field Marshal Bernard Montgomery's Eighth Army stayed largely in the coastal planes of eastern Sicily. Augmenting the amphibious assault, American and British airborne troops were dropped hours before, intent on capturing key terrain and preventing Axis reinforcement around the southeastern parts of the island.

Over 3,200 ships, craft, and boats made up the Allied naval forces, of which more than 1,700 represented the Western Naval Task Force.[3] American forces landed on three separate beach locations, all part of Lieutenant General George Patton's newly designated Seventh Army. The respective infantry divisions were divided up into separate task forces. 3rd ID under Truscott, designated "Joss Force," was the westernmost formation and planned to land near the town of Licata. Initially tasked with protecting the Allied left flank, Truscott's command would become a key maneuver element later in the Husky campaign. To the east of Joss, and under Lieutenant General Omar Bradley's II Corps command, were Dime and Cent Forces. Dime was placed in the middle of the American trio of task forces that consisted largely of Allen's 1st ID. Coming ashore on Gela Plain, 1st ID landed directly within easy reach of the German Hermann Göring Division and the Italian 4th Infantry "Livorno" Division.[4] On the American right, and to the east of Dime, was Cent Force, with the 45th Infantry Division under Major General Troy Middleton. Landing near the town of Scoglitti, the 45th's area of operations would adjust as the operation unfolded, but its right boundary represented the shared edge of Patton's Seventh Army and that of the British Eighth.[5] Specifically the Americans were to capture the port at Licata, the airfields at Ponte Olivio, Biscari, and Comiso, and then establish contact with Eighth Army.[6] Last, planners had the 82nd Airborne Division conduct a vertical assault landing on D-1 north of Gela. Its mission was to secure the high ground around the landing beaches, disrupt enemy communications and movement, and then link up with 1st ID in the assault on the Ponte Olivio airfield.[7]

Unlike the Torch landings, in which the enemy defensive posture was ambiguous and its allegiance suspect, Allied forces during Husky could definitely count on a hostile reception. With four Italian and two German divisions, the Axis formations on the island numbered approximately 325,000. While the Italian forces under General Alfredo Guzzoni were of low morale and poor quality.[8] The Italian Aosta, Napoli, Assietta, and Livorno Divisions were manned by troops who were poorly commanded, equipped, and trained. However, their Nazi counterparts in the 15th Panzergrenadier Division and the Göring Division on the island were of high quality, well-equipped, and ably led.[9] Guzzoni's German counterpart, Field Marshal Albert Kesselring, was a skilled, competent commander with excellent subordinates willing to take the initiative.

Both Axis commanders correctly identified the southeastern coast of the island as the most probable landing beaches. Despite this correct estimate, Kesselring still had to consider defending the entire 140 miles of the southern Sicilian coastline. This was especially true given the poor state of the Italian divisions and the possibility of them caving at the first sign of Allied salvos. Scattered along the southern coast were individual Italian coastal artillery defenses, minefields, pillboxes, and other defensive obstacles. However, most of these fixed positions were isolated, few in number, and poorly manned and equipped.[10] The Axis defensive strategy was to stop the Allied landings before they could consolidate their various beachheads using Italian forces in a mobile defense. Once the Allied assault was stymied, German divisions would then engage and destroy the remaining amphibious forces. The problem was that the Italian forces were not up to the task and lacked sufficient assets and vehicles to conduct such an operation.[11] Regardless of the ill-prepared state of readiness of the Italian ground forces, and the condition of the fixed obstacles and fortifications, this did not mean the Allied assault would be easy, unopposed, or without issue.

With various planning cells and competing visions for the invasion, another schism occurred between the service components. While the naval and ground components were haggling over courses of action, the air forces were seemingly of their own mind about how to participate in the invasion. Both the USAAF and the Royal Air Force (RAF) were disconnected from the larger joint planning effort and failed to communicate or share their intentions with the ground and naval staffs.[12] Although the staff of the Northwest African Air Forces conducted combined RAF and USAAF air planning, it did little to assist their companion components and were cavalier in their disregard. Regarding the planning of the operation, Truscott claimed the air forces showed a "complete lack of participation at any level below that of the high command."[13] Heading the air component was Sir Arthur Tedder, who, like many of his fellow aviators, believed the best use of airpower was not CAS but instead BAI, striking the enemy in the rear areas. For Tedder, sealing off the island precluded possible enemy movement, resupply, or reinforcement; this was the larger, more productive use of airpower—not the direct destruction of enemy forces per se.[14]

He was not alone, as many airmen believed that aviation assets should remain under control of an independent air commander and not parceled out in support of individual beaches, commanders, or efforts.[15] In what could only be seen as a reluctance to participate in the joint fight, official USAAF history sardonically stated: "US commanders continued to experience difficulty in accepting command arrangements which gave full control to the air commander."[16] Tedder's opinions (and also those of other Allied airmen) regarding the use of air assets was also a published doctrinal construct. A 1943 army field manual, *Command and Employment of Air Power*, firmly established three missions for tactical air forces: gain and maintain air superiority; disrupt hostile lines of communication; and destroy enemy troops and material on the fighting front in cooperation with forward ground forces.[17] Given that CAS was the very last priority, the manual went on to state more specifically that, "in the zone of contact, missions against hostile units are most difficult to control, are the most expensive, and are, in general, least effective. Targets are small, well dispersed, and difficult to locate. . . . Only at critical times are contact zone missions profitable."[18] While the definition of "critical times" is open to interpretation, to the soldier on the ground taking fire or fighting armor the definition would be fairly obvious. Taking this construct to heart, and certainly to an extreme, air support during this amphibious assault would be left wanting.

The organizational structure of the Allied command also played a role in the absence of air assets over the assault. While US XII Air Support Command was placed in direct support of Seventh Army, it exercised very little authority over its organic squadrons. Its six squadrons of fighter-bombers and ten squadrons of daytime fighters were all under the operational control of the RAF's Malta Command of the North African Tactical Air Force. Its taskings reflected Tedder's larger concern over neutralizing enemy air and operational targets, with little interest in covering troops landing on the beaches and even less to CAS. During the operation's first two days, not one CAS mission was flown in support of Seventh Army objectives.[19]

While naval aviation assets were used during the North Africa landings and were a key part of the WTF's success, for this next assault Hewitt's fleet lacked any aircraft carriers. The sea battle for the North Atlantic precluded any naval air support for Husky, as the small escort carriers so effective in Torch were equally useful in fighting U-boats. As the small carriers provided convoy escort duty, only ground-based aircraft were available for Husky. With no naval aviation assets and given NWAAF's lack of coordination and its vision regarding the use of airpower, the amphibious assault and Allied fleet were largely at the mercy of Axis airpower. While the official USAAF history claims that some fighter support was provided over the invasion beaches, it conceded that the air support provided was limited. Reflective of its support during the landings, the official USAAF account provides a host of excuses as to why it did not support the landings.[20] When NWAAF's plan was finally published in late June, just weeks before the 10 July invasion, one US commander remarked that it was the "most masterful piece of uninformed prevarication totally unrelated to the naval and military joint plan."[21]

An exception to the USAAF's tactical contributions to the assault landings was the innovative use of L-4 aircraft as naval gun spotters. Flying at low speeds and altitudes, they would help naval gunners and army artillery identify and engage targets ashore. While they were used effectively in North Africa, a more innovative approach was their placement aboard amphibious vessels. Since the L-4's range was limited, in-theater naval engineers affixed a makeshift runway to an LST, allowing the planes to operate from sea-based platforms. Tested in the waters of Lake Bizerte only six days before the Sicilian invasion, *LST-386* was modified with a small flight deck just 216 feet long and 10 feet wide, fixed topside. On 4 July an L-4 was hoisted onto the LST, and once under way the ship turned into the wind. On the very first attempt the brave pilot advanced the throttle to maximum power and took off with room to spare. Successful, the innovative design also allowed the ship to carry a compliment of up to ten L-4s that worked in pairs.[22]

Regardless of its reception by the ground and naval components, the NWAAF's air plan for Husky somewhat reflected the tenets of the newly published *FM 100-20, Command and Employment of Air Power*'s three-phased approach. Phase one of the air campaign called for hitting ports, airfields, and railroads on the Italian mainland, Sardinia, and Sicily. This would seal off the combat zone from further Axis support, resupply, and reinforcement. In this effort, B-17 Flying Fortress and B-24 Liberator heavy bombers struck targets on the island and the Italian mainland. The second phase was establishing air superiority over the island and attacking Axis airdromes and aircraft and removing them as a threat. In the third and final phase, airmen would focus on supporting operations on Sicily by utilizing captured German airfields for further on-island missions.[23] In this effort, daylight raids by B-25 Mitchell medium bombers hit the Gerbini, Trapani, and Sciacca airfields and other locations. In addition, twin-boomed P-38 Lightning fighters attacked targets of opportunity on the western and southeastern parts of the island. During 3–9 July, in preparation for the assault, USAAF heavy and medium bombers flew over 1,300 sorties.[24]

Even on D-Day, NWAAF still focused on targets beyond the beachheads with A-36 Apache dive-bombers along with P-38s. Despite the lack of USAAF representation during planning and over the invasion beaches, rudimentary air coordination took place. Such coordination came in the form of fighter control units (FCUs) embarked aboard Hewitt's flagship USS *Monrovia* and the USS *Ancon*. These floating FCUs were to provide warning and direction for defensive air cover. But the shipboard FCUs fell short. The FCUs were not empowered to order planes into the area, control aircraft entering the area, or request support for offensive operations.[25] The FCU cell was at the mercy of external commands with no real direct tasking authority and provided mostly visibility on executed sorties. Furthermore, the air representation aboard had limited VHF/RT (very high frequency/ radio transmitter) communication capabilities, possessed inadequate command-and-control equipment, and was located in berthing spaces incompatible with the mission. The FCU spaces were so small that one man could not move until the others in the cell did.

Further air representation came in other forms. Defensive aerial support during the night came in the form of a sector ship with a Ground Control Intercepts (GCIs) cell equipped with radars mounted on LSTs.[26] These GCI LSTs were modified, with the ship's bow doors welded shut, working spaces installed in the vessels tank deck, and radios, radar, and other associated gear. Required aerials and antennas were affixed topside for effective communication, with elements of the ship's superstructure removed or modified to reduce electromagnetic interference.[27] However, overall coordination between these sea-based units was also poor, as was their authority to control the aerial defensive battle.[28]

For offensive air operations ground forces were augmented with air support parties (ASPs) equipped with radios and landed just after the initial assault waves to service CAS requests. However, during the landings poorly trained radio operators, small frequency bandwidths, and other factors militated effective CAS requests and support. Five ASPs landed on D-Day but had problems communicating given the mountainous terrain.[29] Even if these organizations were fully capable, CAS taskings were still a low priority given the Allied air forces' visions. Without sufficient air cover during the initial assault phase, Allied antiaircraft artillery gunners both ashore and afloat grew increasingly nervous as enemy aircraft continuously appeared overhead. This was supposed to be a coordination mission for the FCUs, but again their performance fell short, as there was no central air control. In the words of one observer, AAA support was a matter of "every man for himself."[30] This lack of central control conditioned the gun crews to think that all aircraft over the amphibious force were hostile. Such assumptions would eventually result in unfortunate consequences. The lack of CAS, and of air cover, and the failure of airmen to articulate their intent left a bad taste in everyone's mouth.[31]

Although Hewitt and navy historian Samuel Eliot Morison did give credit to the NWAAF for shaping the environment, the latter quipped: "If the XII Air Support Command (ASC) had taken a more active part in the initial planning of the campaign and had been less desirous of showing its independence vis-a-vis the Army, difficulties might have been obviated."[32] Hewitt was even more direct: "The weakest link in the joint planning of the US Force was almost complete lack of participation by the Air Force." The Seventh Army's after-action report echoed the same sentiment.[33] Complaints even came from USAAF personnel aboard ship who did not receive the published air plan until D-1. One air representative noted:

> We did not know what the patrol plan was, [and] we did not know where on that patrol line the aircraft might be at any time. We did not know whether they were simply flying up and down the beach or whether they were going to land or out to sea. And, believe it or not, there was no one aboard the ship who could tell us! There were no grid maps prepared for pilots use so when we wanted to give the pilot a vector, we first had to get them to orbit over an obvious check point so we would know where they were.[34]

This lack of air support was a glaring deficiency. Reflective of the USMC–USN relationship regarding air support in the Pacific, Hewitt rather pointedly quipped that, "where practicable, naval aviation should be used for close support in amphibious operations." While this was relatively easier, as navy and Marine units had a shared understanding of airpower in an amphibious environment, this was unfamiliar territory for the USAAF. Hewitt went even further to refute tenets of *FM 100-20* and believed that army aircraft supporting an amphibious assault should be under operational control of the CATF.[35] He was not alone in his displeasure. A frustrated General Patton, remembering his previous Torch experience, quipped: "You can get naval air to do anything you want, but we can't get the Air Force to do a goddam thing!"[36]

In addition to the lack of air support during the landings, there were no preparatory fires along the beachline or the objective areas. While on-call and preplanned targets were designated, the army still believed that tactical surprise had value in amphibious operations. Assuming it did not have overwhelming firepower, the army believed in the value of tactical surprise.[37] Although two deception operations played a role keeping Axis formations committed in Sardinia and the Balkans, maintaining tactical surprise with the large flotilla was an unrealistic expectation. The movement of additional Wehrmacht forces to the island indicated that the Germans were already aware of the potential for an invasion, with elements of the Hermann Göring Division and *Fallschirmjäger* paratrooper formations arriving from France.[38] Regardless of the large troop movements, an Allied after-action report hinted that surprise might have been achieved, but the same report also stated that it was impossible to maintain such after H-1.[39]

Furthermore, with the planned paratrooper assault in the vicinity of Gela and Scoglitti, army planners worried that errant NSFS might strike elements of the 82nd AB once it landed.[40] Hewitt believed this was a mistake, but army planners clung to their belief in a stealthy approach. Despite joint training between the two services in fire direction and control procedures weeks before the Torch assault, the army was still reticent to allow such bombardment.[41] This was a significant departure from Marines landing in the Pacific, where frontal assaults were almost always preceded with pre–D-Day bombardment and in daylight. It would take lessons learned in the next few amphibious assaults to realize that shaping the AOA with a prelanding bombardment outweighed the element of tactical surprise.

While the Allies engaged in strategic deception in the form of Operations Fortitude (the larger strategic deception operation for all of Europe) and Mincemeat (another deception operation in the Mediterranean along with Barclay), there was also a deliberate effort at the tactical level for Husky. Task Group 80.4 was designated a demonstration element with a flotilla of ten damage control ships and one patrol boat. These modified ships carried a host of special deception equipment along with specifically trained personnel. The plan was to conduct a diversionary operation off the western coast of the island near Point Granitola. However, heavy seas and 20–30-knot winds precluded the mission from taking place. Another larger effort, code-named "Fracture," was also planned for the Marsala–Mazzara area, but a delay in communication precluded its launch. While these operations did not precede the landing, days later Task Force 80.4 would conduct limited operations on D+2/3.[42] Despite this delay, prelanding feints would become a standard tactic for American amphibious operations in the ETO.

While Axis forces posed a threat, so did the weather. As the Allied force got underway, the US Navy's Aerology Section reported that the weather conditions, while still conducive to an assault, were not perfect and would eventually cause considerable difficulties.[43] In the area from Licata to Gela, skies were clear, but a northwest wind of seven knots created swells of two to three feet and a surf of two to six feet. Such conditions would hamper landing operations and cause seasickness among embarked troops, but they were not enough to preclude the assault. The conditions at Scoglitti were less favorable. With clear skies, the Cent Force experienced a northwest wind of ten to sixteen knots generating swells of ten to twelve feet with a surf also two to six feet.[44] These same conditions would also cause difficulties during later amphibious movements. However, weather in the following days was expected to remain favorable for unloading and transport activities across the beaches. This was especially important, as the planned logistics over the shore was dependent on good weather. Any adverse weather conditions might seriously degrade the building of combat power ashore.

Joss

Relieved of his duties as LANCRAB, Rear Admiral Conolly assumed command of Naval Task Force 86 and moved Truscott's 3rd ID, an armored combat command, and two Ranger elements to five designed beaches that bracketed the town of Licata. The assault force had forty of the new LSTs, along with fifty-four LCIs and eighty-five LCTs, and represented the westernmost element of the American and Allied forces. The town itself had a small artificial harbor was too well defended and covered by supporting fires to serve as a landing beach.[45] Red Beach, located five miles west of the town, was used by the 7th RCT. A few miles to the east of Red, elements of the 15th RCT accompanied by a Ranger battalion landed on beaches Green 1 and Green 2 and made for Licata. To the east of the town the remainder of the 15th RCT came with more Rangers landing on Yellow Beach. These units were also to march on Licata and secure it with their companion units from Green. In the very east of the 3rd ID area was Blue Beach, with the 30th RCT aiming to take the high ground at Monte Desusino and tie in Dime Force and II Corps to the east.[46] For fire support, the navy had numerous platforms in direct support of the Joss landings. To organize the AOA, designated naval fire support areas established offshore were intermingled between the landing approaches and on the flanks. At these locations were eleven vessels awaiting requests for fire support.

Action at Red Beach began when 1st Battalion, 7th Infantry landed in a rough surf at 0400, seventy-five minutes late. The unit achieved tactical surprise but received enemy fire only after it had cleared the beach. Forty minutes later the 2nd Battalion arrived, clearing out Italian defensive positions.[47] Initially many of the positions on the beach were already deserted, but LCIs of the second wave took both machine-gun and artillery fire from Italian troops, creating casualties and causing one vessel to proceed out of control at full speed. With the craft landing backward, its troops disembarked over the stern. By 0500 both Red Beach assault waves landed, with the LCIs returning to sea. As the third wave came in, it received enemy fire while fighting a rough surf. One LCI coming ashore lost its troop ramps, leaving soldiers to flounder in the surf, some drowning. The craft then took a direct hit that killed several sailors. To accomplish his mission, the LCI's skipper deliberately beached his charge and had the remaining soldiers unload over the portside.[48]

As morning light came Italian artillery began pounding the beaches. Beachmasters ordered the halt of subsequent assault waves and requested NSFS. In quick fashion the destroyer USS *Buck* answered the call, silencing the enemy guns.[49] Eager to get armor and artillery units ashore and build combat power, these units arrive by 0630 and pushed inland. Enemy artillery fire continued, with the beachmasters again closing the landing site temporarily. This time the cruiser USS *Brooklyn* provided additional counterbattery fire and finally silenced the enemy guns on Monte Sole, located between Green Beach and Licata. All NSFS in the Joss area was accomplished without the aid of shore fire control parties but used the spotter planes that took off from the makeshift flightdeck on *LST-386*.[50]

Assisting in the targeting effort was how enemy positions were poorly concealed and clearly visible, with most pretargeted.[51] By 0715 enemy beach action ceased, the remainder of the landing force coming ashore and securing the lodgment. Combat engineers accompanied the assault wave and removed obstacles, mines, and other defenses.[52] With the silencing of enemy guns and routing of the few Italian defensive position present, by midmorning the beachhead was firmly established.

With the assault successfully conducted, the new amphibious shipping began to unload their cargos. Assisting in this effort was a decidedly low-tech and simple littoral application that made the operation even more efficient. Given the runnels and shallow gradients at various coastlines, naval engineers developed floating pontoons that could bridge the gap between surf and sand. As early as 1940 Captain John N. Laycock of the navy's Bureau of Yards and Docks, presented this idea to deal with natural, shallow-water obstacles.[53] While pontoons had been used during the time of ancient Greece, the navy developed and adopted floating, unpowered causeways that could carry up to 800 tons.[54] Affixed to the bow ramps and then strung together, pontoon sections easily breached natural littoral obstacles. On this day LSTs married to pontoon bridges were put in place, allowing the tanks to roll off by 1000.[55] Impressively, for the entire Husky operation pontoons allowed more that 10,000 pieces of rolling stock to come ashore.[56]

The landings on Green Beach went as planned, with 3rd Ranger

A 1944 photo of an L-4 "Grasshopper" (a military version of the Piper Cub) aircraft on the improvised flight deck of LST 906. Such aircraft provided naval gunfire spotter services and were perhaps the only USAAF aircraft found directly over the beaches during the first days of the Husky amphibious assault. (US Navy photo)

Battalion arriving at 0300 and again achieving tactical surprise. A battalion from 15th RCT and an artillery battery came ashore only minutes later.[57] Moving inland toward Licata, the Rangers accepted the surrender of resident Italian troops before moving into town. In trace, other elements of the RCT occupied the high ground of Monte Sole to the west of the town. Once secured, the American troops took down the Italian flag and replaced it with the Stars and Stripes. While there were no ground casualties in this assault, the minesweeper USS *Sentinel* was hit in the engine room by an enemy dive-bomber. It was attacked four more times and struck a second time, dooming the ship. Over half the ship's complement became casualties, with ten sailors killed and fifty-one wounded.[58]

Yellow Beach, east of Licata, had the remainder of 15th RCT

Spent shell casing litter the deck of the USS *Brooklyn* after providing NSFS
to Joss Force troops ashore on 10 July 1943. Composed of 3ID and Ranger
formations, Joss Force was the western most task force and constituted the left
flank of the Allied landings. (US Navy photo)

debarking from LSTs and landing at 0430. Once ashore, troops
again found positions abandoned, but one battalion did receive light
machine-gun fire.[59] In a marked improvement of amphibious capability, the LSTs arrived and began offloading tanks directly to the beach,
with the full complement ashore by 0914. 30th RCT landed at 0415
on Blue Beach, with the remainder of the command ashore by 0422.
Troops again received some light machine-gun and mortar fire on the
beach.[60] Focused on the high ground of Monte Desusino some 6,000
yards from the landing beaches, USS *Brooklyn* again fired. With the
help of a spotter plane and a rising sun, the cruiser expended 713 rounds
of high explosives and hit enemy artillery batteries that could have
ranged the American landing at Gela.[61] The USS *Buck* again engaged
targets ashore, helping 30th RCT and hitting enemy positions at Monte
Gallidoro. Regarding NSFS for Joss, Truscott reported that "shooting
honors go to the navy's cruisers[,] which destroyed remaining enemy
batteries."[62]

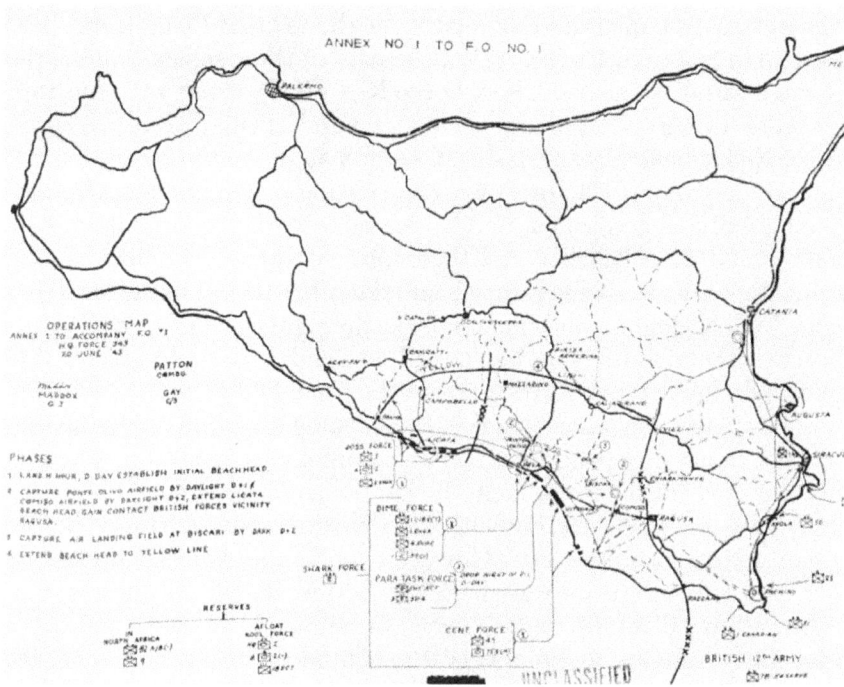

Map of the American landings on 10 July 1943. Joss Force to the northwest landed near Licata as Dime Force came ashore near the Gela plain. Cent Force landed on a wide frontage in the southwest bracketing the town of Scoglitti. (CARL Digital Archive)

With growing interservice cooperation, by 0530 DUKWs were swimming ashore, followed by LCTs an hour later. By 1000 engineers commenced shore-party operations, unloading more tanks and artillery. Regardless of incoming enemy fire that closed the beaches temporarily, the D-Day objectives for 30th RCT were accomplished with Licata secured by noon.[63] Joss Force easily achieved its assigned mission, but that success was not reflective of the other two landings.

Dime

Approximately ten miles to the east, Terry de la Mesa Allen's 1st ID landed near the town of Gela. Objectives for the division included the Ponte Olivo airfield, the town itself, and a linkup with Colonel James

Gavin's 505th Parachute Regiment near the town of Piano Lupo. The initial Dime assault force consisted largely of three separate units: the Ranger battalion labeled "Task Force X" (TF X), along with the 26th and 16th Infantry Regiments, using six beaches (Red, Green, Yellow, Blue, Red 2, and Green 2). TF X landed at Red and Green, located directly in front of the town, with an existing pier serving as a boundary between assault elements. To the right 26th Infantry landed on Yellow and Blue Beaches and then split, with one battalion moving toward Gela to assist the Rangers and the other taking Route 117 to occupy high ground behind the town. On the right flank of Dime Force's beaches, the 16th Infantry landed at Red 2 and Green 2 and planned to move northeast to meet troops from the 82nd AB.[64]

The airborne assaults on the early morning of 10 July were the second use of paratroops in support of an amphibious operation. The earlier use of vertical envelopment during the landing of the CTF during Torch was a clear failure, but with the Sicily invasion paratroopers were given another opportunity. However, while the American airborne performance in Husky was markedly better, it still fell far short of expectations. Planning to drop over 3,000 men of the 504th ahd 505th Parachute Infantry Regiments (PIRs) behind the beaches at Gela, the unexperienced aircrews piloting the C-47s had difficulties en route to the landing zones. Navigation errors, strong winds, enemy ground fire, and other factors precluded accurate drops. Given these difficulties, less than 200 men made it to their objective area, located on the high ground around Gela with many troops scattering in the Sicilian countryside.[65] An after-action report regarding the initial drops argued: "I do not believe that the losses of men and planes involved in the use of airborne troops can be justified unless and until the Air Corps is trained to bring these people in and drop them over the proper targets at the proper time."[66] Intended to block advancing Axis forces making their way to the landing beaches, the airborne forces teamed up as best they could despite their few numbers. They cut telephone lines and intercepted couriers despite the scattered sticks. However, this widespread landing area caused the enemy to overestimate the numbers, viewing them as a much bigger threat that they actually were. Through initiative and effective leadership, the paratroopers made a difference in several tactical actions and helped delay the Axis forces.[67]

Transported by Task Force 81 under Rear Admiral John Hall, the assault flotilla included fourteen LSTs and twenty LCIs, all arriving offshore after midnight. As the Rangers made their way toward the town, Italian defenders blew up the pier as searchlights illuminated inbound landing craft. As TF X made its landing at 0245, it received machine-gun fire from the town and returned fire as best it could. Quick action from the destroyer USS *Shubrick* targeted the lights and then, along with USS *Savannah*, engaged coastal positions engaging the Rangers.[68] Landing at 0335, elements of the 39th Engineers removed obstacles and other defensive measures. While experiencing casualties from beach mines and machine-gun fire from prepared positions, the Rangers entered the town, captured enemy costal batteries, and established defensive positions. By 0800 TF X held the city, captured 200 Italian soldiers, and turned the enemy's serviceable coastal guns inland for additional firepower as motorized artillery units landed to augment their position.[69]

To the southeast of Gela was Yellow and Blue Beaches, with H-Hour set for 0245. 26th RCT landed and met little opposition. The battalions split up to reinforce TF X and establish defensive positions on Route 117. As in the earlier Copy Book rehearsal, some boats went astray, with one landing five miles from the assault beaches. But by noon the 26th tied in with the 16th on its right.[70] Landing on Red 2 and Green 2, the 16th RCT's initial wave arrived unopposed, but once troops began debarking, Italian positions opened with machine-gun fire. Having little effect, the enemy fire quickly ceased, with the initial wave moving inland and passing Italian pillboxes near the shore. However, after 0300, subsequent assault waves received additional machine-gun and mortar fire from the bypassed pillboxes. An hour later NSFS from USS *Boise* and USS *Jeffers* targeted the fixed positions, with the regiment moving toward the town of Piano Lupo.[71]

While the initial landings at Gela went well, the Axis was not without a response. Lacking sufficient air cover, an attack from a German Junkers Ju 88 bomber at 0500 hit the destroyer USS *Maddox*, sinking it and taking most of the crew to the bottom.[72] Since the NWAAF provided little to no air cover over the beaches, enemy air attacks continued throughout the day, but caused limited damage.[73] However, Axis aircraft continued to be a nuisance throughout the operation, with eighty-nine raids disrupting offloading operations, harassing the fleet, sinking two vessels along with dozens of landing craft, and at times precluding spotter aircraft operations.[74]

After the initial assault, Italian counterattacks began around 0900. Advancing from the vicinity of Priolo near Route 115, the Italian armor was a mix of captured French Renault tanks and accompanying Italian Fiat designs. With only infantry weapons, soldiers of the 16th blunted the enemy attack with help from a forward observer in an L-4 calling

Axis aircraft attacked the invasion flotilla at Sicily with impunity. Fortunately, most of their bombs missed their mark but such attacks disrupted operations and movement ashore. (US Navy photo)

in NSFS at 0910. The combined effort fully thwarted the Italian advance.[75] Shortly afterward a two-pronged, second Italian attack came from Butera Road north of Gela and from Route 117 northeast of the town. The USS *Shubrick* engaged Italian armor on Route 117, while the Rangers manned their newly captured Italian guns and opened on the enemy infantry formations coming from Butera.[76] The Italian attack on Butera road was soundly repulsed not only by the captured guns, but also from NSFS, mortars, and anti-tank weapons. However, enemy armor coming from Route 117 succeeded in making it to the town of Gela. Navigating the narrow streets without infantry support, the Italians were now at a disadvantage. The tanks began a cat-and-mouse game with the Rangers in the town's close confines. Using hand grenades, dynamite, and bazookas the Americans leveraged to urban terrain destroying the tanks and neutralizing the threat.[77]

The first American encounter on Sicily with German armor forces was near the towns of Priolo and Piano Lupo. Around 1400, 16th Infantry linked up with paratroopers from the 82nd AB and were making defensive positions. Located on the high ground northeast of the landing beaches, elements of the Hermann Göring Division attacked with panzers and dismounted infantry. Naked against the armor and without heavy weapons or antitank guns, the Americans called for naval fires from destroyers in the Gulf of Gela. The German Mark IVs and Mark VIs were no match for the NSFS, and the attack stalled under a rain of steel. By 1600 the 16th Infantry reported "the tanks are trying to withdraw" and hours later in much the same tone transmitted that the "tanks are withdrawing . . . it seems we are too much for them."[78]

With Allen's desire for more armor ashore, LSTs were sent to unload the heavy vehicles, but the runnels and sand composition precluded their beaching. By noon none of the artillery or armor had made it ashore. At 1400 2nd AD received orders to land on Yellow and Blue Beaches. However, both of those colored beaches were mined. As a result, the much-needed armor came ashore on Red Beach 2. But the building up of combat power ashore remained slow, and by nightfall only three LSTs had been fully unloaded. Compounding the problem was that many LSTs required pontoon sections to overcome the runnels. Adding to the delay was that some pontoon sections had accidentally been set adrift with no ability to recover them.

Enemy air and artillery fire precluded arrival of American heavy calibers. With the other beaches closed, Red Beach 2 quickly became congested with equipment. Overcrowding and disorganization at the beach saw landing craft return to their ships still loaded, as there was no place for them to land. Hewitt noted after the invasion that a large number of craft were stranded while waiting to unload on beaches, and with such poor beach organization most crews unloaded the boats themselves. Many transports reported that their boats were ordered away from the congestion, and few armor assets made it ashore as more enemy tanks sat just beyond the Gela Plain.[79] By 0200 the next morning some addition infantry formations had made it ashore, but stalled medium tanks languished in the rough surf. Moreover, the rising sea state precluding additional armor from coming ashore.[80]

DUKWs brought artillery and supplies ashore efficiently. In an after-action comment on the Husky landings, one officer reported that "these 2½ ton amphibians were praised everywhere . . . they can carry ashore a 6-pounder [artillery piece] complete with gun detachment or a jeep, and [they] have proved [to be] admirable recovery vehicles."[81] However, once ashore these vehicles were often commandeered by ground commanders for other tasks, complicating beach-party functions.[82] Disorder on the beachhead was again an issue. As in previous assaults, shores became awash in men and equipment. One observer noted:

> There was an endless, confused mass of men, of tiny jeeps, huge, high-sided DUKWs, and more jeeps and heavily loaded trucks, stuck and straining in the thick sand or moving clumsily on the wire netting that the engineers had laid down in places as road. . . . From every conceivable direction there was the roar of motors, the sound of spinning wheels, the puttering of craft, the buzzing of planes overhead, shouts of drivers, the curses of soldiers, mechanics, gun crews, [and] officers. . . . I saw abandoned trucks, overturned jeeps and smashed boats, and on the sand were blown up cars, a tank with its tread off, heaps of bedding rolls and baggage with soldiers sitting on them waiting for transportation. . . . Trucks, floundering to their hubcaps in the sand, futilely raced their engines as jeeps, jerking this way and that, tried to pull them out."[83]

Hewitt would also note that "gasoline, ammunition, water, food, and assorted equipment were strewn about in a hopeless mass." The admiral's complaint of not enough exercise of beach-party functions during the Copy Book workups had proven prescient as this confusion occurred at multiple locations. Junior naval officers trying to support their brethren on the ground were often countermanded by senior army officers ashore that precluded efficient organization and processes.[84] Even Ike made a specific comment about the lack of effective shore parties, reporting "supply requirements [ashore] were equally pressing. . . . Part of the difficulty arose from the limited time and opportunity for thorough advance training for all shore parties which combined naval and military elements."[85] Some soldiers even commandeered local fishing vessels to reach supplies afloat and bring them ashore themselves. Obviously both services still had not mastered combined beach- and shore-party functions.

On 11 July (D+1) the Germans tried again as they drove down Routes 117 and 115, each with a Kampfgruppen equipped with tanks and armored vehicles combined with infantry. Estimated strength of the German formation was thirty to forty Mark IV and VI tanks. In a separate and uncoordinated effort, the Italians again launched their own armor assault near Route 117 toward Gela. With few antitank assets available, the RCTs had to rely on the 33rd Field Artillery Battalion, which had made it ashore, along with NSFS support. USS *Savannah* and USS *Boise* again engaged enemy formations along with the shore-based artillery.[86]

The Gela Beaches after the initial Husky landings. A Western Task Force LST offloads onto a pontoon bridge. Such bridges were instrumental in breaching runnels that paralleled the shore-line precluding ships from beaching themselves. In the foreground are Italian prisoners about to be embarked on opportune lift to Algeria. Note to the left and right of the pontoon bridge are sunken landing craft. (US Navy photo)

The combined arms effort stopped the Italian advance. Two more Italian attacks occurred later that morning, under the observation of Patton, and finally stopped in the same combined arms manner.[87]

However, the German formation in the west driving along Route 117 was making progress and began to move across the Gela Plain to join the other Kampfgruppen traveling along Route 115. Wehrmacht formations along Route 115 bypassed American positions near Priolo and made their way to the fringes of the American beachhead.[88] The panzers threatened to penetrate the established beachhead and came within 1,000 yards of the shore and for a time were too close to friendly forces for NSFS. All the men on the beach—sailor and soldier alike—were now involved in the defense, including the newly arrived 32nd Field Artillery Regiment and 16th Infantry Cannon Company (an organic 105mm company assigned to the Infantry regiment). Deploying their guns and lowering muzzles in direct fire, and along with a recently arrived platoon of Sherman tanks from Company I, 67th Armor Regiment, the German attack was stopped.[89] The German counterattack was a near disaster for the entire operation but was successfully defeated through quick action and individual initiative. Retreating German armor was then engaged by NSFS, leaving sixteen tanks as smoking hulks on the Gela Plain with an estimated one-third of the Göring Division's armor destroyed.[90] Hitting these mobile targets while the gun-target line was also moving displayed exceptional skill on the part of the navy crews.

At Gela the joint coordinated defense of army artillery and NSFS made a difference. Part of this successful effort was that a fire direction center aboard USS *Samuel Chase* stayed in contact with 1st ID batteries and managed the joint fires.[91] Even after the initial landings, naval gunfire continued making significant contributions to the division's push inland. They were especially effective in the defeat of both German and Italian armor formations in the first two tenuous days in the Dime sector. Such effective joint fires became a hallmark of American operations in all theaters of the war, especially when air eventually became part of the effort. In his after-action report Admiral Hewitt remarked: "The destruction of this armored force by naval gunfire delivered by US cruisers and destroyers, and the recovery of the situation through naval support, was one of the most noteworthy events of the operations."[92] More important was a note from Patton to an Admiral Davidson extolling NSFS: "The gunfire support that you provided has been of inestimable value."[93]

Reminiscent of the failure of air/surface coordination during the planning phase of Husky, another instance occurred on the night of 11 July (D+1). With the Axis counterattacks on the Dime beaches, Patton decided to reinforce his position around Gela and asked for a second drop of paratroopers. Despite the poor airborne execution on D-1, the 504th PIR loaded aboard 144 C-47s from the 52nd Troop Carrier Wing in bases in North Africa. Flying a route that took them near the Allied armada, the aircrews and paratroopers expected a smooth ingress. The 82nd AB commander, Major General Mathew Ridgeway, attempted to ensure the navy would provide an air corridor for the safe passage over the Allied fleet.[94] Meanwhile ground-based AAA crews were informed of the inbound C-47s and were warned not to engage. However, word of the night's airborne reinforcement was not passed in time to the naval AAA crews afloat. Sailors were already jumpy from previous Axis air attacks earlier in the day that had dropped bombs over the beaches and the offshore fleet. While most of the Axis bombs missed the targets, one found its mark, hitting and sinking a Liberty ship, the USS *Robert Rowan*. Loaded with ammunition, the ship exploded with a huge plume of smoke easily visible for miles that smoldered for hours. As a result of the day's previous aerial attacks, naval crews interpreted any overhead aircraft engine noise as hostile.[95]

Another Axis air raid at 2150 occurred minutes before the 504th paratroopers were to arrive over their drop zones. While the first wave jumped during a lull in the aerial fight overhead, the second and third waves were not so lucky. Despite the earlier warning to army AAA gunners, naval and ground-based batteries opened up. Captain Willard Harrison of the 504th PIR observed: "As soon as this firing began, guns along the coast as far as we could see toward Punta Socca, opened fire and naval craft laying off-shore . . . began firing anti-aircraft guns."[96] Following formations broke up as the C-47s tried to evade the AAA as commanders ashore helplessly watched the slaughter of American soldiers from friendly fire. Of the 144 aircraft that took off that night, twenty-three were lost and thirty-seven badly damaged, a 16 percent loss rate. More important, the 504th suffered 229 casualties that night including eighty-one dead, 132 wounded, and sixteen missing.[97] Ike ordered an investigation, but a board of officers at Allied Force Headquarters could not definitively conclude who was at fault. However, given the earlier misdrops and events during the night of D+1, serious reconsideration was given regarding to the value of airborne operations.[98] Perhaps the most memorable observation of the D+1 drops came from a NWAAF pilot: "Evidently the safest place for us tonight while over Sicily would have been over enemy territory."[99]

After D+1, the beachmasters started to organize the shore, with more pontoon bridges being established allowing the LSTs to unload with equipment moving inland. With stiff enemy resistance reduced, the Italian defenders surrender the Ponte Olivo airfield the morning of 12 July with 1st ID continuing inland.[100] With the Dime force objectives attained, transport ships unloaded their cargos and returned to North Africa as NSFS assets remaining on station. Dealing with an influx of POWs, the Americans leveraged the returning ships, moving thousands of Italians to internment camps in Algeria. Engineers continued to improve the Gela location as LSTs unloaded supplies and equipment. By the end of the first two days, the American beaches moved 80,000 men and 7,300 vehicles/trucks along with 900 guns.[101]

Cent

On the far right side of the American sector and sharing a left boundary with 1st ID was Cent Force, composed of the 45th ID and carried by Combined Task Force 85 under Rear Admiral Adam Kirk. With the largest contingent of soldiers in Husky (26,000), it included the Thunderbird Division, a National Guard unit with a large population of Native Americans from Oklahoma, Colorado, and New Mexico filling its ranks. The division was the first to go through amphibious training at Camp Edwards in 1942 and was the first of the four army-trained divisions from the stateside ATC to conduct an amphibious assault. Coming directly from the states, they had a short stay in Algeria for a quick amphibious rehearsal before entering combat. For their first combat operation they were to capture two airfields located at Comiso and Biscari. Comiso was the primary objective, located eleven miles inland, with the division expected to occupy it by D+1. Biscari was further inland, with planners predicting it would be seized by D+3.[102]

Sharing a boundary with the British army on its right, the 45th landed on five designated beaches (with three as additional as assigned) with Red, Green, and Yellow north of the town of Scoglitti.[103] This stretch of beach was known as "Wood's Hole." South of the fishing village, referred to as "Bailey's Beach," were Green 2, Yellow 2, and Blue 2. With three regimental combat teams—the 157th, 179th, and 180th—Cent Force landed in a relatively uninhabited area of the island containing a few scattered pillboxes and coastal artillery positions. The 180th was to land on Red Beach, move toward the town of Ponte Dirillo, and meet up with elements of the 82nd AB dropped earlier that night. The 179th had two battalions that were to land at Green and Yellow, with one heading to the Comiso airfield following the capture of the town of Vittorio. The second battalion utilized Yellow Beach and was to immediately head southeast and seize Scoglitti. The 157th planned to land nine miles south of the other two combat teams and operated as its own independent task force. It also split up its battalions, with one heading to the Comiso Airfield to assist elements of the 179th, while the supporting effort seized the town of Santa Croce Camerina and thence to Comiso.[104]

The Cent landing beaches were a poor choice as there were few exits and the soft sand made trafficability for wheeled vehicles difficult. Furthermore, both Wood's Hole and Bailey's Beach were thousands of yards from any roads, meaning vehicles and soldiers were in for a long slog through the dunes and scrub brush.[105] Added problems included

45th ID supplies and equipment coming ashore near Scoglitti illustrating the congestion of the Cent Force landings. (US Navy photo)

the marginal surf conditions in the Cent area. Even before arriving in the transport area, Cent Force was experiencing difficulties. With CTF 85 making its way in the Tunisian war channel (the sea between Tunisia and Sicily; also referred to as the "Sicilian Channel"), the flotilla had to give way to ships in the Eastern Task Force coming directly from the United Kingdom, as well as CTF 81 supporting the Dime landings. As a result of the seaborne traffic jam, Kirk decided that H-Hour, originally designated for 0245, had to slip sixty minutes. In the transport area the sea state made landing craft deployment difficult. With H-Hour reset for 0345, the late change caused confusion, as the scout boats had already been launched based on the previous timetable. Landing craft were already in assembly areas, and others were still in the process of embarkation.[106] Adding to the confusion: just before the landings were underway Axis aircraft arrived overhead attacking the CTF for forty-five minutes. Fortunately, enemy airpower had more bad luck and failed to strike any ships.[107] But the attack exacerbated the existing confusion.

A battalion of the 179th landed at Yellow Beach and was the first to engage. Its rocket-mounted scout boats sent eighty-four projectiles followed by smoke rounds to obscure the enemy's field of vision.

Troops landed twenty yards off the beach on a small runnel and had to wade to shore. With soldiers still making their way in the surf zone, two destroyers engaged enemy shore emplacements. Another battalion landed at Green Beach minutes later after heavy swells during embarkation delayed the process. Despite the difficulty, the battalion at Green Beach put 748 men ashore in four waves, both battalions moving toward their objectives. The 180th at Red Beach had more difficulty. Due to a lack of landmarks, scout boats failed to locate the landing site, and with inexperienced coxswains the battalions landed scattershot. One battalion commander ended up landing at a Gela (Dime) Beach, while part of the command landed at Bailey's Beach south of Scoglitti. Still others made landfall across the frontage of Wood's Hole and at other undesignated locations.[108] Despite this setback, by 0600 the first battalion of the 180th consolidated enough troops to head out for Ponte Drillio/Biscari while attempting to contact 1st Division on its left and the 179th on its right. Fortunately, both RCTs at the Wood's Hole beaches met little enemy resistance.

However, on D-Day the Germans attempted another counterattack using routes in the Cent sector that lead into the Dime area and the Gela Plain. Launching an infantry column supported with Tiger tanks, the enemy travelled southeasterly through the town of Biscari heading to Route 115. Along the way the German force routed the 1st Battalion of the 180th and captured the commanding officer. Continuing to head toward Route 115, the column was in position to access the road and continue west, threatening the 1st ID's right flank. However, the German formation was unexpectedly met by the 3rd Battalion of the 180th just south of Route 115. Given the surprise of the American defensive position, the German column broke ranks.[109]

While American forces moved inland, sea states near Bailey's Beach caused serious problems with embarkation and navigation. Lacking distinctive landmarks to orient, scout boats and destroyers providing NSFS had a difficult time identifying Green 2 and Yellow 2. With these problems, part of the first wave landed on Yellow 2 instead of Green 2. As a result, naval fires hit prearranged targets for the assault without the accompanying landing force. Some landing craft fighting the surf were pushed to the right of Yellow 2 and ran into the rocks of Punta Braccetto. Trying to avoid the hazards, two craft collided and sank, drowning thirty-eight soldiers. In the darkness other boats had similar navigation and hazard problems, with another five boats lost and by daybreak only one wave landing on the correct beach.[110] In fact no boat made it to Green Beach 2, but fortunately enemy actions and resistance was negligible. By 0900 both battalions headed for their objectives and by nightfall pushed some seven miles inland.

By 0625 Admiral Kirk tried to assist by moving his transports closer to the beach to ease ship-to-shore movement. Regardless, the beaches were awash in stranded landing craft, equipment, and supplies. One navy officer quipped that the scattering of landing craft looked like "the shoes in a dead man's closet." Cartoonist Bill Maudlin of "Wille and Joe" fame, observing the 45th beaches, realized: "My first lesson about war is that nobody really knows what he is doing."[111] Given this situation Kirk abandoned the use of Yellow and Green 2 and moved the offloading of supplies to the southernmost beach, Blue 2 on the other side of Punta Braccetto.[112] A survey of boats on 11 July around Bailey's Beach found that only sixty-six of the 175 landing craft were still available (a 63 percent loss rate).[113] To the north at Yellow Beach near Wood's Hole, the situation was equally bad, with hundreds of swamped or grounded landing craft floundering on runnels, salvage crews overwhelmed. An observer from Allied headquarters made the same conclusion, reporting that several salvage vessels were needed to recover stranded craft.[114]

Even when troops and equipment made it ashore at Wood's Hole, the trafficability combined with a lack of outlets inland resulted in log-jams and bottlenecks ashore. When one of Hewitt's transport division commanders went ashore, he reported observing poor seamanship, ineffective-shore party work, and beach exits "completely blocked."[115] When the II Corps commander, Lieutenant General Bradley, finally came ashore and established his headquarters at Scoglitti, he described the invasion beaches as "as dismal sight . . . more than 200 assault craft wallowed in the surf after having burned out their engines in crossing the runnels while coming ashore."[116]

Once again beach-party personnel had a hard time organizing and managing equipment that made it ashore. 45th ID commander Troy Middleton already had a poor opinion of ESB personnel, calling them "rabble" and seeing them as rejects from combat units that were in-subordinate and more interested in their own self-interest that helping in the mission.[117] An after-action report from Seventh Army specifically included the lack of resident knowledge regarding shore control. Supporting Middleton's observation, when Hewitt submitted his after-action report he also called out the shore-party personnel and their lack of initiative, complaining they stood idle or hid in foxholes or within the piles of unorganized supplies, unwilling to help unload and consolidate equipment.[118] He was also chagrined to see that beach

LST 314 is waved ashore by a Beach Group signal man. (US Navy photo)

parties failed to erect markers, identify safe routes through enemy minefields for motorized transport, establish delivery locations for various classes of supply, or enforce traffic control measures and while establishing only weak defensive positions on the perimeter.[119] Another senior officer had much the same to report: "I saw the navy officer in charge was a total loss as what to do and I had difficulty in finding any Army officer in control of troops."[120]

Given the situation at Wood's Hole Kirk ordered all subsequent landings there to take place at Blue Beach, just north of Scoglitti.[121] At this location there were more exits from the beaches, but the sand was equally problematic, with exits also becoming congested. Adding to the confusion, follow-on landing craft became stuck in the surf, with boats navigating around runnels or landing at the wrong location. As with the Dime beaches, many boats returned to their launches still fully loaded given debarkation ashore was impossible. Despite these problems with ship-to-shore movement, the 45th had a toehold in its area. The absence of enemy formations at the landing beaches gave Middleton some breathing room and the ability to establish better lodgments inland. Given the surf problems at both Wood's Hole and Bailey's Beach, these locations were eventually closed on 17 July.

The 45th still managed to make progress inland and attain its objectives: the Comiso airfield, move into position near Biscari on Route 115, and take the town of Scoglitti. The small town's location helped the offload by having space to unload one LCT at a time.[122] NSFS again played an important role in these inland operations by defeating German armor at Biazzo Ridge, hitting enemy defenses between the Acate River and Biscari and helping take the town of Santa Croce Camerina four miles inland. Once again, the joint fires were a key aspect of the campaign.

A student of the war could argue that the American performance at Husky was similar to that of Torch, but doing so would ignore significant exceptions. While the enemy response at most of the beaches was weak initially, 1st ID repulsed competent and capable German armored attacks in the Gela Plain with the help of NSFS, antitank weapons, and artillery in a direct-fire mode. These attacks were not from unmotivated Vichy and Italian forces but competent and well-led Germans. The amphibious ante had been raised, and the Americans responded. Lessons learned from North Africa and at the FAITC resulted in more tactically competent US divisions able to respond quickly to emerging situations.

The battle in the Dime sector was a significant confrontation, one that required not only the landing of armor and artillery in the first hours but also the coordination of NSFS at targets with the gun-target line moving and friendly troops dangerously close. Furthermore, success ashore came without significant CAS from the NWAAF. While Torch's WTF could count on naval aviation to reduce enemy positions, tactical units in Husky had no such air support. This fact was not lost on Ike: "One of the major lessons should never be lost sight of in future planning . . . that during the critical stages of landing operations, every item of available force including land, sea, and air must be wholly concentrated in support of the landing force until troops are position to take care of themselves."[123]

The innovative use and construction of aircraft capable LSTs to spot naval fires helped make up for the lack of offensive tactical airpower. Despite the placement of air support parties ashore, CAS was absent during the initial assault waves. Additionally, the operation was conducted without aid of air cover, as persistent Axis air attacks affected landing operations and fleet activity. With ships sunk and disruption of landing operations, enemy air activity hampered Allied operations and contributed to the friendly fire incident killing airborne troops in the attempt to reinforce Dime.

Despite the logistical quagmire at the shorelines, initial landing support occurred without use of significant port infrastructure and with poorly chosen beaches. With no harbors available, new amphibious vessels like the LST, LCI, and LCT, combined with DUKWs and the use of pontoons, made a significant difference in the building of combat power. Such vessels and applications became a mainstay of American amphibious operations for the rest of the war. Of particular importance was the ability of the LST to carry large cargos and discharge them directly on the beach (or reach them via pontoons). DUKWs, LCIs, and LCTs, while much smaller, also had beaching capability but would find further utility as shuttles between deep-drafting Liberty ships or for LSTs that could not fit in restrictive areas. Had such a capability been absent, future amphibious assaults would have been difficult, if not altogether impossible. The United States was then, as it remains today, the only country that can power project from the sea in such a robust capability. These material solutions provided perhaps the biggest advancement in amphibious assault capability.

Even with the new platforms and the training that occurred at FAITC, coxswain performance was still wanting. As for the surf and the environment at various beaches, Hewitt observed:

> In considering the large number of boats stranded or capsized in the initial assault waves, it must be recognized that the combination of the notorious characteristics of the beaches and the high cross-surf running required a greater skill on the part of boat coxswains than the majority of them possessed, for the most skillful surf-boatman

would have found the problem of safely beaching the loaded craft a difficult one. . . . Training of boat crews is an ever-present requirement; it is indicated that training must emphasize night and bad weather landings of loaded boats, and training in retraction and salvage methods. Relief boat crews require as much training as regular crews; this is important.[124]

With these new vessels and the ability to move large amounts of gear and supplies from the fleet, the logistics over the shore methodology was "good enough" despite the difficulties. Such building of combat power through mass was a critical capability for Allied amphibious operations. Additionally, while many landing craft were caught on runnels, a more robust salvage operation occurred with enough supplies and equipment making it ashore. The "logistics over the shore" method would be used again in many subsequent landings with pontoons helping to overcome the runnel issues. Regarding the low-tech pontoons, one observer claimed "they proved a great success."[125] Although use of a fixed port with cranes and other infrastructure was more efficient, Husky proved that enough supplies could be provided over an unprepared beach to support multiple divisions ashore.

However, the issue of beach-party organization, establishment, and coordination between the two services was still problematic. Its importance was recognized at the Engineer Amphibian Command back at Camp Edwards, as an updated training guide specified:

Supplies [over the shore] must be moved rapidly. Battle experience on the beaches of North Africa and Sicily proved that victory is dependent upon a continuous flow of all types of supplies and equipment across the beaches to the assault troops ahead. Unnecessary congestion at the critical stage of the attack meant disaster. There is no place where the lives of men depended more upon the coordinated activities of their fellow soldiers than in the movement of men and supplies across a hostile beach. When the time comes, it will not matter how well the tactical commander has planned, nor how skillfully the boat companies have brought their waves in to the right beach at the right minute . . . if beach organization breaks down, the battle is lost.[126]

The use of airborne forces was again a debacle, but they did play a role in the establishment of the beachhead and the defeat of enemy counterattacks at Gela. Given the extensive losses at the hands of friendly fire, poor navigation, and weather decisions, confusion reigned during execution of these operations. Despite the difficulties paratroopers did make a difference. A far cry from the failed use of airborne troops during Torch, the 82nd AB in Sicily checked German counterattacks, cut lines of communication, and bolstered beachhead defenses during the first few days. Use of airborne troops in subsequent amphibious operations would improve from the Husky experience—although they still had their own problems. One observer noted: "I admit the value of airborne troops, but only if the Air Corps can be given sufficient training to allow them to perform their function efficiently."[127] Paratroopers were used months later in Salerno and were again a key aspect in defense of the beachhead. In the following months, the methods used in the amphibious assaults on Italian shores and in France came from lessons learned on the nights of 10 and 11 July.

All the Husky strategic objectives were achieved. Subsequent operations on the Italian mainland continued to reduce Axis formations and tie up divisions the enemy could ill afford. The next step for US amphibious forces was the Avalanche assaults at Selerno. Conducted weeks after the closing of Husky, there was little time for the Avalanche effort to formally assess the lessons learned from the Sicilian operation, but significant changes did occur.[128] While Overlord/Neptune was still almost a year away from execution, the Allies would have more experiences to sift through and would distill even more lessons before the amphibious assault against the Wehrmacht's coastal defenses in Normandy.

5

As Much as Could Be Expected

Salerno, September 1943

As a continuation of the Mediterranean strategy, the Allies' next few amphibious operations targeted locations on the Italian mainland. The decision for the Salerno invasion came during the Trident Conference in May 1943 in hopes of fully removing Italy from the war. Despite turmoil at the highest echelons of the Italian government, the removal of Mussolini, and the fall of the fascist government, the Germans were in no mood to cede control of the Italian territory. Even with the Italians seeking an armistice, there were still plenty of German troops resident on the peninsula to challenge the Allied advance. Shortly after the announcement of Italy's armistice, the Germans executed Operation Achse and disarmed/captured Italian army units occupying strategic military positions throughout the country. Much of the nation was now held hostage by its former Axis ally. The loss of a onetime political and military collaborator had severe implications for the Wehrmacht. It now inherited the requirement to occupy and defend the peninsula with forces it could scarcely afford. In addition to having to occupy Italy, the tide was turning, and by 1943 as Germans were beginning to face the juggernaut of Allied manpower and industrial production while experiencing their own strategic shortfalls.

As a progression from Husky, on 3 September British and Canadian forces from Montgomery's Eighth Army jumped across the strait from Messina to the "toe" of Italy at Reggio Calabria. Code-named "Operation Baytown," the movement initiated the Allied presence on the mainland as they slowly began pushing northward. An accompanying landing code-named "Operation Slapstick" had additional UK forces make an assault along the Italian "heel" at Taranto. Despite the Allied lodgment on the Italian "foot," the resident German forces believed that the next main Allied assault might be aimed directly at Rome via surface assault and airborne operations. Establishing defensive

141

positions along the peninsula, Wehrmacht forces made the most of the mountainous Italian terrain.[1]

The assaults on the Italian mainland came on the heels of the Sicily landings, with very little time for a wholesale assessment of the Husky operation. Acting only a few weeks after the Allies marched into Messina, the Americans landed on the beaches of Salerno in much the same fashion as they had at Gela. Initial assault waves were to be supported by armor while logistics support was to come over the shore. Despite this methodology, there were some obvious lessons garnered from the Joss, Cent, and Dime landings. Conversely, there were still some lessons that had yet to be learned, with little time to implement changes. Regardless of the similarities or differences, this littoral operation was more fraught and closer to failure comparatively.

The Allied landing on the shores of Salerno was the next logical step given the theater geometry. Rather than a bold jump to take advantage of Axis political and military turmoil, the landing initiated the subsequent drive to Rome with a difficult slog up the peninsula.[2] While an assault north of Naples might be the most direct route to Rome and potentially trap German formations in the south, it was beyond the range of Allied air cover. Despite the disconnect between the NWAAF and the rest of the Husky task force, the requirement for air cover was still understood. Looking more to the south and having an appreciation for hydrography, the beaches at the Gulf of Gaeta near Naples had poor beach gradients, continental shelf buildup, and shoals making amphibious operations difficult. The city of Naples was another option for the Allies but was considered too well defended with coastal guns that covered seaborne approaches. Beaches at both these locations were also heavily mined, as German intelligence had identified these shores as probable locations for an Allied landing.[3] Given these concerns, the Gulf of Salerno, approximately fifty miles south of Naples, offered advantages for an amphibious assault.

While the town of Paestum not as close to Rome as the other locations, assessment of the beaches nearby included good surf and weather conditions, a conducive offshore gradient, a nearby road network for movement inland, and a shoreline facilitating the building of logistical support.[4] With promising hydrography, the Gulf of Salerno housed only a few coastal artillery positions. However, beach surveys reported that the dunes, the streams, and a marshy hinterland resident in the AOA posed a problem once troops were ashore. Furthermore, the entire gulf was surrounded by easily defendable mountainous

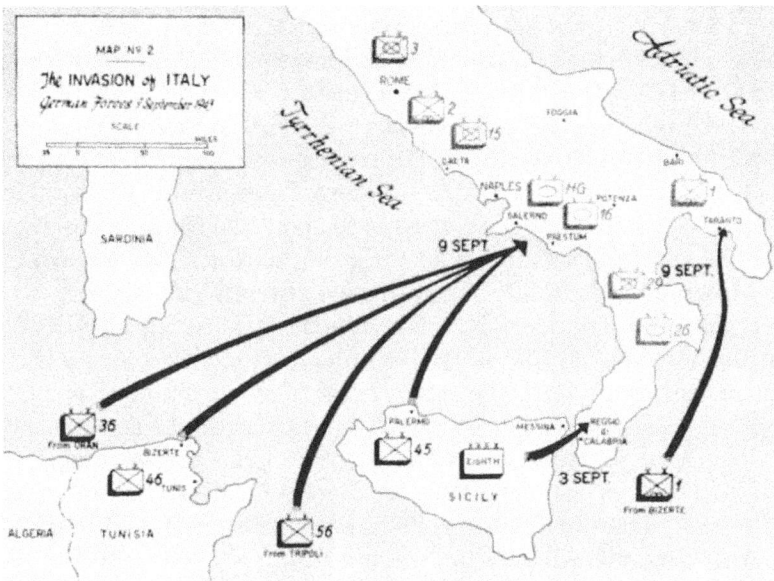

Movement of the major allied units into southern Italy in September 1943. The 36th and 45th Divisions are United States while the 46th, 56th are British formations. Included are British operations with the 8th Army crossing the straits of Messina in Operation BAYTOWN and the 1st AB landing at Taranto in Operation SLAPSTICK. (CARL Digital Archive)

terrain. At the southern end of the gulf was Mount Soprano, which featured a 3,000-foot sheer cliff providing excellent views of the invasion beaches. In addition to Mount Soprano, other summits dominated the beach along with foothills that assisted German defensive efforts. While coastal gun positions were few, Allied forces would eventually find well-equipped and capable German forces at numerous locations in the vicinity of Paestum.[5]

Code-named "Operation Avalache," the assault on Salerno was again a combined effort with US and UK forces landing abreast on a coastal plain. On the northern side of the Gulf, the British X Corps was to land separate from the US VI Corps, with the Allies using the Sele River as the operational boundary. Violating the principle of mass, the split between the two corps at the Sele came about because of runnels and sandbars that precluded possible landings near the river's mouth. While the designated landing sites allowed a ten-mile gap between the Allies and precluded a contiguous effort, the distance was to be closed once forces moved inland and covered by indirect fire assets.[6] Ironically, the sea space offshore the river's mouth served as a naval gunfire support area capable of supporting both corps. Just to the north of the British sector, a single US Ranger element was to seize and hold Nocera–Pagani Pass between Salerno and Naples. Initial British objectives included the Monte Corvino airfield, the rail and road network of Battipaglia, and Route 19. Once ashore, the combined formations would work their way north and drive toward Naples. Additionally, in the southern half of the gulf, the Americans were to contact Montgomery's Eighth Army driving north from Calabria.

To split German defensive power on the peninsula, the Avalanche plan also included an amphibious feint. Littoral operations use the sea as maneuver space, with the mere threat of an amphibious assault almost as powerful in affecting enemy courses of action as an actual landing. The feint included a combined flotilla from the Western Naval Task Force under the command of Captain Charles Andrews aboard USS *Knight*. The small task force's intent was to trick the Wehrmacht into thinking the Allies were landing near the Volturno River approximately forty miles northwest of Naples for an immediate drive to Rome.[7] While the Germans considered the location a possible Allied next step, the Volturo location provided the most direct route to Rome.[8]

The Avalanche deception effort included a US destroyer, two Dutch gunboats, six launches, and other smaller vessels along with a contingent from the 82nd AB into the Gulf of Gaeta. While the feint's objective was to paralyze German decision-making, part of the operation included the capture of Ventotene Island, housing a German radar station. The small assault succeeded in capturing ninety Germans and surrendered Italian troops.[9] Although the Germans had their own internal dysfunction, they remained unsure as to the scale and location of the Allied landings and main effort. With the situation unfolding, the German Tenth Army commander, Colonel General Heinrich von Vietinghoff, delayed the movement of reinforcements to the Salerno area, still fearing a landing closer to Rome.

German units in the vicinity of Naples included the 2nd Fallschirm-jäger (Paratrooper) Division and the 3rd Panzergrenadier Division. In addition to these formations were the two that recently escaped Sicily and made it across the Strait of Messina—the 15th Panzergrenadier and the Göring Divisions. Both units had been reorganized after Husky. Given the concern over a larger amphibious assault landing elsewhere, Vietinghoff had much of 15th Panzergrenadier ordered to assemble along the Volturno River. Similarly, the remnants of the Göring Division, located in the vicinity of the Gulf of Gaeta, also remained uncommitted and in place.[10]

Assigned to the southern part of the gulf was the US VI Corps under the command of Major General Ernest Dawley. The VI's initial assault wave consisted of Major General Fred Walker's US 36th ID, with a reserve that included Middleton's 45th Division, the 34th ID under Ryder, and Ridgway's 82nd AB, along with Major General Ernest Harmon's 1st AD. The 36th was one of the few American divisions that went through the curriculum at the Camp Edwards ATC stateside but had yet to actually see combat. With the 36th as the initial assault element, the 45th would come ashore fresh from its combat operations in Sicily with the 34th, having landed during Torch. Naval support for VI Corps came under Rear Admiral Hall as Task Force 81, while Admiral Hewitt served as the overall naval commander for Task Force 80. Serving as the CATF, Hewitt's CLF counterpart was Lieutenant General Clark in his first combat command as head of Fifth Army.[11]

In support of the operation at Salerno, FAITC also conducted an amphibious exercise code-named "Cowpuncher." Held on 26–27 August the 36th ID made an "assault" at the beaches located between Port aux Poules and Arzew. The location's terrain was similar to that of the Salerno beaches, with the exercise using the same plans for the upcoming invasion whenever practical and substituting local geographical names for the actual ones. The 34th ID served as the defending force for the "invasion." While the 34th participated in Torch, it was fitting that the green 36th conduct a landing in-theater before heading into combat at Salerno.[12] However, large portions of Task Force 81 were absent during the exercise, and this would have unfortunate consequences during the actual assault.[13]

Despite the joint training, and much like the pre-Torch loading and preparation, the army still had not fully understood the art and science of combat loading and embarkation. With the army operating the port at Oran, they exerted authority of loading ships and scheduling. However, preliminary load plans were not coordinated with the amphibious force commander. During Husky it was obvious that with Transportation Quartermaster personnel displayed a complete lack of knowledge of combat loading, resulting in confusion and mistakes. Additionally, late changes in load plans and last-minute revisions were often impractical. As a result, cargo loading for the upcoming Avalanche assault was

Lieutenant General Mark Clark and Admiral Kent Hewitt survey maps during the invasion of Salerno in September 1943. (US Navy photo)

again done poorly, creating problems for accessibility of supplies and equipment at key times during the operation.[14]

With D-Day scheduled for 9 September and H-Hour set for 0330, the invasion forces, consisting of some 600 ships, departed from various locations in sixteen different convoys. Leaving from Oran, Algiers, Bizerte, Palermo, Termini, and Tripoli on 5–6 September, the force was divided into multiple convoys and then converged in the Gulf of Salerno. Given the theater's geometry, the flotilla did not require inclusion of ammunition, tankers, and other cargo vessels, as ports in Sicily and North Africa provided stockpiled supplies within easy transit.[15] Air cover supporting the convoys along the route included the NWAAF and five smaller Royal Navy escort carriers (*Unicorn*, *Battler*, *Attacker*, *Hunter*, and *Stalker*) that were then replaced by the fleet carriers HMS *Illustrious* and HMS *Formidable*.[16] Despite the short distances from ports of embarkation to the objective area, the invasion fleet was easily discovered by the Luftwaffe. Initial Allied intelligence assessments correctly reported that Luftwaffe strikes against Allied shipping would occur if the flotilla was discovered. Even before the invasion force sortied, German planes attacked ships anchored in Bizerte.[17] Similar attacks occurred while en route to Sicily and again when passing near the coast of Capri. Regardless of the Luftwaffe efforts, the Allied vessels made it to the objective area with only one LST being hit with a dud bomb.[18]

Like the American commanders from previous assaults, Walker refused to use pre–H-Hour/D-Day fires to support the landings and soften up enemy defenses. The operation plan specifically forbade any supporting fires until H-15 unless directed by assault commanders. Admirals Hewitt and Hall argued against Walker's decision, as naval planners developed a list of 275 targets worthy of servicing ashore.[19] In studying reconnaissance photos the 36th ID commander saw no hardened positions and believed that any prepared defenses would be quickly overrun with the planned armor wave. In a form of institutional arrogance, Walker thought the navy did not fully understand subsequent ground operations, as naval planners targeted bridges, crossroads, fords, and towns. Walker believed that these features might prove useful once the division made its way inland. After the landings he expressed concern regarding rounds falling short and hitting the landing force.[20] Perhaps it was Walker's lack of recent combat experience or unfamiliarity with NSFS that led him to such a decision. Regardless, Clark respected Walker's decision as the 36th ID would be the initial assault wave going ashore with the corps commander acceding to Walker's prerogative. It was a regrettable decision. Unmolested by preliminary bombardment, German defensive positions remained intact and readily engaged when the initial assault waves came ashore.

Much like Husky, the Allied air forces shaped the battle by attacking enemy airfields, supply routes, logistics nodes, and railroads around central Italy and adjacent areas.[21] While the defensive positions remained unmolested by NSFS, Allied airpower succeeded in significantly reducing the Wehrmacht's logistics. While USAAF BAI made noteworthy contributions in the pre–D-Day battlefield shaping, there was still plenty of German combat power resident ashore. Similarly, the Luftwaffe would again establish a presence over the assault force and landing beaches, causing havoc and delays.[22] Intelligence estimates concluded that Junkers Ju 87s, Ju 88s, and Heinkel He 111s would be present on D-Day to harass both the fleet and the landing forces.

However, in a significant departure from Husky, tactical air cover from both British carriers thirty miles off the coast and the land-based NWAAF made a presence over the beaches on D-Day. Allied aircraft were visibly present over the assembled fleet and remained in support.[23] While Salerno was also chosen because it fit under the range fan of NWAAF fighter cover, P-38s and A-36s were still at their limit of endurance, even with the installation of drop tanks. As a result, their endurance in the AOA remained limited.[24] Flying from Sicilian airfields almost 150 miles away, the use of external tanks increased loiter times from thirty minutes to one hour.[25] Despite this restriction, the combined air cover planned to span daylight hours from 0900 to 1950, with four to forty aircraft over the landing force. Patrolling altitudes between 6,000 and 20,000 feet, during the first nine days of the operation the NWAAF flew over 9,000 sorties.[26]

Adding to the joint nature of air/surface cooperation, Hewitt's flagship, the USS *Ancon*, embarked the commander of XII Air Support Command, Major General Edwin J. House, a staff of thirteen officers and forty-two enlisted men, and manned the Air Support Control Center (ASCC). Tried initially during the Husky landings, the shipboard ASCC served as the FCU during the assault phase, but this time the organization's berthing spaces were much improved. This arrangement also included the addition of offensive air support in addition to defensive functions. Assisting were two fighter-control ships provided by the Royal Navy, equipped with radar that passed information to the air cell aboard *Ancon*. However, for defensive operations the British vessels lacked height-finding radar and required augmentation for their two GCI LSTs. Additionally, the defensive FCUs did not have their own designated VHF radio network, and communications within this network reduced the ability to effectively pass along information for effective intercept.[27]

More significant was the coordination of offensive air from a sea-based platform. With a more robust suite and communications capability aboard *Ancon*, the ASCC coordinated support for troops in need of air support. The ground formations notified their divisional headquarters, which then passed the request to the ASCC aboard ship. Once received, it could then task inbound or patrolling aircraft within the AOA. The ASCC was a precursor to the modern Joint Air Operations Center and included radar, radio, and command-and-control equipment.[28] On-call air support was normally serviced within five minutes, and such responsiveness would be a key component countering future German counterattacks.[29] While marginally effective in the previous operation, a more capable and robust air cell afloat improved air/surface coordination. Along these same lines, to help assist USAAF pilots, navy representatives went to XII ASC locations to help school army aviators on spotting procedures and how to assist in calls for NSFS.[30] In fact, subsequent naval gunfire spotting using P-51 Mustangs was reported as "exceptionally successful."[31]

In addition to these advances, air and ground commanders began having daily meetings to determine targets and missions for the next day. Furthermore, the operations saw an increase in the use of air support teams with jeep-mounted radios.[32] Perhaps the biggest concession from the air component was the consideration of basing aircraft within the AOA. Planners hoped to use an existing airfield near Paestum, but it was under enemy artillery fire and was of limited value during the operation's initial phases. While the airfield could not be used given the tactical situation, consideration of such an effort alone was a significant advancement in joint interoperability. When the United Kingdom captured the airfield at Monte Corvino, an American squadron of Spitfires flew ashore on 20 September.[33]

While such air cover was appreciated by the landing force, deliberate CAS during the amphibious assault remained unplanned.[34] While incidents of A-36s dropping ordnance on German armor did occur, true deliberate combined arms integration of NSFS, air, and ground combat power in an amphibious assault was still beyond the army's capability. Deconfliction of airspace by time or altitude was still too complex in an already complicated operation. Regardless, when ASPs went ashore at Paestum, they helped establish links between air and ground forces once forces moved inland. Forward air controllers (FACs) overhead were employed to assist in CAS missions. Up until Avalanche, only the RAF had employed such a technique, but with the recent experience of Husky and the North Africa campaign, the Americans adopted the practice. Called "Rover Joe" by US troops, the FAC team consisted of an experienced pilot and an army ground officer flying above the front lines in an observation plane. Ground troops requiring assistance radioed the Rover Joe, which then passed the request to the shipboard control units. Once a request was approved, the Rover would guide the inbound aircraft in locating the target.[35] This was an important advancement in combined arms coordination.

On the eve of the assault, 8 September, the news of the Italian armistice was announced, with the Germans initiating Operation Achse. While the armistice was not a complete surprise to the Germans, Field Marshal Albert Kesselring, commander in chief of German forces in the south, was disgusted with Italian "treachery" and believed that the

Wehrmacht could still defend the peninsula even after the surrender of Italian forces.[36] With German troops starting to occupy former Italian army positions, the announcement made no immediate difference to the actions at Salerno.[37] Avalanche was already well underway—only hours from launching the landing craft—when the news broke. Welcomed by many men aboard ships in the Allied convoy, the news provided a false hope that the amphibious assault might occur in a benign environment with little or no combat.[38] They were wrong.

In the immediate Salerno area the 16th Panzer Division was alerted to the change in the Italian disposition. The 16th was relatively new to the theater, having been reconstituted after serving earlier near Stalingrad on the Eastern Front. While not at its full authorization in men and equipment, the unit was still sizable:17,000 men, 100 tanks, three dozen assault guns, and three artillery battalions. As an organization the unit fought the Red Army in the harshest of environments, but many troops in the freshly reconstituted command were without combat experience.[39] New to the Salerno area, the division arrived ten days earlier from Bari on the southeastern coast. Equipped with ample armor and heavy gun assets, the division was still spread thin, with a large frontage of twenty miles. This broad defensive coverage became even more problematic, as Achse required the unit to assume previously held Italian coastal defensive positions.[40]

Much like 16th Panzergrenadier, the Luftwaffe, while still formidable, was not the force it once was. The number of planes available in the geographic area for combat operations against the Allies dwindled in August from 1,100 airframes to less than 600. Approximately 1,000 aircraft had been left or abandoned on Sicily, with more and more called back to Germany to defend the homeland. By this stage of the war the Luftwaffe was described as fighting a "poor man's war." With logistical and manpower shortfalls, the Luftwaffe in the Mediterranean could support only fifty to a hundred sorties a day.[41] At this point of the war the best it could do was save its strength and conserve what combat power it still had. Despite this disposition, the Luftwaffe would make its presence felt in new ways.

For the defenders, the plan was to keep the invaders in the coastal plain and prevent them from achieving a foothold in the surrounding hills. However, with equipment and personnel deficiencies, the German defense was not as well-coordinated or well-planned as it might have been. With sea mines presenting planning and execution problems for the American landing craft and NSFS platforms, landmines ashore were few, barbed wire and other obstacles were scattered, and armored assets were piecemealed throughout the defense. Additionally, the 16th made no effort to establish central control or coordination, and the fragmented defense curtailed combat power. Had the Germans massed armored forces during the initial American assault or further developed a synergy of obstacles with direct and indirect fire, the landings might have failed.

In addition to organizational and planning challenges, trees, walls, ditches, and man-made and natural obstacles reduced the mobility of German armor. Furthermore, to avoid NSFS, many tanks were positioned in hull defilade, further reducing their effectiveness. Although the defenders occupied the advantageous high ground, any counterattack would be made downhill and in full observation of Allied guns. Limiting German options, not just in Salerno but along the entirety of the Italian peninsula, was a lack of gasoline. While the Germans were pioneers in mechanized mobile warfare, this logistics shortfall had serious implications for potential Axis courses of action during the later phases of Avalanche and in subsequent operations.[42]

Execution of the initial assault was like those that preceded it. Thirty-six LSTs, each with six davits carrying LCVPs along with LCIs, launched much of the assault force as other LSTs brought critical supplies and equipment to shore. Shortly after midnight transport ships lowered the landing craft from the davits, and it took some three hours for troops to climb down cargo nets onto landing craft and then arrive in the rendezvous area.[43] But this time the H-Hour was met. Some coxswains again had a difficult time finding guide boats directing them into their correct lanes, but most of the assault waves made it to the correct beaches. During the movement ashore troops were again drenched in water, inhaled exhaust fumes, and, given the motion of the landing craft, became seasick. As recommended from the FAITC, the soldiers' individual load was minimized to allow better mobility. Troops went ashore with only a mess and toilet kit, one day of rations, and two bandoleers of ammunition for riflemen.[44]

A significant obstacle during Avalanche was a sizeable naval minefield laid along the invasion beaches. To clear the field at 2200 on D-1 twenty-two navy minesweepers of Task Group 81.8 attempted to sweep the established approach lanes of German sea mines.[45] However, the minefield was too large for the number of boats assigned. The remaining sea mines would cause a serious disruption of ship-to-shore movement. More important, it kept many naval surface fire platforms ten miles off shore and out of radio and gunfire range during the assault. The mines also deterred the larger LSTs carrying armor and heavy equipment from beaching.[46] This simple low-tech defense was effective and remains perhaps the biggest problem for future amphibious operations.

The landing craft made their way to four designated beaches whose frontages covered some two miles. The northernmost beach, Red, was 800 yards long and was adjacent to Green at a mere 500 yards. The two southern beaches, Yellow and Blue, were approximately 1,000 yards and 1,500 yards, respectively. Red and Green Beaches were assigned to the 142nd RCT, while Yellow and Blue to the 141st, with both regiments organized into six separate assault waves. Following the 142nd RCT two hours later at Red and Green, the 143rd RCT was scheduled to land in support. Objectives for the two RCTs included high ground off the beaches from Ponte Sele, Altavilla, and Rocco de Aspide, to Magliano. On the two southern beaches the 141st's objectives included contacting the 142nd to the north at Mount Vesole and then occupying high ground to the southern end of the landing at Agropoli.[47]

Scout boats were sent to each designated beach and positioned a few hundred feet from shore. Once in position they signaled to the incoming landing craft by blinking their beach's respective color every five seconds to guide the inbound coxswains.[48] Even before the first landing craft made it to shore, scout crews could hear armor and mechanized vehicles moving into defensive positions ashore.[49] The scout boats were followed by minesweepers that cleared the approach lanes for the landing force. Once the sweepers passed, the landing craft traversed seven to ten miles over calm seas. The landing craft were equipped with compasses that were calibrated in ten-degree increments, but given the distance required to arrive at the beach, even a small navigation error could prove catastrophic.[50] Favoring the execution sequence, the weather on 9 August had a light breeze with relatively still waters.[51] So far all seemed to go as planned as the first assault waves landed with minutes of each other and at the designated times with follow-on schedules met.[52]

Initial assault waves consisted of twenty-four LCVPs per RLT element along with an engineering unit to help remove beach obstacles. Seven minutes later a second wave was to land, followed eight minutes later by a third wave with heavy weapons, medical support, and naval beach parties. Larger weapons such as 40mm, 75mm, and .50-caliber guns along with beach-clearing bulldozers were to arrive at H+50. An hour after the initial landings, the reserve battalions were scheduled to

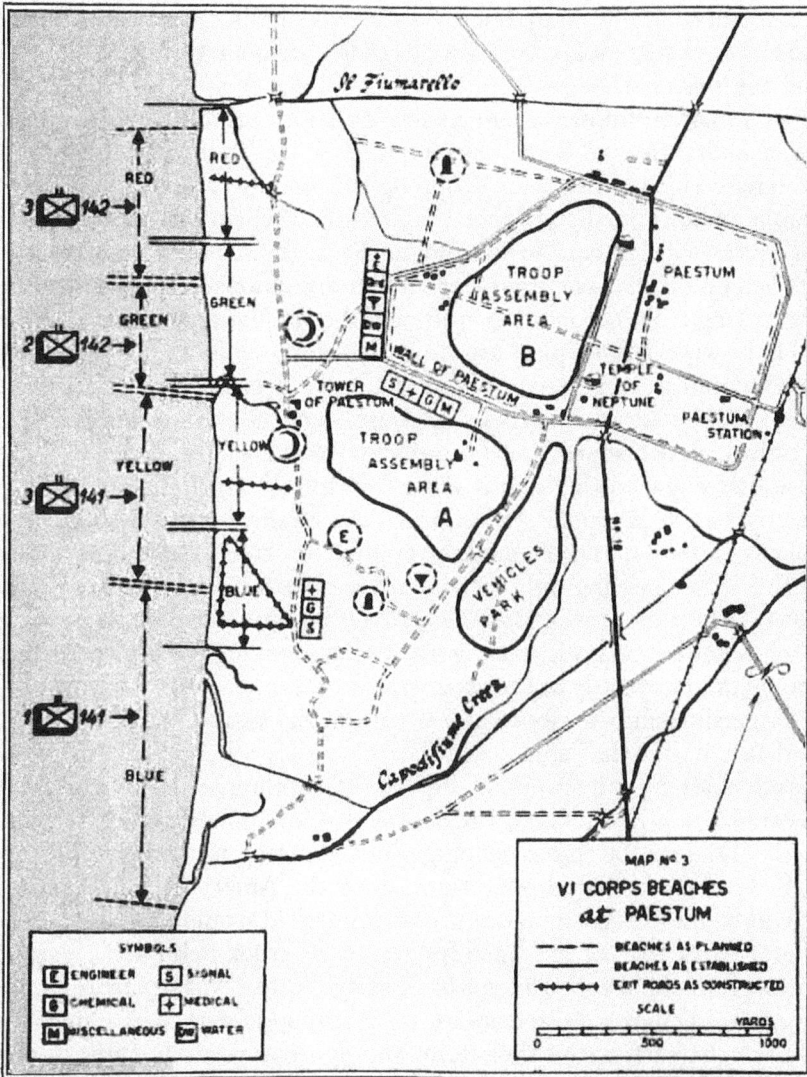

Landing beach plan for 9 September as elements of the 36th Infantry Division came ashore on four colored beaches. Yellow and Blue would prove to be the most difficult and heavily defended. Note the depiction of various classes of supply and their planned location ashore. (CARL Digital Archive)

come ashore, followed by DUKWs carrying artillery and ammunition. The reserve battalion waves were to follow in much the same sequence and composition.[53]

In a marked improvement in ship-to-shore movement from previous assaults, the 3rd Battalion, 142nd RCT landed as scheduled on its designated beach. But after dropping the loading ramp on Red Beach, troops were immediately met by awaiting Wehrmacht troops shooting flares with tracers to illuminate the darkness. German defenders opened up on the assault wave with 88mm cannons and machine guns. Debarking from the landing craft, and despite lighter individual loads, soldiers were left to plod ashore in the surf while enduring withering incoming fire.[54] Given Walker's early decision to preclude any pre–D-Day fires, the German positions were fully intact and ready for action. Unlike the previous Husky and Torch assaults, enemy defenses furiously engaged the assault waves.[55] While Vichy and Italian coastal defenses created some issues in previous assaults, German defenders at Salerno anticipated the American approaches and prepared clear fields of fire. After moving only a few yards ashore the soldiers were pinned down. The only cover available on the beaches were small drainage ditches and a few rock walls, with soldiers seeking concealment from the incoming rounds in the scrub.[56]

Regarding ship-to-shore movement, initial assault waves made it to Red Beach, but the same could not be said for all the landings. Many assault craft turned around in the face of the intense fire, while others became stuck in the surf, caught on fire, hit mines, or drifted aimlessly. Despite the minesweeping effort, existing parts of the obstacle field severely hindered operations along the American beachfront. It would be midmorning before the sea minefield would be fully cleared. Elements of the second wave for Red were stuck behind the parts of the sea minefield that had yet to be fully cleared.[57] Many men jumped from stricken vessels and swam to shore, and important equipment sank in the surf, with other items simply floating away. Important to building combat power ashore, many mortars and their accompanying rounds failed to land, leaving the initial wave with the barest of weapons.[58] With landing craft striking sea mines, a navy patrol boat closed approach lanes for the subsequent assault waves at Red Beach. Individual coxswains took the initiative and ignored the patrol boats' instructions. Some of them steered past the patrol boats and traversed the sea minefield and headed inland.[59] As more men and material arrived on the beaches, the shore became crowed with boats, troops, and equipment all in a disorganized manner. Beachmaster support was nonexistent, with crews unloading their vessels without help or any real organization.[60] However, with all the confusion and chaos, Red Beach had it easy.

As the sun rose, Allied aircraft arrived overhead in the form of British Seafires, along with American A-36s and P-38s.[61] Unlike at Gela or Scoglitti, American troops could now claim they indeed saw friendly airpower over the invasion beaches on D-Day. While enemy aircraft did attack troops ashore during the landings, causing delays and disruptions, the arrival of Allied fighters was indeed a welcome addition.[62] Based on their respective performance capacities, the fighters were given designated altitudes to patrol. With friendly planes patrolling a fifteen- to twenty-mile patch of airspace, they gave warnings to surface vessels of any inbound enemy aircraft. Despite the Allied air cover, the Luftwaffe was still a credible threat. Hewitt's flagship, USS *Ancon*, which also carried Fifth Army's commander, General Clark, was attacked by enemy aircraft thirty times in a thirty-six-hour period in which near misses occurred almost two dozen times.[63]

German air attacks disrupted beach operations and inflicted damage to ships in the fleet. Such raids employed a new weapon that made a significant impression. Launching "Fritz X" radio-controlled glide bombs at 20,000 feet from specially equipped Dornier Do 217 bombers, German aircraft damaged three US and two UK ships.[64] One of the American ships hit was USS *Savannah*, which previously had provided effective fires on the Kasba during the Torch WTF. Once the Fritz X was released, a remote-control joystick in the Do-217 mothership allowed the bomb to be steered to its target with precision. While such weapons had been seen previously, this was the first time they were used prolifically against naval forces.[65] Such groundbreaking technology helped lay the foundation for future precision-guided munitions.

In the center of the American beaches was a medieval tower named Torre di Paestum serving as a German observation post and defensive position. Wehrmacht snipers in the tower disrupted movement inland while also spotting for German artillery fire. Adding to the defensive fires on Green Beach, elements of the 16th Panzer concealed themselves in a grove of saplings, fired at will, and pinned down troops. Such enemy fire reduced American unit cohesion. With ground forces outgunned, antiaircraft weapons aboard one LST near Yellow Beach helped by providing heavy-caliber support driving off enemy armor individually. Despite the chaos, men still moved forward, with engineers clearing beaches of mines and other obstacles while preparing for the reception of follow-on units and equipment.[66]

Engineers were loaded into six LCVPs per beach, and despite having lost much of their equipment in the ship-to-shore movement or during debarkation, they did their best to clear the beach under intense enemy fire.[67] Ninety minutes after H-Hour the first twenty DUKWs came ashore at Red Beach, with much-needed artillery and antitank pieces. Given the unfolding situation, the 125 DUKWs assigned to land at the other colored beaches remained at sea, circling while German fire precluded their beaching, until finally directed to land at Red Beach.[68] The amphibious trucks would again prove their utility and were in constant demand during the assault. However, as at Husky, local commanders often commandeered the trucks and disrupted offload operations.[69] Shortly after 0640 the 143rd RCT began landing on the same patch of sand at Red Beach and also received incoming fire.[70] As dawn broke, German armor engaged the landing forces, with US infantry fighting them off with what was available including bazookas, grenades, and machine guns. Fortunately, and surprisingly, the bazooka turned out to be a fairly effective defensive weapon.[71] American armor and heavy artillery were supposed to land before daybreak, but much of that was still afloat on landing craft in approach lanes.[72] Eventually soldiers moved forward in small sections, making it into the town of Paestum and the nearby railroad line as snipers in the town made movement even harder.

The first tank platoon did not make it ashore to Red Beach until 0830, followed by three more from 1000 to 1330.[73] Additional armor- and tank-destroying units arrived in the afternoon and engaged enemy vehicles approaching from the north.[74] Eventually navy destroyers were able to breach the sea minefield and sailed within radio and gunfire range. Providing much-needed fire support until the tanks arrived, naval spotters from the 4th Naval Beach Battalion (NBB) assisted in repelling German armor.[75] By midmorning the light cruisers USS *Philadelphia* and USS *Savannah*, along with four destroyers and a Royal Navy surface combatant, navigated the water hazards and provided much-needed firepower ashore. When USS *Savannah* finally established communications with shore-fire parties, it alone answered eleven calls for fire support, expending 645 rounds of 6-inch ammunition. Included in its supportive fires was a 23,000-yard salvo against a German railroad gun.[76] USS *Philadelphia* also contacted naval shore parties and engaged enemy armor, flushing out thirty-five tanks, hitting seven and causing the remainder to retreat.[77] At 1020 over a dozen German Mark IV tanks approached 142nd Command Post from the north. In a rare case of full combined arms coordination, a DUKW towing a 105mm howitzer arrived just in time to engage the tank; an A-36 attack aircraft also joined in the defense. Additionally, a destroyer that navigated the minefield also provided additional support. Engaging the armored column, the combined effort of air, land, and sea assets destroyed five tanks, causing the remaining ones to retreat.[78]

With all the confusion, chaos, and destruction, the 142nd and 143rd RCT landings at Red Beach were successful in attaining their D-Day objectives and pushed over a mile inland. Given the ferocity of the defense at the other colored beaches, Red Beach began receiving the bulk of ship-to-shore deliveries. As in previous landings, the shore became inundated with equipment, supplies, and men. Landing craft had a hard time finding space to drop ramps, with previously delivered stockpiles awash in the surf. Army shore parties again failed to establish order, with few troops available to provide the labor required. Navy crews and coxswains were left to clean up the mess despite Admiral Hall's request to General Clark that the army provide 1,000 additional men for the task.[79] By late afternoon, Hewitt recalled, most beaches were closed due to congestion and enemy fires, any movement of equipment being brought to a virtual standstill. An Engineer Special Brigade did not arrive at Red Beach until 1630, and only then did the unit begin to assist in clearing the beach and organizing supply dumps.[80]

Located just to the south of Red Beach and north of the Paestum tower, the 2nd Battalion of the 142nd constituted the first wave on Green Beach. Much like the other assault waves, troops coming off the landing craft were met with withering defensive fires from 88mm cannons and machine guns. The Paestum tower easily provided fields of fire and observation as it bisected the adjacent Green and Yellow Beaches. The forward observers in the tower effectively adjusted German mortar and artillery fire on the beach.[81] However, supporting the initial landing at Green Beach was a specialized landing craft support (LCS) rocket boat. Moving within 80 yards of the shore on the beaches' left flank, it fired a series of rockets that ranged up to 750 yards, helping to neutralize machine-gun nests that had pinned down the first assault wave. The rocket salvo created a lull in enemy fire, which allowed the first wave to make progress inland. A captured and dazed German machine-gunner later testified to the demoralizing effect of the salvo. Again, this support was key, as no preparatory fires had been allowed to shape the battlefield before the introduction of troops.[82]

The follow-on assault waves were still slowed by the existing minefield causing landing delays and mixed up sequencing.[83] *LST-386* attempted to land on Green Beach, only to hit a mine, causing forty-three casualties. By 0500 a series of DUKWs arrived offshore but were waved off by control vessels, as enemy fire was still too intense.[84] At 0545 all LSTs were ordered to wave off landing at Green Beach and to await NSFS.[85] But twenty-five minutes later thirty DUKWs made it ashore, bringing in much-needed 105mm howitzers along with ammunition. Unloaded behind the dunes, the amphibious trucks returned to sea. On D-Day alone over 120 DUKWs landed on the four designated beaches between 0530 and 0730.[86] The DUKWs delivered much-needed firepower in the initial landings when armor remained afloat and before the NSFS came into range.[87]

Ashore, elements of the 2nd Battalion, 142nd RCT were slowed by enemy fire, barbed wire, and mines but eventually pushed inland and contacted companion units at Red Beach to the north.[88] By 0640 elements of the 143rd came ashore on Green and proceeded inland.[89] As the morning passed, infantry and armor streamed inland and combat engineers went about preparing the beach for follow-on operations. The plan was for one company of engineers to work with each battalion combat team in its designated sector. With troops searching for landmines, bulldozers began clearing lanes, preparing supply areas, and developing beach exits while under constant enemy fire. The engineers' larger equipment was an especially attractive German target, with one bulldozer hit by German 88mm fire, destroying the vehicle and killing the crewmen. Even if engineers completed their assigned tasks, the situation was so tenuous that teams were at times forced to retire when enemy fire became too intense.[90]

The two southern beaches, Yellow and Blue, proved the most problematic as German strongpoints supported by over a dozen Mark IV tanks stopped the initial assault waves and precluded building up combat power.[91] So confident were the Wehrmacht defenders that it was reported they announced by loudspeaker in English to the landing troops: "Come on in and give yourselves up. We have you covered!"[92] Met with fierce enemy artillery and armor upon landing, elements of the 141st RCT on the southern beaches would be pinned down for hours, the German fire preventing LCTs from delivering much-needed armor ashore.[93] In addition, men in the initial assault waves—ignoring FAITC doctrine and the lessons learned from previous assaults—were often separated from their heavier equipment and weapons and struggled to find it if they made it ashore. Incoming supplies were dumped wherever the coxswains might safely find land, often without beachmaster support.[94] This only added to the confusion.

Given the enemy armor at the southern beaches, the 141st assault

US soldiers pinned down by enemy fire at Salerno with an explosion in the distance. Engineers did much of their work at Salerno under enemy fire. (US Navy photo)

was stopped cold. While the RCT's command post was established ashore, the beaches were still under constant enemy fire. Well-placed German artillery hit within fifty yards of Blue Beach and sealed off the shore operation from receiving follow-on shipping. Troops landing on Blue Beach advanced, but only as far as 500 yards, and were quickly stalled. While the first two assault waves made it ashore, the third had to land elsewhere due to German fire. Of three self-propelled 75mm howitzers planned for Blue Beach that morning, only one made it ashore, with one destroyed by a mine and the other remaining aboard a landing craft that turned away from the action. The single howitzer ashore was put into action and scored hits but was soon damaged.[95]

While armor was scheduled to land as early as 0630 at Blue Beach, the LST carrying it struck a mine and withdrew.[96] Four of six LCTs carrying tanks were hit by German 88mm cannons, but *LST-389* rigged a pontoon bridge to get the much-needed armor ashore.[97] Although subsequent assault waves landed elsewhere, the few soldiers from the first two assault waves made their way to the Solofrone River; others remained pinned down.[98] Fortunately, by noon USS *Ludlow* engaged targets at Blue Beach.[99] Despite the introduction of tanks, the beach remained closed until 1600.[100] The RCT Command Post was bracketed by German cannon fire until the arrival of NSFS destroyed the enemy battery.[101] With the 142nd and 143rd making good progress inland, during the day the 141st barely made it past Highway 18, a movement of only a few hundred yards. Troops on Blue did not establish contact with their adjacent units until 1825, the beach eventually being abandoned on D+1.[102]

On Yellow Beach, the 3rd Battalion was pinned down by enemy fire after moving only 400 yards inland. Troops clawed their way forward under machine-gun and mortar fire. By daybreak they had moved 300 yards from the shoreline. Like before, initial attempts to call for NSFS went unanswered, as ships were safely beyond German sea-based mines, and out of radio transmission range.[103] When communications were finally established, NSFS hit tanks and German artillery ashore.[104] A boat carrying out wounded at the beach was hit by mortar fire and sunk before it was fully loaded. Other landing craft attempting casualty evacuation were turned back.[105] Fortunately all the beaches staved off any sort of rout, as light artillery and antitank guns delivered by DUKWs after sunrise helped build combat power. By the end of D-Day troops advanced two miles inland, with the beaches finally opened for follow-on assault waves.[106]

Given the disruption of the landing waves, the resistance at Yellow and Blue Beaches, and German defensive fires, the landing force's equipment piled up on the two northern beaches, Red and Green.[107] Once again beachmaster support had broken down in the heat of battle. In the afternoon Brigadier General John O'Daniel, former head of the FAITC, took charge of beach organization and began establishing order. Red Beach especially was awash in boxes, material, and equipment. As with Husky, some landing craft could not find the space to lower ramps, with beachmaster troops few and disorganized, leaving boat crews to do the unloading. The situation got so bad at one location that, once one of the few beachmasters came ashore, he refused any LCVPs landings without working parties. By late morning Admiral Hall contacted General Clark to help clear the beaches.[108] Not until 21 September did navy beachmasters attempt to reconcile the ships' manifests of high-priority equipment required ashore.[109]

Although the organization of the beach remained a problem, the loss of landing craft was significantly less than previous assaults. While the distances covered from ship to shore were longer, the surf condition was conducive to surface movement. Despite the incoming enemy fire and the sea minefield that had only been partially cleared, only eleven landing craft were abandoned, a far cry from the initial landings at Torch and partly during Husky.[110] Progress had been made with the in-theater training in North Africa, clearly influencing the proficiency of coxswains and naval personnel, Hewitt reporting that "these crews are deserving of the greatest praise and credit."[111] The navy, too, was learning.

By the end of the first day the green 36th ID had done well considering the ferocity of the defense. In all, the division incurred only 500 casualties, with 20 percent fatalities, but attained all of its objectives except for Blue Beach.[112] The Allies controlled the plains south of the Sele River and pushed inland up to five miles. Yellow Beach remained tenuous, but more men and supplies were coming ashore on the northern approaches. NSFS was again a key element in establishing the lodgment and fired 11,000 shells to support the landing force. Although beachmaster and engineer support again was poor and slow to develop, by dusk beach exits were being prepared, supply dumps organized, and communications networks established, with General Walker requesting the commitment of the reserve ashore.[113] Despite nuisance raids by the Luftwaffe, the NWAAF provided enough air cover over the landing beaches. A repeat of the Husky experience was avoided despite the introduction of the new German radio-guided bombs. Given the events of D-Day, General Clark was pleased with the overall results and reported: "[I] felt that we had achieved as much as could be expected."[114] However, what the Fifth Army commander did not know at the time was that the Germans still had plenty of fight left in them.

While US VI Corps made a successful landing and was expanding the beachhead, the established Allied toehold did not necessarily mean that the amphibious operation was over. By 11 September the German defenders realized the Allied scheme of maneuver and began committing its reserves to the Salerno area. The 26th and 29th Panzer Divisions came from the south in advance of the British Eighth Army as it moved north up the peninsula, while the Göring and 15th Panzergrenadier Divisions moved south, taking positions near the Gulf of Gaeta. Eventually six German divisions entered the Salerno defense, with their formation counterattacking at several locations.[115]

The two Allied corps remained separated by the ten-mile gap along the Sele River. Supposedly covered by indirect fire assets, this area remained an Achille's heel for the Allied command. Recognizing the danger, Clark shifted the American boundary past the Sele River and had an RCT from Middleton's 45th ID fill the battlespace.[116] Unknown to the American commander, Wehrmacht soldiers struck at the existing gap just as Clark committed the RCT to the area. If the Germans could exploit the area along the Sele, they might easily advance to the sea, drive a wedge between the Allied forces, and destroy either the US or the UK beachheads. Four German divisions pushed into the gap and exposing Allied flanks. The Allied situation became tenuous. Middleton recalled years later: "The Germans could have broken through us and gone right down to the beach. Why they didn't, I'll never know."[117] Despite Middleton's recollection, the German 16th and 29th Panzers made significant gains along the Sele River, coming within three miles of the landing beaches. By 13 September the American inland frontage was pushed back approximately four miles.[118]

The situation was getting desperate as support troops at the shoreline were sent inland to assist in a defense. On the afternoon of 13 September, a lone A-36 pilot landed at the Licata airfield on Sicily directly from the Salerno front. Upon landing he hand-delivered a personal letter from Clark to the 82nd AB commander, Major General Mathew Ridgeway. Given the German counterattack, the letter requested a RCT drop immediately south of the Sele River to help fill the gap, with an addition call for a battalion to jump on the town of Avellino the following day.[119] Acceding to the request, C-47s and C-53 Skytroopers carrying the 504th Parachute Combat Team avoided flying over the Allied fleet and made their way along the Italian coastline, averting a repeat of the friendly-fire catastrophe at Gela on 11 July.[120] To preclude such a reoccurrence, Clark also gave specific direction that all AAA firing after 2100 was prohibited and all barrage balloons were to be taken down, with officers sent to the firing batteries to ensure the word was passed.[121] Dropping troopers over the Sele River, insertions occurred with no aircraft losses with troopers landing in the designated drop zone. The Avellino drops occurred the next night, followed by another combat team jumping into the Sele River area. Following insertions were also successful but not as efficient or precise.[122]

Regarding AAA control during Avalanche, the ASCC aboard *Ancon* also managed AAA units, both shore- and sea-based. In this effort AAA gunners were ordered not to engage anything above 3000 feet unless cleared by *Ancon*'s control center. Furthermore, both army and navy AAA officers were represented in the center on a constant basis with radio communication networks. Additionally, flight crews were briefed that AAA gunners would shoot any aircraft under 5000 feet. As a result, there was a 2000-foot buffer between the AAA crews and

Allied aircraft.[123] If unidentified aircraft were intercepted by Allied fighters, ASCC controllers warned the appropriate AAA battery to hold fire and vice versa if no aerial intercept was available. As a result, only four friendly-fire incidents occurred, two of them P-51s flying low over the beach after a German fighter had been in the area.[124]

For the next few days, the two sides hammered away, the situation in doubt. NWAAF heavy and medium bombers were diverted to strike targets behind enemy lines at important road junctions, towns, and railroads. Tactical air also played a significant role starting on 13 September and began bombing and strafing targets of opportunity. A-36s and P-38s hit troop concentrations, vehicles, roads, and bridges around the towns of Battipaglia, Eboli, and Avellino. During 12–15 September strategic and tactical aircraft dropped more than 3,000 tons of bombs, with an average bomb density of 760 tons per square mile.[125] Additionally NSFS added powerful 15-inch guns from over a dozen battleships, with smaller-caliber fire provided by cruisers and large destroyers. USS *Philadelphia* alone fired approximately 1,000 rounds until relieved by USS *Boise* expending 600 rounds fired at eighteen different targets.[126] Allied NSFS was key in thwarting the German counterattack, General Vietinghoff noting: "With astonishing precision and freedom of maneuver, these ships shot at every recognized target with very overwhelming effect."[127] The use of combined arms in all three domains succeeded. The Allies held, and by 15 September the German counterattack failed.[128]

When the issue was still in doubt, Clark considered an amphibious withdrawal.[129] As German forces counter-attacked, the Fifth Army commander prepared for the removal of the corps in a kind of mini-Dunkirk. While the army leader recoiled at the suggestion, Hewitt was dismayed at the request, and with his staff immediately informing army counterparts that such a task was no easy feat. Clark's staff did not realize that it was not as difficult to land a loaded assault craft into the sand and then withdraw it from the beach when it was significantly lighter and devoid of men and equipment. This task was much more difficult in the reverse—and even harder under possible enemy fire.[130] Neither the US Navy nor Army had any practice with large-scale amphibious withdrawal. Removing up to 150,000 men and material was an entirely different challenge, and neither service was prepared to conduct.[131]

Hewitt informed Admiral G. N. Oliver, Hall's UK counterpart in the Northern Task Force, about a potential withdrawal. Oliver was dismayed and suggested it would be suicide, as shortened Allied gains

German counterattacks from 11–15 September were a serious threat to the Avalanche beaches causing General Mark Clark to consider an amphibious withdrawal from the objective area. (CARL Digital Archive)

might allow enemy artillery to range the established beachheads as troops pulled back. Hewitt noted a "thorough [British] dissatisfaction with our withdrawal idea."[132] In an example of understanding the "supported–supporting" relationship between the CATF and the CLF, and despite his dismay and apprehension regarding the potential tasking, Hewitt took preliminary actions by stopping the unloading and planned for the possible movement of ships beyond enemy artillery range.[133] When 15th Army Group commander Sir Harold Alexander heard of the potential withdrawal, he curtly replied "there will be no evacuation." Fortunately, the Allied forces held, another Dunkirk-like operation was avoided, and they denied the Germans a much-needed victory. Unimpressed with Dawley's handing of the crisis, Clark took over tactically and personally and moved units to solidify the beachhead and thwart the German counteroffensive.[134]

The Allied assault of Salerno succeeded despite the immediate German response at the beach and the subsequent counterattacks. While the victory was indeed in jeopardy and the situation precarious enough to warrant consideration of an amphibious withdrawal, the joint operation succeeded. Although Avalanche came on the heels of Husky, with very little time for an in-depth review of the preceding assaults' lessons, there remained significant variances between the two operations. Either by circumstance or by deliberate design the two amphibious landings illustrated significant advancement—but also new challenges in littoral operations.

First, the assault on Salerno was done against a determined enemy with sufficient combat power in easily defensible terrain. The German defenders succeeded in shutting down almost half of the invasion beaches on D-Day for periods of time and seriously disrupted the initial landings. While Torch involved combat operations at certain locations, Vichy forces quickly capitulating. Although the taking of the Kasba required significant effort on the part of Truscott's Goal Post force, the situation was never as grave or in doubt. Similarly, the Husky landings were against mostly Italian coastal units that had little stomach for a fight and offered largely token resistance. Although Göring Division panzers and Italian armor did make advances on the Gela Plain on D+1 and came close to collapsing the Dime beachhead, the German thrust was a counterattack after the initial landings. Conversely, Salerno was heavily defended with prepared positions and armor just off the beachline. Again, the amphibious ante was raised, this time significantly. US troops on the southern beaches were pinned down in the sand after making it only a few hundred yards. These beaches remained closed, with some elements failing to achieve D-Day objectives.

Second, in concert with the landings at Salerno, the navy conducted a feint in the Gaeta Gulf near the Volturno River in an effort to draw away enemy defenses from the actual assault area. The ruse had the desired effect, preventing the early commitment of other German units on D-Day. While Kesselring and other German commanders feared an assault farther north, and were predisposed to the idea, this was the first significant use of an amphibious feint in the MTO/ETO. While Task Force 80.4 was supposed to provide a feint for Husky, it was canceled while a larger follow-on operation occurred after the landings.

Third, given the paucity of ground-based air assets over the invasion beaches of Sicily, the NWAAF made a deliberate presence during the Avalanche landings. As the NWAAF again shaped the operational area outside the AOA, it also provided a fighter cap above the objective beaches on D-Day. Stacks of P-38s, A-36s, and Royal Navy Seafires assisted in protecting Allied forces both ashore and afloat. While Luftwaffe forces still leaked through, conducting harassing raids and dropping the new radio-guided bombs, Allied air was clearly present over the beaches. Although advanced weaponry posed new threats, the Allied air efforts to protect both ground and sea forces was indeed progress. In addition, the air component provided CAS and served as spotters for naval fires as the beachhead expanded and then countered enemy thrusts. Another significant advancement in the joint arena regarding air was the employment of FAC and expedited relay of requests for air support and assistance in locating targets. For the first time, USAAF assets were used in an ETO amphibious assault, with this development illustrating that the air component was also learning. Perhaps this new air-ground coordination represented the single biggest advance in amphibious combined arms integration.

Similarly, the establishment of a joint ASCC on board a naval vessel was a huge step forward for MTO amphibious operations. The placement of Major General Edwin House, commanding XII ASC, represented a significant level of USAAF commitment. From a ship-based platform, both ground- and carrier-based aircraft were managed by sea-based direction centers during the assault period. The USAAF also established standby and auxiliary control centers on other ships for surge operations or in case of shipboard losses due to enemy action. Additionally, reconnaissance taskings were placed under the ship-based control center for both planned and on-call missions, with pilots reporting out upon departing the AOA.[135] Furthermore, much like a landing force commander who transfers his flag ashore, the ASC commander did much the same once USAAF fighters were established on airstrips in the area. With ground-based aviation in the AOA, the ASC commander would collocate with Fifth Army HQ as much as practicable.[136] These were significant advances considering where the services were during Husky just a few months earlier.

Another positive development from previous assaults was the use of airborne troops. Unlike Torch, where navigation errors and weather precluded the success of airborne forces, and certainly in a departure from the Husky friendly-fire incidents, Avalanche saw the effective use of the 82nd AB in defense of the Salerno beachhead. Designated as a part of the reserve, the insertion of the PCTs was effective in helping to thwart the German counterattack between 11 and 15 September and was done without fratricide or significant navigation errors or mistakes due to weather conditions. With the 82nd experience in Husky still fresh, the execution of the Avalanche drops seemed to indicate that lessons had already been learned without any formal doctrinal changes.

However, with the progress made, some of the same issues remained as new ones popped up. Regarding ship-to-shore movement, both the fleet and the landing craft had to deal with relatively new threat: sea mines. While mines were not a new technology, they had not been a significant problem in previous amphibious operations in the MTO. However, starting with Avalanche sea mines had a significant effect on the assault force and its execution of the plan. Not only did the German minefield preclude effective NSFS by keeping ships out of radio and gunfire range; mines closed approach lanes, damaged landing craft, and affected both wave composition and scheduling. Hewitt planned for clearing the mines, but Task Force 81.8 was too small and limited in capability to fully clear the field before H-Hour. If the Germans were to make regular use of this defense, Allied amphibious operations needed to include a counter to this simple yet effective threat.

Unfortunately, logistical lessons were still left unlearned from the previous operations on how to combat-load ships for quick access in the AOA. Many of the cargo ships supporting Avalanche were loaded at Oran, for which the army had responsibility. Ignoring Hewitt's recommendations about navy assistance in loading ships, army personnel embarked supplies and equipment, placing emphasis on maximizing cubic area, not accessibility, while afloat. This required a difficult sea-based game of Tetris that affected landing schedules, altered lift priorities, and slowed support to the beaches. By the end of D-Day only 17–65 percent of cargo and equipment was unloaded.[137]

Beachmaster support during the first hours of the assault again remained problematic, many boat crews having to unload their charges. While tactical actions certainly affected the efficient offload and organization of supplies and equipment, this function remained an unsolved problem. With the beaches awash with gear and equipment, the assault was in jeopardy due to lack efficient organization ashore. Even with the former commander of the FAITC ashore and deliberate requests by Admiral Hall for support, the two services still had not fully addressed this deficiency.

In addition to beachmaster issues, army commanders remained unconvinced that preparatory fires were more important than the element of surprise. Unscathed German forces lay in wait for American landings. As a result, naval guns engaged over 132 targets on D-Day alone.[138] While on-call fires were successful in both Torch and Husky, army leaders held to their established paradigms. Even after the clear success of NSFS in defeating the German counterattacks at Gela, Patton quipped afterward that naval gunfire was "no damn good." The remark is ironic given his specific laudatory mention of it to Admiral Davidson following Husky. He was either insincere in his praise or forgot the key role it played in the defense at Gela. In a quick retort to Patton, Truscott boldly replied: "[It] saved us at the landings on Sicily."[139] The same could be said about Salerno. With no prelanding fires, the 16th Panzer went unaffected, making the VI Corps fight ashore more difficult. The combination of both air and naval assets kept the landing force from being pushed back into the sea. As naval officers pushed for preparatory fires, army officers still held onto their beliefs, with unfortunate consequences.

6

The Anzio Highway
Central Italy, January 1944

After the failure of the German counterattack at Salerno, General Clark and the Fifth Army began a slow advance up the Italian peninsula. Although the Avalanche landings were successful, VI Corps commander Dawley was seen by many officers as weak and indecisive. While Ike harbored some suspicions of the corps commander's leadership abilities before the operation, other general officers visited Dawley during Avalanche and were also unimpressed with his demeanor, indecisiveness, and poor exercise of command. With Clark initially confident in Dawley's skills, he began to doubt them as the Salerno operation unfolded. When pressed by Clark as to what the VI Corps commander was going to do given the German resistance on the beaches, Dawley responded pathetically: "I'm praying." Clark's response was pointed: "That's OK, but you better do something else besides."[1] When Ike visited VI Corps ashore, the Allied commander was dismayed with Dawley's comportment. After a briefing by Dawley regarding his troop dispositions, Ike quipped: "How did you ever get your troops into such a mess?"[2]

When 15th Army Group commander Sir Harold Alexander visited Clark on the Salerno beachhead on 15 September, the Fifth Army commander reported his dissatisfaction with Dawley's handling of the situation. In their conversation Alexander told Clark: "I can tell you definitely that you have a broken reed on your hands and I suggest you replace him immediately."[3] On 16 September Clark informed Ike that the corps commander needed replacement: "He appears to go to pieces in emergencies." Ike concurred with the assessment, and Clark formally replaced Dawley on 20 September. Dawley was temporarily replaced by Clark's deputy, Matt Ridgeway, with both Ike and George Marshall deferring to the Fifth Army commander's prerogative.[4] Upon his relief Dawley, appointed as a general officer only temporarily, reverted to his permanent rank of colonel. His ignominious departure was made worse when he made a call on Ike's headquarters before leaving the theater. However, Ike was absent when Dawley arrived, and the only reception he received was the Allied commander's formal withdrawal of this temporary rank. Sent stateside, Colonel Dawley soon found himself commanding the army's Tank Destroyer School and remained in the army training establishment. But many saw Dawley as a mere scapegoat for Clark's own failings as a leader and planner. Regardless of the sentiment over Dawley's ouster, Major General John P. Lucas was soon placed in command of VI Corps and would become the next unfortunate victim of Clark's amphibious ambitions. Ironically it was Lucas who, as commanding general of 3rd ID in 1942, quipped that army amphibious training at the time would only end up in a disaster.

Unfortunately for both Lucas and Clark, the Germans were hardly finished defending the Italian peninsula. As late summer turned to autumn, the Wehrmacht effectively used Italy's defensible terrain to its advantage. South of Rome the Germans established a series of defensive lines laterally spanning the peninsula from the Adriatic Sea to the Tyrrhenian Sea. One of these lines was a series of screening positions nicknamed "Barbara," with the so-called Winter Line behind it and other defensive positions constituting the main German defenses. As an extension of the Winter Line, the Gustav Line proved the toughest and stymied the US Fifth and British Eighth Armies. Given the valleys and draws in this mountainous region, there was very little room for movement or maneuver. The topography of the central Apennine Mountains channeled offensive action to existing roads and narrow corridors. Seemingly the only way to make progress was through brute force: using massive amounts of firepower followed up with small unit action traveling up ravines to engage individual positions. Such actions were time-consuming and costly.[5]

After having stormed the flat, smooth beaches on the initial assault waves at Salerno, the 36th ID now found itself slugging it out in mountain passes. Given the number of bridges and narrow roads, the Germans did their best to frustrate the Allied advance by demolishing infrastructure or laying mines. Mother Nature seemed to work against the Allies, bad weather making the mountain fighting even harder.[6] Reflecting his disgust with the emerging tactical situation, the 36 ID's commander, Major General Fred Walker, wrote: "The Italian campaign will not be finished this week, nor next. Our wasteful policy or method of taking one mountain mass after another gains no tactical advantage, locally. There is always another mountain mass beyond with the Germans dug in on it, just as before. Somebody on top side, who control the required means, should figure out a way to decisively defeat the German army in Italy, instead of just pushing, pushing, pushing."[7] While some characterized the campaign as a "slogging match," the new VI Corps commander wrote "we haven't got enough troops to go very fast."[8] Given this situation, the Allies looked for alternatives. Not only had the offensive stalled, by December 1943 time was running out.

The British "Soft Underbelly" strategy focused on North Africa, Sicily, and Italy was now giving way to the all-important cross-channel invasion scheduled for 1944. While the Italians had surrendered and the Mediterranean Sea line of communication was restored, many questioned the strategic value of continuing the campaign. However, Churchill was still pressing for the capture of Rome as a capstone to the entire endeavor.[9] Inexplicably making an ambiguous connection between Italy and the invasion of France, he claimed it was folly to leave the Italian campaign only half-finished. He went as far as to claim: "What . . . could be more dangerous than to let the Italian battle stagnate and fester for another three months."[10] By winter 1943 Churchill was insistent on continuing the Mediterranean strategy and hectored Allied leadership to accede to his request.[11]

The Normandy invasion was no longer merely a debate between Churchill, FDR, the Joint Chiefs of Staff, and the Imperial General Staff. As a result of the Casablanca, Quadrant, and Tehran Conferences, Overlord was agreed to by the Big Three powers and tentatively planned for May 1944. With Overlord in the offing, the effort in Italy would soon take a backseat to larger strategic imperatives. The Normandy invasion would quickly siphon off men, material, ships, and individual talent. Some might view what was left in the MTO was the second string. With Ike's departure to become head of the Supreme Headquarters Allied Expeditionary Force (SHAEF), he was replaced in the MTO by Sir Henry Maitland "Jumbo" Wilson. Despite the United States hitting its production stride and churning out the sinews of war, various operations in other theaters were vying for many of the same resources. The Italian campaign would soon feel the effect of this competition. Valuable landing craft and ships were needed for the cross-channel invasion, and the assets resident in the Mediterranean were destined for Northwest Europe and the planned Normandy assault. Equipment sets were needed not just for Europe but also for the Pacific. By this time in the Pacific both General Douglas MacArthur and Admiral Chester Nimitz were beginning their thrusts toward

Japan. Given the larger strategic requirements of the global conflict, Clark and the Fifth Army could not expect many more resources to come their way. Time was one of them.[12]

On 1 October Clark triumphantly entered Naples to the cheers of locals. Capturing the port city meant that the Allies now had a logistical hub for future operations. However, before the Germans evacuated the port they sabotaged quays, cranes, and the harbor. The resident tugs were sunk along with fifty-eight vessels moored at the port's sixty-eight berths. Some ships were submerged completely, while others were partially visible with their masts or superstructures just above the water's surface. Railroad cars and cranes were pushed into the water and the entire port laden with mines or other booby traps. According to one engineer the damage was done "by a man who knew his business."[13] While the Salerno beachhead was again supported by the logistics over the shore method, the requirements for sustaining the entire Fifth Army mandated a port and its accompanying infrastructure. Before the port could be utilized as a sustainment base, army engineers had their work cut out for them.

As mentioned above, amphibious operations allow a commander to use the sea as maneuver space and bypass enemy ground defenses and/or geographic barriers. Additionally, amphibious landings can be made at the discretion of the landing force, giving the sea-based offensive the initiative as to where and when action will occur. Defending forces are left largely to speculate. With the Allies pinned down, 15th Army Group looked for alternatives to the Gustav Line problem. Given the amphibious assaults' unique characteristics, Alexander devised an end run to solve his Gustav Line dilemma. By outflanking the Germans with an amphibious assault in their rear areas, the 15th Army Group commander believed he could put the Wehrmacht in a defensive posture. Use of an assault on the Italian coast might cause the Germans to reorient some Gustav Line units to counter a landing in their rear. While a previous amphibious operation had been considered to turn the enemy flanks in the Gulf of Gaeta in October, the operation was canceled at the last minute.[14] But another, deeper penetration might help break the Gustav Line stalemate.

If an amphibious attack drew forces from the Gustav defensive line, a renewed ground offensive against the weakened German positions might finally return the operational initiative to Allied forces.[15] This proverbial left hook strategy utilizing an amphibious operation held promise for Allied forces looking to expedite the offensive. Alternatively, and reflective of the Allied thinking, the German high command asked: "Where can the enemy land?" "Everywhere" was the response, with senior officers replying that "the enemy is not tied to any season."[16] As a result, the Germans were keenly aware that another amphibious assault was a threat. However, for the Allies, questions remained: How much combat power and shipping were available? Would it be enough? Would the Germans react as expected? More important, what if it failed?

Earlier at the Quebec Conference in August 1943 the Combined Chiefs of Staff agreed that sixty-eight of the ninety LSTs in the Mediterranean were required for other offensives or taskings. However, with the stalling of the Italian campaign and possibility of a left-hook amphibious assault, Ike retained them in the Mediterranean until 15 December.[17] Later in November at the Sextant Conference the Chiefs allowed the December date to be pushed to 15 January.[18] Even with the LSTs' departure time pushed back, planners doubted the feasibility of both a ground offensive and an amphibious offensive. As a result, the possibilities of the proposed left hook dropped considerably. However, Churchill remained insistent on the capture of Rome. Given the slow advance against the Gustav Line, Churchill, at a Christmas Day meeting in Tunis, pressed the issue again with American leadership, who finally acquiesced to the prime minister's concern. With the green light given for the landings at Anzio, LST departures were delayed again, to 5 February. However, even with this later date came the understanding that the LSTs and associated assets would not be available for long-term sustainment of the assault force. Sufficient shipping for the proposed landing and its subsequent operations would be limited. Given the other strategic requirements, after D+2 Clark was informed that he would have only six LSTs available for additional lift, and that number itself ignored the possibility of operational losses due to enemy action. However, the six LSTs would eventually grow to twenty-four after Churchill's badgering on 8 January. Regardless of the fourfold increase, shipping constraints remained a major planning consideration. In this regard, the cart was ahead of the proverbial horse. The Annex A (Task Organization) of the operation was reflective of the resources available, not necessarily the requirements.[19]

The proposed Anzio assault, code-named "Shingle," was a joint endeavor assigned to Clark, along with naval counterpart Rear Admiral Frank C. Lowry and XII ASC's Major General House.[20] Initial planning occurred at the Royal Palace at Caserta north of Naples on 12 November and was headed by General Donald Brann, Fifth Army assistant chief of staff for operations. Assisting the effort was former FAITC

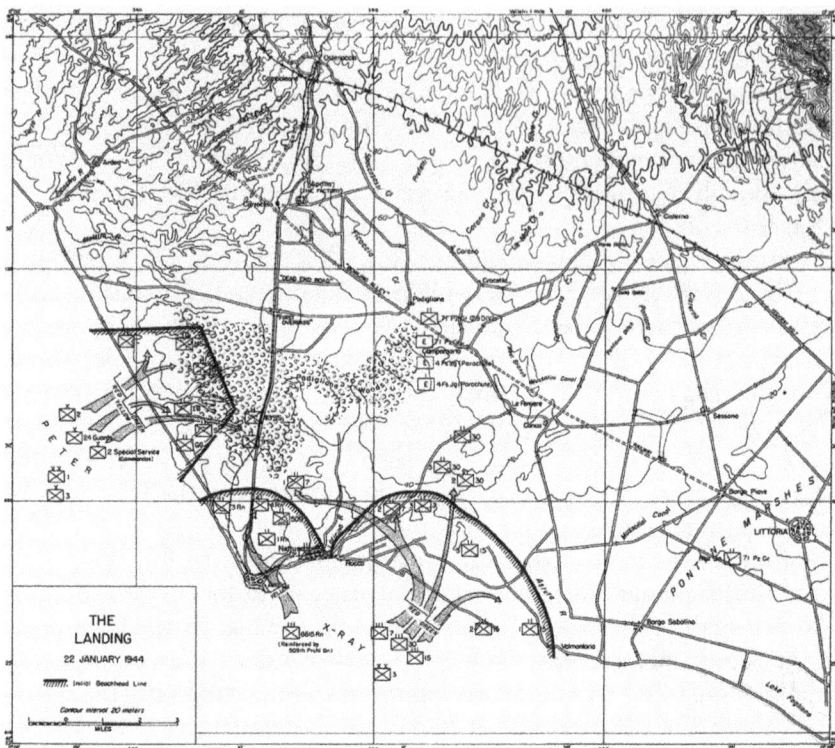

Planned assault for Operation Shingle. The 1st UK Division would land north of Anzio at "Peter" Beach while the 3rd US ID landed at X-Ray Beach. A separate ranger landing at Yellow Beach would secure the town and its port. (CARL Digital Archive)

head and Salerno veteran, Brigadier General O'Daniel, assigned to the Fifth Army G-3 as head of its special amphibious section.[21] The naval component consisted of Lowry's Task Force 81, with the final Combined Fleet composition consisting of two command ships, five cruisers, twenty-four destroyers, two antiaircraft ships, two gunboats, twenty-five minesweepers, four Liberty ships, eight LSIs, eighty-four LSTs, ninety-six LCIs, and fifty LCTs.[22] The initial US contingent afloat included three Ranger battalions, the 3rd ID, 751st Tank Battalion, 509th PIB, and 504th PIR.

Analysis of German defenses and the hydrography showed that the beaches by the coastal towns of Anzio and Nettuno might provide the best sites for executing the end run. In addition to a port, the beaches at that location had a steep underwater gradient with suitable beach exits.[23] Another attractive feature was that the region fell within range of Allied air cover, now based on the Italian peninsula.[24] Designated "X-Ray Force," the Americans would land south of Anzio at a 5,600-yard stretch of shore, with "Red" and "Green" beach designations, while three Ranger battalions seized the town's port and city, coming ashore south of the city at "Yellow." Simultaneously the British were to land 1st Infantry Division north of the town. Code-named "Peter," the UK formation also used three beaches with the same color designations.[25] The American beach gradients were very shallow, averaging from 1:80 to 1:110. Given this hydrography, the navy determined ships no larger than an LCT could land in the 1:80 gradients with only LCAs and LCVPs at 1:110. With these limitations, the beaching of LSTs and the disgorgement of equipment could be done only instream at a much slower pace or through use of pontoon bridges. However, the port might still be made LST-compatible. Of additional concern was the Italian January coastal weather that might hamper offload operations. Forecasters expected to have clear weather for no more than two out of seven days.[26]

Considering the size of the initial landing force, the planned beachhead area was seven miles deep and fifteen miles wide with a perimeter of twenty-six miles.[27] Located within thirty miles of Rome, the area was a low coastal plain, lightly defended, with drainage ditches and farm fields devoid of the steep terrain often advantageous to the defense. Rolling wooded hills were just to the northwest of the proposed AOA and would be the designated area of operations for the British 1st Division going ashore at "Peter Beach."

With the concern over lift and the threat of bad weather, Fifth Army realized that combat loading would reduce the amount of cubic area a given ship could take to the AOA. As a result, less equipment and supplies could be shipped. With ships sortied from North African ports providing much of the supplies for Shingle, others vessels brought equipment and materials from the recently cleared port of Naples.[28] In addition to the increased importance of combat loading and given the limited time the LSTs were available, army planners came up with a new transport method. Trucks were loaded up to their five-ton capacity at supply depots in Naples, driven aboard their designated LSTs, and then debarked ashore to VI Corps supply points. This made the most of the vehicle space available, facilitated quick offload, and expedited turnaround. Using 1,500 trucks, this procedure was not a single lift but a continuous process.[29] During the initial weeks when the clock was ticking on the LSTs' time in theater, 300 empty trucks from Anzio would drive aboard the ships, transit down to Naples, reload with supplies, and reembark aboard the amphibious shipping in a twenty-four-hour period. By 28 January six LSTs moved daily from Naples to Anzio carrying preloaded vehicles with various classes of supply. This efficient use of lift reduced debark time from one day to one hour.[30] The newfound use of mobile-loaded trucks was a determining factor in the expeditious offload of equipment.[31] Dubbed the "Anzio Highway," the round trip between the AOA and the port in Naples kept VI Corps well-supplied.[32]

Since the operation was envisioned to be of relatively short duration, when the assault bogged down new methods of ship embarkation were created. Each six-ship convoy moved 1,500 tons of cargo and given a shortage of artillery ammunition; Class V (ammunition) comprised 60 percent of the load. The remaining 40 percent was split between Class I (rations) and Class III (petroleum). Class V was placed on an LST's weather deck along with any mobile-loaded vehicles carrying explosives and flammable materials for quick access once the ship arrived at Anzio.[33] Such embarkation practices were frowned at by the navy and considered unsafe and dangerous. However, necessity overruled normal safety procedures. In addition to the mobile-loaded LSTs, fifteen LCTs made weekly turnarounds between Anzio and Naples along with Liberty ships from North Africa. According to the leading historian of the campaign: "What made life possible at Anzio is the midst of death was the logistical lifeline that pumped a steady stream of supplies to the beach head."[34]

While fully loaded LSTs could not land in the shallow surf, the small port at Anzio could berth some vessels. The facility was enclosed with a 600-yard breakwater that might be able to accommodate vessels drafting less than ten feet, but ability remained limited.[35] Included in the landing plan were port construction engineers who would land at H+15 on D-Day then improve, modify, or repair the Anzio port for possible use by LSTs. Leveraging a port facility would result in even quicker debarkation and offload operations.[36] If the port was determined to be unusable, pontoon causeways would again be used to move assets ashore. However, if the causeways were used, that placed tonnage restrictions on the LSTs given the shallow beach gradient. With these restrictions the invasion force's LSTs would initially rely on the LCIs, LCVPs, and DUKWs available to VI Corps to move men and equipment from ship to shore.[37] With the lift available, planners concluded that it would take three days for the ships of the initial landings to turn around and then embark the corps reserve, consisting of the 45th Division and a combat command of 1st AD.[38]

The landings were scheduled in concert with other 15th Army Group operations along the Gustav Line. With only two divisions making the assault, the remainder of the US II Corps, British X Corps, Eighth Army, and a unit of the French Expeditionary Corps would attack the Gustav Line and hopefully push the German Tenth Army back into Liri Valley. If successful the Allied ground offensive would make a link with the Anzio beachhead.[39] As previously envisioned, VI Corps making the Anzio landing would draw German units away from the Gustav Line and then establish defensive positions as the rest of Fifth Army moved north. An issue that lingered was the strength of the combined US/UK divisions going ashore and its rather ambiguous mission.

Important objectives of the landings included the German lines of communication heading south from Rome to the Gustav Line. These lines consisted of two highways that also paralleled rail lines linking the capital city to the defensive positions. If the landings could establish a beachhead, push inland, cut the transportation links, and defend itself against German counterattacks, they could create a defensive dilemma for the Wehrmacht. Key to this effort was holding the Alban Hills high ground at Colli Laziali about twenty miles northeast of the Anzio beaches. The hills were located between both Rome–Gustav lines of communications and were essential to the German defense.[40]

Given the shortfalls of amphibious lift and logistical support after D+2, would the Allied formations be robust enough to establish and defend the beachhead, continue all the way to the Alban Hills, and then hold them? The objective of the assault was still somewhat unclear. While the initial plans called for seizing the Albans, a subsequent order by Clark required VI Corps to merely advance on them. While a seemingly minor semantical issue, there was a difference between advancing to the hills and seizing them.[41] Would the Allied assault be strong enough to hold off German counterattacks while waiting for Fifth Army to move through the Gustav Line? What if the Fifth Army failed to break through the German defenses and join with VI Corps? Might the Allies have to conduct an amphibious withdrawal or, worse yet, be annihilated by Wehrmacht forces?

These questions and other planning considerations lingered. Considering the small size of the amphibious assault, naval historian Samuel Eliot Morison derisively reported that "either this was a job for a full army or no job at all; to attempt it with only two divisions [one American, one UK] was to send a boy to do a man's errand."[42] Lucas's chief of staff, General Alfred Gunther, characterized the plan as "a forlorn hope."[43] Even Clark realized that a larger force was required, with the plan canceled on 22 December.[44] However, it was revived days later at the Christmas meeting by Churchill, reiterating his support for the Italian campaign and quipping: "Whomever holds Rome[] holds the title deed of Italy."[45] When pressed by a senior officer about the risks, a callous and cavalier Churchill replied "of course there is risk, but without risk there is no honor, no glory, no adventure."[46] With the British prime minister insistent, Avalanche was reinstated. A subsequent planning effort was organized on 31 December to update and modify the plan after its revival.[47]

Despite the risks and ambiguities, the plans were finalized and approved by 8 January 1944, with D-Day set for 22 January. The small invasion force, limited in lift and logistics and with a somewhat ambiguous tasking, resulted in a less than sanguine VI Corps commander. In his diary, Lucas wrote: "Unless we can get what we want the operation becomes such a desperate undertaking that it should not, in my opinion, be attempted."[48] He went on further to compare the effort to the World War I disaster at Gallipoli and that the planning was that of an amateur.[49] According to one historian: "He was well aware of Shingle's bastard provenance, the equivocal offspring of an insistent Churchill, a compliant Alexander, and an ambitious Clark, with Eisenhower playing the midwife."[50] Even Clark hinted at possible failure of the entire operation by advising the VI Corp commander "don't stick your neck out the way I did at Salerno."[51] Hardly stirring words of confidence.

Again, XII ASC provided air cover for the operation with 2,600 airframes. Like it had during Husky and Avalanche, the air component shaped the environment, with BAI hitting rail and marshaling yards, road networks, bridges, and industrial targets. Conducted in a three-phase air effort, the first occurred from 1–13 January, focusing on transportation networks. During the pre–D-Day aerial attacks the newly established Mediterranean Allied Air Forces (MAAF) dropped over 5,400 tons of bombs against Italian lines of communication is isolation of the battlefield. The MAAF structure came into existence at the beginning of 1944 and subsumed the NWAAF organization. Unlike Husky and Shingle and in a modification of *FM 100-20*, Allied air attacks leading up to the landings did not initially focus on Luftwaffe bases. German airfields and plans were attacked during phase two and occurred up to D-Day. Although *FM 100-20* placed air superiority as the priority, during Shingle this mission was given secondary status. Planners assumed that the enemy could not mass enough airpower to affect the landings and might muster as little as 270 aircraft in Italy with a few hundred more in France and the Balkans.[52] The MAAF flew over 9,000 sorties in pre–D-Day bombardments, with the air plan's final phase including air cover over the landing beaches and the amphibious fleet and CAS for troops ashore.

Only days before the actual assault, VI Corps initiated landing rehearsals. Between 4 January and 19 January assigned assault units carried out night operations, conducted speed marches, and practiced amphibious embarkation/debarkation procedures. Part of the preparations included a corps-size landing exercise code-named "Web Foot" (17–19 January). Conducted on beaches six miles south of Salerno, the exercise reflected the recent Avalanche experience, as the training included assaults against fixed positions and movement through minefields.[53] Underscoring the dangers of an amphibious assault during winter, Web Foot led to the sinking of an entire battalion of 3rd ID's howitzers loaded into forty-three DUKWs. Nineteen guns, along with fire control equipment and seven 57mm and two 37mm antitank guns, were unloaded from their berthing ships into the hapless DUKWs. Heavily loaded, and too far from the beach in a high sea state, the DUKWs floundered. The mishap saw the loss of the guns and a number of soldiers, although most were rescued. A chagrined Admiral Lowry claimed: "The accidents were so many that it appeared impractical on the face of it to make the assault without further training."[54] When Clark was informed, he was appalled at the "overwhelming mismanagement by the navy."[55]

Furthermore, the Web Foot exercise was limited in scope, with only eleven LCTs participating and no testing of communications networks or NSFS procedures. H-Hour for the exercise was 0200, and when Truscot went ashore at 0800 he again found units landing on the wrong beaches and all of them late. No armor or tank destroyers had yet made it ashore despite their planned landing before daybreak. After the exercise the 3rd ID commander grimly observed: "No single battalion landed on time or in formation . . . [and] transports were so far offshore that assault craft required three to four hours to reach the beach. . . . Not a single battalion landed on its correct beach."[56] He went on further to gripe how, "against opposition, the landing would have been a disaster."[57] Disgusted, he called off the exercise by 0930 and again chastised the navy for its "obvious lack of control and training."[58] While Truscott pressed for another rehearsal given the poor showing, the request was rejected, with the operation already given the green light and scheduled.[59] Regarding the debacle, Lowry assured Truscott that "the navy would do its utmost to set matters straight and to put [the division] ashore exactly as [he] wished."[60]

As with Avalanche, the Shingle plan also included an amphibious feint. Originally planned for Ostia Lido near the mouth of the Tiber River, it was changed to Palo and then finally to the coastal town of Civitavecchia.[61] The change of location was ordered by Clark himself, as he believed the Osta Lido site would needlessly draw enemy forces into the area of the actual assault. The plan included use of dummy vessels and dumps created on Corsica and fake radio transmissions.[62] On D-Day the Civitavecchia location was attacked by a group of destroyers at H-Hour and then again the following day by a force of navy cruisers and destroyers. In addition to the naval effort, the air component also contributed to the feint, with A-36s attacking docks at Civitavecchia.[63] The feint apparently had some success, as a Luftwaffe pilot flew over Civitavecchia at 0830 on D-Day, asking "where is enemy landing force?"[64] However, in the larger picture Field Marshal Kesselring did not take the bait with no major German ground movement toward the feint locations.

The Gustav Line assault by 15th Army Group began days earlier on 12 January and was led by the French Expeditionary Corps attacking Cassino. This assault was followed by the British X Corps five days later, moving near the Garigliano River. On 20 January US II Corps initiated the American advance in the center, with the 36th ID attacking and establishing a small bridgehead across the Rapido and Garigliano Rivers.[65] If the Germans were to bolster their defenses along the Gustav Line and commit their reserves, it might enable the Anzio operation to fully establish a beachhead and move to the Albans.[66] However, harkening back to the ambiguous nature of the entire endeavor, such a commitment of German formations would thwart Fifth Army movement north, which ironically was the more decisive action. The 36 ID cross-river assaults were the key component to the entire plan. Furthermore, the entire Fifth Army needed to reach the Liri Valley and assist the isolated beachhead before a possible German counterattack turned on the two Allied amphibious divisions.

Adolf Hitler dictated that the Gustav Line was to be held at all costs, expecting "the bitterest struggle for every yard."[67] As hoped, with the Allied offensive on 18 January Kesselring committed his two reserve divisions to bolster the Gustav Line. However, with this commitment the British X Corps attack stalled, as did the French. In the American effort torrential rain swelled the rivers, making resupply and movement across the raging waters difficult. After only two days the Rapido beachhead was abandoned, as 36th ID casualties mounted, losing 1,700 men. Clark's orders to cross the river have been heavily criticized. Years after the war the 36th ID Association published a resolution stating: "The crossing of the Rapido River was a military undertaking that will go down in history as one of the colossal blunders of the Second World War." However, German fire was not the only danger these men faced. During the eventual retreat, one veteran recalled the difficulty of trying to cross back over the river:

> They [Germans] had their artillery blow up the pontoon bridge, trapping all of us. . . . Machine gun fire increased and the "screaming meemies" [nickname for Nebelwerfer rocket launchers] started up and continuously pounded our position. . . . Voices of other GIs I could hear were saying lets swim for it. . . . As I approached the river . . . three men had already entered the water preparing to swim to the other side . . . only one made it to the other side . . . [the other two] got to the middle and the current was too strong . . . one by one I saw these poor guys sink. I could do nothing to save them. I witnessed five or six drownings that day.[68]

Given this failure, the objective of Liri Valley remained beyond Allied reach, making the Anzio landings even more of a gamble than before.[69] By the time VI Corps launched its amphibious assault on 22 January, the Allied ground offensive to the south had already ground to a halt. Despite the Allied failure in breaching the Gustav Line, the Germans did commit their reserve just as the Allies had hoped. As a result, the Anzio and Alban areas were lightly defended—but not for long.[70]

While the Germans bolstered their defensive line, what the Allies did not know was that the Wehrmacht had a planned reinforcement. They observed the Allied buildup in January at the reclaimed port of Naples but failed to sight the flotilla's movement. Despite this intelligence failure, Kesselring moved forces from France, Germany, and Yugoslavia to Italy. While an amphibious landing was just as dangerous as a breakthrough at the Gustav Line, the immediate issue was the Fifth Army attack from the south.[71] Before the start of the Allied offensive, the 1st Fallschirmjäger Division and the 29th and 90th Panzergrenadier Divisions were brought in to defend the Gustav Line.

The Hermann Göring Division remained an operational reserve in the Rome area. While not physically located at the beach at the time of the allied assault, the newly arrived German forces could be called forward. These additional forces were a serious oversight to the Shingle plan. While having committed some reserves to the south along the Gustav Line as the Allies had hoped, the Germans planned to move newly arrived troops to the Allied beachhead.[72]

Sortied from the Gulf of Naples on 21 January, the American component of Lowry's fleet consisted of forty-two LSTs, forty LCTs, and 250 DUKWs.[73] With Liberty ships from North Africa in support, the convoy carried enough supplies of all classes for three days.[74] For the journey north the weather was fair with calm seas, with the only aircraft overhead being Allied air cover. H-Hour was set for 0200 the next day, with a waning quarter moon providing limited illumination.[75] Truscott's 3rd Division, as the main American force, planned to land three regiments at Red and Green Beaches. Scout boats marked the sites for incoming landing craft using colored blinking lights.[76] After the initial landings the 1st Naval Beach Battalion was to come ashore and start improvements for the introduction of heavy vehicles and pontoon causeways. Yet again army commanders felt that the element of surprise negated the use of preparatory fires. However, like Avalanche, they did allow the use of three LCT(R, for "rocket") rocket barrages just minutes before the troops were to come ashore.[77] Such rocket barrages had been effective at Salerno's Green Beach, silencing German machine-gun positions at the contested shoreline.

The first American forces to land were the Rangers at Yellow Beach at the town of Anzio. A small folbot marked the beach with its lamp forty-five minutes before the incoming troops arrived. At H-10 a British LCT(R) was one of the three barges scheduled to fire its 798 rocket tubes in support of the landings. However, the ship arrived late and, fearing that its salvo might hit the inbound Rangers as they headed to shore, held its fire. Fortunately for the Americans, the town was undefended, with the assault achieving total surprise. By 0645 the Rangers were fully ashore and the town secured.[78] Heading inland, the Americans captured German engineers who had planned to destroy the breakwater, rubble parts of the town, and create obstacles for the Allied forces.[79] In preventing the sabotage, the small port could now quickly be modified by engineers for use by Allied LSTs.

For the main US landings, a British submarine led minesweepers to the objective area. Arriving the evening before, the twenty-three sweepers had a limited antimine capability and leveraged captured

Vichy French and German gear. Finding only a few mines in the area, they completed their work only minutes before the assault force arrived. At 0153 rocket-bearing LCT(R)s fired in support of the 3rd ID. The initial assault waves landed as scheduled on Green and Red Beaches at 0200.[80] The only enemy troops they encountered were slumbering or drunk Germans at the few resident positions. The 509th PIB and 504th PIR landed and headed south, taking the town on Nettuno a few miles away. Follow-on assault waves came ashore in LSTs, with one hitting a runnel. When an LCVP came to assist the grounded vessel, machine-gun fire opened up from a shoreline position, causing several casualties.[81] Despite this singular enemy action, follow-on assault waves continued ashore, with all the LCTs landing by 0643. All the organic division artillery and a significant part of the 751st Tank Battalion landed before daylight. The landing was largely unopposed and might be more accurately characterized as an amphibious movement.[82] Truscott moved his flag ashore with the morning sun rising.[83] While the enemy eventually reacted with some artillery fire for inland positions, Truscott described the incoming fire as "slight and harassing."[84]

However, after daybreak at 0748 a request by a shore fire control party had the destroyer USS *Mayo* hit several buildings with sixty rounds.[85] Shortly afterward the Luftwaffe appeared, with aircraft breaking through the Allied fighter cover. Dive-bombing Red Beach, they set fire to several mobile-loaded vehicles. Attacks later that morning saw Fw 190s dropping bombs among the pontoon causeways and landing craft offshore, hitting one LCI and causing it to sink. For the next few days air attacks continued, with USS *Plunkett* hit, a near-miss registered by USS *Brooklyn*, with British ships also being targeted. Errant mines also took their toll as USS *May* struck one and suffered serious damage, with five casualties. These incidents in the first three days recorded the naval flotilla's most expensive Mediterranean experience, with four destroyers knocked out of action within twenty-four hours.[86]

Regardless of the air attacks, the MAAF flew more than 1,200 sorties on D-Day, with bombers continuing to attack lines of communication and fighters striking enemy troop movements. However, even with all the MAAF sorties and support, Shingle still suffered from a lack of direct control of aviation assets in the AOA. While a fighter-direction team was present with Task Force 81, the codes identifying friendly from enemy aircraft had not been passed from higher headquarters. Adding to the confusion was that the senior air commander for the invasion was not aboard the HMS *Ulster Queen* that housed the afloat

American armor comes ashore at the port of Anzio via an LST. Using the existing port facility was key in the generation of combat power ashore. (US Navy photo)

ASCC but was aboard USS *Biscayne*. As a result, radar plots were a mass of contacts from which friend or foe could not be discerned. This caused unneeded air raid warnings, placed friendly aircraft in peril, and disrupted offload operations. This situation was more oversight than a deliberate step backward, but it caused problems with real-time coordination with the naval or ground forces until such control could move ashore.[87]

With communication a specified component of amphibious assault, for more effective command and control of formations the landing force employed a new radio, the SCR-300. This new radio provided communications for division units, and soon proved itself worthy of the task.[88] A backpack-size radio, the SCR-300 was a key link between forward observers and fire-support assets. With a three-mile range, the radio was easy to use and robust enough to withstand the rigors of combat. So important was this new capability that use of the SCR-300 was included in preinvasion training.[89] While a tactical asset, it made a difference in command and control not just for amphibious assaults but also for extended land operations.

Casualties were remarkably light, with VI Corps experiencing thirteen killed, forty-four missing, and ninety-seven wounded. As the hours passed, the 3rd ID, the Rangers, and UK forces all contacted each other, tied in their defensive fire plans, and established the Allied beachhead. A survey of the port was conducted, and naval engineers determined that the harbor could berth two LSTs and, with some modification, six more.[90] At this point Shingle could be classified as an unqualified success, especially after what had transpired during the Web Foot exercise.[91] Truscott went so far as to quip: "After the almost disastrous performance during the rehearsal, our Navy comrades gave us one which was almost unbelievable smooth and accurate."[92] Clark visited the landings on D-Day and was pleased with the initial assault, but he was still unsure of Lucas's aggressiveness.[93] Despite Clark's disposition, at the end of D-Day 36,000 men and over 3,000 vehicles made it ashore, including 90 percent of the assault loads. By 0800 on 24 January the entire assault convoy was unloaded.[94]

Regardless of the German air efforts, service troops continued to improve the beach and port facilities. The 36th Engineer Combat Regiment (ECR) cleared the Anzio facility of the few small ships deliberately sunk by the Germans and made the facility ready for LSTs to disembark their cargos. By the beginning of February, the small harbor in Anzio could accommodate eight LSTs, eight LCTs, and five LCIs simultaneously. However, the Liberty ships were still too big, remained offshore, and unloaded instream with LCTs and DUKWs.[95] With only a handful of LCTs available, LCIs were used as a stopgap measure to move supplies from ship to shore. An effort was made to encourage Liberty ship captains to come closer to shore so DUKWs and LCIs could more readily unload supplies ashore. However, given the German artillery, many remained reluctant.[96]

Use of the existing port was a key component in building combat power during the early phase of the operation. Admiral Lowry went so far as to admit that the loss of a pontoon causeway from the enemy airstrike might have doomed the beachhead if it were not for the engineers' efforts to improve the Anzio port.[97] While debarkation was clearly a success, Lucas worried that a hit on an LST might block the cleared channel or the port's berthing capabilities, causing significant delays. He reported that this was his biggest anxiety at this part of the operation.[98] While the initial weather was better than expected, a gale-force wind hit on 26 January, forcing the movement of causeways to safe harbor. Several landing craft floundered, with the wind and surf creating new runnels along the beach.[99] The meteorological conditions slowed the debarkation process while also requiring salvage operations for several floundering landing craft. Debarkation was also interrupted or slowed with additional incoming German artillery or when the occasional errant mine stuck a vessel.

To facilitate beach-party functions, Admiral Lowry assigned his deputy, Captain Robert Morris, the task of coordinating unloading and salvage operations. His army counterpart, Colonel George Marvin of the 540th ECR, was placed in charge of the Anzio port and the X-Ray Beach network.[100] Despite the wind, artillery, mines, and air raids, by the end of the month some 201 LSTs and seven Liberty ships had been offloaded, with almost 2,000 tons moved over X-Ray Beach, more than 1,260 tons at Yellow, and the bulk, some 6,350 tons, via the Anzio port.[101] As the weather held, the much-needed reserves, composed of the 45th ID, parts of the 1st AD, and other attachments, moved from Naples and landed ashore by 1 February.[102]

The 540th ECR and 1st NBB operating at X-Ray beaches quickly cleared minefields, bulldozed sand dunes, and created beach exits. Roads were constructed, supply points organized and built, with Anzio's beaches capable to handle large, heavy vehicles. As army engineers established a base of supply, manual labor was now at a premium. Italian civilians from Naples were recruited and brought to Anzio to help clean up the beaches and assist in building supply dumps.[103] The soft sand required the use of pontoons as DUKWs unloaded the equipment from the larger ships offshore and often became mired. With the beach developed, Corps level supply dumps were created inland. Given force on-hand, a twenty-six-mile perimeter was determined to be the extent of Lucas's combat power ashore as the Allies secured bridges over the Mussolini Canal.[104] However, they had yet to acquire the Alban Hills and sever the important German lines of communication.[105]

Despite the Allied movement, the Germans were not idle. While the initial landings took Kesselring by surprise, he adroitly surmised the real objective were the Alban Hills and the associated lines of communication.[106] On D+1 elements of the 4th *Fallschirmjäger*, 71st Infantry, and 3rd and 29th Panzergrenadier Divisions were sent to the Anzio Plain along with regiments of the Göring and 15th Panzergrenadier Divisions. While multiple German units converged on the Allied beachhead, at this time they were still largely overmatched and were merely a patchwork of units thrown together.[107] Though surprised,

A task force of the 504th Paratroop Infantry Regiment comes ashore from USS *LCI-38*, during the initial landings near Anzio, 22 January 1944. (US Navy photo)

Kesselring's initial shock wore off by 23 January, as the Alban Hills remained in German hands. The Allies focused on establishing and consolidating their beachhead and had not conducted a bold offensive action. German reports reflected this disposition: "[The Allies] limited themselves to reconnaissance and patrols . . . [and] on 22 January and the following day, an audacious and enterprising formation of enemy troops could have penetrated into the city of Rome itself without having to overcome any serious opposition. . . . But the landed enemy forces lost time and hesitated."[108]

Focused on building combat power ashore and establishing a beachhead rather than exploiting the element of surprise, Lucas lost a fleeting opportunity.[109] But given the ambiguity of the situation, his prudence was certainly warranted. While a disingenuous Clark had warned Lucas not to stick his neck out, the Fifth Army commander also penned that "Lucas must be aggressive."[110] It appears that Lucas was faced with a fateful choice: risk the entire VI Corps in an aggressive manner, or slow-roll the offensive with a methodical approach, thereby allowing the Germans time to reorient and reinforce defenses south of Rome. It seems as if Clark's personal instructions to Lucas were as ambiguous as the formal orders issued to VI Corps. Lucas's earlier concerns of an overreach and Clark's desire for aggressiveness were both well-founded, if not contradictory. In the postmortem of the Anzio operation, it appears that the Germans were in no position to counter a quick thrust into Rome. But that could only be determined afterward. At the time, Clark or Lucas could only speculate as to the German ability to sever the IV Corps line of communication. Churchill, who insisted on the operation in the first place, was displeased with the initial result, complaining "I had hoped we were hurling a wildcat onto shore, but all we got was a stranded whale."[111]

A small counterattack was thwarted by NSFS from USS *Brooklyn* on 23 January at 0859, hitting a German assembly point near the town of Littoria.[112] Despite this small action, Kesselring had already made plans to respond and initiated Operation Richard, starting the movement of German reinforcements to Anzio. A significant intelligence oversight on the part of the Allies, such Wehrmacht reinforcements were already coming from Germany and Italy with more called from as far away as Yugoslavia and France. In a few days the Anzio beachhead would face five German divisions, with more coming.[113] Soon the bantamweight amphibious assault of two divisions that was supported by a tenuous sea-based logistics chain would be up against a heavyweight foe.

On 24 January the 3rd ID and British 1st Division advanced to occupy key bridges and expand the perimeter to the towns of Cisterna and Campoleone in preparation for an assault on the Albans at Colli Laziali. When met with aggressive fire from both the Göring Division and 29th Panzergrenadier Division the Allied forced withdrew.[114] By 29 January the Allied offensive was paused as the Allies took time to regroup and await the arrival of the corps reserves.[115] The Gustav Line attacks and the Anzio assaults were now effectively checked by Wehrmacht forces. Any chances of a quick and speedy linkup between II Corps forces and VI Corps was fading, and it was painfully obvious that the original two-division effort was far short of the requirement.[116]

As in Avalanche, the Luftwaffe used Fritz X radio-controlled bombs and hit several ships, causing many to retreat. Massing more aircraft than expected, on 29 January at 110 Dornier Do 217 and Ju 88 bombers, along with Messerschmitt Me 210 fighters, attacked and sank a Liberty ship, a British cruiser, and one hospital ship while damaging a second.[117] Such successful attacks might have direct correlation to the lack of aircraft identification on the fighter direction radars on HMS *Ulster*. The Luftwaffe was fond of early-morning attacks, as Allied fighters could sortie only in the daylight and then had to travel 100 miles from their bases in the south to reach the AOA.

DUKW amphibious trucks bring cargo ashore at Anzio. They were used
as lighters for unloading shipping in stream. The Liberty ship seen in
the background was unable to navigate the shallow waters near the beach.
Additionally some of Liberty ship captains refused to come closer to shore
because of the incoming German artillery. (US Navy photo)

However, in a new development, this threat was countered when
engineers repaired an existing 3,000-foot airstrip near Nettuno soon
occupied by Spitfires of the USAAF's 307th Fighter Squadron. With
the forward basing of Spitfires, air cover could be provided on the spot.
This was a deliberate effort to get ground-based aircraft ashore in the
AOA during combat operations. However, as German forces arrived in
strength, Wehrmacht artillery fire eventually forced the withdrawal of
the squadron. Such forward basing was intended for the Salerno landings, but the German artillery fire precluded such support.[118] In yet
another advancement for air-ground interoperability, air cover was not
restricted to just daylight hours. With the German use of dusk or dawn
attacks, eventually the British provided night fighter coverage in the
form of twin-engine Bristol Beaufighters and specially trained Spitfires.[119] Such twenty-four-hour coverage was also a new development.

Additionally, as the beachhead developed and commands transitioned ashore, representatives from XII Tactical Air Command (TAC)
met nightly with VI Corps planners to identify and determine future

targets and the sequencing of attacks.[120] In addition, they developed new methods of support, classifying targets as either "prearranged" or "on-call." Request for prearranged support were initiated twenty-four hours in advance and at the division level, with liaison officers determining enemy dispositions and aircraft requirements, with the request forwarded to VI Corps. Corps weighed such requests based on upcoming operations and then forwarded validated submissions. Once Fifth Army received the request, it was considered by a joint Army–Air Force targeting board. The board sequenced and coordinated the overall tactical effort and prioritized targets.[121] The nightly conference brought together various unit representatives to review the day's activities and requested targets, then conferred with the various air commands accepting requests based on availability and capacity.

After the conference, air planners developed directives for the next day's mission set.[122] Once approved, orders were sent out in as little as two hours via teletype or other conveyance. Sent to the squadrons servicing the request, crews received a brief on enemy dispositions, callsigns, weather, and the latest on safety-control measures. If images were available, pilots could review photos and maps and study key/prominent features of the target area. Once the mission was flown, intelligence debriefings allowed for an update to the current situation, bomb-damage assessment, and enemy activity, with the entire prearranged process starting again for the next day.[123]

On-call missions were initiated via radio and were based on the current or developing situations or for targets of opportunity. Coming from the division level, the request bypassed corps and went right to the joint Army–Air Force control center at Fifth Army. While listening to the incoming on-call request, corps-level approval was assumed by Fifth Army (if it did not object to the submission). If approved, taskings were sent to the appropriate airfields that were standing at alert status. The goal was to service such requests within a ninety-minute time frame.

Leveraging the Avalanche experience, A-36s and Spitfires were again used as spotters for NSFS. In addition, L-5 "Sentinel" observation aircraft serving in what was termed "Horsefly" missions. Flying above the battlefield, these small liaison planes helped spot for the aircraft servicing a target request and could also help walk artillery rounds to a target.[124] Air support also came in the form of "Pineapple" missions that focused on moving targets. Once a reconnaissance aircraft identified a moving target, he reported it the Air Control Center, which then tasked the designated unit standing on Pineapple alert. Such requests were reportedly very efficient, with requests serviced in as little as fifteen minutes.[125] Rover Joe missions, initiated during the previous Salerno operation, also continued and represented sustained growth in the combined arms effort.

To support the coordination of USAAF air personnel introduced a host of radios, transmitters, and procedures to handle the communications requirements. The SCR-299 radio was by far the most used high-frequency (HF) radio model. Vehicle-mounted, it covered a wide range of frequencies and proved dependable. First introduced during the North Africa campaign, it had a range of almost 2,300 miles. Combined with the SCR-193 and other communications equipment, it gave signal personnel ample coverage and frequencies to support coordination activities. These radios proved especially useful for immediate requests and on-call missions. However, not all requests had to be made verbally via tactical radio frequencies. The air component also found the use of teletype equipment to be very useful at higher echelons tasking subordinate commands. This reduced demands on the electromagnetic spectrum and the equipment required.[126] Such communication was useful for sending the next day's target lists, mission sets, and other field orders.

VHF radios were the standard for fighter communications, but as air became more integrated and deployed during amphibious operations, the number of frequencies available became limited. In the aircraft, the SCR-522 radio had the capacity for up to four channels. However, two of the four channels were used for air–sea rescue and for "guard" (common emergency frequency for all aircraft). As a result, half of their capability was reduced, leaving only two channels for actual combat operations. In a report submitted in late 1944, signal personnel addressed how XII TAC fighters' SCR-522s were inadequate given the four channels with two already assigned. With only two remaining channels, the follow is a listing of the available networks working on the same frequencies:

Channel 1—Fighter Control
Channel 2—Fighter-Bomber
Channel 1—XII TAC Common Frequency
Channel 1—Bomber Escort
Channel 1—Bomb Group Control
Channel 2—Artillery Spotting

As a workaround, some units recrystallized their radios for specific missions to avoid congestion on the preset channels. While the SCR-522s were excellent radios, airborne channels remained limited.[127]

While Lucas's initial landing faced minimal opposition with only a few enemy troops present, by 30 January the Wehrmacht's 14th Army was estimated at 71,500 troops and established itself around VI Corps, which had 61,332 men. Commanded by General Friedrich Mackenson, as Wehrmacht reinforcements arrived they began pummeling the Allied beachhead with 88mm and 170mm artillery.[128] Having observers in the Alban Hills the German guns rained shells on the Allied troops at will. Augmenting this firepower in March, the Wehrmacht eventually brought in a Krupp K5E railway cannon that weighted 218 tons and launched 280mm shells. Called "Anzio Annie," the weapon could easily range the beaches from its position near the Alban Hills.[129] So confident were the Germans in collapsing the beachhead that the voice of German propaganda, "Axis Sally," called Anzio "the largest self-supporting prisoner-of-war camp in the world."[130] Given their clear observation ability and fields of fire, the Germans held the upper hand during the day, forcing Allied troops underground. Troops made for cover in basements and in root and wine cellars. Even the VI Corps headquarters had to be moved to an underground position. At night US and British troops came up from their underground protection and conducted reinforcement operations as ship-to-shore movement brought more support to the amphibious toehold.[131]

A week after the initial landings, the corps reserve, consisting of Middleton's 45th ID and a combat command from 1st AD, arrival at Anzio and replaced the 3rd ID, the Rangers, and the paratroopers in the beachhead security mission. Now Lucas had the equivalent of four divisions under his command and, with his combat power now doubled, finally decided to go on the offensive toward the Alban Hills and the German supply routes.[132] Relieved of their initial security responsibilities, the 3rd ID, Rangers, and paratroopers were scheduled for a 30 January offensive. Preparing the battlefield, Lucas requested air, artillery, and NSFS for an assault on the German positions at Cisterna. The area around the town contained several road intersections to include an important Highway 7 junction along with the associated railroad line that supplied Gustav Line positions.[133]

Unknown to the Allies, the Germans were also looking to go on the offensive. A planned counterattack had to await the arrival of reinforcements, as Allied bombing disrupted surrounding transportation networks. Beating the Germans to the punch, the Allies went into the

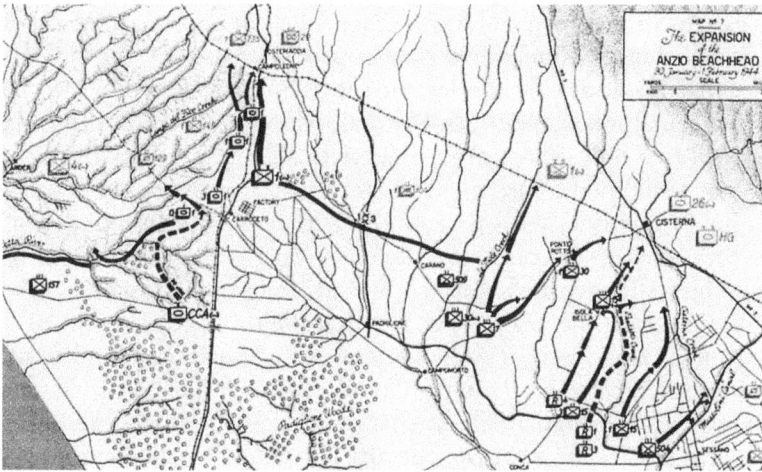

VI Corps offense of 1 February 1944. The UK's 1st Division attacked north to Campoleone while the US 3rd ID, Rangers, and paratroopers to Cisterna. (CARL Digital Archive)

attack with a multipronged American assault, the main effort diving toward Cisterna. The plan was for the 3rd ID for move toward the town of Velletri in the Albans, with 1st AD under Major General Ernest Harmon (Combat Command A) to the left of the British effort, focused on taking the high ground above Marino. In addition, the British 1st Division was positioned to push up to Campoleone to the south slope of Colli Laziali.[134]

Leading the attack to Cisterna were two Ranger battalions crossing the L/D an hour before the main force of 3rd ID initiated its advance. Another Ranger element supported by infantry would follow the first element along the road leading to the town. Flank security and diversionary attacks came from other elements of 3rd ID on the left and by the 504th PIR on the right. While the initial elements made good progress under cover of darkness, once daylight arrived the Rangers ran into well-concealed German reinforcements from the 1st *Fallschirmjäger* Division that also included armor from the Hermann Göring Division. US intelligence believed Wehrmacht positions south of Cisterna were merely a delaying action. Instead of a thinly constructed set of defenses, the Americans ran into well-prepared ones with fresh troops and combined arms. Recognizing the importance of the town and its lines of communications, the Germans set their main defenses in front of the town, not behind it.[135] By noon the Rangers were caught in the open and were either killed or captured. Of the 767 men in the Ranger attack, only six escaped.[136]

The 3rd ID attack to the left of the Ranger infiltration also met strong German resistance. While it gained one mile on the first day, it was still two miles short of its objective. The next day, with the full weight of combined arms, 3rd ID again moved forward, but the Germans held their line, with part of the 26th Panzer Division arriving from the Adriatic to bolster the defense. To the right of the Ranger assault the 15th Infantry Regiment moved along the Cisterna Creek in an effort to block the bridges but were unable to move elements of the Hermann Göring Division. The same occurred with the 30th Infantry as it attempted to reach Pantatto Creek, 1,500 yards west of Cisterna. Meeting with German artillery, this advance was also checked. After three days of offensive action, the 3rd ID and other elements of Lucas's command were spent. While the Americans gained a few miles, they could not breach the new enemy defenses that secured the town and its important transportation networks.[137] German combat power continued to grow, and by mid-February the tables would be turned.

While fighting occurred during the first few weeks of February, the Germans organized themselves for a larger offensive effort. On 16 February the Wehrmacht initiated a four-mile-front assault that included motorized infantry, Panzergrenadiers, and other armored formations totaling some 120,000 troops, intent on cracking the beachhead defenses. Once breached, an exploitation wave would follow the first, which consisted of additional grenadiers and panzers, with more battalions driving down the main avenues to Anzio and Nettuno.[138] By the end of the first day the German offensive was blunted, but on 17 February the Germans renewed their offensive, and for the next three days intense combat ensued. VI Corps held the line, with the Germans suffering over 5,000 casualties and the Allies 609. With L-5 spotter planes, the Americans countered with artillery along with tanks from the 1st AD and stalled the German offensive.[139] By 20 February the enemy gained only two and a half miles.

While the Wehrmacht offense was also a failure, so too was Lucas's performance. Understanding his position, the VI Corps commander wrote that he "was afraid that the top side is not completely satisfied with my work, I can't help it." He went on admit to General Jacob Devers, commander of North African Theater of Operations, United States Army, that "he should have gone as fast as he could to disrupt enemy communications."[140] Obviously hindsight is 20/20.

Disappointed in the lack of progress by the Allied effort, Clark arrived at Anzio and sentenced Lucas to the same fate as Dawley. Flying up to the small airfield himself, Clark relieved Lucas from command on 23 February. The Fifth Army commander again deflected any criticism of himself and claimed that Lucas "had no flash."[141] Military historian Carlo D'Este concluded—as had Lucas at the time—that his force was "simply too small to establish and maintain a defensible beach head and seize . . . Colli Laziali at the same time."[142] In his memoirs Clark deflected any blame and claimed that Lucas was "ill" and "tired physically and mentally from the long responsibilities of command in battle."[143] However, such an assessment was Monday-morning quarterbacking, as Lucas had to address the situation with the information he had at the time. He could have risked all of VI Corps with an aggressive move to Rome or the seizure of the Albans. But he remained cautious; unsure of enemy dispositions, did not want to risk his own extended logistical lines. But the real fault lay with Churchill, Alexander, and Clark. Replacing Lucas was the ever-capable veteran of multiple amphibious operations, Lucius Truscott. Given this responsibility, the new VI Corps commander felt as if he was to "pull someone else's chestnut from the fire."[144] In the next few weeks, Truscott would also find command of the VI Corps beachhead problematic.

With Truscott now in charge, he coordinated land-based artillery and NSFS to counter additional German offensives. While much of the fighting occurred beyond the range of NSFS, it provided essential support during early German counterattacks. The joint effort again succeeded in thwarting the Wehrmacht offensive, but the entire campaign's objectives were now beyond reach. The left-hook gamble resulted in a stalemate not only at Anzio but also along the Gustav Line proper. Only after Operation Diadem in conjunction with the USAAF's "Strangle" air interdiction effort in spring 1944 did the Allies finally break through the Gustav Line with accompanying movement from the beachhead. Rome fell to the Allies only two days before the Normandy landings—some five months after the initial Shingle assault.

Using the sea as maneuver space is a proven method to get at an enemy's lines of communication and exploit vulnerabilities. However, such actions require proper weighting, meaning the sufficient combat power required to attain the assault's main objectives. From the review of the Shingle operation, clearly Clark and Alexander were attempting an economy-of-force operation limited to the initial two divisions that were constrained by the amphibious-lift shortage. Additionally, Allied intelligence assumptions regarding German troop strength and the ability to reinforce the Gustav Line and the area around Rome were clearly mistaken. However, those operations in January and February fell far short of the objectives. Militarily the liberation of Rome was inconsequential, even after a month of stalemate, Churchill's goal of taking Rome would finally be realized. Years later the prime minister would finally admit that "Anzio was my worst moment of the war. I had most to do with it."[145] Militarily the liberation of Rome was inconsequential, even after arriving in the capital, vicious fighting continued up the peninsula into spring 1945.

However, the operation did provide another opportunity to exercise amphibious operations and develop additional tactics, techniques, and procedures. Key to sustaining this operation was the use of mobile loads and the efficient movement of supplies via rolling stock. Trucks were loaded with gear at the Naples port, then embarked aboard ships, driven ashore at the Anzio port, unloaded, and then returned in the same fashion for an expedited turnaround. Such mobile methods and efficient combat loading were key in developing power ashore and sustaining the operation—ill-conceived as it was.

Also given the paucity of amphibious lift available, a more efficient use of assets was required, with logistics personnel maximizing both cubic area and weight. The loading of Class V supplies on LSTs topside, while dangerous, also expedited the movement of critical supplies to the AOA. While Class V loads were certainly a fire and explosive hazard to any ship, the army surmised that so, too, was combat. Such creative embarkation practices illustrated an army learning the art of combat loading and of leveraging the assets and space available.

While there were problems with controlling air in the objective area, engineers created an expeditionary airfield near Nettuno for resident air cover. Placing a fighter squadron in such a forward area was a new approach, as most air bases were safely placed out of enemy artillery range. Although the Luftwaffe again enjoyed successes over the beach and the assembled fleet, having on-the-spot fighter support was a new development in air-ground coordination. Despite the effort to provide such air support within the AOA, the squadron had to be withdrawn due to the enemy's indirect fire. However, and with much of the same intent, air planners at least entertained the idea of building more bases within the beachhead area. While initially proposed during the Salerno landing, the actual building of the airstrip certainly was a change in the USAAF's attitude and methodology.

In addition to embarkation procedures, the Americans refined their CAS methodologies with on-call targeting, daily coordination of air and ground staff regarding priorities and missions, and continued use of spotter aircraft. L-5 liaison planes assisted not only NSFS but also artillery and attack aircraft. The cleavage that occurred during the Husky operation between air and ground forces was clearly addressed, with true combined arms coordination becoming a reality. Air Control Centers helped manage airspace and priorities while forward observers guided inbound aircraft. As German combined arms capability regarding air began to wane, the Americans continued to refine and develop such practices.[146]

Although the initial Anzio landings might be classified as an amphibious movement due to the lack resistance ashore on D-Day, the reception of follow-on assault waves, the development of the beach and port, and the relative ease of building combat power ashore reflected improved Army–Navy coordination. Unlike the previous landings, at Anzio there were few, if any, reports lamenting beach/shore party coordination for follow-on assault waves and supplies. The messes witnessed at various beaches in Sicily and Salerno were largely avoided at Anzio. While the German defense did not begin in earnest until days later, and certainly was an important consideration, the quick and efficient offload of men, supplies, and equipment illustrated that many lessons had been taken to heart by both services. Alternatively, one could argue that such a methodical process came at the cost of an aggressive offensive thrust on the Alban Hills or Rome itself. Had Lucas pushed beyond the initial beachhead and not focused on its development, the entire operation might have a different history.

7

The Friendly Invasion Before D-Day
Operation Overlord, 1943–1944

The events that occurred early on the morning of 6 June 1944 on the beaches of Normandy have been covered in hundreds (if not thousands) of books, essays, and documentaries. Accounts and descriptions regarding the amphibious assault and the struggle to breach the Atlantic Wall are readily available in book and electronic formats. These accounts are inspirational and terrifying and remain a testament to the bravery of the men who stormed the German defenses. This work's opening account of Harold Baumgarten's experience in Dog Green Sector is indicative of these heroic accounts and the sacrifices made by such men.

However, less well known is how the Allies developed such an amphibious assault capability against the most formidable beach defenses ever constructed. No other assault in history was as large and complex and pitted against such lethal and well-prepared defensive positions. This was truly a unique event in history that required extensive planning, training, and organization. Taking lessons from the MTO, the Supreme Allied Command undertook countless initiatives to ensure the six elements of an amphibious assault were sufficiently addressed given the German threat. Supporting this operation, the Allies gave specific attention to command relationships, ship-to-shore movement, NSFS, air support, establishment of a beachhead, and especially to communications and logistics. Given that the invasion required Allied forces to drive deep into occupied Europe, logistics and the establishment of a beachhead were paramount concerns.

At the 1943 Casablanca Conference, the Imperial General Staff agreed to a redoubled effort for a cross-channel invasion, with the final commitment made at the Quebec Conference. As a result, Allied focus began to shift. While US, UK, and French forces continued to fight up the Italian peninsula, Ike and much of his staff relocated to

England for Overlord's planning and preparations. Arriving in London on 16 January 1944, he was subsequently designated Supreme Allied Commander and given the authority to order, direct, negotiate, arm-twist, or accede to the differences of opinion between the two nations regarding this most important operation. After years of political wrangling, compromise, and disagreement, the Supreme Headquarters Allied Expeditionary Force set forth the formal mission statement:

> The object of Operation Overlord is to secure a lodgment area on the continent from which further offensive operations can be developed. The lodgment area must contain sufficient port facilities to maintain some twenty-six to thirty divisions and enable that force to be augmented by follow-up shipments from the United States and elsewhere of additional divisions and supporting units at the rate of three to five divisions per month.[1]

This mission statement is clear in that the Allies were going to have to build and maintain the biggest beachhead of the war. This would require the six functions of amphibious assault to be exercised on a scale never seen before. Fortunately, by 1944 the American industrial machine had fully ramped up production of material for operations in the Pacific and in Europe as the draft filled the ranks. With this manufacturing and manpower bounty, the scale and scope of American amphibious assaults grew. Considering that Churchill's desire for Rome and Operation Diadem in Italy was still taxing Allied resources, one of Ike's first communiqués in his new position as Supreme Headquarters Allied Expeditionary Force stated "convinced that in all discussion full weight must be given to the fact that his operation marks the crisis of the European war. Every obstacle must be overcome, every inconvenience suffered, and every risk run to ensure that our blow is decisive. We cannot fail."[2] With this he put the ongoing Mediterranean campaign aside from his desire for a possible simultaneous June assault of the French Riviera.

In 1942 the United States had already begun setting the stage by initiating Operation Bolero, sending men and material to the United Kingdom. Establishing an air bridge across the Atlantic and sailing convoys through U-boat–infested waters, the Americans were increasingly becoming a presence in the British Isles. Early Bolero movement focused largely on moving or flying aircraft across the ocean for Operation Pointblank (as a part of the Combined Bomber Offensive against Germany).[3] While the cross-channel invasion was postponed until 1944, the Americans continued to send more and more personnel and equipment to the United Kingdom in preparation for the MTO landings and the eventual Normandy assault.

As early as January 1941, representatives from the Army Staff and Chief of Naval Operations began a series of meetings addressing a possible US presence in the United Kingdom, the American–British Staff Conversations. This initial effort established joint discussions and developed courses of action against the Axis should the United States commit to war.[4] On 8 June 1942, six months after Pearl Harbor, the United States established the European Theater of Operations, United States Army (ETOUSA) with a mission to direct the buildup of American troops and supplies in the United Kingdom for an eventual cross-channel invasion.[5] Using the Army–Navy Board's "Rainbow" series of plans as a starting point, the structure for the US buildup was based on a modification of the Rainbow 5 scenario with an enlarged presence in the United Kingdom.[6] This was only a starting point for planning purposes, as the Americans and their British Allies were now required to do the hard staff work, detailed planning, and orders generation for the joint/combined operation.

In January 1943, months before the Husky landings and after the Quebec Conference, the Combined Chiefs of Staff initiated the detailed work of the cross-channel invasion. Discussion and coordination for the endeavor continued in late spring 1943 as Allied representatives met at North Devon in the United Kingdom at the Conference on Landing Assaults. In this monthlong meeting, Allied representatives addressed the issues facing them and outlined preparation requirements. In the introduction by ETOUSA commander Lieutenant General Jacob Devers, he declared that they had one goal: "Crossing the English Channel with properly organized and properly trained assault teams, ready to seize, to hold, and maintain beachheads through which might land a major invasion force to advance against the enemy."[7] The conference was comprehensive and subdivided into several parts: Orientation, Discussion of Doctrine, Exercises, Preparation of Proposed Training, and Adaptation of *FM 31-5*.[8] Because Torch was the only American assault experience against the European Axis at the time of the conference, part of the orientation was a summary of that operation and few other landings already conducted, including Dieppe, the Aleutian Islands in Alaska, and a recent British exercise code-named "Kruschen" held near Dunwich Heath.

At the conference the ETOUSA G-5 outlined a number of initial assumptions that would drive Overlord and its naval component,

Neptune. Preliminary assumptions included the expectation that this assault would be made against a strongly defended and prepared beach. The initial landings would require two US divisions followed by three for subsequent operations ashore. The force required amphibious lift for five US divisions. The average distance from the near to far shore was 100 miles.[9] Unlike previous assaults in the ETO, the extensive fixed positions and defensive firepower at Normandy posed a serious concern. Given German preparations, the plan now called for aerial bombardment of the objective area and prelanding NSFS.[10] While NSFS had been withheld prior to landings in previous assaults to leverage the element of surprise, by the time of Overlord the Allies had overwhelming firepower that lowered the requirement for tactical surprise.[11]

To support the influx of US forces, the army's Services of Supply Branch was tasked to provide a host of cross-channel support operations. These functions included reception of troops, transportation, quartering of American units, establishing training centers, building ranges, depots, vehicle parks, ammunition dumps, bulk fuel storage farms, and hospitals, and a host of other administrative requirements. For armor training alone the United States requested over 190,000 acres in southern England. While the British minister of agriculture howled at such a request, the Americans still obtained 141,000.[12] Given that the British were already experiencing rationing and limitations on the necessities of life, the introduction of hundreds of thousands of American troops required great diplomatic finesse and tact. By May 1944 over 1.5 million US troops arrived in the United Kingdom, along with 5 million long tons of cargo and over 4,000 ships of various classes.[13] This number included twenty-seven infantry divisions, including eleven armored, four airborne, eight separate parachute regiments, four armored composite groups, and one light armored group, plus two Ranger Battalions.[14] In addition, the USAAF established new airfields in the central and western parts of England to base the 9th Air Force's Troop Carrier, Fighter, and Tactical Air Commands.[15] Given the introduction of so many Americans on the British Isles the buildup was sometimes referred to as the "friendly invasion."

Billeted in the "sausage camps" in southern England, dozens of these bivouac sites dotted the formerly quiet and placid English countryside. When given passes for off-base travel, these Americans "invaded" the many cities, towns, and villages of southern England.[16] The mixing of Yanks with British subjects made for an interesting clash of cultures. Teenager Brenda Devereau from the port city of Bournemouth recalled her experiences with the Americans by stating "they swaggered, they boasted, and they threw their money about." Unlike British men who acted with more refinement and tact, Brenda was "captivated" by the Americans: "How we loved it!"[17] With US forces receiving better pay than their UK counterparts and an appetite for the few comforts available in wartime England, their presence was not always welcomed. A British newspaper poll claimed the Americans were less regarded than the Czechs, Dutch, Russians, French, and the Italians.[18] With such an influx of so many young, eager Americans at the peak of their reproductive capabilities onto the island, many Englishmen derisively found the US soldiers "overpaid, oversexed, and over here."[19]

To ensure a common vernacular and staff functioning between the two militaries and even within their various branches, in January 1943 the Services of Supply Branch established the Quartermaster Course, or what was referred to as the Quartermaster or "Q" School at Norfolk House, St. James Square, London. This school trained a pool of US and British officers in the others' doctrines, organization structures and strengths, planning processes, and staff procedures.[20] Toward this end, there existed fundamental differences between US and British planning methods. Key differences were that the British prescribed details to lower echelons that the Americans left to subordinate commands. While the Americans tended to delegate command and leverage individual initiative, the British were more directive, leaving nothing to chance. One senior American commander observed: "Our system of command was to tell the fellow what you wanted him to do and why you wanted him to do it." This approach allowed the subordinate to figure it out, whereas the British were less inclined to allow such freedom.[21]

Furthermore, for the British there remained a lack of standardized order formats and publishing of plans.[22] Aside from the staff process differences, the twelve-day course also included topics such as development of amphibious planning, landing tables, beach maintenance, support for subsequent operations, and civil affairs. In the next few months almost 500 officers attended, most of them holding key planning or tactical unit leadership positions.[23] While a seemingly tedious and mundane course of instruction, the combined effort required using common and shared planning processes, vernacular, staff functioning, and orders generation methods. Although the Americans came and worked with great haste, the British were more careful and analytical. One historian described the Americans' perspective of their counterparts as "old fogeyism." Countering this narrative, a senior

British officer quipped "the yanks are new to this game and have the enthusiasm of beginners."[24]

While Neptune was a joint and combined effort, operational and tactical control of the fleets remained largely along national lines. Royal Navy Admiral Bertram Ramsay was named the Allied Naval Expeditionary Force Commander, but US Navy Admiral Alan G. Kirk served both the Omaha and Utah Beach assault fleets as the Commander of the Western Task Force (designated CTF 122) and established his flag on USS *Augusta*. Prior to the assault Ramsay set up his headquarters at Southwick House near the Portsmouth docks, with both Kirk and Ike becoming frequent visitors to address combined action and coordination.[25] Two task forces supported the US effort. Under Kirk, "Force O," supporting the landings at Omaha, was led by Rear Admiral John Hall aboard USS *Ancon*. USS *Bayfield* carried Admiral Don Moon, commander of "Force U" assaulting Utah Beach.[26]

To assist in further Anglo-American cooperation, US Admiral Harold Stark was named Commander Naval Forces Europe. In this role he served as the liaison between the British and American naval forces and overall administrator for logistical support for CTF 122 vessels. His mantra to his staff was "get to know your opposite number," as the Americans required significant host-nation assistance.[27] As in North Africa, the navy created an organization to oversee the handling, basing, and support of landing craft. Rear Admiral John Wilkes, Commander Landing Craft and Bases, assumed control of existing craft, oversaw port organization, and established new bases while ensuring the logistic support of amphibious forces. Both men were very effective in their responsibilities; 99.6 percent of the American flotilla sortied on D-Day as ordered (2,480 of 2,493 vessels so ordered to set sail).[28]

Ground forces worked much the same way. Field Marshal Bernard Montgomery was named head of 21st Army Group, with General Omar Bradley assuming command of US ground forces of the First Army upon activation. Under Bradley were two numbered corps, V and VII. VII Corps was commanded by Major General Lawton Collins, and V Corps was under Major General Leonard Gerow. Both corps commanders were respected officers with excellent reputations. Given the division of labor, CAS and BAI for the American sectors were accomplished by a combination of the 8th and 9th Air Forces. Under the respective commands of Lieutenant General Jimmy Doolittle and Lieutenant General Lewis Brereton, both airmen were subordinate to Lieutenant General Carl "Tooey" Spaatz, the overall head of US Strategic Air Forces While the 8th Air Force's support of Overlord was temporary in nature, the 9th was specifically assigned to support ground forces.[29]

Like the army's earlier need for stateside Amphibious Training Centers (ATCs), the Americans required new amphibious in-theater training areas. By July 1943 an army study determined that units designated for the invasion had not conducted training in tide, surf, and beach conditions similar to Normandy.[30] With input from General Daniel Noce, who established the first ATC at Camp Edwards in 1942, ETOUSA had to coordinate with UK national and local governments for acquisition of civilian areas for military use.[31] After looking at numerous locations, the Americans settled on a stretch of beach in North Devon near the towns of Woolacombe and Appledore. This site provided 8,000 yards of beach on Bristol Channel, with another 4,000 on Taw Estuary. The location had tidal variations and shorelines similar to those in northern France, even with hedgerows that were comparable to the Normandy bocage. Furthermore, the location included a twenty-five-square-mile training area for inland operations. When the facility opened on 2 April 1943, units undergoing instruction at the new location were assumed to have already experienced combat action or received specialized training in amphibious operations.[32] The site was host to the earlier 1943 Conference on Landing Assaults that helped lay the foundations for the combined effort. Much like the stateside ATCs, the UK site advanced and developed methods and doctrine to include ship-to-shore movement and in-stream offload.[33] Part of the ATC's tasking specifically mentions the requirement to "develop and keep up to date doctrine and methods covering the assault of enemy held coasts, particularly western Europe."[34]

However, it was not the only training site established. Scores of others were set up at Rosneath and Falmouth in Cornwall; Dartmouth, Teignmouth, and Salacombe in Devon; and Milford Haven and Penarth in South Wales. The Rosneath and Dartmouth locations conducted extensive NSFS training and exercises. In addition to training the landing forces, many of these facilities provided instruction for navy coxswains, maintenance personnel, and ship's companies.[35] Several locations also served as modification centers for American landing craft and assault equipment. These modifications included upgrades suggested from previous assaults such as incorporating new radios, bow doors, side-loading capabilities, and additional AAA.[36]

Amphibious training areas at the UK ATC included structures representative of German defenses in Normandy with concrete strongpoints, pillboxes, and bunkers. With realistic combat environments, these training fortifications and exercises were much different than the previous stateside ATCs.[37] According to one observer: "The ATC provided very realistic training to prepare the infantry and supporting assault troops for all known aspects of the Normandy invasion. The training was tough, and some men were killed in attacking the simulated fortified positions with explosives and conventional weapons—including airpower."[38] Regarding these facilities a soldier who helped build the ATC facility remembered: "We made an utter mess of this beautiful old golf course while building pillboxes and other concrete defensive structures as we converted several separate areas into the Assault Training Center. . . . We rebuilt the fortifications in 'Normandy France.' We rebuilt the fortifications after each assault group had blasted into rubble all of our recent construction efforts."[39]

Training at the location began in September 1943 for divisions in the initial Overlord assault waves. The 29th ID conducted training first, followed by the 4th ID and elements of the 1st ID. The flotilla carrying the 1st and 29th IDs constituting Gerow's V Corps landing at Omaha Beach as part of Force O. On the initial wave, 1st ID was already a veteran of both Torch and Husky and undertook training at the Fifth Army Invasion Training Center in 1943. The Big Red One's 16th Regimental Combat Team planned to land on the eastern part of Omaha tied in with the 29th Regimental Combat Team, with 116th Regiment to its right. Like the 29th, 4th ID had not experienced combat but did receive amphibious training stateside at Camp Johnson. Upon arrival in the United Kingdom it participated in additional landing exercises.[40] Collins's VII Corps consisted of 4th and 90th IDs and embarked aboard ships of Force U. Landing at Utah Beach, both Force U divisions had yet to see combat but had received extensive training in the United Kingdom.

Perhaps the most important training area available to American forces was on the southern coast of England at Lyme Bay in the English Channel. This location served as the "far shore" for American training efforts and served as a live-fire amphibious assault area. In a meeting on 6 July 1943 at the Admiralty in London, a joint US–UK assault training area selection committee determined the requirements and a plan of action for such an establishment.[41] Up to a dozen locations were considered, and the timeline was short. Eventually the committee selection the Slapton Sands location in southern Devon County. Hoping to begin establishing the training facility by the fall and start exercises shortly afterward, this new amphibious exercise area forced thousands of locals to evacuate ancestral homes, villages, and lands. While rumors spread among the locals, official word was passed to the inhabitants in early November with a 20 December deadline. In just six weeks the lifelong inhabitants had to find accommodations elsewhere. This meant the evacuation of residents from over 30,000 acres across six parishes, along with the closure of 180 farms.[42] It was an enormous undertaking, with expenses paid by the Crown with additional help from the United States. Leaving their community, one local left a note pinned to the Slapton Church door asking a favor from the new inhabitants: "This church, this church yard, in which their loved ones lie at rest, these homes, these fields, are as dear to those who have left them as are your homes and graves and fields which you, our Allies, have left behind you. They hope to return one day, as you hope to return to yours, to find them waiting to welcome them home. They entrust them to your care."[43]

With Slapton Sands established, US units would embark at various ports in the United Kingdom and then set sail for a mock assault at the location. With a seven-mile stretch of rough sand and a shingle that was overlooked by cliffs, Slapton Sands's shoreline and topography were eerily similar to the Omaha and Utah Beaches in Normandy.[44] Exercises reflected the scheme of maneuver for the naval assault. The larger LSTs and Attack Transports (APAs) would remain offshore during the assault's initial phases. Meanwhile, LCIs, LCTs, and LVCPs went ashore carrying men and material under fire. The larger APAs required a port for berthing but could still unload troops over the side (in-stream) as in previous assaults. The LSTs were far too valuable to risk during the initial landing exercises and remained offshore. Once the beachhead was established with approach lanes cleared and marked, only then would the LSTs beach themselves ashore and disgorge precious cargos.

Embarked aboard LCVPs, LCAs, and LCIs, American units landed on the exercise beach with live fire accompanying the assault waves. Although all was designated as training, combat action occurred within Lyme Bay on 27 April 1944. During Exercise Tiger, German E-boats crossed the English Channel and attacked the training flotilla as the landing craft approached the beach. In the action, the Germans sank two LSTs, damaged two others, and killed 749 sailors and soldiers plus another 200 injured.[45] Public information regarding the attack was limited but not completely silenced. The Supreme Allied Commander feared that word of the attack might tip off the enemy as to their level

An English girl waits by a sign announcing the evacuation of Slapton Sands village, England, on 29 December 1943. Slapton Sands was evacuated to permit realistic invasion practice on its beaches. (US Navy photo)

of success and possibly divulge the nature of the training. Ironically, the German attack yielded positives as Allied forces developed better communication skills via common radio frequencies, emphasized life jacket usage, and improved escort procedures.[46]

Developing an appreciation of the impending threats ashore and assisting in amphibious planning, intelligence gathering required a robust and well-coordinated effort. Sharing of information between the United States and United Kingdom was critical in creating a clear picture of what lay ahead. Liaisons were established between the Allies, with key information disseminated to the task forces. Air reconnaissance was conducted in force by the Ninth and Second Tactical Air Forces flying at least eight missions per day over France north of the Siene. Mosaic images of the entire coastline were taken from 3,500 feet.

Additionally, USAAF commands sent out aircraft over the invasion beaches, taking photos at various altitudes and at wave-top height so that ground commanders might get a peek at the objectives from the same angle they would see it on D-Day. Furthermore, reconnaissance planes took pictures of most of the defensive positions, as well as the areas immediately behind them, and then returned at a later time to ensure the most up-to-date images were available.[47]

Assisting in the ship-to-shore navigation, assault vessels and landing craft received a "monograph" packet that included a compendium of weather, sea, and tidal info, enemy orders of battle, schematics of defensive positions, ports, and other facilities ashore. These were disseminated to as far down to the LST level. Additional information included hydrographic sketches for coxswains and navigators, with 17-by-22-inch charts that depicted adjacent landing areas, bombardment and gunfire plans, and listings of established priorities.[48] The dissemination of aerial photographs and the packets was a significant advancement from Husky and other MTO assaults.

At the 1943 conference, observations from Torch regarding coxswain performance were given full address. Despite the numbers of landing craft arriving on the wrong beaches, naval representatives still considered the training adequate, but they partially blamed faulty compasses aboard the landing craft for the navigation errors.[49] The conference addressed the compass issues along with development of new navigation aids for crews. However, such material solutions did not fully address the issue, as crews still needed better seamanship and landing craft training. Regardless of the new compasses and improved training, a navy representative predicted that "crews will still be relatively inexperienced, and navigation of landing craft will not be of high order."[50] In agreement with this naval counterpart, the commanding general of the 29th ID, Major General Norman Cota, disparingly quipped: "The landing craft aren't going in on schedule and people are going to be landed in the wrong places. Some won't be landed at all."[51]

To help mitigate problems in ship-to-shore navigation, CTF 122 set up the Naval Scout Boat School to train landing craft crews on how to recognize coastline silhouettes and significant landmarks. Such training was valuable, especially given the meteorological conditions of 5–6 June. With new navigation equipment, intelligence packets, and specialized training, coxswains were more prepared than before. Along with pre-assault training, scout boat personnel also assisted control vessels in directing landing craft through obstacle gaps and to their landing beaches during the actual assault while helping armor move ashore in the initial waves.[52] Additionally the presence of roaming control and scout boats helped manage sea-based traffic during the movement ashore in a rather crowed AOA.

Actual ship-to-shore movement was determined by several factors. First was the position and range of enemy coastal artillery and its ability to engage assault transports and the inbound landing craft. Included also was the ability of coxswains to observe known terrain features, their navigation abilities, and finally the ocean currents at the respective beaches. Movement of landing craft from the larger transport vessels was a complex task and could easily be delayed by mechanical problems, operator error, or slow unit movement into landing craft. Transport areas for the assault were roughly 20,000 yards offshore. At this distance they remained safely out to sea yet far enough for coxswains to potentially make serious navigation errors. Once seaborne embarkation was completed, assault waves were set up to depart at ten- to fifteen-minute intervals. Strong ocean currents pushed vessels astray on both beaches, and navigation errors occurring at Omaha with smoke obscured many terrain features. The initial assault waves at Utah and parts of the 116th at Omaha landed up to 2,000 yards southeast from of their target beaches. But many units did land in their intended locations to include B and D Companies of the 116th in the second assault waves in Dog Sector.[53] While there were indeed mis-landings, most of the assault force landed near their designated areas and largely on time despite the high sea states, adverse weather, and incoming enemy fire.[54]

Although American shipyards were building new vessels, there remained a shortage of landing craft for the cross-channel operation.[55] The originally planned day of 1 May was changed to 31 May and then pushed back again to obtain more shipping and other embarkation needs.[56] A concern during the Anzio operation, this deficiency became a point of contention between the two nations because the Americans were insisting on the proposed amphibious assault of southern France initially entitled "Anvil." Envisioned to coincide with Overlord, the Anvil plan hoped to split German defenses in France. With Allied forces coming from both northern and southern France, the US planners believed the operation would put the Wehrmacht in a defensive dilemma regarding allocation of forces. A southern assault would also have the benefit of providing another major port facility in France for the introduction of troops, supplies, and supporting equipment. Ike was a key proponent of this simultaneous landing as early as January 1944. But, this second landing reportedly needing as many as 72 LCIs,

47 LSTs, and 144 LCTs.[57] Given the premium placed on amphibious lift, the simultaneous assaults seriously tasked Allied capabilities.

However, the Imperial General Staff roundly rejected the Anvil plan because the assault on the French Riviera would preclude Churchill's desire to continue the Italian campaign using the Istrian peninsula and Ljubljana Gap to push toward Vienna.[58] Furthermore, the Imperial General Staff believed the two operations were too geographically separated to have the intended effect.[59] Additionally, to pay the bill on the proposed Anvil assault, the Normandy assault would be shorted fifteen LSTs.[60] Given the controversy over the numbers and the Mediterranean strategy, both General Marshall and Chief of Naval Operations Admiral Ernest King sent representatives from their staffs in Washington to mediate. Meeting in London on 13 February they initiated the Landing Craft Conference including representatives from SHAEF HQ and Admirals Kirk and Hall. With the Anvil plan still in the offing, the attendees agreed to asset allocations.[61] Given the number of landing craft required for the southern France operation, on 21 March Ike acceded to the Imperial General Staff's request and cancelled the operation, thereby removing the requirement for two sets of amphibious fleets landing simultaneously. However, Anvil was not necessarily a dead issue.

Much like Hewitt observed before and after Husky, and then witnessed again during Avalanche, the deficiency of beach party operations and logistics remained a concern. Learning from the Copy Book and Web Foot exercises and subsequent invasions, training for an amphibious assault required more than just storming the beach in mock assault waves and moving inland. To address the problems, the army established three European-based Engineer Special Brigades (ESBs) that received additional training before the invasion. These units grew in both size and mission. By the time of the June assault, army ESBs grew from approximately 3,000 personnel to a strength of 15,000 with an additional port company, quartermasters, MPs, and other special attachments.[62] Initially the 1st ESB was the only such brigade in the theater. However, to support Overlord two other brigades were included and began arriving in late 1943 with similar augmentation of personnel and capabilities.

These ESBs also trained at UK locations and practiced various beach party functions by setting up dumps, constructing beach exits, undertaking salvage operations, and conducting supply support inland.[63] Joint interoperability at the beach was evident, as the ESBs were also accompanied by three Navy Beach Battalions (NBBs)—the

2nd, 6th, and 7th. As joint training occurred for army and navy battalions at the regiment and division levels, they also began working together in the pre-assault exercises. Another exercise, Exercise Beaver, provided the opportunity for assault force engineers to conduct full-scale rehearsals.[64] Utah Beach support consisted of the 1st ESB working with the navy's 2nd NBB; Omaha Beach was supported by 5th ESB with elements from both the 6th and 7th NBBs. The remainder of the engineering units went ashore in the afternoon of D-Day, with the commands transitioning to the Engineer Shore Brigade on D+2. Despite the very checkered history of beach party support, CTF 122 reported such functions were well executed on both beaches, with Utah organization in place and operating smoothly on D+1 and on Omaha by D+2.[65]

Pre-D-Day training and exercises also ran along national lines, but US forces still had to leverage host-nation support and trained at various locations in the British Isles.[66] At the Slapton Sands location, exercises were divided into three types. The first set included exercises requiring troops from different units to work together on assault and supply challenges. This series of exercises addressed different aspects of the invasion to include embarkation, landing, and beachhead consolidation. The second set included smaller exercises focusing on individual units and their role in the larger operation. The third set served as large-scale dress rehearsals for the assault.[67] The ATC and the newly established 11th Amphibious Command ran units through training, with the Americans holding numerous exercises in and around the United Kingdom. Starting in January 1944, small-scale exercises such as Otter I and II, Mink I and II, Muskrat I and II, Chevrolet, Jeep, Teal, Mallard, Gull, and Jalopy occurred with larger ones including Duck I, II, and III, Fox, Beaver, and Fabius I and VI.[68] V Corps commander Gerow was dismayed at his command's performance during the early exercises and worried that embarkation took too long, supplies were late, and troops had packed too much gear.[69] Full-scale rehearsals for Force U were held 24–28 April and Force O 3–8 May. Ironically the 29th ID, untried and leading the assault on Dog Sector at Omaha Beach, was unable to participate in the early phases of DUCK due to a temporary lack of shipping. Eventually the division was able to conduct practice assaults at Slapton Sands as well as rehearsals that included movement of combat-loaded transports of LSTs, LCIs, escorts, and gunfire support ships along with follow-on forces.[70] Unlike Copy Book and Web Foot, these exercises included use of beach parties and engineering support and not just combat arms functions.[71]

Exercise Muskrat held at the Firth of Clyde in Scotland focused on initial assaults while also including the use of engineer detachments and operations. In support of the more logistically applicable functions, Exercises Chevrolet, Jeep, and Jalopy focused on embarkation, staging, and supply functions and occurred at locations in Northern Ireland.[72]

The massive scale of the operations taxed UK facilities, requiring use of most any coastal port regardless of its capability. Some vessels were loaded at ports as far north as Belfast. To embark V Corps, the 1st and 29th IDs used ten UK ports including Poole, Weymouth, Torquay, Brixham, Dartmouth, Salcombe, Plymouth, Fowey, and Falmouth/Helford. At these locations the naval forces berthed, launched, and trained with 3,500 landing craft of various designs. However, many of these locations housed relatively small ports, having no real embarkation facilities, and were subject to large tidal variations.[73] Using such limited facilities, movements to the embark points, staging of equipment, and loading had to be carefully timed to avoid congestion ashore and afloat. With many ports having limited infrastructure, the Royal Navy constructed loading ramps (referred to as "hards") to facilitate embarkation that were determined to be "invaluable." With problems identified during these exercises and landings, army and navy forces refined their combat loading, adjusted embarkation scheduling, and solidified plans by D-20. With this refinement effort, the plans and schedules of the two services (army and navy) had no ship requiring more than forty-eight hours of preloading time.[74]

Traffic loggerheads were a concern at the ports surrounding communities, as the UK road networks were often limited and narrow. Many of the relevant areas had unpaved roads with only trails or paths available. Some routes were capable of single vehicle traffic or the occasional horse cart. While the Americans helped build and improve roads and other infrastructure, there were reports of 24,000 traffic accidents, with a large percentage at speeds less than five miles per hour.[75] Movements from "sausages," or marshaling areas, to ports of embarkation with thousands of men and vehicles often clogged existing road networks and threatened planned movements. With local British subjects already tolerating the friendly invasion and large American presence, in April Ike asked the British government to ban all nonmilitary traffic between southern England and the rest of the island. Acceding to this request British authorities forbade any civilians from visiting the coast between Norfolk and Cornwall.[76]

To deconflict and manage traffic between the national fleets in the English Channel, American forces staged at ports from the Isle of

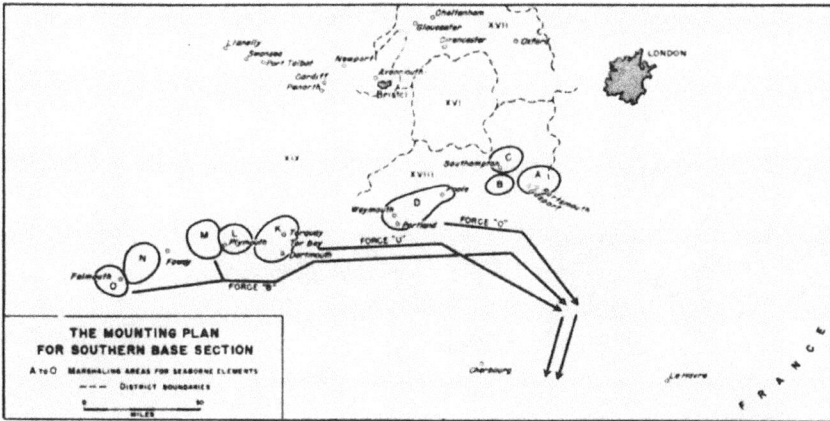

Marshalling areas and movement of American convoys from the western UK ports to the Channel assembly area. (CARL Digital Archive)

Portland west to Falmouth. UK forces generally staged in the east from around the Isle of Wight. Given this disposition, American troops traversed longer transit routes, with some troops at sea in landing craft up to H-39 hours.[77] Convoys proceeded based on the tactical plan and tides, with sailing speeds reflective of their cargos or mission sets. The management of movement required an intricate dance of ships and timing. Fire-support ships and transports sailed at twelve knots while landing craft such as LSTs, LCMs, and LCTs used for the assault moved slower at only five knots. The slow movement ensured convoy integrity, with many of the LSTs also towing causeway sections and other lighterage used for amphibious movement ashore. Such convoys included hundreds of ships. For example, the Task Force O convoy consisted of 11 LSTs (with lighterage in tow); 2 LCIs; 168 LCTs; 84 minor vessels (control craft/scout boats); and 28 escorts (destroyers or patrol boats).[78] Navigation within the Channel was well orchestrated, with minesweepers marking approaches, a special QH (Gee Navigation System) radio beacon installed on some ships and landing craft, and an additional beacon operating at Pointe de Barfleur. Navigation was a key component for traffic control and timing. Fire-support ships needed to arrive four and a half hours before the landing vessels to be in place providing naval gunfire support at H-Hour or before. Additionally, LCTs carrying tanks also had to arrive in time to launch the armor and allow it sufficient time to swim ashore with the initial assault waves.[79]

Considerable discussion was given to the timing of the landings.

US troops coming ashore at Slapton Sands UK during exercises conducted by US forces in preparation for the cross-channel invasion. (US Navy photo)

Approaching Normandy under cover of darkness was generally agreed upon. However, given the Germans had placed extensive underwater obstacles and mines, debate ensued about the best time and dates for the assault. Normandy's spring tidal variations were as large as twenty feet, and at Omaha Beach the low ebb created a tidal flat of 300 yards. These high and low tides occurred twice during a twenty-four-hour interval. If the landings came in at high tide, amphibious craft could travel closer to shore and deposit assault forces nearer to the objectives. However, the submerged defensive obstacles would likely disrupt landing craft ingress and prematurely attrite assault forces even before they reached the shingle. If assault forces waited until low tide, the landing craft could avoid the exposed obstacles and land safely short of them. But by landing short, soldiers would have to debark farther from dry land and then be exposed to enemy fire in the open tidal plain while trying to make it to the Normandy shingle.[80]

Additionally, at low tide NSFS vessels would be farther from the targets, possibly precluding effective inland targeting. Furthermore, at the British beaches (Gold, Sword, and Juno) rocks and natural obstacles created additional problems within the surf zone. With all these variables at the five landing beaches, planners determined that the best window of opportunity was 5–7 June. Complicating the decision was that all landings were supposed to occur simultaneously.

Given the hydrographic differences of the assault beaches, planners also concluded that H-Hour should occur at different times based on tidal variations at individual assault beaches. However, they also believed that the ordered H-Hours should not vary more than an hour between the British and American sectors.[81] Eventually planners determined that the best aggregate tidal conditions for the Allied assault occurred at 0630.[82]

Taking their experiences from Husky and other operations, the Allies determined that the initial landings were to take place in daylight, as NSFS and CAS were vital, with both applications requiring visual targeting. This contrasted from the early-morning H-Hour times for previous MTO assaults and was a significant change to US amphibious operations in the ETO. Troop movement was not necessarily under cover of darkness (although much of the landing craft embarkation was), making wave assembly and formation easier; NSFS and CAS could be employed with visual sighting methods, with overall situational awareness improved. While some radar targeting was used, visual sighting was preferred with troops "danger close." In previous assaults amphibious planners felt they did not have overwhelming strength in both air and sea, thus requiring the cover of darkness.[83] However, by the time of Overlord the material momentum had shifted in favor of the Allies. Given the size and capability of the Overlord amphibious force, the element of surprise was not considered as important, with joint fires integration occurring before landing.

A significant change from all preceding assaults was the prelanding bombardment of the objective beaches with NSFS. Preparatory fires had been frowned at by army commanders, as the element of surprise was seen as more important. This was a topic of much debate between CATF and CLFs, with the ground component having final say in the matter. Such decisions yielded unfortunate consequences, especially during the Salerno landings. Overlord would be different, at least in terms of planning and intent. Use of pre–H-Hour fires was a significant development of the invasion, with the CTF 122 commander determined that, during "pre–H-Hour bombardment and in the close support of troops fighting inland, naval guns lived up to our highest expectations."[84]

However, such a claim requires some nuance depending on which beach a soldier landed at what time. Initial assault waves going ashore at Omaha certainly could make a case that the pre–H-Hour fires were largely ineffective, with most enemy positions intact and manned. For safety, NSFS was to cease once troops were ashore, with ships directed not to fire unless exceptionally definitive targets appeared or until a liaison was made with shore-based fire control parties.[85] With such measures in place and given the incoming fire many of the men landing in the Dog Sector at Omaha would probably disagree with CTF 122's observation. Most, if not all, of the hardened and prepared German defenses on Omaha remained intact, unhit by the aerial bombing or naval guns. Many of the Germans' defensive Widerstandsnester (resistance nests, or WNs) were of robust construction and cleverly concealed, avoiding the superior Allied firepower.

While the prelanding bombardment was planned, getting the platforms required proved problematic. Despite the importance of the operation, at the beginning of 1944 Admiral Kirk at CTF 122 made numerous requests for battleships and other gunfire support ships without much success. Frustrated, and taking advantage of a Chief of Naval Operations representative attending February's 1944 Landing Craft Conference in the United Kingdom, he and Admiral Hall of Task Force O approached Rear Admiral Charles Cooke of King's staff. During their meeting the theater commanders strongly expressed displeasure at Washington's lack of response regarding fire-support assets. Support from destroyers, battleships, and other surface combatants was an imperative, especially since the landing forces expected pre—H-Hour fires. According to Hall: "I banged my fists on the table and said 'It[']s a crime to send me on the biggest amphibious attack in history with such inadequate support. . . . All I'm asking you to do is to detach a couple of squadrons of destroyers from some transoceanic convoy, give them to me, [and] give me a chance to train them in naval gunfire support for the American Army at the Omaha Beaches.'"[86] As the CLF, Bradley also was frustrated with the paucity of fire support ships assigned, writing: "I begged the navy to stack the odds more heavily on our side. Eventually Washington agreed to Kirk's bombardment fleet. . . . It could not be called a formidable force in terms of the Pacific naval campaign, but at least our pinchpenny days were ended." Successful in his approach, Kirk was able to finally secure a bombardment fleet consisting of at least three battleships, three heavy cruisers, six light cruisers, and twenty-two destroyers.[87]

While the larger US ships had maximum ranges from 18,000 to 33,000 yards, with the destroyers having 18,000, the published fire plan placed supporting battleships and cruisers 6,000–12,000 yards from the beach and potentially out of range of enemy artillery fire.[88] As H-Hour passed, the incoming tide allowed naval platforms to move closer to the beach. With this tidal variation, NSFS also was able to

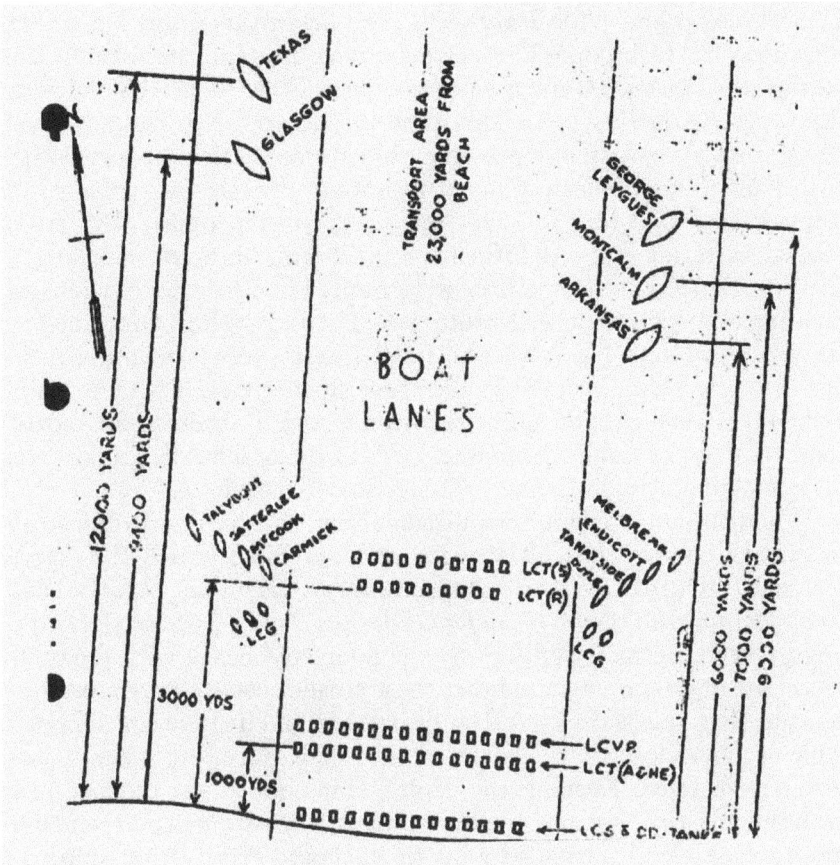

Initial fire support schematic for V Corps on D-Day. Note the distances offshore and the organization of the initial waves. (CARL Digital Archive)

move nearer the enemy positions and provide additional firepower ashore. As per the plan, such support was broken into three phases. The first was targeting counterbattery fire on German artillery and fixed positions. The second focused on defensive obstacles and positions. And the third was largely on-call and tasked dynamically. While many of the prelanding fires were ineffective, during the third phase naval fires were invaluable and reduced many WNs, pinning down assault forces ashore. As in previous operations, naval fire control parties accompanied landing forces, thereby providing an important link to the fleet and valuable information on targets, locations, and adjustments.[89]

American ships providing fires for Task Force O were the battleships

USS *Arkansas* and USS *Texas* with nine destroyers from Destroyer Squadron 18. Task Force U received similar assets in the form of the battleship USS *Nevada* and the heavy cruiser USS *Tuscaloosa* along with destroyers from Destroyer Divisions 34 and 20.[90] French and Royal Navy ships also assisted in providing much-needed fire support. With fire channels swept clean of mines inshore of the transport area, naval assets moved into position and began receiving incoming fires from coastal batteries at 0535. Fifteen minutes later at 0550 prearranged fire commenced, but some fires were limited in effect, with defensive positions too robust or well-protected. The larger ships continued to fire after H-Hour, but it was the smaller destroyers providing timely and efficient on-call NSFS. While these smaller vessels were initially tasked to screen the invasion fleet from enemy U-boats and E-boats, many destroyers came within 800 yards of the beaches to support the assault with only a few inches of water under their keels.[91]

When the pre–H-Hour bombardment at Omaha failed to destroy or silence enemy guns, destroyers such as USS *Emmons* (DD-457), *Carmick* (DD-493), *McCook* (DD-496), *Doyle* (DD-494), *Baldwin* (DD 624), *Harding* (DD-625), *Frankford* (DD-497), and *Thompson* (DD-627) engaged the German WNs along the contested beach with great effect. One naval officer stated that these smaller vessels were more important than the larger capital ships in terms of effective fire support. Able to move closer to the beach, their 5-inch guns were accurate and expertly handled. Keeping the capital ships out at sea reduced risk from enemy fire, but the smaller ships were easily more expendable and replaceable. To assist in joint fires, aboard every firing ship was an army artillery officer with information regarding the location of troops ashore. On land the forty-four Naval Shore Fire Control Parties (SFCP) were to maintain contact with ships by radio link and then designate each target by map grid. Ships' crews controlled the firing, with SFCP spotting the results and adjusting fire. Of course, if the SFCP did not make it ashore or had been incapacitated, calls for fire could not be generated.[92]

The destroyers provided support during H-Hour and beyond. Assisting the landings in Easy Red and Fox Green Sectors, USS *Doyle* expended 364 rounds of 5-inch general-purpose rounds at 0650 with additional salvoes minutes later hitting gun batteries ashore. USS *Carmick* silenced an enemy position at 0647 in support of 116th RCT with USS *Thompson* hitting field guns at 0716 with the latter (along with *McCook*) providing addition fire support at noon at the mouth of the

Vierville Draw.[93] In the same sector a SFCP requested and received fire support from USS *Carmick* at 0810. *Carmick* provided additional support to the advance into the Vierville Draw, shooting targets on the bluffs engaged by ground forces. Despite the lack of radio contact with forces ashore, the ship fired salvos in areas targeted by troops ashore and shifted fires as required.[94] Later that morning USS *McCook* also provided support to Dog Green, coming as close as 1,300 yards of the beachline to engage targets.[95] USS *Frankfort* serviced targets on Easy Red without actual calls for fire. At 1036 and firing from a distance of 1,200 yards, *Frankfort* hit an enemy mortar battery that had pinned down assault forces. Observers on deck reported smoke rising from the targeted position and enemy troops surrendering.[96]

Dedicated to silencing enemy positions, many destroyers sailed so close to shore that they received enemy machine-gun and rifle damage to their hulls and superstructures.[97] USS *Baldwin* reported direct hits from 88mm or 105mm shore batteries near Fox Green at 0820, returning fire minutes later.[98] While the navy provided NSFS in the sector, not having established radio contact with landing troops resulted in small cases of fratricide. In one instance light signals were used by troops ashore to order a cease fire.[99] Offshore near Fox Green USS *Harding* received a request at 1854 targeting the steeple located in Colleville. Expending sixty rounds at a range of 3,500 yards, the naval guns hit the steeple and leveled parts of the town. However, in the process the incoming fires inflicted casualties on US troops in the vicinity.[100] Despite this unfortunate episode, CTF 122 found any reports of large-scale fratricide by the landing forces to be "completely inaccurate."[101]

With German defenders delivering withering fire on the landing force, Admiral Charles Bryant on the USS *Texas* radioed nearby destroyers: "Get on them, men! Get on them! They [the enemy] are raising hell with the men on the beach, we can't have any more of that! We must stop it."[102] As the morning progressed, smaller ships continuously engaged targets of opportunity, with *Frankfort* servicing targets in direct support of the 116th at Dog White and Dog Red.[103] Other ships came within a few hundred yards of the beach, and by noon calls for fires and servicing of targets of opportunity increased as troops moved into the E-1 and E-3 draws.[104] In addition to the destroyers, USS *Texas* aimed at the town of Vierville, keeping German positions pinned down. With Wehrmacht troops dazed from the incoming 14-inch naval shells, they surrendered as elements of the 29th finally moved inland.[105] Indeed, the price was high in men and material, with chaos in some sectors of Omaha Beach, but the integration of NSFS enabled the landing force to reach its D-Day objectives.

While the navy was skimping in its allocation of naval fire platforms given the importance of the landing, by this time the army and navy established great trust regarding joint fire applications. With some fires executed by visual and ad hoc means, the established method to call for fire was through use of SFCPs. Nine were assigned to each infantry division along with others assigned to individual Ranger or airborne battalions and field artillery headquarters.[106] Each team consisted of one army and one naval officer, with twelve enlisted men equipped with two SCR-609 radios and a frequency modulation set landing in the early assault waves or with paratroopers. Able to observe fires, these teams helped describe the target, identify its location, and walk fires to the designated targets ashore from ships at sea. Similarly, naval platforms providing fires had an accompanying SCR-608 radio, and the combination of the two sets proved reliable and flexible. In addition, a naval gunfire liaison officer was assigned to each artillery battalion's fire direction center to coordinate and direct the activities of the three SFCP in his sector, with similar representation at the division artillery headquarters.[107]

Supporting these naval fires was the use of the aerial spotters that had been so effective in previous assaults. Planes from the Royal Naval Air Service, RAF, US Navy, and USAAF flew as spotters and operated in the AOA during the assault. Beginning to arrive approximately an hour before the preparatory fires, the planes were to establish contact using multiple frequencies designated for CTF 122 spotting.[108] Once on station, spotter aircraft worked in pairs, with one adjusting fires while the other served as a weaver providing escort protection for the other. Loiter times were planned for a forty-five-minute run over the assault area. However, only 42 percent of the spotting missions flown adjusted fires, as weather, communications, and mechanical failures precluded a larger application. As a result, coverage suffered at times.[109] Nevertheless, when employed it was very effective. Out of the 229 shots conducted with aerial spotting, 75 percent neutralized or destroyed the intended target. While this is an impressive statistic, CTF 122 was disappointed with the number of calls for support from aerial spotting missions, as more were expected. Regardless, this was a proven concept, with CTF 122 concluding that "spot and deliberate fire cover over a long period are required to neutralize and destroy concrete batteries or strong points."[110]

In addition to the more traditional forms of fire support, CTF 122 also used a host of specialized landing craft to provide specific types of effects during the invasion. Numerous Landing Craft Gun (Large) took station on the flanks of assault waves to engage beach defenses as soon as possible with continuous fire. Modified LCTs were fitted with two 4.7-inch guns and have been referred to as "mini destroyers," providing quick NSFS. Of similar size was the Landing Craft Tank (Rocket), provided High Explosive fire on targets approximately 600 yards off shore using multiple rocket launchers. Again, using the LCT as the base platform and affixed with a radar for range-finding, the vessel could launch approximately 1,000 5-inch rocket in salvos to saturate area targets. Landing Craft Support (Medium), also stationed on the flanks of the assault waves, provided additional firepower. This craft carried an array of weapons and was especially useful in laying smoke to obscure the landing force from enemy observation. The vessel also included a complement of heavy machine guns and mortars. Finally Landing Craft Flak (LCF) provided antiaircraft cover against low-flying aircraft. All these vessels fell under command of CTF 122.[111]

The placement of specific troops to certain vessels involved meticulous and laborious planning. Troops in assault waves and their associated gear were the only units assigned to a specific craft of ship. However, planners generally avoided splitting up tactical units from their equipment.[112] With the experiences in the MTO, both armies learned that assaulting troops had to move fast off the landing craft and get ashore as quickly as possible. While individual troop equipment sets were cut down to lighten the soldiers' loads, assault units were also reconfigured. Like the navy's suggestion years earlier about a smaller-size division for amphibious operations, the recommendation was now partially accepted. Battalion organizational overheads and logistics were also reduced, with the traditional infantry structures adjusted for the ship-to-shore movement and assault. Rifle companies were reconfigured as teams, with platoons split into two assault sections, each with twenty-nine men, as that was all that could fit on one LCVP.

Assault teams reflected more of a combined arms mix that included bazookas, flamethrowers, a Browning Automatic Rifle section, 60mm mortars, and an attachment of engineers. Companies were given 81mm mortars and heavy machine guns as additional support. After the platoons made it to shore, the formation would revert to its traditional structure.[113] Taking lessons from earlier operations, care was taken to reduce the soldiers' loads for better mobility once ashore. Troops were issued only three K-rations and three D-rations but came ashore with plenty of ammunition. Riflemen carried ninety-six rounds, with each Browning Automatic Rifle team transporting nine hundred. Also, 60mm mortar crews came ashore with twenty rounds, with all soldiers carrying five hand grenades.[114]

While infantry battalions were pared down organizationally, in return each infantry regiment received a battalion of tanks in direct support to help spearhead the assault. With the introduction of the amphibious-capable tanks and LCTs, planners expected ample armor to support infantry in the initial wave.[115] However, getting the armor ashore provided its own challenges. Armor was to be delivered by two methods: one used specifically modified LCTs that beached themselves under enemy fire, and the other required the tanks to "swim" to shore. The LCTs taking armor to the beaches, designated LCT(A, for "armor"), were designed to carry two M4 Sherman tanks on a ramped, elevated platform, allowing them to fire over gunwales as a form of offensive fire. These vessels were also equipped with additional protection for the more vulnerable parts of the ship.[116] Plans had the armor shooting High Explosive rounds at visible targets inbound and as permitted. When approximately 2,000–3,000 yards out, tanks with T34 Calliope rocket launchers affixed to their hulls were to drench area targets.[117] The second method discharged armor offshore with specially designed skirts allowing the tank to float. These tanks included a Dual Drive (DD) capability that operated a shaft from the engine driving propellers located at the tank's rear. With three armor battalions in direct support, planners hope to place sixty-four tanks ashore in the first few hours.[118]

DD tanks were to be launched from their landing ship at the discretion of the army commander present, with the 70th Tank Battalion swimming 3,000–5,000 to Utah Beach. Twenty-eight tanks made it ashore fighting with the 4th ID conducting combined arms operations.[119] Similarly, elements of the 741st Tank Battalion successfully landed on Omaha Beach's Easy Red and Fox Green Sectors, providing armor support to the 16th Regimental Combat Team. At H-Hour five DDs landed on Easy Red and immediately went into action. Ten minutes later A Company landed under fire (less three tanks) astride Easy Red and Fox Green and hit enemy positions and targets of opportunity, assisting in the assault of the bluffs near and above the beachline. For the next few hours these tanks knocked out prepared defensive positions near the E-3 exit between WN 61 and WN 62, with more of the battalion's assets coming ashore throughout the day.[120]

However, the Dog beaches at Omaha saw the unloading of DDs some 6,000 yards from the beach and having to travel the distance with 10–18-knot winds and three- to six-foot waves. The decision to launch the tanks this far out was made before (H-50 hours) by the B Company and C Company commanders of the 743st Tank Battalion.[121] The decision was ill-advised; of the thirty-four tanks launched at sea and headed for the Dog beaches, twenty-seven were swamped, with only two swimming the full distance. Three more tanks came ashore on LCT(A)s, with a total of five landing in the sector.[122] One veteran observed that, of the few that made it ashore, most in the initial wave never made it past the sea wall, hit mines, ran in to obstacles, or took direct hits from enemy fire.[123] However, eight tank bulldozers of A Company made landfall after H-Hour at Easy Green and Dog Red near exit D-3 and drew enemy fire away from exposed troops coming ashore or on the beach.[124] While the assault beaches were awash in men, vehicles, and material, combat power continued building as the morning passed. With more armor making it to shore in subsequent assault waves, and as part of the combined arms fight, in fighting near Le Moulins the commanding officer of 2nd Battalion, 116th Regiment remembered that "tanks saved the day. . . . They shot the hell out of the Germans . . . and got the hell shot out of them."[125] The next day, D+1, the 747th Tank Battalion rolled ashore, moving up the Vierville Draw and supporting operations inland and movement toward Isigny.[126]

The LCT(A)s were not the only landing craft taking armored vehicles ashore. Self-Propelled LCTs (SPs) were modified to carry the tank-chassised M7 105mm artillery pieces. Much like the M4s shooting over the gunwales, when embarked the M7 self-propelled artillery could be used while afloat in direct and indirect modes. Ammunition expenditures while en route for LCTs carrying M4s and M7s were not to expand the vehicles' normal combat load. In this regard shooting while en route required additional magazine storage aboard the landing craft in accordance with the ship's capabilities. The ship's magazine stock was separate from the vehicle's organic supply of rounds.[127]

However, use of the weapon en route still required a forward observer with alternate means of communication. The observer had to be within the same wave and able to call cease fire when the LCT(SP)s came within 1,000 yards of the beach. While the armor in Dog Sector was decimated and smoke precluded effective NSFS, providing direct support to the 116th was the 58th Armored Vehicle Battalion. The unit splashed into the water, took position offshore, then commenced firing from landing craft afloat from H-30 to H-5. With liaison personnel going ashore by 0700, the unit hit targets in Dog Green Sector at a time when NSFS was suspended due to the close proximity of ground forces. As a result, it was the only unit providing supporting fires to this area of the landing beaches that morning.[128] By noon, the 58th had eleven guns ashore and by evening was supporting the 116th as it pushed inland.[129]

Many other modifications were done to various landing craft, especially to quickly develop combat power ashore and establish beachheads. Taking lessons learned from the MTO, the army found that certain types of landing craft were more efficient in disgorging selected payloads than others. To expedite debarkation at the assault beaches, LCVPs and LCIs transported troops, while vehicles and equipment landed via LCMs and LCTs. In support of the requirement for quick debarkation, all the LCTs of the Western Naval Task Force were installed with a Mulock Ramp that decreased the angle between the craft's ramp and the beach, facilitating quicker discharge ashore.[130] As during the Anzio landings, use of mobile loads on LCMs and LCTs was a far quicker way to debark material than having coxswains hand-deliver supplies ashore from smaller landing craft.

Airpower increasingly became an integral part of ETO amphibious assaults. At the 1943 conference the US Army Air Corps representative, Brigadier General A. C. Candee, agreed that the invasion required a "well[-]trained and efficient air staff organization and air–army–navy teamwork [to] permit the whole operation [to be] controlled by the supreme tactical commander."[131] He argued that close liaison between the tactical air force and the assault force was essential. This required a joint air headquarters in the United Kingdom, with others afloat to liaise directly with ground and naval commanders. In addition, he outlined the use of air support parties ashore with the ability to communicate with the air headquarters afloat and with aircraft overhead. This capability took the form of Jeep-mounted SCR-193 radios as during the previous campaigns.[132] General Candee's points were echoed by Hewitt's post-Husky recommendation: "Where practicable, naval aviation should be used for CAS in amphibious operations. Where it is not practicable, Army dive bomber forces should be assigned under the operational control of the naval commander to carry out vital CAS missions until the ground forces are firmly established ashore."[133] The USAAF balked at such a suggestion, as BAI and CAS efforts were handled by the air personnel. But by this time the air component realized that air planning and execution had become an increasingly joint endeavor.

Regarding composition of airpower allocations during the assault, Candee argued that 50 percent of the striking force should be designated for predetermined targets, with alternates assigned. Also, 25 percent should be held on alert status controlled by the air support control center afloat, with the remaining 25 percent used when circumstances dictated. While this was his conclusion in 1943, operations on the Italian peninsula proved invaluable, as both air and ground planners started developing methods for more effective air support and dynamic taskings. USAAF planners began focusing on transportation targets to preclude the movement of German reinforcements and to isolate the battlefield. Aviation's ability to shape the battlefield, cover ship-to-shore movement, and support subsequent operations ashore was coming to fruition, eventually fulfilled by the direct assignment of the 9th and 8th Air Forces.

Pre–D-Day and pre–H-Hour attacks were a key element of the shaping operation, as discussed at the 1943 conference.[134] Unlike in the Sicily operation, air planners learned from the Salerno and Anzio operations of the need for air superiority in the AOA.[135] While the Luftwaffe had free reign over the Husky flotilla and managed to mount a presence over the Avalanche and Shingle operations, reduction of the enemy air threat on 6 June was clearly a requirement. To the credit of the USAAF, by the time of Overlord, air superiority was established within the AOA, with only minor night raids reported and little enemy presence over the beaches or the fleet during the day.[136] According to the Luftwaffe's own reports, the Allies had an overwhelming numerical superiority of all types of aircraft with an overall ratio of 20:1. When major combat operations commenced, the ratio became even more stark and was estimated at 40:1.[137] While air superiority was always a concern for the Allied air forces and was clearly established, it enable other tasks outlined in *FM 100-20*. As a result, support to ground forces in direct contact was no longer an afterthought but rather a deliberate part of air planning and the campaign. Although the USAAF might have been lacking airframes and capability in the MTO, its capabilities in summer 1944 were more robust, competent, and effective. This establishment of air superiority was largely a result of the attritional fight the USAAF had been waging directly against the Luftwaffe since February 1944.

Given the previous assaults and campaigns, the requirement for effective air-ground coordination quickly became evident. Reflecting this need, in the United States the army established the Joint Air-Ground Action Ground Liaison Officer School in January 1944. With the school's mission of training specialized liaison personnel for such operations, the mere establishment of such a facility was a recognition of the importance of combined arms integration.[138] However, not all airmen were of the same mind. Many remained steadfastly devoted to the concept of daylight strategic bombardment. In the weeks leading up to the 6 June invasion, the US 8th Air Force conducting the strategic campaign over Germany allocated 84 percent of its assets to the cross-channel operation. Many USAAF officers objected to this allocation and saw it as a distraction from the ongoing Pointblank Combined Bomber Offensive. For many, the strategic effort was a separate endeavor from the other domains. As Commander, US Strategic Air Forces, Spaatz complained about the use of strategic bombers to shape the Normandy battlefield. He thought the war would end quicker by continuing to hit targets in greater Germany to reduce Nazi morale and production capabilities.[139]

While the postwar US Strategic Bombing Survey equivocally concluded Spaatz's claim was inaccurate, many airmen at the time failed to understand the decisiveness and importance of the cross-channel invasion.[140] The role strategic bombardment played in the overall victory was argued for years, with those in Air Force blue claiming a dubious success. Strategic airpower advocates protested the use of bombers to support the Normandy landings. Butting heads with airmen who resisted such taskings, Ike concluded that he needed to exercise command over all Allied assets (including the US Strategic Air Forces), and if he could not, then he should "simply have to go home." By 7 April Ike won the argument and received authority to direct the US Strategic Air Forces and the RAF to support the landings and participate in this most important operation of the war.[141] Regardless of the USAAF's strategic bombing efforts, in his role as Supreme Allied Commander Ike had to exercise his authority, take the reins, and yoke his air commanders into the larger joint fight.

USAAF targeting was predicated on the G-2 (Intelligence Section)'s assessment that the German defense on the coast was a thin "crust" with large amounts of artillery and concrete fortifications. This defensive crust was designed to take the first shock until augmented by Field Marshal Irwin Rommel's inland-based mobile armor reserve.[142] Attacking Normandy's road and other transportation networks was a key part of the pre–D-Day USAAF mission sets to preclude the movement and reallocation of German forces. Called the "Transportation Plan," the intent was to make the 100-mile radius around the assault beaches of northern France a "railroad desert."[143] Both the 8th and 9th Air Forces along with the RAF were used in pre–D-Day bombings and dropped a total of 76,200 tons on railway centers, bridges, and open lines.[144] The 9th Air Force alone sortied an average of 1,000 aircraft a day against Atlantic Wall targets.[145] In the two weeks before the invasion, the 8th Air Force dropped 13,000 tons of bombs and damaged twenty-three rail centers so badly that fifteen needed no additional attacks.[146] In addition, strategic bombers hit tactical targets to shape the AOA. From D-4 to D-1, 8th Air Force continued to hit coastal areas in northern France, with 3,386 bombers dropping 9,387 tons of bombs.[147]

In the three months preceding the invasion, the aerial shaping operation included the following targets:

Enemy aircraft factories and assembly plants, ball bearing and aircraft accessory plants, and aircraft on the ground.

Strategic rail centers, in particular those that included servicing and repair facilities essential to the enemy for the maintenance of rail communications in northern France, the Low Countries, and western Germany.

Enemy coastal batteries, Crossbow (V-1 flying bomb) launch sites, and naval installations.

Airfields and installations within 130 miles of Caen and in the Brest–Nantes area.[148]

Transportation targets were generally located around the coastal cities of Rouen, Dieppe, and Lillie along with inland towns such as Nantes, Tours, and Orleans. Attacks in general support of Neptune and the associated landings occurred over Caen, Saint-Lô, and Cherbourg.[149] By 4 June all ten rail bridges between Rouen and Conflans were knocked out as well as thirteen out of fourteen road bridges. Allied planes claimed the destruction of forty-six locomotives with another thirty-two damaged.[150] Train destruction was so effective that some rumors surfaced that French railroad engineers began calling in sick to avoid going to work. As D-Day neared, the USAAF shifted to enemy airfields, reinforcements and reserve formations, and signal and communications centers.[151] Such targeting intended not only to reduce enemy air capability but also to prevent the movement of formations and reserves in an around Normandy. Preceding the invasion, the 9th Air Force flew 2,300 sorties in just twenty hours protecting the cross-channel movement, preparing the area for the landings, and neutralizing coastal defenses while attempting to deny enemy movement to the objective area. [152]

Despite his displeasure of allocating strategic bombers in support of the amphibious landings, after Overlord Spaatz reported that "the interdiction of German rail movement to the Normandy area was effective . . . and opened the door for the invasion."[153] Supporting this statement, one German General recalled: "The main difficulties that arose for us at the time of the invasion were the systematic preparations by your air force: smashing of the main lines of communication, particularly the railway junctions."[154] Echoing the sentiment, General Fritz Bayerlain, commander of the Panzer Lehr Division in Normandy, said it took eighty hours to travel a normally twelve-hour journey to the front. When he did arrive, his command's firepower had been reduced by half. Field Marshal Gerhard von Rundstedt also complained that the constant Allied fighter attacks on transportation networks, combined with bombing of communications centers, prevented shifting German reserves that could have successfully repulsed the Allied assault.[155]

However, the results of the effort were similar to that of the entire strategic bombing effort: equivocal. While there were German reports addressing the "catastrophic effects" of the Allied effort under the Transportation Plan, subsequent reviews were not as positive. A July report from 9th Air Force stated the opposite claiming the campaign had no decisive effect.[156] Such contradictory evidence might be the result of personal perception, predisposition, stage of operation, or limited analysis. While the bocage in the Normandy region created its own difficulties for Allied forces, German resistance inland in the weeks after the Overlord landings might indicate that the Transportation Plan was less than effective. After the landings, German formations seemed able to redeploy to assault areas, although reportedly at a much slower pace. Such delays of Wehrmacht forces might have indeed been the difference in the early and tenuous phases of the assault. This was certainly true for troop movements and supplies. As a result, enough interference of tactical traffic provided precious hours to pass, allowing beachhead establishment and the reinforcement of forces ashore.[157] Even if only for a few days or even hours, delays in German movement of assets were a key component in building combat power. Debates aside regarding the Transportation Plan's overall effectiveness, airpower used in various forms was a significant part of prelanding operations as well as part of the amphibious assault.

US Army Air Force Operations for D-Day. Heavy and medium bombers were to attack targets near the shoreline while fighters were staged at various locations around the objective area conducting CAS and interdiction missions. (US Air Force map)

Providing air superiority, BAI, and various other missions, the integration of airpower along with NSFS, armor, and infantry ashore overwhelmed enemy defenses. Validating such applications, the Joint Air-Ground Action Ground Liaison Officer School after the war emphasized the importance of preinvasion air attacks combined with naval bombardment.[158]

In an untried use of airpower, on D-Day the USAAF planned to strike shore positions at night with medium bombers attacking at H-34 minutes until H-Hour in conjunction with heavy bombers attacking specific targets earlier on the assault beaches at H-314 minutes to H-44 minutes. Day strikes included dropping 860 tons of bomber per beach.[159] During this pre-assault bombardment, landing craft remained 1,000 yards offshore and were directed to maintain a five-minute interval between the last bomb dropped and the initial landings.[160] 9th Air Force delivered a final pre-assault aerial attack at H-20 to H-5 minutes along with other specific targets. Throughout the day, a 9th Air Force fleet of 1,900 aircraft continued providing CAS by responding to requests from forward observers and air liaison officers. By the end of D-Day, Allied fighters had flown nearly 2,000 sorties.[161] Similarly, strategic bombers from 8th Air Force during the first six days of June hit tactical targets, dropping more than 14,000 tons of bombs on coastal areas.[162] While the bombers were above the cloud layer and out of sight, men of the 116th Regiment saw RAF Spitfires and other aircraft protecting them from Luftwaffe attacks.[163]

To prevent fratricide the USAAF requested a larger window of time for its aerial assault. However, the request was rejected as it would affect the carefully considered H-Hour.[164] Although the use of strategic bombers was a welcome addition to amphibious assault, the effect of bombardment on D-Day is debatable, as the bombers missed the beaches with some estimates claiming that less than 2 percent of German positions were hit. In many cases the bombers dropped long, meaning they released their payloads after the aim point to deliberately avoid hitting American troops.[165] Perhaps the biggest effect of the aerial assault was psychological, one historian stating that "the encouragement of our own troops of such a tremendous show of airpower was of immense moral significance during critical hours of the assault."[166] While such was a rather fanciful claim, joint air forces integration within the larger framework of fire support was a significant change from preceding MTO operations. In another example of the increased joint interoperability between the naval and air components, 9th Air

Force submitted continuous and accurate reports of the situation over the invasion beaches to naval forces in direct assistance to surface landing operations.[167]

In addition to support from the air forces, appreciation for subsequent support was evident when ground planners included the possibility of creating airfields in the AOA only days after the initial assault. The 29th ID's operations order identified eight locations suitable for airfield operations shortly after the landings. While the nearest Luftwaffe base was in Bayeux, the 29th's operations order specified that expeditionary airfields might be established at St. Pierre Du-Pont on D+1, Colleville on D+3, and Cardonville on D+9. In addition to those named, five others were identified by grid coordinates.[168] So valuable was airpower that the first emergency landing strip (ELS-1) was established at Pouppeville southeast of Utah Beach by 2115 on D-Day, with the first Advance Landing Ground airfield becoming operational a week later.[169] By D+24 (June 30) American engineers established nine expeditionary airfields in northern France and finished seventeen more by D+89 (29 August).[170] Clearly, appreciation for what airpower could bring to the fight during the amphibious assault and in subsequent operations ashore was understood.

Supporting NSFS and air-ground coordination required a robust communications network. The size and scope of communications requirements had grown exponentially along with Allied amphibious capabilities. One narrative claimed that communications requirements for Overlord were "perhaps twenty-five times greater than it had for Torch."[171] The invasion plans called for the use of over 90,000 transmitters within the same AOA. Making matters worse was the increased use of radars and other sensors that might interfere with voice communications. To help address this problem, communications personnel reduced the number of kilocycles for ground-based units from 5kc to 4kc, which required grinding down radio crystals. In addition, SHAEF published twenty-one detailed sets of instructions, annexes, charts, and other documents laying down policies and other technical orders.[172]

SFCPs communicating with vessels offshore carried SCR-609 and SCR-284 radios with fire-support ships directed to use the initial crystal settings for their shipboard SCR-608 sets. Designated FM and AM frequencies were assigned to Force O and Force U units, with the assignment of channels having been developed to avoid stepping on each other due to similar kilocycles or megacycles. Facilitating identification of transmitting/receiving parties, each ship and shore liaison element was assigned a specific three alpha-numeric call sign. For example, USS *Nevada*'s call sign was "DVN," with a shore party counterpart with the 1st Battalion, 116th RCT (SFCP 3) assigned "KRD."[173]

In another example of better air-ground coordination during an amphibious assault, air representation at sea was more robust than in previous operations. Air support parties were established within each regimental combat team, division, and corps headquarters and were planned to have vehicle-mounted VHF/HF radios that could range to the Allied Expeditionary Air Force Advanced Headquarters Combined Control Center at Uxbridge.[174] While these teams had the ability to communicate with aircraft overhead, they were discouraged from doing so as it would preclude effective management of the larger effort. Much like before, Air Operations Centers were again located on flagships coordinating joint fires during the assault.[175] However, as Overlord unfolded, centralized control from Uxbridge was not as responsive as expected, with the air element aboard *Ancon* subsequently receiving directive authority over aircraft.[176]

Air planners anticipated the need for on-call targets and directed ASPs to radio directly to the Combined Control Center at Uxbridge. However, during the embarkation planning the ASPs assigned SCR-399 HF radios, with a range of 100 miles, had to be mounted on a 2½-ton truck. Given this requirement, the SCR-399 radios were determined to be too large and vulnerable. As a result, they were replaced with smaller, less capable SCR-284 radios that had a range of only twenty-five miles.[177] Given this limitation, air representatives on the CTF flagships at times ended up relaying requests from the ASPs to Uxbridge. As at Salerno and Anzio, Fighter Direction Tenders (FDTs) and GCI-LSTs served as the eyes and ears of the invasion fleet. Again they filled the gap, providing defensive coverage and acting as forward controllers until those functions were passed ashore.[178] Again placed in the shipping lanes, these vessels provided defensive and offensive fighter control functions for the respective beaches during the assault phase.[179] For the airborne drops, the IX Air Support Command's Visual Forward Direction Post was designed to direct day fighters over the 101st AB.[180] Facilitating the air–sea coordination, up to eleven communications networks were established to connect 9th Air Force, CTF 122, and Task Forces O and U with a host of other frequencies.[181]

With the introduction of the SCR-300 radio at Anzio, communications for units at division level and below improved dramatically. Training on this piece of equipment was a required part of the Overlord prelanding syllabus.[182] However, in addition to the various radio

nets created for the joint force, providing reports of ammunition consumption and supply in forward areas, a more low-tech solution was
also adopted. The Neptune operations order included an assignment
to 282nd Signal Pigeon Company to provide cross-channel communications. With lofts located on the southern coast of England, accompanying lofts for 300 pigeons were established far ashore by D+6
with full capability by D+18. This ancient form of communication was
used by army ordnance and quartermaster officers in forward dumps
and supply trains to submit their daily reports. Quartermaster reports
were submitted by releasing two pigeons daily with coded messages
in duplicate. Replacement birds were forwarded to these ammunition
units daily in sets of four. This method was also expected to be used
during communications emergencies when other forms had failed or
when radio silence was ordered.[183] Planners determined that the birds
could cover distances incrementally: 10 miles in 30 minutes; 30 miles
in 45 minutes; or 60 miles in 75 minutes. As a caution, handlers were
warned that the pigeons' homing instincts were unreliable at night and
during bad weather.[184] This was a joint endeavor, as pre–D-Day training occurred with birds released from LCTs twenty miles offshore and
even used during many planned exercises.[185] With all the Allied technical prowess, time-proven methods still held some validity.

Similar to Husky and Avalanche, airborne operations were part of
the assault phase and played a key role in neutralizing enemy units inland. With the 101st AB and 82nd AB Divisions flying from the United
Kingdom on D-1/D-Day to the Cotentin Peninsula, care was taken to
avoid the tragedy of the initial Husky drops and the D+1 insertions.
H-Hour for the airborne landings was set for 0130 on 6 June, with
approximately 13,000 paratroopers dropping into the Cherbourg area.
Although the initial plans attempted to avoid C-47s and towed gliders
flying over the fleet risking friendly-fire incidents, many last-minute
changes caused the 101st Airborne Division to pass over Force U.
However, in this instance the flight path changes were disseminated
by CTF 122 to the task force in an efficient and timely manner. With
over 1,000 planes and gliders passing over, none were fired at by Allied
ships.[186]

As in previous operations, feints and deceptions were included as
part of the cross-channel assault. Operation Bodyguard was a deliberate
attempt to deceive the Germans and cause them to make faulty strategic decisions regarding Allied actions.[187] Although the Allied deception effort conveyed possible landing locations as far away as Norway,
the Balkans, and eastern France in direct support of the cross-channel

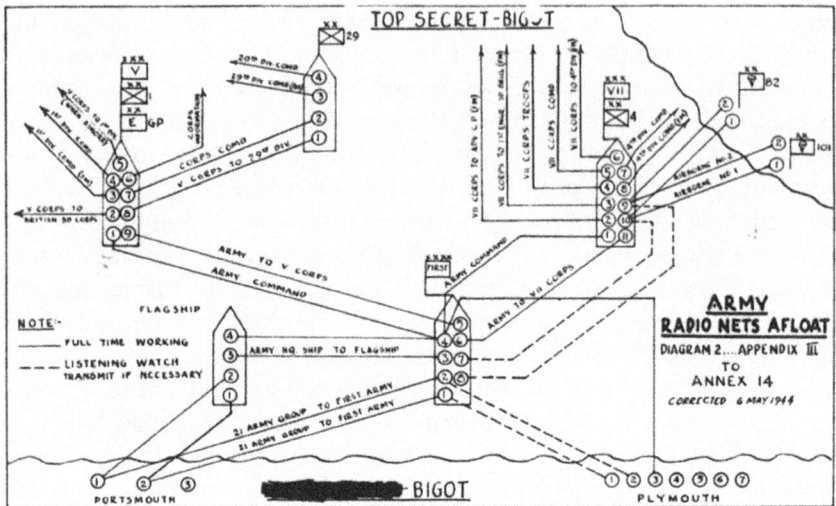

Note the number of radio nets established at the Army level to provide effective communication and coordination. Joint coordination and communication made significant improvement since Torch. (CARL Digital Archive)

invasion, Operation Fortitude (South) created a fake First United States Army Group. The nonexistent assault force was built around General Patton with decoy tanks, barges, equipment, and bogus radio traffic. The Fortitude (South) effort served to reinforce many German commanders' preconceived notions that the main attack would be at Calais at the narrowest point of the English Channel.[188] Similar to the Avalanche and Shingle operations, Neptune included diversion efforts to delay the commitment of Wehrmacht reserves and draw potential enemy naval action away from the objective area.[189] Neptune included three separate deception efforts. The first, code-named "Taxable," was focused miles east of the UK landing beaches at Cap d'Antifer. Another, code-named "Big Drum," was a counter-radar operation focused on the northeastern part of the Cotentin Peninsula. A third effort code-named "Glimmer" focused on the shore of Boulogne near Calais, feeding German preconceptions.[190] Whether it was German inclinations regarding a Calais assault, or Hitler's amateur suppositions, or these individual efforts, the fact remains that the Wehrmacht delayed the movement of its reserves and armor forces from the Calais region to Normandy.

Logistics support for the initial assault included preloaded packages of supplies and equipment from D-Day to D+2. Joint Army–Navy shore/beach parties handled the initial supply movements ashore. This was a massive undertaking, and the first two days alone saw almost 130,000 troops come ashore with 17,000 vehicles. The total plan eventually involved over a million personnel and a quarter-million vehicles.[191] Given the Allied experiences in the MTO and the large number of personnel and equipment, the use of ports and fixed facilities was important to subsequent land operations. While port facilities were the most effective for moving men and material ashore, they were vulnerable to enemy sabotage, battle damage, and poor maintenance that might limit effectiveness. Initial plans for Overlord required a minimum of 6,000 tons of supplies per day starting on D+4, growing to 9,000 tons by D+10 and 12,000 by D+16.[192] Eventually the plan called for the use of seven captured facilities in the Brittany area weeks after the initial landings. Torch made the ports and fixed facilities objectives in their own right, whereas Husky, Avalanche, and Shingle (to a degree) had used an expeditionary, over-the-shore capability. The scale and scope of Overlord and its subsequent operations inland were much bigger, suggesting novel solutions requiring a significantly more robust logistics effort.

Supplementing the logistics effort during the assault phase and providing emergency resupply, CTF 122 planned to load twenty 1,000-ton barges and haul them to the assault areas. These onetime car barges were towed across the Atlantic and were remarkably resilient to high sea states. While only sixteen barges were eventually built, they were towed into the Norman surf at high tide and then allowed to dry out (meaning settle into the sand as the tide subsided). During ebb tides, vehicles that made it ashore drove out into the surf and retrieved the prestaged supplies. While it was intended to use these on multiple occasions once the barge was empty, a lack of tugboats precluded their repeated use. When a storm precluded ship-to-shore movement, these seaborne caches proved their worth. Additionally, left in place, they found a second life as barges for subsequent ship-to-shore movement weeks after the initial landings.[193]

To allow the further prosecution of subsequent operations ashore in support of expanding the beachhead, many merchant vessels lay in reserve after the initial landings. Hours after the initial assault, the vanguard of 126 preloaded ships with 90,000 tons of supplies was already making its way to US forces.[194] In a new approach to ETO amphibious operations, a prolonged buildup period of several weeks followed the initial assault. In the effort to initiate a thrust toward Germany proper, Allied forces needed a continuous supply of vehicles and equipment

across the landing beaches.[195] Although not a part of the initial assault or the invasion flotilla, merchant vessels were preloaded with US
equipment and staged in the Bristol Channel or near the Isle of Wight.
These vessels, along with surviving LSTs, LCTs, and LCIs, began a
constant cross-channel shuttle operation. Initial estimates determined
that these supplies and lift capabilities were sufficient to counter most
enemy actions, but admittedly there was very little room for error.
This shuttle service was planned for twenty-four days until more robust facilities were established on the far shore. The vessels again were
combat-loaded and reflected anticipated priorities, with accessibility
being a key embarkation concern. Again, with combat loading, much
of a cargo vessels' available cubic space was lost as expeditious access
and prioritization remained the larger concerns. This emphasis on
combat loading was a lesson drawn from the earlier assaults, with the
tradeoff being less cargo moved but high-priority items readily available and accessible in the ships' holds.[196]

Scheduling and traffic management of follow-on shipping was accomplished via Shuttle Control aboard ship on HMS *Capetown* and
HMS *Ceres*. Shuttle Control was anchored in a mineswept area of the
English Channel with the two ships working together. *Capetown* was
anchored seaward, received inbound convoys, and directed them to
unloading berths or offshore anchorages. *Ceres* was inshore and controlled unloaded ships in return convoys to a northern assembly point.
These ships kept ground commanders informed of inbound supplies
and arrivals and assisted with unloading priorities. In executing the
mission, Shuttle Control command also had a small flotilla of escort
and dispatch ships to help guide inbound vessels to anchorages and
established beaches.[197]

In addition to the escort ships, a Naval Officer-in-Charge was located at every unloading beach working with ESBs and NBBs. Addressing the issue of poor beach party support and coordination seen
on other assaults, the Naval Officer-in-Charge served as the vital link
between naval and ground forces. Furthermore, he reported to Shuttle
Control about the status of anchorages, offload beach conditions, and
the flow inland.[198] As a result there was two-way communication to
manage seaborne traffic to and from Normandy.

Supporting the establishment of the beachhead and providing logistical requirements, a cross-channel organization had to oversee
the flow of men and material between the two shores. With ports in
the United Kingdom filled with vessels supporting expeditionary logistics, and ships headed to and from both locations, a prioritization

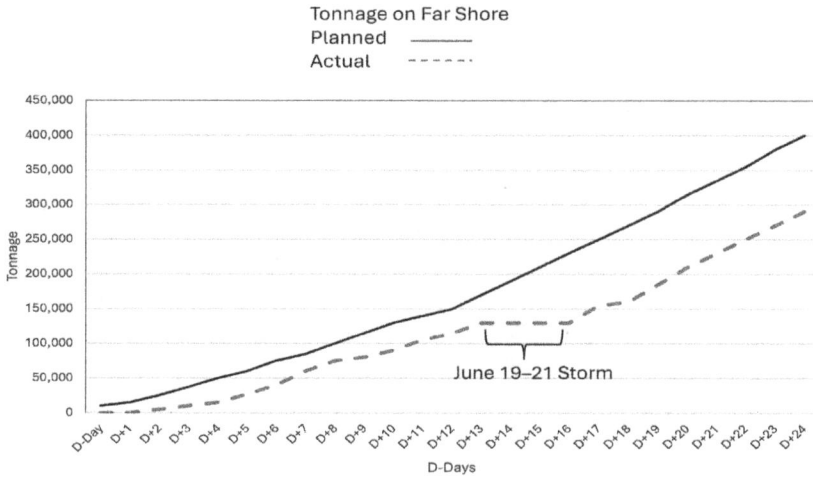

Tonnage on Far Shore
Planned   ———
Actual   - - - - -

June 19–21 Storm

D-Days

CTF 122 tonnage ashore during the first month of the Normandy campaign. (CARL Digital Archive)

and scheduling system was required. Given the combat environment, planners only could forecast requirements and available shipping.[199] However, after the assault the movement of ships and their arrival at far-shore locations required positive control and could not be subject to the vagaries of subordinate unit requirements or ship captains. With this kind of amphibious traffic cop assigning prioritization, controlling berth management, and facilitating the development of combat power ashore, the Allies also established the Build Up Control (BUCO) organization.[200] While not tasked with loading or sailing for the assault force, it worked in support of the commands on the far shore and their requirements after landing. Located at Fort Southwick near Portsmouth, the organization consisted of American and British personnel representative of all three domains—land, sea, and air.[201] Its reach was extensive, as it gave permission for units to move to their embarkation points, assigned them movement priorities, and then directed them to available shipping.

Working under BUCO was Movement Control, which gave permission for units to head to their embarkation points, thereby attempting to avoid overtaxing UK roads. Additionally, Turn Around Control oversaw the movement of ships from far-shore locations back to their original embarkation/loading points.[202] BUCO facilitated tactical requirements at the request of the actual First Army ashore and then set up what was referred to as "Little BUCO" on the far shore. Initially attached to the G-3 of 1st Army, this section kept the army group commander advised on the status of troops and equipment back in the United Kingdom.[203] The BUCO system provided an important link between the tactical level commander and the larger operational logistics infrastructure in the United Kingdom.

As the Allies expanded the beachhead and pushed inland, the logistical requirements ashore would rise exponentially. Initially, French ports were viewed as unavailable for logistics throughput due to German sabotage or battle damage. To address the logistical requirements during this crucial period, the British devised the idea of building a so-called synthetic harbor. Such a facility would handle follow-on shipping requirements in the weeks immediately after the assault, filling the gap between early Overlord requirements and the planned use of fixed ports in Brittany and Cotentin. Given the gap of time between landing and the use of available ports, British Commodore John Hughes-Hallett, who led the ill-fated Dieppe Raid in 1942, quipped: "Well all I can say is, if we can't capture a port we must take one with us."[204] With this idea in mind, at the Quebec Conference in 1943 UK representatives proposed the solution of creating a man-made breakwater to house the synthetic harbor.

The idea was championed by the British and Churchill, who had a penchant for such experiments during the war. Despite the effectiveness of the US-developed expeditionary logistics capabilities using the proven LSTs, LCTs, and other amphibious vessels, the synthetic harbor provided another alternative. Despite American skepticism over the effort, such a harbor required the development and integration of numerous complex and massive structures. Providing a breakwater for the harbor, the Allies built structures with creative names such as "bombardons," "corncobs," "phoenixes," and "gooseberries," each with a specific function in the littoral environment.[205] Inside the man-made harbor, the British developed the Lobnitz Pier, also referred to as a "spud pierhead," which served as a sea-based berth. These pierheads serviced deep-draft vessels and could also offload LCTs and LSTs offshore. Servicing amphibious vessels, pierheads could avoid the problem of stranded vessels at low tides, decrease offload times, and congestion on the shoreline.[206] Connected to the spud pierhead were "whale" roadways linked to the shore, expediting roll-on/roll-off operations. Each whale was an 80-foot steel section of bridging linked together and withstood wave action and tidal variations.[207] With these feats of naval engineering, planners expected the capability to move to 1,000–5,000 tons per day by D+20.[208]

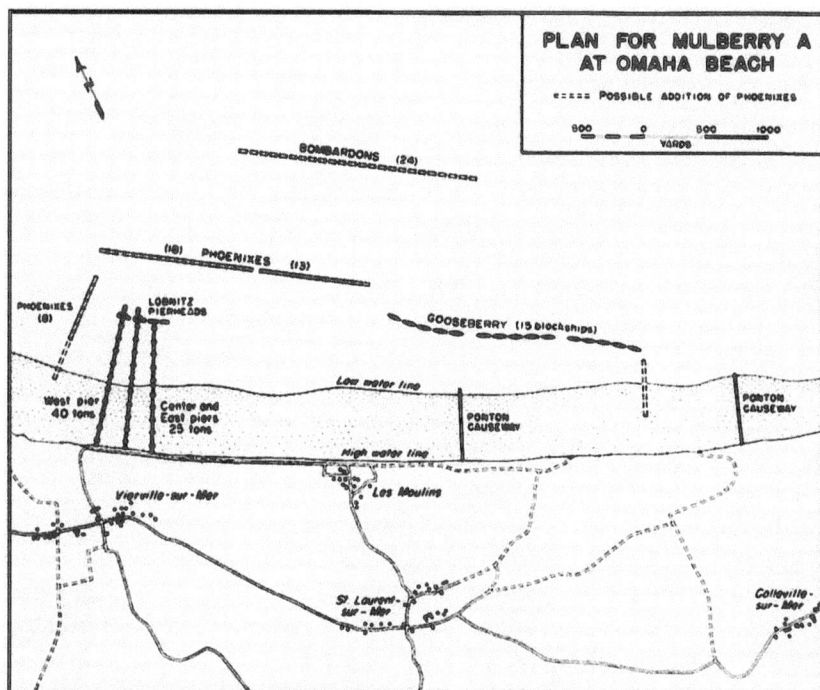

Graphic of the planned Mulberry harbors with the "phoenix" breakwaters, "Lobnitz" pier heads, and "whale" roadways linking strategic sealift to operational ground forces. (CARL Digital Archive)

Despite American skepticism about the massive undertaking, the Allies built two of these man-made harbors, one in each nation's sector. In the American sector at Omaha Beach, the man-made port, designated "Mulberry A," was planned for construction starting on D+3, with operations beginning on 16 June. Similarly, its UK counterpart, designated "Mulberry B," was placed near Arromanches-les-Bains on Gold Beach.²⁰⁹ However, these man-made harbors were heavily damaged in a 19–21 June storm. During the three-day lashing the Americans saw the seas tear Mulberry A's bombards from their moorings, along with twenty-six of the thirty-two huge phoenixes. With the breakwater failing, incoming wave actions forced the pierheads to separate from their accompanying whales, wreaking havoc on the entire system. Smaller vessels and parts of the structure were tossed about, with some landing at the highwater mark and remaining there until the tide eventually washed them back out. Taking the full force of

Mother Nature, the American synthetic harbor lay a wreck, the damage irreparable.[210]

Before building Mulberry A and in the week following the assault, debarkation of men and equipment fell short of the planned figures. Established orders called for landing 22,869 troops, but by 12 June only 17,000 had arrived. Similarly, of the 12,700 tons of supplies required, only 9,896 made it ashore, with only 2,645 vehicles out of the 4,000 scheduled. Once the Mulberry was in place, unload times for an LST or larger vessel went from twelve hours to less than two. Furthermore, the simultaneous berthing of ships and the debarkation of cargos added to increased throughput. With the pierheads and whales, the total discharge time of an LST was reduced to just over an hour, without the need of having to wait hours for the tide to come and go.[211] While this new capability was expected to sustain the force, the Mulberry's demise was feared as a huge logistical loss.

While this new ability was short-lived, conventional offload methods on the Normandy shores resulted in a marked improvement from previous operations. Soon every LCT, LCM, and DUKW was engaged in the ship-to-shore movement of supplies. These efforts, combined with the beaching of LSTs, were moving men and material ashore at a rate that planners had not foreseen and underestimated inherent throughput capabilities.[212] Despite the loss of the Mulberry, American logistics efforts in Normandy rebounded after the storm. Full resumption of offload operations started on 23 June, with both landing beaches surpassing their previous performances by unloading 10,000 tons of supplies on Omaha and 6,400 on Utah.[213] While the offload rate never fully caught up with the totals planned, enough men and material made it ashore.[214] Just over a week after the storm, both beaches handled over 161,000 tons of supplies, and by 30 June totals reached as high as 289,827. During this same period, using only conventional methodologies, Omaha processed 115 percent of its planned tonnage capacity, with Utah reaching 124 percent.[215] At the end of the month, 78 percent of planned troop movements made it ashore, along with 80 percent for supplies and equipment and 65 percent for vehicles.[216]

Supporting the logistics effort at the landing beaches, the Americans also leveraged numerous smaller ports and locations to augment offload operations. Ports at Grandcamp and Insigny were captured by D+4, with one at Carentan two days later. Facilities at all three smaller locations were intact but still required the removal of mines, minor repairs, and dredging. Grandcamp and Insigny were functioning by 23 and 24 June, respectively. Both locations were planned to have a capacity to unload only a few hundred tons a day but ultimately grew to between 1,000 and 1,500 tons.[217] Other Normandy ports used for debarkation operations included Saint-Vaast-la-Hougue and Barfleur.[218] While these smaller ports never fully reached their planned potential, they did add to the overall effort. Until the major seaport at Cherbourg became useable, Omaha and Utah remained the best beaches for logistical support. Although the American formations ashore remained short of the envisioned requirements, enough men and material made it to France. The numbers making it to the beachhead and supporting subsequent operations are indicative of how efficient and capable American expeditionary logistics had become. While the Mulberrys were an innovative effort and did gain some efficiencies, previous American methods were refined, augmented with additional organizations and men, with other innovations adding to the effort. In all, these methodologies proved sufficient to meet the combat need.

The buildup period of the Normandy operation proved to be an apex of large-scale expeditionary logistical support during the war. The movement of supplies and equipment to shore, reception on the beach, and subsequent organization were significant problems from Torch all the way through Avalanche. However, the services took careful note of the deficiencies, made organizational changes, created new methodologies, and developed new technologies to address the requirement to support the large armies ashore. Such innovations made the Overlord operation a success as American and British troops raced across northern France into greater Germany. These subsequent operations were not possible without creative solutions to the tyranny of cube, weight, and distance.

This huge effort included the three combat domains—air, land, sea—combined with the integration of every possible warfighting function in an expeditionary environment. The Overlord assault had to address each of the six characteristics of an amphibious assault on a scale never envisioned, much less attempted. While the Marine Advance Base concept initiated the American vision of forceable entry from the sea, the development of the actual application was a bloody and painful process. Compounding the problem, this endeavor also required the cooperation from the Allies, who did not always see eye to eye on problems, solutions, or strategies. The CTF 122 report of the D-Day operation specifically calls out the many lessons of previous assaults and the important role they played in the development of the Neptune/Overlord plan. Specifically, the report stated: "As our experience has accumulated, we have learned in what strength to assemble forces and how to attack positions which earlier seemed impregnable. In achieving this progress, we are but confirming historical precedents."[219]

Perhaps the most telling observations came from German Commander-in-Chief (West), Field Marshal Gerd von Rundstedt, in his report on the assault. In a 20 June communiqué, he reported:

> Four Facts must be emphasized:
> (1) The enemy's complete mastery of the air.
> (2) The skillful and large-scale employment of parachute and airborne troops.
> (3) The flexible and well directed support of the land troops by ship's artillery of strong English [Allied] naval units ranging from battleship to gunboat.
> (4) The rehearsal of the enemy invasion units for their task; most precise knowledge of the coast, of its obstacles and defense establishments, swift building of superiority of numbers and materials on the bridge [beach] head after just a few days.[220]

He went on to report what many soldiers on the ground observed: "Before the landings there was a heavy bombardment of extraordinary intensity from the sea and air, with weapons of all calibers. The consequence was that all the field defenses were more or less knocked out and "ploughed down" so that for the most part only the solid fortifications remained intact. The enemy seeped through the gaps without trying to attack the fortifications or strong points."[221] The field marshal went on to specifically address naval fires, commenting on their rapid fire capabilities, range, and ability to engage armor.[222]

A common narrative about the Overlord operations is that the armor floundered in the channel waters, the air effort missed targets, and the NSFS was ineffective. Such perceptions are superficial, devoid of detailed analysis, and ignore the contributions made along the entire V and VII Corp sectors at various times during the assault. Clearly, armor was effective and available at the 1st ID and 4th ID sectors, helping clear out enemy positions. Indirect fire assets supported the 116th RCT during the near-disaster in Dog Sector, with additional armor eventually supporting operations ashore with the 29th ID. Additionally, only a handful of Luftwaffe fighters patrolled the AOA with the USAAF controlling the skies.[223] Such presence over the fleet and the landing force allowed the Neptune armada to move with impunity; ship-to-shore movement was countered only by mines or enemy surface fires.

While Normandy posed different problems compared to the Mediterranean and North Africa landings, previous experiences helped lay foundations for new and innovative solutions. Despite many challenges over three years the United States Army became the largest amphibious assault force in the world. Although the execution of Overlord/Neptune was rife with mistakes, miscommunication, confusion, and downright incompetence, the highly complex and complicated operation succeeded despite many detractions. Even with the confusion and chaos that occurred during the landings, the Allies generated sufficient combat power, flexibility, and logistics support to overcome the prepared German defenses. As the men embarked on CTF 122's landing craft, it was the culmination of a process that had been underway for only a few short years. Despite disagreements and arguments, the new capability was ultimately successful in both scale and scope. If historians wish to characterize the landings as a flawed victory, then their judgments are overly harsh and fail to appreciate the requirements of such and impressive effort.

8

Faultless on a Large Scale

Operation Anvil/Dragoon, August 1944

Even with the initial success of Overlord, the Americans still favored a double envelopment of France with a landing near the Riviera. First addressed during the Quadrant Conference in May 1943, it was promised by FDR to Stalin at the Sextant Conference in Tehran later that year. Supportive of the operation, Ike envisioned this accompanying operation in southern France to coincide with the cross-channel invasion.[1] Characterized as the worst-kept secret of the war, this second invasion could provide a one-two punch to split German forces and put them into a defensive dilemma.[2] Originally code-named "Anvil" (later changed to "Dragoon"), the envisioned operation had Allied forces landing near Marseilles or Toulon before driving north to meet with the US First Army and UK Second Army, both of which fell under Montgomery's 21st Army Group. This assault would become the apex of interservice cooperation in the ETO and exemplified how far the Americans had come regarding amphibious assault in the short span of two years.

For Ike the southern France operation held larger implications than just operational maneuver. If northern French ports were found to be too small or too damaged to support Allied army groups as they pushed east toward Germany. The Anvil plan provided access to the port city of Marseilles, adding another logistical hub and point of debarkation for follow-on forces. Marseilles was a hundred miles closer to Germany from Cherbourg, and the city was connected to rail and road networks heading inland. Having a major port in southern France was an important consideration given the course of the war, with much hard fighting still ahead.[3] With this operation, SHAEF hoped to introduce additional divisions onto the continent. For Ike, this second port was of "transcendental importance," and he saw the southern invasion in-extricably linked, describing the two operations as "one whole."[4] While German ground combat power was beginning to wane by 1944, it did not mean that ultimate victory was clearly in sight or that the Weh-rmacht was not an effective and deadly foe. In April 1944 Allied intelli-gence reported: "The enemy is now incapable of mounting an attack by surface ships against an Allied task force [and thus] the greatest threat is from the air, from enemy controlled bombs and missiles."[5] Wanting to keep the pressure on German formations required another port of debarkation for the introduction of more Allied troops.[6]

Planning for this second assault on France began on 29 Decem-ber 1943.[7] However, much like at Anzio, the issues of amphibious lift, troops required, and available supplies and equipment were significant. The ability to support both assaults on France simultaneously while conducting offensive actions in Italy was a difficult proposition.[8] De-spite the soundness of the double envelopment and the growing size of the Allied forces by 1944, there were still material and manpower limitations to consider. For the British the southern France assault was seen as a waste of resources, with the accompanying Overlord operation too far away from the Riviera to be mutually supporting. Furthermore, Churchill still held to his belief that a second assault on Germany should come from an Italian-based southern route, and he was dead set against the American proposal. For the prime minister, his preferred strategy was to stay the course in Italy and use the Istrian Peninsula and Ljubljana Gap with a following push toward Vienna.[9] Despite Churchill's earlier call for the ill-fated Anzio landings and the capture of Rome as a precursor to Overlord, the prime minister still stuck to his favored Italian strategy. However, Ike and the American Joint Chiefs of Staff remained insistent on its vision for the dual inva-sion strategy.

As the Supreme Allied Commander, Ike had to consider military strategy and operational limitations on available men and materials. Understanding the importance of the cross-channel invasion and the implications of its potential failure, he was forced to allocate the re-quired assets (predominately LSTs) to the Normandy assault and forgo the simultaneous dual invasion strategy for the time being. Given the assets available in the ETO at the time, the cross-channel invasion was by far the main Allied effort in the bid for strategic success. In addi-tion, the Allies were still planning a May offensive in Italy that would require additional assets. While not necessarily acceding to Churchill's ideas of a continued Ljubljana Gap strategy, the planned simultaneous Riviera operation was canceled on 21 March for lack of shipping and equipment.[10]

However, that did not necessarily mean the Anvil plan was dead. The plan also allowed Free French divisions to contribute to the war effort and illustrated unity of effort. While Allied forces were indeed growing, there was still a paucity of troops given the task ahead. The use of French troops helped to alleviate some of the Allied manpower demands. This was seen as a way to leverage formations into the larger fight and reinforced the strategic message of liberation. Furthermore, FDR was eager to keep his promise to Stalin and conduct a second landing in France to help alleviate the pressure on the Soviets on the Eastern Front. Agreeing at the Tehran Conference, the American president, as well as George Marshall, wanted to keep the shotgun marriage with the Soviet Union on good footing in hopes of receiving future assistance if necessary in the war against Japan.[11]

Prior to the March decision to cancel the second assault, the Americans were already deep into planning. Lieutenant General Jacob Devers, instrumental in developing support for American forces in the United Kingdom, was reassigned as deputy theater commander in the Mediterranean, working under Jumbo Wilson. Despite the US–UK rift regarding future MTO strategy, Devers tasked Lieutenant General Alexander Patch, the new Seventh Army commander to plan the additional French landing.[12] Previously, Patch had been heading XIV Corps in the Pacific, commanding a joint force of two army and one Marine division. In this role he relieved the beleaguered US 1st Marine Division at Guadalcanal and finally secured the jungle island in February 1943.

With his return to combat, Patch oversaw rudimentary planning that envisioned an assault occurring in May 1944 with at least three US divisions and several French formations. Not only did French formations contribute to the overall war effort; they were an ideal choice to liberate towns under Nazi occupation.[13] While the French divisions were receiving training in North African at Arzew and hoped to lead the assault, the language barrier with the American landing crews and coxswains was too great. As a result, they would follow American formations ashore.[14] In addition to the liberated formations, Patch's landings could also count on further support from French Forces of the Interior (FFI). This was a collection of civilians that had long conducted resistance operations in occupied France and had been cultivated by the British and Americans. The FFI was estimated to be

75,000 strong in southern France, provided excellent intelligence on German dispositions, and conducted guerilla action and harassment raids on Wehrmacht forces.[15] In history, books, and film, this force would become renowned as the "French Resistance."

With Allied forces in Italy stuck along the Pisa–Rimini Line and the Normandy beachhead stalled at the bocage, the southern France invasion was resurrected on 24 June 1944. Given the impasse between the United Kingdom and the United States regarding the next steps in the MTO, FDR threw his weight behind Ike's plan, with the prime minister finally acceding to the Americans. On 2 July the Combined Chiefs of Staff ordered Wilson to execute the invasion of southern France with a designated D-Day of 15 August.[16] The original code-name was changed from "Anvil" to "Dragoon" on 1 August, as some feared the plan had been compromised by German intelligence. Supposedly the new name was a result of Churchill's disdain for the plan, claiming he had been "dragooned" into it.[17] Regardless of the Allied infighting, Ike got his southern France assault and with it the ports he desperately desired.

The amphibious fleet was once again commanded by Vice Admiral Kent Hewitt serving as Naval Commander Western Task Force. He ordered the US Eighth Fleet staff to begin work on the plan using experiences at Casablanca, Sicily, and Salerno. Dragoon would again be a joint/combined operation, the various functional area planners gathering in Algiers. Given the priority of operations in northern France, this next amphibious assault would be sourced from units largely located in the MTO, with the Italian campaign becoming the "bill payer" for Dragoon.[18] Detailed planning began at École Normale in Bouzarea, Algeria; accompanying Hewitt's fleet staff was part of Patch's Seventh Army Headquarters.[19] Located at Palermo, elements of the Seventh Army staff displaced to North Africa on 12 January to assist planning. Under Seventh Army, Truscott's VI Corps would serve as the assault force, its staff well-versed in such operations. Rounding out the joint planning effort, representatives from XII Tactical Air Command under Brigadier General Gordon P. Saville were equally cooperative when they arrived. The planning cell for the operation, designated "Force 163," included all the service components and understood the importance of close joint planning. With VI Corps headquarters in Naples, Truscott also understood the utility of joint planning and had Force 163 move to his location.[20] The cell embarked aboard Hewitt's flagship USS *Catoctin* and joined VI Corps in Italy. Upon arriving at the port city, Force 163 set up at Castel dell'Ovo and continued detailed planning. Located in a building dubbed the "blockhouse," the placement of all functional component planners at one location was a great improvement over the disparate planning efforts during Torch and Husky. According to the official navy account, the Naples location allowed Admiral Hewitt "to walk out one door and in the next to be able to consult with the General and vice versa."[21] With Free French participation in the planning occurring in March, the various components obviously had learned the importance of joint and combined staff functioning and planning.

Patch's task was to establish a beachhead, capture the ports of Toulon and Marseilles, and then head north to Lyon and Vichy and eventually link up with the army groups from Normandy.[22] The first issue planners had to address was determining the beaches for the assault. The coastlines near and around the port cities of Marseilles and Toulon were attractive, as they provided easy access to the infrastructure to support VI Corps operations inland. However, the enemy also saw these locations as possible landing sites and placed significant obstacles along with 240mm guns overlooking areas of the beaches. Additionally, beach gradients and surrounding channelized terrain also looked to be problematic for assault forces moving inland. Similarly, and like the Naples beaches during Avalanche, these more western beaches were beyond Allied air cover.[23] Ground-based tactical air support had to fly all the way from Corsica some 100 miles away, a distance too far for effective support. In addition, planners wanted to avoid approaching the assault beaches that were surrounded by the islands of Porquerolles, Levant, and Port Cros. Given these considerations, the landing beaches had to be shifted well east of Toulon and Marseilles.[24]

The Riviera is known for its picturesque seascapes, temperate weather, and blue waters. These same features also provided ideal landing sites. The beaches east of the Hyeres Islands from Cape Negre to Cannes provided the best option for an assault. The initial coastline was relatively flat and conducive for amphibious operations, with sufficient exits points for movement inland to Toulon, Marseilles, and the Rhône River Valley. The surf itself was also favorable for assault, with tidal variations of less than a foot. Equally attractive was the area's deep water, making the placement of underwater obstacles and mines difficult. Truscott requested a reconnaissance of the beaches to locate possible obstacles. But Hewitt assured him that the tidal variations and depths precluded Normandy-like obstacles and did not want to risk revealing to the enemy possible landing sites. In addition to the lack of tidal currents, the late-summer weather and sea states in the

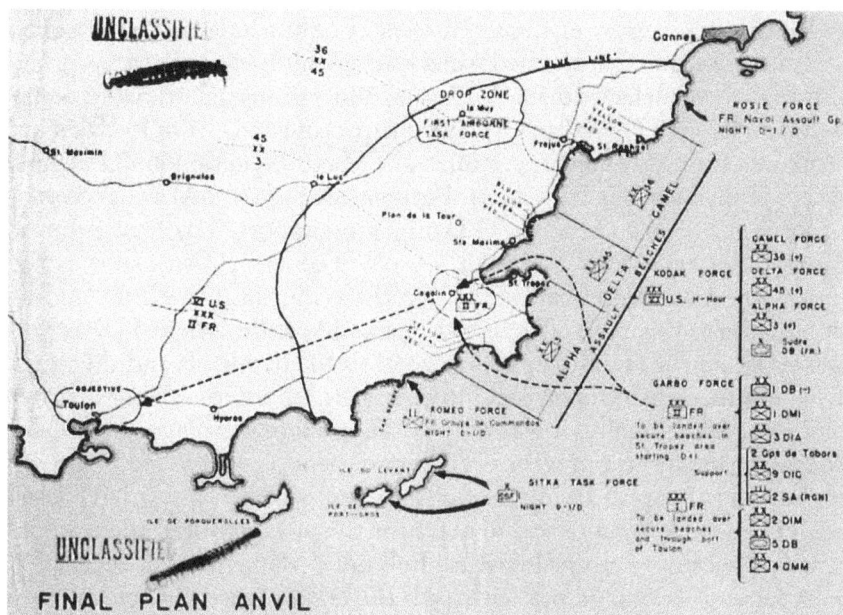

The overall course of action for the three-division assault of Anvil/Dragoon with accompanying airborne and commando actions. (CARL Digital Archive)

Western Mediterranean were expected to be good, posing little concern. Furthermore, given the water depths there was a distinct lack of reefs, sandbars, and runnels that so often frustrated prior debarkations on the shoreline.[25]

However, nearby hills and terrain provided defenders good visibility, channelized terrain, and several chokepoints that might isolate the landings. Additionally, the shoreline itself and known German defenses precluded the three divisions from landing fully abreast. The independent US landing forces would be isolated from each other during the assault, violating the principle of mass. Some beaches were as far as eight miles from another landing, with beach frontages ranging 80–4,500 yards.[26] But the expectation of weak German defenses mitigated the risk. When all three sites were finally identified, the proposed beachhead extended roughly east of Hyeres to just short of Cannes, with its center extending to Le Muy and Le Luc. In all, the landing area was some forty-five miles wide with an inland depth of twenty. Outlining the AOA, planners established what was referred to as the "Blue Line." This control feature marked the extent of the initial objectives for the assault.[27]

By this time, army and navy in-theater commanders were seasoned and experienced. The planned American assault included a three-prong simultaneous surface attack. VI Corps units going ashore were designated as "Kodak Force" and included three divisions.[28] On Kodak's left flank was the 3rd ID under command of Major General John O'Daniel, who was promoted in May 1944. Former head of the FAITC and organizer of the Salerno beaches, O'Daniel was supported by Rear Admiral Betram Rogers's Task Force 84 vessels. The 3rd ID was seen as the most experienced and capable of the three divisions, with its landing designated as the main effort. Code-named "Alpha," the 3rd ID assault was to land near St. Tropez and seize both the peninsula and the town. It would then introduce French formations ashore for subsequent operations. Additionally, it was to take the town of Cavalaire, secure the coastal road, and tie in with French commandos near Cape Negre on its left and the 45th ID on its right. When ordered, the 3rd ID along with French formations was to make for the port city of Toulon, where it would serve as a major logistical hub until Marseilles was secured.[29]

A second set of landings with 45th ID, code-named "Delta," were in the Kodak Force's center. Landing east near the St. Tropez–Bougnon area was Major General William Eagles, commanding the veteran 45th ID, with his naval counterpart Rear Admiral Frank Lowry and Task Force 85. Initially sending two regiments abreast ashore with a third in reserve, it was to seize the town of Ste. Maxime at end of the Gulf de Tropez and the surrounding high ground. After establishment ashore, the 45th's regiments were to move inland and head toward the Argens River eight miles north of Ste. Maxime. It was to make way for French formations and the introduction of such units into their homeland. Additionally, the division was to assist the 36th ID in the capture of the town of Frejus on its right and then tie in with 3rd ID on its left. Upon making contact, the landing force began consolidation/establishment of the beachhead and eventually joined with paratroopers dropped inland before H-Hour.[30]

Finally, on the American right was Camel Force, comprising the 36th ID, experienced from the Salerno landings. These were veterans of Avalanche and the fight up the Italian peninsula, combat-hardened, but haggard. However, unlike the division itself, the 36th's commander, Major General John Dahlquist, was new to combat. Supporting the 36th was a flotilla under Rear Admiral Spencer Lewis and Task Force 87. At H-Hour it was to land one regiment east of St. Raphael and one battalion three miles away at Antheor Cove that included a

French armored division. Another regiment would follow the first two and land at 1400 at Red Beach, a heavily defended stretch at the mouth of the Argens River. The Red location was strategically significant, as it provided an entrance into the Argens River Valley for the planned advance north. On D-Day Camel's objectives were manyfold: occupy the towns of Agay and Frejus, move inland to LeMuy, meet up with paratroopers, and prevent a German counterattack. In addition, Camel would protect Kodak's right flank by tying in with a French commando force blocking German reinforcements coming from the east. Once in place it, too, would consolidate and establish the beachhead.[31]

In addition to the American forces, seven French divisions under General Jean de Lattre de Tassigny were available and planned to land afterward to assist in the drive north. If the 3rd ID landings were successful, the first French army would land on the same beaches on D+1. Four French divisions were to follow in trace (behind): the 1st Infantry, 3rd Algerian, 1st Armored, and the 9th Colonial, with the remainder of the French II Corps arriving around D+25.[32] These formations would assist in the assaults at Toulon and Marseilles, but planners did not expect the towns to be in French hands until D+40. In addition to these traditional military formations, Seventh Army coordinated actions with the FFI to conduct harassment and guerrilla actions in support of the landing.[33]

Much like previous landings, the plan called for the use of airborne forces in support of an amphibious assault. Dragoon used a vertical envelopment of the First Airborne Task Force (FABTF), a combination of US and UK troops. It consisted of a UK paratroop brigade, a US para regiment, two US para battalions, a glider, and two para 75mm howitzer battalions.[34] The airborne force fell under a separate command during the assault and was not initially a VI Corps asset. While the landing beaches had many attractive features, the surrounding terrain allowed for an enemy to easily isolate the beachhead. The narrow coastal roads and beach exits could be readily blocked.[35] Instead of VI Corps, Seventh Army exercised control over the FABTF along with three troop carrier wings with thirty-two squadrons of C-47s and 350 gliders.[36] The task force of over 5,000 paratroopers was to arrive over the drop zone four hours before the amphibious assault. With beacon ships providing navigation aid en route, C-47s and their compliment of gliders were to depart from ten bases near Rome on Italy's western coast. They headed to a drop zone eighteen miles north of the beaches near the town of Le Muy in the Argens River Valley. Once in place the combined force would prevent possible German reinforcements heading to the landing beaches. Fortunately, a quarter moon rising at 0315 provided sufficient lighting for a planned drop.[37]

Much like the Normandy operation, planners envisioned that, after a quick beach assault, the seaborne forces (specifically Camel Force's 36th ID) would meet up with the airborne assets. Once combined, they would then drive toward the Blue Line. Truscott had the same concerns as his predecessor and was afraid of overextension and did not want to make the same error as at Anzio. While the Anzio landings were laterally separated, the Riviera's shoreline precluded mutually supporting landings. For Truscott the massing of combat power was a paramount concern. As a result, the Blue Line control measure was put in place to help keep his combat power consolidated.[38]

Other units were involved during the pre–H-Hour period that did not fall under the control of VI Corps. In addition to the main assault, over 2,000 troops from the First Special Service Force code-named "Sitka" were to land on the Hyeres Islands (specifically Levant and Port Cros) southwest of the 3rd ID's Alpha Beaches near St. Tropez. Composed of Americans, Canadians, and 800 French commandos, this effort focused on islands that housed German troops, with the Ile du Levant reportedly having 164mm guns directly overlooking Alpha's ship-to-shore movement. Once the island was captured and the enemy guns neutralized, Allied forces planned to place a radar site at the location.[39] Furthermore, another commando unit designated "Romeo" planned to land on the mainland around Cap Negre and seize the coastal road and high ground between Toulon and Frejus. This effort would seal off possible German reinforcement.[40] A third commando force code-named "Rosie" was to secure the coastal road to prevent German reinforcement from Cannes. Once in place on the invasion's right flank, it was to link up with the 36th Division.

Even after staggering the dates of the Allies' Overlord and Dragoon assaults, the latter effort was still deficient in amphibious lift. With Overlord complete, as late as June Hewitt remained short sixty-five LSTs, 160 LSIs, a number of APA troop transports, and a host of other littoral support craft. To address the shortfall the navy dispatched twenty-eight new LSTs to the MTO, with Ike sending an additional twenty-four along with several LSIs, APAs, and LCI(L)s. This still left a shortfall of thirteen LSTs. However, creative embarkation and juggling of resources partially made up for the deficiency. While assault shipping was covered by a thin margin, an adjustment in the overall composition of the assault force ship mix was still required. Given the lift deficiencies, follow-on merchant vessels that were not classified as surface combatants were now required in the AOA during the actual assault. With German defenses expected to be degraded, the introduction of these vessels was a calculated risk given their lack of defensive armament. As a result, sixty-four merchant ships were a part of the D-Day convoy and even assisted in landing French forces as early as D+1.[41]

With the Allied assault and the planned counterattack in Normandy, the Wehrmacht's defense of southern France was a lesser priority, with troops siphoned off to counter the first Allied landings. Both the Kriegsmarine and the Luftwaffe were increasingly impotent at this time of the war, with the USAAF and combined Allied fleets decimating German services. The VI Corps G-2 overestimated Luftwaffe strength in the area, reporting that it had only approximately 255 combat aircraft, but in reality it had significantly less. Even the air planners determined that a large counter air effort was unnecessary given the poor state of the German air fleet.[42] In this predicament the Wehrmacht was left to carry the burden of defense along the Riviera beaches. Despite growing Allied combat power, the invasion beaches still included pillboxes, barbed wire, and coastal guns augmented with thousands of landmines. However, the focus of German construction material and labor in the south went to the more strategically relevant submarine pens in Marseilles. While such positions still posed a threat, German measures along Dragoon's invasion beaches were not nearly as formidable as those along Normandy. Given the defensive positions and with Overlord freshly in mind, the Allies had plenty of experience dealing with beach fortifications.

In addition to the practical experiences from previous assaults, the US Army and Navy created a joint board in Naples to address the problem of littoral obstacles.[43] The board pioneered what would eventually be called "daisy cutters." These weapons had extended fuses that detonated above ground to clear barbed wire and other obstacles. One of the board's unique innovations was the creation of the Apex drone boat filled with explosives designed to neutralize underwater obstacles. Packed with 8,000 pounds of explosives, the vessel was remotely piloted and then detonated in the target area with Navy Combat Demolition Team available to fill in.[44] In addition to technological solutions, the board also developed and introduced an eight-man engineering team in DUKWs to widen and mark gaps through the underwater obstacles for the first assault waves. These teams were also trained in removing the obstacles if the Apex boat failed.[45]

Facing VI Corps was the Nineteenth Army under the command of General Friedrich Wiese. Commanding up to nine infantry divisions, Wiese's formations often lacked transportation, logistical, and other administrative support.[46] Despite these shortfalls Wiese correctly identified the location of the future Allied assault east of Toulon and designated a third of his force to coastal defense. He then assigned his best two divisions as a mobile reserve and could expect reinforcement from an additional panzer division.[47] If his forces could contain the beachhead, the panzer division might provide a significant blow. Wehrmacht forces in southern France were estimated at between 285,000 and 300,000 but remained a mixed bag regarding quality, as many soldiers were draftees from Eastern Europe.[48] Referred to as "Ost" (East) troops, these impressed soldiers did not have much fight in them by this stage of the war. In the war diary of one German naval officer, he wrote: "It can hardly be hoped that an invasion can be beaten off by our forces, which are much too weak."[49] Despite detractors the Germans still posed a considerable threat. Although the German high command directed that the coast be held at all costs, withdrawal plans were already being drawn up before the Allies landed in the south. In the VI Corps operations order, the G-2 concluded "it appears that [the enemy] cannot prevent our landing on most of the beaches . . . [and] he is not likely to have sufficient forces available to interfere seriously with the accomplishment of our mission."[50]

H-Hour was set for 0800, and for the first time in the MTO the army allowed the operation to launch during daylight hours, making embarkation and ship-to-shore navigation much easier. Furthermore, daylight landings allowed for the more efficient use of NSFS. Since first light occurred at 0610, pre–H-Hour fires had almost two hours to sight and hit designated targets.[51] Ironically, and unlike Avalanche, Hewitt did not request a pre–D-Day naval bombardment, and nor was he an advocate of a planned large-scale aerial bombardment. He assessed that there was very little to gain from such attacks given the German defenses, and he expressed concern that they might cause forest fires generating smoke and obscuring targets during the actual assault. In somewhat of a reverse of his previous stance, he instead opted for the element of surprise that the army had long subscribed to regarding amphibious operations.[52] However, Hewitt's decision did not fully preclude the Mediterranean Allied Air Forces, which fell under

Lieutenant General Ira Eaker, from conducting operations in the AOA prior to the landings. But the admiral was still concerned about "tipping the VI Corps hand" regarding location of the assault beaches. Given this concern, MAAF agreed to stretch out the aerial assault in both time and location to mask Seventh Army's intentions. In this regard MAAF hit targets all the way from the Po Valley to Genoa and the Marseilles–Toulon area.[53]

For its part of the Dragoon effort, MAAF provided support through the Mediterranean Tactical Air Forces, under which XII TAC fell.[54] Allied airpower started targeting the area as early as 28 April with raids against Toulon and Marseilles. From that time until 10 August it flew more than 6,000 sorties and dropped over 12,000 tons of bombs.[55] Much like in Overlord, strategic bombers attacked lines of communication, bridges, ports, infrastructure, and airfields in an effort to isolate the invasion beaches. Specific target areas included the region near Cap d'Adge to Montpellier, the planned assault beaches, and the Italian Riviera. By the time the of the assault, five of the six major railway bridges across the Rhône River were destroyed, double-track rail lines along the river were cut at various places, and the Allies were neutralizing Luftwaffe airfields in the area.[56]

Tactical air P-47 Thunderbolt fighters went after Wehrmacht coastal defensive positions and radar stations under the auspices of Operation Nutmeg. Nutmeg was the pre D-Day aerial interdiction effort, with attacks focused on the landing sites but extending to other areas to avoid revealing the intended assault beaches to the enemy.[57] By D-Day all Nutmeg tasks had been completed, with the MAAF sending 5,406 sorties of strategic and tactical assets.[58] In addition to the pre–D-Day attacks, MAAF operations included three more phases. From D-5 to 0350 before H-hour airpower focused on main coastal defense batteries in the assault area and radar stations. From 0350 to H-Hour (Operation Yokum) it focused on coastal defenses by using the full weight of XII TAC's fighters and bombers along with naval air. And after H-Hour, air support (Operation Ducrot) focused on troop concentrations, enemy ingress routes, bridges, and enemy beach facilities.[59] In a new interservice development, Saville's XII TAC was responsible for all CAS during the landings. In this capacity it also had operational control over both land- and carrier-based air assets in direct support of assault forces.[60] Such a command relationship was another significant step in joint and combined interoperability. While a D-Day overcast limited air operations, the XII TAC flew 4,249 sorties, of which 3,936 were CAS. By the end of the first week the number of sorties grew to 9,646, dropping 3,881 tons of bombs.[61] Given this performance it was clear that the air component had established air superiority, with the Luftwaffe largely absent.

Much like previous operations the ASCC exercised a sea-based coordination offshore for the invasion's aerial effort. Offensive fighter-bomber support was controlled from Hewitt's flagship USS *Catocin*, with spaces specifically built for this purpose handling both carrier and land-based aircraft. Here navy and USAAF personnel made direct contact with all inbound and outbound fighters while assisting in other dynamic mission taskings. This cell remained afloat until finally moved ashore by D+4. Similar to Overlord, the air effort included a separate fighter direction ship afloat for defensive operations that was handled by a Fighter Direction Tender.[62] While Luftwaffe operations were negligible during the landings, FDT-13 picked a location providing the maximum radar coverage possible for the coordination effort. Afloat it handled defensive air control requirements until the function was passed eventually ashore on D+6.[63]

With the invasion force departing from various ports in Italy and North Africa, the island of Corsica served as an intermediate support base for all the services.[64] While ammunition, tankers, and "reefer" refrigerated cargo ships were a part of the invasion force, Corsica housed a logistics hub and enabled the MAAF to place airfields and infrastructure.[65] As early as May navy and MAAF personnel began building air bases and ports to handle support operations. In mid-June XII Air Force Service Command stocked more than 136,000 bombs, 3.5 million rounds of ammunition, and 2,500 external fuel tanks with stocks sufficiently maintained throughout the invasion.[66] By 10 August the Allies had fourteen airfields on the island housing fighters, fighter-bombers, and medium bombers with the capacity of supporting eighteen air groups of tactical aircraft.[67]

Planned fire support was ample, with four battleships, nine cruisers, twenty-nine destroyers, and a host of other vessels with various armaments.[68] In addition to the USAAF, the flotilla included nine US and UK escort carriers to provide CAS, fighter protection, and spotting services. The naval air component working under the command of XII TAC planned to have over 200 F4F Wildcats, Seafires, and F6F Hellcats providing up to 300 sorties per day.[69] NSFS priority targets included counterbattery fire and guns that could range the flotilla and landing craft, observation posts, and minor defenses. After H-Hour, targets shifted to calls for fire, targets of opportunity, and active enemy

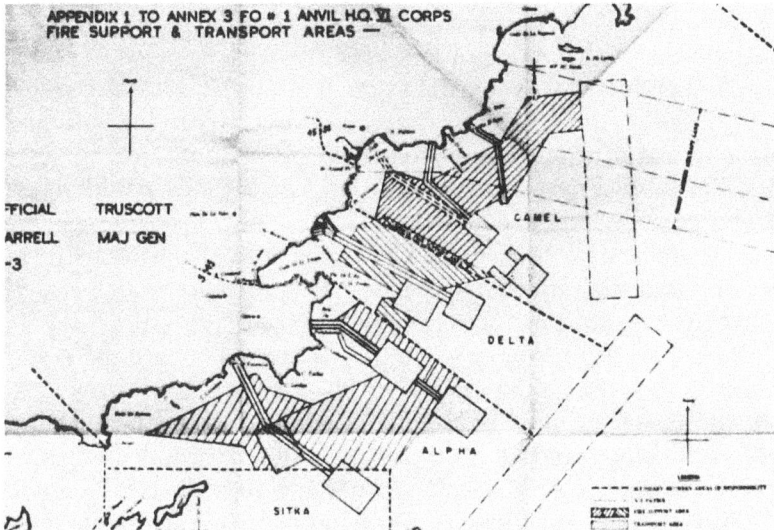

Fire support and transportation area overlays for the 15 August assault.
Note the location and approach of the three task forces and their
associated beaches. (CARL Digital Archive)

batteries. Shore fire-control parties were to land in the initial assault
waves and were robust, with nine allocated to each division and two to
three for the other landing forces. Floating fire-control parties were
also planned from H-10 to H+60 while their shore-based counterparts
were still being established. Leveraging the joint force, other organizations providing observation support included USAAF P-51s, L-4
spotters, and the United States Navy/Royal Naval Air Service fighters
operating from carriers.[70]

As a testament to the development of joint interoperability, Anvil's
three domains (air, land, sea) were commanded by coequal yet independent flag officers, all working under the direction of Seventh Army.
Taking this to an even deeper level, Hewitt divided the NSFS vessels
among the assault divisions and put them in direct support of the respective CLF. However, after the initial landings, these vessels would
then be collected under a single naval command.[71] More important,
given that no corps-level entity was established with Hewitt's Eighth
Fleet, each division commander (acting as CLF) was responsible to his
corresponding naval task force commander (serving as CATF) during
execution. Given this situation, Truscott insisted that both the assault
and naval force commanders be on the same ship with the CATF in

the superior position. In support of this arrangement, he wrote later: "I have no doubt that much of the difficulty that attended the Salerno landings was due to the confused command organization during the assault phase. I sincerely hope that we do not repeat that mistake."[72] While this was a fractured arrangement, each landing force was its own entity, but both services understood that army troops would revert to Truscott's command once he moved his flag ashore. While command authority and transfer can indeed be a tricky and delicate matter, the Dragoon arrangement could only have been possible through close and familiar relationships between the two services.[73]

Both army shore and navy beach parties began training and working together before the assault. In early March, Seventh Army had established the Beach Control Board composed of officers from both services establishing standard operating procedures for unloading supply ships. Located at École Normale, the organization was instrumental in providing guidance for logistics and assault support. In the execution of these responsibilities, one army combat engineer regiment of 1,900 troops along with one navy beach battalion with 445 sailors were assigned to each assault division and its landing beaches. These organizations conducted pre-assault training jointly and in the same manner assigned for the operation. As a result, the joint Army–Navy teams established familiarity between the commands before the assault and understood how each component operated. To avoid confusion, a clear division of labor was established. The army engineer commander assumed the responsibilities as the beach group commander, while his navy counterpart served as the beachmaster. In this arrangement the army was responsible for all beach and unloading activities while the navy handled control of landing craft, beaching directions, and ship-to-shore communications concerning unloading operations.[74] Again the two services had come a long way since the landings of Torch, Husky, and Avalanche.

Since the ports of Marseilles and Toulon were subsequent objectives after the initial landings, logistics support would have come over the shore. Existing facilities within the AOA were too small or insufficient, with major ports unavailable until D+25. Cargo vessels were to be offloaded, with equipment sent to beach dumps managed by beach and shore party personnel with enough stocks for thirty days.[75] In the first month six convoys arrived and gradually built up supplies ashore. Each of the convoys brought amounts over the calculated consumption rates so that the entire landing force would have a twenty-day reserve at depots and another ten days as a theater reserve.[76] For the total lift

Army shore party and navy beach masters working together during Dragoon. Joint cooperation on the beach had come along way since Torch and Husky. (US Navy photo)

requirement, the plan called for 336,000 personnel and 56,051 vehicles ashore by D+30 and twice that number by D+65.[77]

Once Allied forces captured Rome and moved north to the Po Valley, the 3rd, 36th, and 45th IDs were subsequently detached from their duties on the peninsula and became part of Patch's Seventh Army on 15 June.[78] The FAITC originally established in North Africa at Port aux Poules was also displaced and moved to the shores of Salerno in spring 1944. Given the mission of preparing Kodak Force's three American divisions, it also was placed under Seventh Army command. Each participating division received three weeks of training before the assault that included organizing boat teams as combined arms units with flamethrowers, heavy weapons, and rockets. The 45th and 36th IDs trained at the Paestum beaches at Salerno starting 28 June, while the 3rd conducted landings in the Gulf of Gaeta near Pozzouli on 3 June.[79] Since 3rd ID was well versed in amphibious assault, its training tailored to the unit's experience with additional support from 1st Naval Beach Battalion.[80] Pre–D-Day training included the exercising of the assault forces and, as Hewitt had suggested earlier before the Avalanche landings, navy beach and army shore parties as well as fire

LSTs loaded in Bagnoli Italy on 8 August in preparation for the Dragoon D-Day of 15 August. The lack of LSTs remained an issue even after the Normandy landings. The utility of these vessels was paramount to Allied assaults throughout the war. (US Navy photo)

control personnel. NSFS live fire was conducted with white phosphorus shells, reduced-charge mines, and rocket barrages. Such exercises were done at beaches south of Salerno, with full-scale rehearsals occurring 31 July–6 August.[81] These exercises, code-named "Shamrock," "Cowpuncher II," and "Thunderbird," were unlike previous training evolutions that included embark, landing, and supply functions. These rehearsals were well received by the senior commanders, Admiral Lowry remarking that the amphibious force "could have made the landing without an operation order." Patch was suitably impressed with all three divisions' pre-assault performances.[82] Additionally, the FABTF conducted pre–D-Day airborne training at Lido de Roma that was conveniently collocated with the Provisional Troop Air Carrier Division.[83]

Deception again was utilized in the operation, as dummy paratroopers were dropped and combined with naval efforts to draw the enemy away from the intended AOA.[84] The airborne effort included five C-47s departing the airfield at Ajaccio Corsica on D-Day at five-minute intervals at 0210 to 0230. After arriving over the French coast, they released "window" (chaff) to confuse enemy radar as to the actual size of the inbound airborne force. In addition to the American window effort, three RAF Wellington medium bombers flew elongated tracts conducting similar radar deception operations. Meanwhile 500 miniature dummies were dropped by American aircraft northwest of Toulon. This preceded the real airborne operation placing 8,631 paratroopers (some in gliders) to the east around Le Muy.[85]

In addition a special operations group led by the destroyer USS *Endicott* along with a flotilla of smaller vessels streamed reflector balloons near Baie de la Ciotat between Marseilles and Toulon to simulate a landing farther west of the actual landing beaches. It was intended to project a convoy twelve miles long, and the German radar at Cap Side near Toulon was deliberately left off the target list so it might report these electric observations. Alternatively, a special operations group consisting of a small contingent of gunboats, some patrol vessels, and a fighter-direction ship were to feign a landing near Genoa. This eastern effort included a fighter escort to deter enemy reconnaissance aircraft and three PT boats in case German E-boats arrived. The gunboats fired shells eastward, while the fighter-direction ship transmitted electronic noise to simulate a landing away from the actual AOA.[86]

Ships of the invasion force came from numerous locations including Naples, Brindisi, Taranto, Malta, Palermo, and Oran and set sail between 11 and 13 August. With the slower vessels leaving first, the invasion fleet experienced no enemy encounters en route.[87] On D-Day Hewitt's flagship carried Generals Patch, Truscott, and Saville as well as Secretary of the Navy James Forrestal.[88] Landing forces boarded the Western Naval Task Force's 800-plus ships, including over 1,500 landing craft of various sizes. After arriving in the AOA, they began moving into position and divided up into their respective assault lanes as a morning mist obscured the beachline.[89] Minesweepers again preceded the landing craft as scout and beacon vessels made their way to the beaches and NSFS ships took position. The Sitka, Romeo, and Rosie commando forces also took up their assault positions to support the larger landings.[90]

Originally the Western Naval Task Force was allocated sixty-six davit LSTs distributed evenly to the three assault forces. With this complement each division planned to lift four assault battalions. However, the landing force was given only fifty LSTs, thus requiring reallocation. As a result, twenty remained with 3rd ID, as Alpha Force

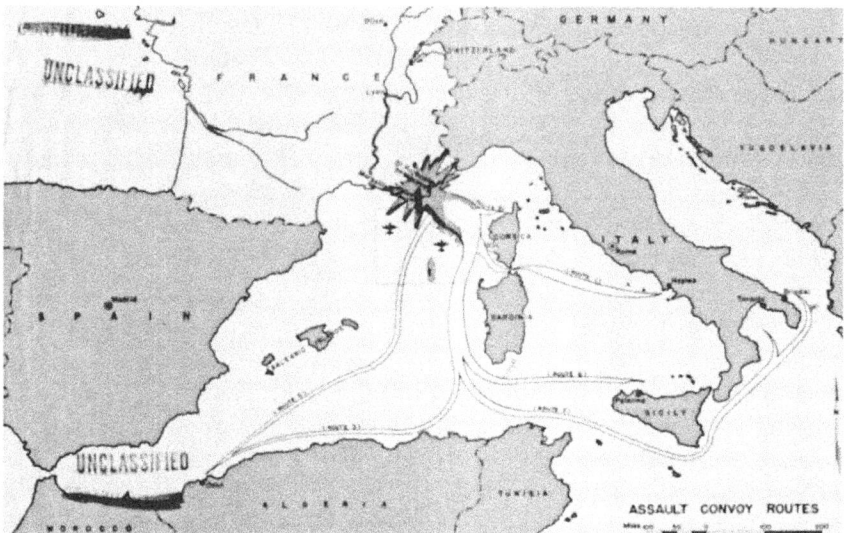

Convoy movement of the Dragoon fleet from various Mediterranean ports.
(CARL Digital Archive)

was designated the main effort for the operation. The reminder were
divided evenly between 45th ID's Camel Force and 36th ID's Delta
Force.[91] Despite the shortfall, the juggling of lift assets assigned to Dragoon made up for the deficiency.

In the hours preceding the amphibious landing, the FABTF echeloned in dropping from C-47s or landing in gliders. Pathfinders used
navigation beacons, lights, and smoke and set fire to trees to help identify landing zones for the follow-on sticks of paratroopers. Low clouds
created navigation problems and obscured some of the intended landing zones. Despite the meteorological impediments, most of the force
landed within ten miles of Le Muy, with some scattered within the
lateral limits of the AOA. Establishing themselves in the area to prevent a German counterattack, they awaited the amphibious assault's
movement inland.[92]

Pre–H-Hour fires began as scheduled, hitting coastal defenses and
scoring direct hits on designated targets. Naval bombardment began at
0630 and lifted only when Allied aircraft reported in the area. Given
coordination between NSFS and air, it is clear that the services understood the effect of combined arms operations and could now effectively
sequence and manage this most difficult tasking. In the prelanding
bombardment naval gunners fired 15,900 projectiles and continued

up to 0750, just before the landing forces were to arrive. At H-Hour, NSFS shifted and engaged locations on the landing forces' flanks while LCT(R)s then went in, launching their rockets as a final preparation for the introduction of assault troops.[93]

In coordination with the surface barrage, aviation provided additional support in the form of naval aviation along with Seville's XII TAC.[94] As dawn broke, Allied fighters executed the Yokum phase of the air plan and prowled the AOA. While the tactical aviation effort hit various targets, strategic bombers pummeled the beaches with 1,000 pounds of explosives for each ten yards of beach just before H-1.[95] Once finished at the landing beaches, aviation assets continued attacking enemy targets inland, with one squadron from the escort carrier USS *Tulagi* claiming destruction of 487 vehicles plus another 114 damaged.[96] The Navy–USAAF cooperation was so effective that General Saville wrote Hewitt: "I would like to express my appreciation for the outstanding work they [naval aviators] have done and for their perfect co-operation. I consider the relationship and co-operation of this force to me a model of perfection and [to serve as a] standard for future operations . . . well done and thanks!"[97]

In another testament to the join aerial campaign, after the landings both Patch and Truscott attributed the aerial assault with saving the ground forces "many losses."[98]

Prior to H-Hour the commando forces of Sitka and Romeo conducted raids on the AOA's left flank and the offshore islands. Sitka landings on Port Cros met with German resistance that held out until D+1. This action delayed the placement of radar equipment, but it neutralized the enemy guns that had ranged the landing force. Romeo Force landed on the mainland on Kodak's far left and was tasked to destroy enemy positions, seize the coastal road, and hold high ground in the area. They landed by stealth and destroyed several enemy positions. Despite some confusion with subsequent assault waves, by 1300 on D-Day the commandos accomplished their mission and established contact with the 3rd ID.[99] Rosie commandos landed on the AOA's far right near Pointe des Trayas. However, this force ran into barbed wire and mines and attempted to withdraw. Surviving elements eventually contacted the 36th ID after it came ashore, but the mission was a failure.[100]

Along with the 0800 H-Hour came clear and calm weather with only a slight breeze. While a coastal fog bank initially hampered air support operations, it eventually cleared. However, the smoke from preparatory fires replaced the fog and obscured much of the beachline.[101] For most of the landings, the respective units hit the beaches only minutes apart. The first assault waves received very little enemy resistance, with mines causing damage to DD tanks and landing craft.[102] Fixed positions along the beaches had been either abandoned or destroyed, accompanied only by the occasional sound of token enemy fire from the Wehrmacht's 242nd and 148th Divisions. Enemy shore batteries with 88mm and other guns in casements were in place but found to be unmanned, with some small garrisons surrendering. While small pockets of resistance engaged, the ensuing firefights were short-lived.[103]

An exception to enemy ground action that day occurred near St. Raphael on Kodak Force's right flank and in Camel's designated area. The 142nd Regiment was set to land on Red Beach just east of the town of Frejus. At this location the Germans had built significant defensive positions with 88mm guns and pillboxes along with a sea minefield strung across the Frejus Gulf. With the assault scheduled to go ashore at H+6, minesweepers preceded the landing force by hours but were met with heavy enemy artillery fire and driven off.[104] To silence the enemy guns, and in an excellent display of interservice cooperation, a flight of ninety-three B-24s came over the beach, dropping 187 tons of bombs. Waiting fifteen minutes after the bombers cleared, the minesweepers moved back into the gulf to clear the assault lanes but were again met with incoming fire and had to move off. Naval fires were brought in this time in the form of four destroyers, two cruisers, and a battleship, all firing for forty-five minutes. In addition, twelve of the newly developed Apex remote-controlled boats were also launched. The Apex boat attack failed, with only three exploding as planned. As a final contribution, LCT(R)s were also brought in just minutes before the 142nd Infantry Regiment's planned assault. However, sending troops into such stout defensive fires offshore seemed ludicrous, and the assault was delayed until 1430 by order of Task Force 87's commander, Admiral Lewis.[105]

While the CATF is responsible for ship-to-shore movement to the designated landing beaches, the decision to land at an alternate beach really belonged to the CLF, in this case the 36th ID's commander. Such an arrangement reflected the existing supported/supporting relationship. However, General Dahlquist was already ashore by 1000 and incommunicado, leaving Admiral Lewis alone to make the decision as the 142nd offshore remained afloat in over 100 landing craft. Making a command decision, the admiral chose the planned alternate location and had the regiment land on Camel Green Beach, a violation of the understood CATF–CLF agreements. Following orders, the landing craft turned right from the Gulf of Frejus and subsequently came ashore without loss. Nevertheless, once Dahlquist heard of Lewis's decision, he replied: "I appreciate your prompt action changing the plan when obstacles could not be breached. . . . Opposition irritating but not too tough so far."[106] This episode again reflect the development and growth of joint operations in the ETO. Despite this cordial command relationship, Truscott was dismayed when the assault of Frejus from the ground delayed the introduction of follow-on formations key to subsequent operations ashore.[107]

The only other significant enemy action occurred later in the evening when Luftwaffe bombers sortied and attacked in Camel Force's sector. Approaching from 15,000 feet, the bombers leaked through the Allied defensive air umbrella and dropped their payloads. The Germans again used Fritz X radio-controlled bombs, which hit an LST laden with ammunition and 36th ID artillery. While the strike created an impressive explosion resulting in forty casualties, it was the only Allied ship casualty on D-Day.[108] In all the Luftwaffe flew no more than sixty sorties that day.[109] Unlike previous MTO assaults, the air above the invasion fleet was not filled with enemy aircraft hampering ship-to-shore operations or beach party functions.

Regardless, the amphibious assault moved quickly. On the left flank Alpha Force met with Romeo commandos by 1330 and secured the beachhead's western flank, then proceeded to the neighboring high ground. By that evening 3rd ID had moved six miles inland. Truscott moved the VI Corps Headquarters to shore, as many D+2 objectives were already being attained. German opposition manifested in various places during the evening on the far left near Cape Negre and inland at the Argens Valley but was readily dealt with. Additionally, the 45th Division established itself in the central position between Alpha and Camel. While the 36th Division on the right flank continued to struggle with the Wehrmacht defenses in Frejus, it eventually secured the town and moved inland.[110] Meanwhile, beach/shore party personnel arrived and began building combat power ashore for subsequent operations, successfully moving 60,000 men, 6,700 vehicles, and 18,500 tons of cargo onto dry land.[111]

By the end of D-Day all combat elements of VI Corps were ashore and moving inland. The first day resulted in capturing 2,041 prisoners with landing beaches secure. The following day, 16 August, General Patch transferred the Seventh Army Headquarters flag ashore and established himself on the continent. The initial assault made much more progress than expected, with losses reported to be an amazingly low number: ninety-five killed and 385 wounded.[112] Following the American landings, French army elements came ashore on D+1, and by 18 August these formations began pushing west along the coast on the VI Corps left flank. They were heading toward the objective cities of Toulon and Marseilles, and the lack of enemy resistance allowed the French formations to reach the cities by 22 August.[113] According to the Seventh Army after-action report: "During the assault phase the operation had gone according to plan, but in many ways, it had exceeded even the most optimistic expectations."[114]

The subsequent plan called for two drives toward the mouth of the Rhône River and up the Rhône Valley. The breakout from the beach began only days later, and one could easily claim that Dragoon was a tactical, operational, and strategic success. While enemy resistance was light compared to previous assaults, the operation was carried out with great efficiency and a minimal amount of internal friction. Apart from Camel's Red Beach landings, the assault was largely executed as planned. The quickness of the assault led naval historian Samuel Eliot Morison to compare it to the Tinian assault in the Pacific: "If Tinian in the Pacific was the 'perfect amphibious assault' on a small scale, Dragoon was the nearly faultless on a large scale."[115] This last major seaborne amphibious operation in the ETO was a marked improvement from just a few years earlier.

The assault on southern France was a point of contention between the British and the Americans. But just as American amphibious capabilities grew during the war, so, too, did its ability to influence Allied strategy. With the United States initially coming into the war as a perceived junior partner, the roles had certainly reversed by 1944. With more men and equipment, the United States now had significant skin in the game. While this change was not necessarily verbalized, it was at least realized by the relevant parties. The Americans were now the senior partner, and it was representative of American military capabilities globally.

Dragoon was the apex in the development of US amphibious capability in the ETO. Almost from its inception it embraced many of the lessons learned from previous assaults. By conducting joint and detailed planning, establishing trusted command relationships, and integrating air and naval fires, and with efficient ship-to-shore movement and a robust logistics and communications network, Seventh Army and VI Corps move ashore quickly and efficiently. In Hewitt's report of the Dragoon landings, he specifically mentioned that "the integration of gunfire support and air bombing was planned to a finer degree than was ever attempted in this theater."[116] Even though Wehrmacht and Luftwaffe capabilities had significantly waned by 1944, executing a complex and large operation like Dragoon could not have been done in 1942—either materially or in execution. The problems and losses experienced during Torch against a weak Vichy force were not repeated against the declining German military of 1944. All three services—the US Army, Navy, and Army Air Force—learned to work together efficiently toward a common and unified goal.

Conclusion

Just because the Allies were established on the continent did not mean that amphibious operations in the ETO were finished. As the combined US–UK armies moved eastward, and before they could launch fully into Germany, the Allies had to cross the Rhine River. Given this natural obstacle, the three services, along with their UK counterparts, again conducted joint and combined amphibious operations. Instead of coming ashore from the sea, these final amphibious assaults crossed the Rhine and secured lodgments on the river's far shore. While some American troops had already crossed this important waterway before the last remaining bridge located at Remagen fell on 17 March 1945, many elements of both 21st Army Group and 12th Army Group were still stuck on the western (near) bank. Getting the armies, corps, and divisions across required joint operations with support from both the US Navy and the USAAF. The planned assault required a navy task force of LCVPs, LCMs, and pontoons that also included the use of army amphibious tractors (Amtracs) and DUKWs.[1] In addition, and like previous amphibious assaults, one of the landings incorporated use of airborne forces, with airpower also shaping the battlefield.

Months before the last Rhine Bridge span fell, planners had already anticipated the use of landing craft for the river crossing to support the US First, Third, and Ninth Armies. The three armies were arrayed with the Ninth in the north, the First in the center, and the Third in the south. Navy Task Force 122.5 was attached to Bradley's 12th Army Group, with its LCVPs transported from Le Havre, France, by trucks borrowed from armor recovery units. Once inland the landing craft and crews were staged in Belgium and The Netherlands while training for the upcoming cross-river assaults. Since the LCVPs were not big enough to move armor, over forty-five LCMs were sailed from the United Kingdom to Antwerp, floated down the Albert Canal, and loaded into truck transports.[2]

As the US First Army moved east to the Rhine River on 7 March 1945, it was surprised to find the Ludendorff Bridge at Remagen still standing. For the next ten days, after removing German demolitions designed to blow the span, the 9th Armored Division quickly moved tanks and equipment to the far side. German air and ground forces attempted to drop the bridge until it finally collapsed on 17 March. However, by that time US troops had already established a bridgehead on the eastern (far) bank. Days before the bridge collapsed, ten US Navy LCVPs splashed into the water near Bad Neuenahr and began a ferry service while helping build pontoon and treadway bridges. In addition to their assistance to the army's bridging efforts, the LCVPs had ferried more than 14,000 troops and 400 vehicles across. When the German bridge collapsed, the landing craft helped remove floating debris that might damage the new established army bridges. By 24 March the First Army's bridgehead had grown to ten miles deep and thirty-five miles wide, with units in a position to break out.[3]

A more deliberate and large-scale operation occurred later that month as the US Ninth Army conducted landings near and around the city of Wesel. Set for a 24 March commencement, Operation Plunder had all the same earmarks of earlier amphibious assaults. Pre-assault fires preceded the landings with 9th Air Force bombing targets on the far shore.[4] While not having to debark from APA or LST transports, men and equipment still had to be staged in preparation for movement in boat teams. Like beach landings, Ninth Army used colored designations like "Red" and "Blue" to identify specific crossing sites. Using two divisions, in the north the 30th ID set up three crossing sites using LCMs, LCVPs, and Amtracs, while the 79th ID in the south crossed in two locations with LCVPs, LCMs, and Sea Mule tugs.[5]

With the river at a ten-year low and with a velocity of five to eight feet per second, Ninth Army initiated operations at 0200 as small assault boats crossed the river first. Once ashore troops affixed flashing lights to mark landing site boundaries. Meeting with minimal resistance, succeeding assault waves utilized LCMs, LCVPs, and Amtracs. The naval platforms were especially useful for moving bridging and engineering equipment, along with supporting weapons, to the far side. Following the initial assaults were DD tanks crossing under their own power. Not having to deal with a high sea state of the English Channel, the amphibious tanks made it across. Once sufficient men and material were on the eastern bank, engineers began building bridges for follow-on forces.[6]

Supporting the Plunder effort, Operation Varsity landed XVIII Airborne Corps on the far side of the river near Wesel. This combined effort by US and UK paratroopers was to prevent German

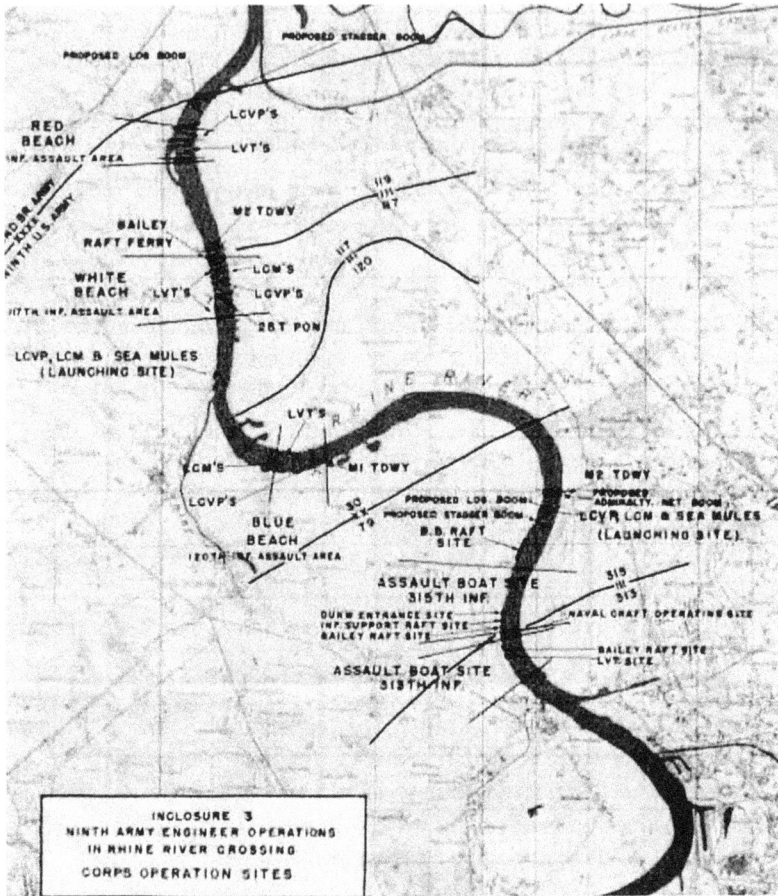

9th Army Plunder crossing sites for the Rhine River on 24 March 1945.
Both 30th and 79th IDs made good use of Navy landing craft in the assault.
(CARL Digital Library)

counterattacks and allow for the establishment of beachheads on the far side. Unlike the deep penetration of the ill-fated Market Garden operation attempting to seize the Rhine River bridges, this drop was within combined arms range and close enough to the landing forces for a linkup in the first twenty-four hours.[7] Varsity was the largest single-day air operation of the war, with more than 21,000 paratroopers flying in 1,600 transport planes and 1,300 gliders.[8] While the airborne drops fought tough German resistance, the paratroopers successfully established contact with the ground forces once across the river.[9]

As in previous amphibious assaults, the USAAF provided support for the crossing operations with BAI and CAS. From mid-February to 21 March heavy and medium bombers flew 1,700 sorties in the area, while tactical aircraft conducted another 7,300 just days before the crossings. Hitting bridges, roads, and viaducts days before the crossings, heavies flew another 3,800 sorties in what airmen referred to as "processing the terrain."[10] Supporting Varsity, 9th Air Force also carpet-bombed landing zones with fragment bombs to neutralize enemy AAA hours before the first pathfinders flew over the area. Additionally, fighter aircraft escorted the C-47s and provided a screening force for frontline cover.[11]

Two days earlier George Patton was on his own timetable. On 22 March the Third Army initiated crossings sites at multiple locations south of the city of Mainz. At around 2200 Third Army units moved into position to cross the river at multiple locations. However, the LCMs and LCVPs did not arrive until 0100 and were floated an hour later.[12] For the next twenty-four hours navy personnel moved 1,000 vehicles and 15,000 troops across the river. Not only did the landing craft move troops, armor, and other equipment; they again were key in helping move bridging equipment and in the building of pontoon and other bridges across the span. LCVPs remained in constant use for the next seventy-two hours, with but two sailors fainting from exhaustion.[13]

Once again, the services effectively conducted joint and complex amphibious operations in the face of enemy resistance. Executing such an assault hundreds of miles inland required coordination and joint planning that was hardly possible just a few years earlier. The traditional interservice rivalry that had existed for decades eventually dissipated after the nation was drawn into the existential crisis. Initially uninterested in amphibious missions, the army had to quickly develop its capability, while the navy was only slightly ahead of it ground counterpart if only because of its habitual relationship with the Marine Corps.

Still a lesser priority in the Navy Department, the "gator fleet" had to grow in both size and capability. Even with the emerging requirement, the two services were still at an impasse as to which was responsible for amphibious training in the MTO/ETO. Only after the agreement between Marshall and King did official joint taskings occur. With further guidance given by FDR in the form of naval construction and prioritization, the two services' amphibious efforts grew while coming to an understanding and then capturing lessons from each assault. As the two traditional services joined forces, combined arms, eventually included the USAAF. In all three domains American assault capabilities grew in both effectiveness and capability. Taking the lessons of combat to heart, the three services collectively innovated, coordinated, and synchronized to develop the most powerful amphibious capability in history. They had all proved their abilities to become learning organizations.

The unsung hero of this development was Kent Hewitt. While army commander Lucian Truscott is certainly worthy of mention as a tactical practitioner, it was Hewitt who took great strides toward developing joint doctrine, training, and capability. Starting with his time at AFAF and then serving as the CATF for four amphibious landings, his force of personality and professional competence drove the amphibious progress that made Overlord possible. During his watch the Mediterranean became a classroom that saw American forces learn not only the art and science of amphibious assault but also how to fight the Wehrmacht on its own terms. Under his tutelage the services develop better combined arms integration, mastered large-scale ship-to-shore movement, built an expeditionary logistics capability, and introduced army- and corps-size structures into a littoral environment. In these efforts he was instrumental in the development and prosecution of subsequent land campaigns that eventually liberated two continents.

Returning to this book's framework leveraging the six prescribed components of amphibious assault, all three services had roles to play in their development in the MTO/ETO. Working together, the synergy provided by each service was greater than the sum of its parts. Most important, this joint effort was bound together by the establishment of command relationships, mutual understanding, and the setting of joint goals and objectives. During the planning and loading for Torch, Hewitt hectored Patton and other army officers to understand the importance of embarkation/debarkation and an appreciation of ship-to-shore movement. While Patton was suspicious of navy capabilities early on, and for good reason given prewar exercises, relationships and respect between these flag-grade officers and their respective staffs grew. The development of joint interoperability was evident before Torch, as Hewitt's Amphibious Assault School was already training army and navy personnel together. Despite the rocky start regarding who was responsible for amphibious training and ship-to-shore movement, by the time of Salerno many of these differences had been reconciled. This interoperability and understanding continued with the establishment of the FAITC, training establishments in the United

Kingdom, and the Quartermaster "Q" School in London. Additionally, establishment of joint boards prior to Dragoon provided further evidence of how the services overcame established parochialism.

The establishment of joint planning efforts and placement of staffs on headquarters ships were also indicative of the growing appreciation of multidomain execution. This included the placement of fire direction centers, FCUs, GCI-LSTs, and ASCCs aboard ship to coordinate joint fires within the AOA. The USAAF also eventually came to appreciate the role it had to play not just in BAI and isolation but also in CAS and defensive counter air missions. Immediately after Husky landings, where the Luftwaffe and Regia Aeronautica had free reign over the Allied fleet, the USAAF and Royal Naval Air Service immediately began allocating assets to such defensive air missions. Additionally, after the friendly-fire incident of the 82nd AB over the fleet at Husky on D+1, future airborne operations were routed around the invasion fleet or had effective communication that prevented another similar incident. Amphibious planning increasingly became a joint affair with collocated major commands developing and generating operations orders that were well synchronized and integrated.

Respecting the supported/supporting relationship, when navy personnel suggested the use of pre–H-Hour fires during various landings, they deferred to the army's preference for stealth over the use of firepower. Thankfully discarded in Overlord, the navy yielded to army concerns despite its unfortunate consequences on the beaches at Salerno. Supporting the CLF, during Husky Admiral Kirk moved his task force transports closer to the shoreline when Cent Force floundered in the rough surf. The same was true of many coxswains and NSFS skippers who during Avalanche navigated the sea mines and landed on a contested beach or provided much-needed fire support. Perhaps the greatest illustration of how the army and navy came to trust and understand each other was the effective organization of multiple CATF/CLF relationships during Dragoon. Not only were there three separate CATF/CLF commands established; they were all successful. This organization was best epitomized at Camel Red Beach when the CATF adjusted the landing site for the 142nd Regiment, only to be complimented by the CLF for his sound judgment. Despite Truscott's dismay at the delay, this action illustrated single-mindedness toward a common objective.

NSFS was one area where the navy was already functionally competent. Naval gunners understood the problems inherent with a moving gun-target line before the war began. However, the use of such fires in support of, and in proximity to, ground forces was something relatively new. The two services had to develop communication networks and a common vocabulary and language. With army officers unfamiliar with the capabilities of naval gun fire, the ground component had much to learn. NSFS proved itself as it took out defensive positions in Torch, saved American troops at Gela, combined with joint fires in thwarting the German counterattack at Salerno, and provided key support to troops in subsequent assault waves at Normandy. While army commanders were initially gun-shy of using such weaponry with troops in the area, the development of aerial spotters, shore fire-control parties, gunfire liaisons, shipboard fire direction centers, and established fire coordination networks, naval fires made the difference in many engagements.

The largest material solutions in the development of amphibious assault were in ship-to-shore movement. In none of the other components did the introduction of new equipment matter more. The design and building of LSTs, LCTs, LCIs, and DUKWs were proverbial game-changers. These platforms allowed a seagoing flotilla to efficiently unload its cargo and personnel and transition into a shallow-water environment. The platforms not only allowed large-scale movement in a littoral environment but also made the building of combat power ashore feasible without need of a fixed port. Although cranes, piers, and other infrastructure certainly expedited debarkation, the Americans could do it over unprepared beaches and fast enough to respond to enemy actions. Use of these littoral platforms determined the success of a landing at the tactical level by moving armor and artillery ashore in short order, and their availability and numbers drove larger strategic initiatives. LSTs proved invaluable, as the inelegant vessels did much of the heavy lifting for the Allied invasions. Without these new landing craft and the number produced, Allied amphibious efforts would have fallen far short if not failed altogether.

In addition to the new landing craft, ship-to-shore movement capabilities also grew because of deliberate efforts to improve the performance of coxswains and crews. Given their poor performances in the prewar exercises and their continued unsatisfactory execution during Torch, the early training conducted stateside obviously fell short. With the establishment of the FAITC in North Africa and various training centers in the United Kingdom, in-theater schools specifically addressed the issue of movement ashore. Coxswain seamanship and navigation skills were improved, with additional steps taken before Overlord. Specialized navigation training, establishment of patrol vessels with the AOA to assist landing craft in their trek toward to the correct shoreline, development of intelligence packets, deliberate study of the shoreline profiles, and installation of compasses all helped improved crew performance. While some boat teams came ashore on the wrong beaches at Omaha and Utah, the problem was not nearly as bad as it was in Torch, and there was not the huge loss of landing craft due to poor seamanship. Considering that many of these coxswains had never seen an ocean before joining the navy or Coast Guard, the services made huge strides in individual competence and seamanship.

Perhaps the biggest advances overall occurred regarding the use of aviation and its integration into the joint endeavor. As seen during Torch, airpower in an amphibious assault was originally a Navy-only affair. Land-based tactical air did not have the range or capability to assist. However, as the size and scope of amphibious assaults grew and airfields in the theater became available, it was clear that the USAAF indeed had a role to play. Smitten with their newfound status as specified in *FM 100-20*, airmen thought of themselves as something wholly different from their surface-based brethren. After a lack of participation in the Husky landings, the USAAF eventually learned to work and play well with others. Initially providing only spotting services for NSFS in lightweight aircraft, airmen only weeks after the Sicilian campaign were over the invasion beaches at Salerno providing a defensive umbrella, effectively coordinating air operations aboard naval vessels, stacking fighters and attack aircraft over the battle area, learning how to spot for naval fires and more effectively executing CAS missions. By the time of Shingle, the air component was coordinating daily with ground commanders on targets, had ASPs ashore, and helped provide on-call support and various forms. Air planners even attempted to forward-base airpower within the AOA on a hastily built airstrip.

With Overlord, airmen also allocated airframes, at the expense of their sacred mission of strategic bombardment, and attacked transportation networks. While this was done because Ike exercised his full authority as Supreme Allied Commander, the use of strategic bombers combined with other combat arms helped pave the way for ground forces. Not only did the 8th and 15th Air Forces hit targets inland to help shape the AOA; they also used four-engine bombers to attack enemy positions ashore prior to landings in France, bringing down the full weight of airpower. While the aerial effort sometimes fell short of expectations, land-based airpower was now clearly a part of the amphibious effort and made significant contributions.

The USAAF also placed entire air forces in direct support of assault troops, providing a host of services, both on-call and planned. During Overlord and Dragoon, tactical aircraft conducted missions over the beaches just before H-Hour and continued to support the landings through BAI and CAS as the beachhead expanded. Moreover, command and control of the aerial onslaught during the assault was executed by control centers afloat and by working in coordination with the other domains. Outside of the six characteristics founded by Marine doctrine, the use of airborne forces in support of the amphibious landing became a staple in the ETO. C-47s with gliders in tow helped secure surrounding areas, caused havoc with German communications, and prevented enemy reinforcement. With these developments US forces establish a truly effective combined arms integration capability in an expeditionary environment.

In establishing a beachhead, the army clearly understood the requirement to consolidate gains after an offensive assault and to establish a defensive perimeter. Such tactical actions were not new or unfamiliar. After seizing the objective area, beachhead defenses worked much the same way. However, after the initial assault the services needed to improve the landing sites to support subsequent operations ashore. It was in this application that the army took its first steps toward amphibious operations. Establishing the Engineer Amphibian Command in March 1942 was the catalyst for many of the service's initiatives. From there it branched out to establish the respective Amphibious Training Centers, but even more important it led to the creation of Engineer Special Brigades. It was these ESBs that served as the army's shore parties to prepare the beachhead for the reception and storage of supplies and equipment, establish travel lanes, emplace control measures, create supply and administrative areas, and improve the physical location. Most important, ESBs also worked with navy beach parties in the reception of vessels, men, and material from the sea. Both the army shore and navy beach parties working in unison, developing combat power ashore and for subsequent operations.

However, of all the functions that seem to be the most problematic, establishing the beachhead was the greatest challenge. The Torch, Husky, and Avalanche landings were awash with equipment, supplies, and men, with subsequent assault waves creating traffic jams, confusion, and chaos on the beaches. Failure to practice these functions during preinvasion exercises had severe consequences that in some cases threatened mission success. Eventually the services begin to understand how to establish these functions ashore, with tables of organization being adjusted and increased troop allocations reflecting the requirement. After Shingle and concluding with Dragoon, shore party missions became better organized, more efficient, and greatly effective. The services also learned that army shore and navy beach parties need to exercise these functions before the assault and build habitual relationships. Such pre-assault exercises between units yielded better results on contested beaches.

The logistics function was obviously tied to the establishment of the beachhead and ship-to-shore movement, and it, too, grew significantly. From the poor delivery of supplies during Torch to the establishment of man-made harbors in Overlord, the United States and its UK ally made significant advancements in expeditionary logistics. The United States went from requiring a port or harbor to support an army to one capable of providing over-the-shore joint logistics. Expeditionary logistics grew to enable sustained combat operations and made possible subsequent operations inland. The introduction of LSTs and LCTs meant that large amounts of supplies and equipment could now be moved ashore without fixed infrastructure and were not necessarily at the mercy of enemy sabotage or poor maintenance. This was a wholly new capability. In addition to the new littoral platforms, combat loading and efficient use of available cargo space expedited the offloading of ships, making supplies readily available while still in-stream. The Anzio Highway typified this creative use of available lift as it sustained VI Corps at a time when it lacked the required LSTs. Through mobile loads and the shuttle system, troops in Anzio were well supplied. While the army had to learn the art of combat loading and team embarkation, once these new methods were joined with a growing and more capable amphibious fleet American power projection ashore was unmatched.

While man-made Mulberrys worked in conjunction with over-the-shore methods, creating this capability in an expeditionary environment was truly unique and original. These innovations along with others worked together and made possible the subsequent movement of army groups onto the continent. In addition to shore-based capabilities, the movement and management of high-priority gear managed by BUCO in support of Overlord was also a key enabler. Merchant vessels waiting at various locations in the United Kingdom were called forward to provide a robust and efficient logistical pipeline across the English Channel. Similarly, the Dragoon invasion fleet also included merchant shipping as a part of the invasion flotilla. The innovation in both material solution sets and in methodology/management of large-scale logistics was a key component of the liberation effort. As the armies moved farther and farther from the beach, these developments kept Allied forces well stocked and connected to the bounty of American factories and production.

And finally, the joint force established communications networks that allowed command and control of invasion forces in all three domains. This required the fielding of new radios, equipment, and modification of existing systems and also the development of joint terminology, especially in the area of joint fires. The first step was the establishment of a joint communications school under Hewitt's command in Virgina Beach that trained sailors and soldiers alike. In addition, as capabilities matured in theater communications, the FCUs, ASPs, and ASCCs also grew to enable the increased inclusion of airpower within the AOA. Communications networks for Rover Joe, Pineapple, spotter, and other air-centric applications were established with dedicated frequencies assigned. Important to this air-ground effort were the mobile SCR-193 radios along with the development of the SCR-300s for ground operations. While the SCR-399 radios at Normandy were too large for embarkation, ASP personnel developed a workaround using SCR-284s to talk directly to air cells afloat and having them relay support requests to the Combined Control Center.

Perhaps the biggest challenge for signal personnel was managing the frequencies given bandwidth limitations and the volume of traffic required to support such operations. To address these challenges American forces modified the crystals in radio sets, used teletypes, and published detailed guidance and technical instruction regarding the networks available. These were key in establishing effective communications networks ashore, afloat, and in the air. Additionally, the Allies made available thousands of short- and medium-range radio sets, along with wire communications for smaller units at the battalion, company, and platoon levels.[14] Again, the ability to shoot, move, and communicate was key to Allied success in the assault and in subsequent operations ashore.

In the end, the American military, backed by a robust industrial base at home, eventually overwhelmed the Axis forces in numerous ways. This is not to say that mass was *the* key to the victory over Nazi Germany. That is too simple an answer and clearly wrong. The victory was not certain until 1945 and came about because the Allies innovated, learned, and understood the emerging requirements and the associated threats. From a ragged performance in Torch to the nearly faultless assault in Dragoon, the US military clearly proved to be a learning organization. Through a constant process of assessment and review, US–UK forces adjusted methodologies at all levels of war and outpaced the European Axis powers. Hewitt himself summarized it best in his official report of the Dragoon operation: "In detail . . . the lessons of previous large amphibious operations in this theater, in all of which this command participated, [were] applied insofar as circumstances permitted."[15] While the Wehrmacht and Luftwaffe were truly innovative during the interwar years and in the first few campaigns of the war, they eventually peaked and then stagnated. They largely ceased in large-scale battlefield innovation and resorted to what they understood from before sometimes with only minor modifications. With a failed grand strategy, the Nazi regime and its associated militaries regressed in both operational and tactical acumen.

Meanwhile the Allies did the direct opposite. The US Army, US Navy, and Army Air Forces beat the Germans at their own game. Through US development of its own methods of movement and maneuver, integrated fires, joint coordination, robust logistics, and use of operational tempo, American forces grew more proficient and capable—much more so than the Germans. Part of this new proficiency included amphibious assault and the projection of combat power ashore in a joint manner. Perhaps the most telling testament came from the CTF 122 commander's assessment of the Normandy assault: "The initial check on the beach was overcome because of the initiative displayed by the gunfire support ships, the assistance of the air force, and the intrepidity of the infantry on the shore line."[16] The men, material, processes, and coordination in developing such a capability was something truly new in warfare and was conducted on a scale never seen before. Only the United States could have accomplished such a feat.

Notes

Introduction

1. Oral Interview, Dr. Harold Baumgarten, www.ww2online.org/view/harold
-baumgarten#loading-up-and-crossing-the-english-channel, National World War
II Digital Archive, New Orleans, LA.

2. Harold Graham Shook, Biography, www.americanairmuseum.com/archive
/person/harold-graham-shook, American Air Museum in Britain Digital Archive,
Imperial War Museum, UK.

3. Oral Interview, Hal Shook, www.ww2online.org/view/hal-shook#d-day-in
-normandy, National World War II Digital Archive, New Orleans, LA.

4. The Amphibious Objective Area is defined as a geographical area of sufficient size to conduct the necessary sea, air, and land operations and within which is
located the objectives to secured by the amphibious force. Department of Defense,
Joint Publication 3-02, Amphibious Operations, www.jcs.mil (January 4, 2019).

5. Oral Interview, Irvin Klimas, www.ww2online.org/view/irvin-klimas#targe
ts-off-normandy.

6. Oral Interview, Irvin Klimas.

7. DD-627, www.hazegray.org/danfs/destroy/dd627txt.htm; Oral Interview,
Irwin Klimas.

8. USS Thompson, Index of Allied Warships during Operation Neptune, www
.dday-overlord.com/en/material/warships/uss-thompson; DD-627.

9. Gordon L. Rottman, *US World War II Amphibious Tactics: Mediterranean and
European Theaters* (Westminster, MD: Osprey Publishing, 2006), 11.

10. Adjutant General, US Army letter to Commandant, Command and General Staff College, Fort Leavenworth, Kansas, Subject: Request for Background
Information, RE: List of Assault Landings made during World War II, 9 Dec 1955,
Combined Arms Research Library (CARL) Digital Archive, No Call Number Assigned, Fort Leavenworth, KS.

11. Department of Defense, *Joint Publication 3-02, Amphibious Operations*, www
.jcs.mil/Portals/36/Documents/Doctrine/pubs/jp302/pdf?ver=CbqCq6-mhWVN
jsXKkqZRwA%3d%3d2019.

12. Jeter A. Isely and Philip Crowl, *The U.S. Marines and Amphibious War: Its
Theory and Its Practice in the Pacific* (Princeton, NJ: Princeton University Press,
1951), 36–44; Alan R. Millett, *Semper Fidelis: The History of the United States Marine
Corps* (New York: Macmillan Publishing Company, 1980), 331; Frank Hough, Verle
Ludwig, and Henry Shaw, *Headquarters U.S. Marine Corps, Pearl Harbor to Guadal-
canal. History of U.S. Marine Corps Operations in World War II, Volume 1* (Historical

Branch, G-3 Division), 21–22. *US Marine Corps, Tentative Landing Manual, 1934,* CARL Digital Archive, Call number N17315.492; Kenneth J. Clifford, *Amphibious Warfare in Britain and America from 1920–1940* (Laurens, NY: Edgewood, 1983), 102–105.

13. Joint Chiefs of Staff, *Joint Publication 3-02, Amphibious Operations,* III-01.

14. *Joint Publication 3-02,* xvi; Department of the Navy, *Fleet Training Publication 167, Landing Operations Doctrine,* 1938, 61–62, www.history.navy.mil/research/library/online-reading-room/title-list-alphabetically/l/landing-operations-doctrine-usn-ftp-167.html#chi-5; Isely and Crowl, 41–42; Clifford, 106.

15. *Joint Publication 3-02,* VII-6; *Fleet Training Publication 167,* 111; Isely and Crowl, 38–39; Clifford, 105.

16. *Fleet Training Publication 167,* 151–152; Isely and Crowl, 40–41; Clifford, 106.

17. *Joint Publication 3-02,* VI-6, GL-9.

18. *Fleet Training Publication 167,* 9; Isely and Crowl, 42–43; Clifford, 106.

19. *Fleet Training Publication 167,* 34–35; 161–168, 201–202; Isely and Crowl, 43–44; Clifford, 106–107.

Chapter 1. Join the Army's Navy: Early Amphibious Development

1. David S. Nasca, *The Emergence of American Amphibious Warfare 1898–1945* (Annapolis, MD: Naval Institute Press, 2020), 35–36.

2. Nasca, 42.

3. Hitch Peabody, "Paramount Interests: Command Relationships in Amphibious Warfare," Naval War College Paper, Newport RI, 18 May 2004, 6–7, https://apps.dtic.mil/sti/citations/ADA425987.

4. Lecture by Commander H. S. Knapp, "The Cooperation of the Army and Navy," delivered in 1907, Archives of U.S. Naval War College, Newport, RI, CARL Digital Archive, Call Number 355.46 K67c 1907.

5. Knapp.

6. Knapp.

7. Knapp.

8. Knapp.

9. Millett, 270–271; Nasca, 8–9, 16, 29.

10. Millet, 271.

11. Millet, 275–276.

12. John A. Lorelli, *To Foreign Shores: US Amphibious Operations in World War II* (Annapolis, MD: Naval Institute Press 1990), 8; Millett, 278–282; Isely and Crowl, 23.

13. Isely and Crowl, 18.

14. Isely and Crowl, 18; Angus Murray, "The Marine Corps and Gallipoli," in Timothy Heck and B. A. Friedman, eds., *On Contested Shores: The Evolving Role of Amphibious Operations in the History of Warfare* (Quantico, VA: Marine Corps University Press, 2020), 160–164; Nasca, 92–93.

15. Isley and Crowl, 25–26; Nasca, 161.

16. Millet, 326; Nasca, 199, 205.

17. Murray, "The Marine Corps and Gallipoli," 155, 160.

18. War Plan Orange outlined American military strategy given a war with Japan. The so-called Color Plans were a part of the Army–Navy Board's effort to outline military courses of action for a given country. Each enemy country was assigned a specific color.

19. Murray, "The Marine Corps and Gallipoli," 148; John T. Greenwood, "The US Army and Amphibious Warfare During World War II," in *Army History*, PB 20-93-4 (No. 27), Summer 1993, 3.

Samuel Eliot Morison, *History of the United States Naval Operations in World War II, Volume 2: Operations in North African Waters, October 1942–June 1943* (Boston: Little, Brown, and Company, 1975 [Reprint]), 2.

20. Isley and Crowl, 37–44.

21. United States Navy, *Fleet Training Publication 167 (FTP-167), Landing Operations Doctrine*, 29–31, www.history.navy.mil/research/library/online-reading-room /title-list-alphabetically/l/landing-operations-doctrine-usn-ftp-167.html#ch2-1; Greenwood, 7.

22. Morison, 2:20–21; Jerry E. Strahan, *Andrew Jackson Higgins and the Boats That Won World War II* (Baton Rouge: Louisiana State University Press, 1998), 29.

23. Gordon A. Harrison, *United States Army in World War II, The European Theater of Operations, Cross-Channel Attack* (Washington, DC: Department of the Army, Office of the Chief of Military History, 1951), 60; Strahan, 29.

24. Strahan, 26.

25. Strahan, 26.

26. Strahan, 26.

27. Clifford, 111; Strahan, 28.

28. Al Hansen to Engineer-in-Chief, June 8, 1937, as referenced in Strahan, 27.

29. Clifford, 112; Strahan, 41–42.

30. Victor "Brute" Krulak would become a highly decorated combat veteran of World War II, Korea, and Vietnam and rise to three-star rank. While many believed he was to be Commandant of the Marine Corps, Krulak was passed over. However, his son Charles become Commandant of the Marine Corps in 1995 and obtained four stars.

31. Clifford, 114; Strahan, 57–58.

32. Richard Overy, *Why the Allies Won* (New York: W. W. Norton, 1995), 139; Lorelli, 37; Blanche Coll, Jean Keith, Herbert Rosenthal, *The United States Army in World War II, The Technical Services. The Corps of Engineers: Troops and Equipment* (Washington, DC: Office of the Chief of Military History, Department of the Army, 1959), 360; Greenwood, 4; Nasca, 189.

33. Lorelli, 36; Greenwood, 4.

34. Harrison, 64; Leo J. Meyer, "The Decision to Invade North Africa (Torch)," in Kent Roberts Greenfield, ed., *Command Decisions* (Washington, DC: Center for Army History, 1960), 179; Lorelli, 36. This number fails to include the requirements for the Pacific War, which would increase the requirement exponentially.

35. Meyer, 179. In all the Higgins Company built approximately that number in support of the entire war effort.

36. Harrison, 13–16, 28–29; Greenwood, 6.

37. Meyer, 183.

38. Overy, 138; Lorelli, 42; Meyer, 174–175, 181; Alexandra Lohse, Jon Middaugh,

US Navy Operations in World War II, Operations Torch: The American Amphibious Assault on French Morocco (Washington DC: Naval History and Heritage Command, 2018), 3. Commander-in-Chief, Allied Expeditionary Force, Report on Operation Torch, 2, CARL Digital Archive Call Number N7290.2. (Referred as AEF Report), 5.

39. Dwight D. Eisenhower, *Crusade in Europe* (Garden City, NY: Double Day and Company, 1949), 51.

40. Overy, 139; Roland G. Ruppenthal, *The United States Army in World War II, The European Theater of Operations, Logistical Support of the Armies, Volume 1: May 1941–September 1944* (Washington, DC: Center of Military History, 1985), 328–329; Lorelli, 26–27; Nasca, 209; Morison, 2:268.

41. Overy, 139.

42. Lorelli, 36.

43. Andrew Whitmarsh, *D-Day Landing Craft* (Gloucestershire, UK: The History Press, 2024), 43.

44. Porch, 345.

45. Russell Weigley, *Eisenhower's Lieutenants: The Campaign of France and Germany 1944–1945* (Bloomington: Indiana University Press, 1990), 42; William Breuer, *Operation Dragoon: The Allied Invasion of Southern France* (Novato, CA: Presidio Press, 1987), 14; Ruppenthal, 182; Harrison, 64.

46. War Department, *Basic Field Manual, Landing Operations on Hostile Shores* (Washington, DC: US Government Printing office, 1942), II: Lorelli, 18; Lohse and Middaugh, 7; Christopher D. Yung, *Gators of Neptune: Naval Amphibious Planning for the Normandy Invasion* (Annapolis, MD, Naval Institute Press, 2006), 25; Adrian Lewis, *Omaha Beach: A Flawed Victory* (Chapel Hill, NC: University of North Carolina Press, 2001), 50.

47. Marshall O. Becker, *The Amphibious Training Center, Study No. 22* (Washington, DC: Historical Section, Army Ground Forces, 1946), 2, CARL Digital Library, Call Number N15036A; Ruppenthal, 328–329; Greenwood, 5.

48. Lorelli, 18, 23.

49. Coll, Keith, and Rosenthal, 355; Greenwood, 5.

50. The Joint Board, *Joint Action of the Army and Navy* (Washington, DC: US Government Printing Office, 1927), 1, CARL Digital Archive, No Call Number Assigned. The 1927 document was superseded by a revision in 1935; Greenwood, 2; Lohse and Middaugh, 9.

51. Morison, 2:2.

52. Greenwood, 5; Lorelli, 31; Yung, 23.

53. *FM 31-5*, 1–2; George F. Howe, *United States Army in World War II, The Mediterranean Theater of Operations, Northwest Africa: Seizing the Initiative in the West* (Washington, DC: Center of Military History, 1993), 39.

54. Coll, Keith, and Rosenthal, 356; US Navy, *Combat Narratives: The Landings in North Africa, November 1942* (Washington, DC: Office of Naval Intelligence, 1944), 12.

55. Greenwood, 2; H. Kent Hewitt (Evelyn Cherpak Ed.), U.S. Naval War College Digital Commons, *The Memoirs of Admiral Kent Hewitt* (Newport, RI: Naval War College Press, 2004), 146 (hereafter referred to as Hewitt, *Memoirs*).

56. Cole, 2; Coll, Keith, and Rosenthal, 358; US Navy, *Combat Narratives*, 12; Lewis, 68.

57. Final Report on Landing Operations LT 3-OT 18, January 8 to January 18, 1942, General Conclusions, Prepared by Major Harry E. McKinney, Fort Devon MA, CARL Digital Library, Call Number R2824.

58. Final Report on Landing Operations LT 3-OT 18.

59. Coll, Keith, and Rosenthal, 357.

60. William F. Heavey, *"Down Ramp": The Story of Army Amphibious Engineers* (Landsville, PA: Coachwhip Publications, 2010 Reprint), 12.

61. Coll, Keith, and Rosenthal, 357; Heavey, 12–13.

62. Coll, Keith, and Rosenthal, 363; Lewis, 67.

63. Merle T. Cole, *Cradle of Invasion: A History of the US Naval Amphibious Training Base, Solomons, Maryland, 1942–1945* (Solomons, MD: Calvert Marine Museum, 1984), 2; Morison, 2:21; Greenwood, 1, 3.

64. Richard Bass, *The Brigades of Neptune* (Devon, UK: Devon England, 1994), 13; Hewitt, *Memoirs*, 134; Harry Edwards, *A Different War: Marines in Europe and North Africa* (Washington, DC: Marine Corps History Center, 1994), 3.

65. Derrill Daniel, "Landings at Oran, Gela, and Omaha Beaches (An Infantry Battalion Commander's Observations)," Armed Forces Staff College, Norfolk, VA, September–January 1947–1948, CARL Digital Archive, Call Number N16759; Howe, 62–63.

66. Lewis, 65; Becker, 1; Cole, 2; Morison, 2:21; Greenwood, 3, 6; Yung, 30. A similar structure with the 2nd Marine Division and 3rd Infantry Division was created on the West Coast along with an accompanying Amphibious Force Pacific Fleet; Hewitt, *Memoirs*, 134; Walter Karig, *Battle Report, Volume 2: The Atlantic War* (New York: Farrar and Rinehart, 1946), 165–167.

67. Lohse and Middaugh, 8; Lewis, 63; George F. Howe, *US Army in World War II, Mediterranean Theater of Operations, Northwest Africa: Seizing the Initiative in the West* (Washington, DC: Center for Army History, 1993), 60; Hewitt, *Memoirs*, 85, 110.

68. Hewitt, *Memoirs*, 138.

69. Combat loading is a methodology in which embarkation and storage of items of equipment and supply are based on their importance in a combat environment. Thus, the high-priority gear is loaded last, as it can be accessed quickly in the assault. Conversely, lower-priority items are loaded first and often in the lower holds of a ship. One drawback is that combat loading does not make the best use of the available space on the ship. Hewitt, *Memoirs*, 147.

70. Headquarters, 9th Infantry Division, Notes on Training an Amphibious Division, 30 October 1942, CARL Digital Archive, Call Number N6148; The Armor School, *Armor in the Invasion of North Africa: A Research Report*, Fort Knox Kentucky, 29–30 CARL Digital Archive, Call Number 2146.43.

71. As referenced in Lewis, 64.

72. Greenwood, 5; Heavey, 10.

73. US War Department, *Basic Field Manual: FM 31-5 Landing Operations on Hostile Shores, June 1941*, 25, www.ibiblio.org/hyperwar/USA/ref/FM/FM31-5/FM 31-5-2.html#s2.

74. *FM 31-5*, 25.

75. *FM 31-5*, 25; Hewitt, *Memoirs*, 136.

76. US Army, *Engineer School Special Text ST 25-1: History and Traditions of the Corps of Engineers* (Fort Belvoir, VA: The Engineer School, 1953), 64; Heavey, 12.

77. Bass, 3; Greenwood, 5.

78. Lorelli, 41; Coll, Keith, and Rosenthal, 361; Ruppenthal, 329.

79. Bass, 3; Ruppenthal, 329; Greenwood, 5–6; Heavey, 10; Lewis, 70.

80. Engineer Amphibian Command, *Engineer Amphibian Troops and Operations: Tentative Training Guide 4* (Camp Edwards, MA, May 1943), CARL Digital Archive, Call Number N15535, 1; Yung, 31; Greenwood, 6.

81. Greenwood, 6; Richard T. Bass, *Spirits of the Sand: The Story of the United States Army Assault Training Center in Northern Devon* (Brighton, UK: Menin House, 2014), 13.

82. Coll, Keith, and Rosenthal, 363; Ruppenthal, 329; Becker, 3; *FM 31-5*, 5; Heavey, 12, 32; Greenwood, 6; Howe, 61.

83. Coll, Keith, and Rosenthal, 362; Ruppenthal, 329; Greenwood, 5; Heavey, 11, 12; Becker, 22.

84. Ruppenthal, 329.

85. War Department Letter to Commandant Command and General Staff School, Fort Leavenworth, Kansas, Subject: Handling Supplies Across the Beaches, 25 October 1944, CARL Digital Archive, Call Number N3562, 1; Bass, 4; Heavey, 46, 96; Greenwood, 8.

86. Ruppenthal, 329–330; Heavey, 11.

87. Engineer Amphibian Command Tentative Training Guide No 7, Engineer Amphibian Troops, The Organization of the Far Shore, 2, CARL Digital Archive, Call Number N15536.

88. US Army, *Engineer School Special Text ST 25-1*, 66; Becker, 23; Lorelli, 35.

89. Heavey, 29.

90. Bass, 7; Heavey, 46; US Army, *Engineer School Special Text ST 25-1*, 65; Ruppenthal, 330.

91. Heavey, 29, 34, 59, 64, 66, 124; Howe, 49–50, 62; US Army, *Engineer School Special Text ST 25-1*, 66.

92. Bass, 3; Coll, Keith, and Rosenthal, 365; Hewitt, *Memoirs*, 145.

93. Heavey, 13; Hewitt, *Memoirs*, 145.

94. Heavey, 13.

95. Heavey, 15.

96. Heavey, 12, 25.

97. Coll, Keith, and Rosenthal, 373.

98. Heavey, 23.

99. Heavey, 23.

100. Cole, 2–3; Coll, Keith, and Rosenthal, 360; Greenwood, 7.

101. Hewitt, *Memoirs*, 135.

102. Coll, Keith, and Rosenthal, 361; Greenwood, 4.

103. Coll, Keith, and Rosenthal, 361; Greenwood 4.

104. Ruppenthal, 331.

105. Coll, Keith, and Rosenthal, 361.

106. Coll, Keith, and Rosenthal, 358; Becker, 5.

107. Greenwood, 3–4.

108. Becker, 1; Coll, Keith, and Rosenthal, 355.

109. Becker, 1; Lorelli, 41; Greenwood, 3.

110. Becker, 1; David J. Coles, "'Hell by the Sea': Florida's Camp Gordon Johnston in World War II," *Florida Historical Quarterly* 73, no. 1 (July 1994): 5.

111. Becker, 1.

112. Becker, 1; Yung, 30; Lewis, 69.

113. Becker, 2.

114. Becker, 1, 8.

115. Greenwood, 5; Morison, 2:27; Yung, 32.

116. Coll, Keith, and Rosenthal, 368; Becker, 24.

117. Becker, 31; Yung, 31.

118. Becker, 2.

119. Coll, Keith, and Rosenthal, 361–365; Becker, 5.

120. Becker, 2; Coll, Keith, and Rosenthal, 379; Greenwood, 5.

121. Becker, 3, 5; Coll, Keith, and Rosenthal, 379; Howe, 61; Yung, 31; Greenwood, 4.

122. Nasca, 225; Coles, 5; Lewis, 71; Coles, 3.

123. Coles, 6.

124. Brigadier General Frank A. Keating, "Narrative" Development of Amphibious Training Center, as referenced in Becker, 5; Coll, Keith, and Rosenthal, 364.

125. Coll, Keith, and Rosenthal, 364; Becker, 7; Heavey, 19; Greenwood, 5.

126. Coll, Keith, and Rosenthal, 364; Heavey, 19–20.

127. Becker, 7.

128. Coll, Keith, and Rosenthal, 374.

129. Greenwood, 6; Heavey, 24. Some evaluation was also done at Fort Ord and Monterrey Bay, California, conducted by the 2nd ESB.

130. Coll, Keith, and Rosenthal, 375; Ruppenthal, 332.

131. Morison, 2:22, 28; Karig, 167, Becker, 3; Lorelli, 38; Howe, 60, 67; Cole, 2; Lohse and Middaugh, 7, Howe, 60; Hewitt, *Memoirs*, 135, 146.

132. Craig Symonds, *Neptune: The Allied Invasion of Europe and the D-Day Landings* (New York: Oxford University Press, 2014), 79; Strahan, 129–131; Hewitt, *Memoirs*, 135, 147.

133. Karig, 173; Strahan, 129; Hewitt, *Memoirs*, 135, 147.

134. Isley and Crowl, 71; Lohse and Middaugh, 7; H. Kent Hewitt, Correspondence to General George S. Patton, August 23, 1942, Coors Personal Apr-Sept 43, Folder 5, Box 2, H. Kent Hewitt Papers, Library of Congress (LOC), Washington, DC; Hewitt, *Memoirs*, 137.

135. Cole, 9; Karig, 167.

136. Karig, 168.

137. Morison, 2:28; George R. Howe, *United States Army in World War II, The Mediterranean Theater of Operations, Northwest Africa: Seizing the Initiative in the West* (Washington, DC: Office of the Chief of Military History, 1957), 12–13.

138. Morison, 2:28–29; Howe, 15; Lohse and Middaugh, 8; H. K. Hewitt letter to Rear Admiral Cooke, August 11, 1942, Coors Personal Apr-Sept 43, Folder 5, Box 2, Hewitt Papers.

139. Morison, 2:28–29; Coll, Keith, and Rosenthal, 356; Hewitt, *Memoirs*, 136.

140. Ruppenthal, 335.

141. H. Kent Hewitt Correspondence to General George S. Patton, August 27, 1942, Folder 5, Box 2, Hewitt Papers; Hewitt, *Memoirs*, 35.

142. H. Kent Hewitt, Correspondence to General George S. Patton September 1, 1942, Coors Personal Apr-Sept 43, Folder 5, Box 2, Hewitt Papers; *Armor in the Invasion of North Africa*, 30.

143. Ruppenthal, 335.

144. H. Kent Hewitt Correspondence to General George S. Patton, August 28, 1942, Enclosure (1), Program for General Staff School, Coors Personal Apr-Sept 43, Folder 5, Box 2, Hewitt Papers.

145. Hewitt, *Memoirs*, 138.

146. Morison, 2:30; Becker, 4; Hewitt, *Memoirs*, 136; Robert von Der Osten, *LST 388: A World War II Journal* (Deeds, GA: Atlanta Publishing, 2017), 17, 19.

147. Hewitt, *Memoirs*, 136.

148. Morison, 2:30.

149. H. Kent Hewitt, Correspondence to General George S. Patton, August 23, 1942.

150. H. Kent Hewitt, Correspondence to Major General Thos. T. Handy, September 7, 1942, Coors Personal Apr-Sept 43, Folder 5, Box 2, Hewitt Papers; H. Kent Hewitt Correspondence to General George S. Patton, August 27, 1942; H. Kent Hewitt Correspondence to General George S. Patton, August 28, 1942, Hewitt Papers; Hewitt, *Memoirs*, 138.

151. H. Kent Hewitt, Correspondence to General George S. Patton, August 23, 1942; Hewitt Papers.

152. Headquarters, Ninth Infantry Division, Notes on Training an Amphibious Infantry Division, October 30, 1942, CARL Digital Archive, Call Number N6148.

153. Dave Gutierrez, *Patriots from the Barrio: The Story of Company E, 141st Infantry Division: The Only All Mexican American Army Unit in World War II* (Yardley, PA: Westholme Publishing LLC, 2018), 56–57.

154. Heavey, 19, 26; Becker, 10, 52; Gutierrez, 56.

155. Heavey, 40; Yung, 31; Gutierrez, 56–57.

156. Heavey, 43; Becker, 12.

157. Camp Gordon Johnston *Amphibian* Newspaper, June 5, 1943. Available on microfilm at the Robert Manning Strozier Library, Florida State University; Undated clipping from *Florida Highways* in Florida Collection, State Library of Florida, Tallahassee, FL. As referenced by Coles.

158. US Army Corps of Engineers Map, 1995 Archive Search Report, Florida Department Environmental Protection, September 2011, Carabelle, Franklin County, Florida 32322, US Highway 98, Camp Gordon Johnston; US Army Corps of Engineers, Defense Environmental Restoration Program, Archives Search Report, Findings of the Former Camp Gordon Johnston, Franklin County FL, Project Number: IO4FL011004, September 1996, 3–4; Coles, 8.

159. Coles, 11.

160. Coles, 5.

161. Omar Bradley and Clay Blair, *A General's Life: An Autobiography* (New York: Simon and Schuster, 1983), 112; Steve Ossad, *Omar Bradley Nelson: America's GI General, 1893–1981* (Columbia, MO: University of Missouri Press, 2017), 87.

162. Coles, 8.

163. Unnamed Camp Carrabelle newspaper, October 16, 1942, as referenced in Coles, 8, 11.

164. Becker, 48; Coles, 14.

165. Becker, 32–45, 58; Coles, 12; Army Corps of Engineers, Archive Search Report, 12.

166. Headquarters Amphibious Training Command, Training Circular 10, December 17, 1942, Synopsis of Events, 38th Infantry Division Landing Exercise, 1, CARL Digital Archive, Call Number N3095.

167. Becker, 63; Coles, 12.

168. Becker, 65; Coles, 12.

169. Becker, 66, 69.

170. Becker, 8.

171. Becker, 8.

172. Becker, 3.

173. Becker, 15; Greenwood, 4; Coll, Keith, and Rosenthal, 378.

174. Joint Chiefs of Staff, 81/1 Distribution and Composition of US Amphibious Forces, 5 Sept 1942, as references in Coll, Keith, and Rosenthal, 378.

175. Greenwood, 7–8; Becker, 17; Coles, WWII Museum, 17.

176. Becker, 72.

177. Lewis, 73; Coles, 15; Becker, 17, 72; Coles, WWII Museum, 18; Army Corps of Engineers, Archive Search Report, 8, 13.

178. Greenwood, 7; Coll, Keith, and Rosenthal, 372.

179. Greenwood, 7.

180. Heavey, 32.

181. Greenwood, 7.

Chapter 2. Hit-or-Miss Affair: Operation Torch, November 1942

1. Morison, 2:135, 190, 223; Worral Reed Carter and Elmer Ellsworth Duvall, *Ships, Salvage, and Sinews of War: The Story of the Fleet Logistics Afloat in the Atlantic and Mediterranean Waters During World War II* (Washington, DC: US Government Printing office, 1954), 134–135; AEF Report, 6; Daniel, *Landings at Oran, Gela, and Omaha Beaches*, 6.

2. Morison, 2:15–16.

3. Meyer, 175; US Navy, *Combat Narratives*, 6.

4. Office of the Historian US State Department, FOREIGN RELATIONS OF THE UNITED STATES: DIPLOMATIC PAPERS, 1942, EUROPE, VOLUME III, "Memorandum of Conference Held at the White House, by Mr. Samuel H. Cross, Interpreter," https://history.state.gov/historicaldocuments/frus1942v03/d471.

5. Howe, 16; Morison, 2:134–135; Reed and Duvall, 135; AEF Report, 2; Assistant C/S intelligence Historical Division, US Air Force Historical Study, no. 105 (AAFRH-5), Air Phase of North African Invasion, November 1944, 1–4, CARL Digital Archive, No Call Number Assigned; US Navy, *Combat Narratives*, 3.

6. Howe, 4.

7. Carter and Duvall, 135; Lohse and Middaugh, 1; AEF Report, 7; Greenwood, 7.

8. Morison, 2:135, 190, 223; Carter and Duvall, 134–135, 138–139; US Navy, *Combat Narratives*, 71; AEF Report, 12.

9. Douglas Porch, *The Path to Victory: The Mediterranean Theater in World War II* (New York: Farrrar, Straus, and Giroux, 2004), 348.

10. The three-dimensional space that is the amphibious objective area, defined above (see Introduction, n.4), referring to the geographical location of an amphibious assault that encompasses all three domains of air, land, and sea, must be large enough to encompass all amphibious operations and is designed for an established period of time.

11. Morison, 2:5–7.

12. Porch, 350; Walter Consuelo Langsam, *Historic Documents of World War II* (New York: Van Nostrand Company, 1958), 52; Hewitt, *Memoirs*, 151, 165.

13. Headquarters Services of Supply, Report of Operations in North Africa, 12 December 1942, 2, CARL Digital Archive, Call Number N6186 (hereafter, SoS Report of Operations); US Navy, *Combat Narratives*, 1; *Armor in the Invasion of North Africa*, 66.

14. Langsam, 53.

15. Correspondence, Marshall to Eisenhower, Ref No-R1573, Directive to the Commander in Chief Allied Expeditionary Force From the Combined Chiefs of Staff, 5 October 1942. National Archives and Records Administration (NARA), as referenced at https://liberationtrilogy.com/books/army-at-dawn/historical-documents/slideshow/.

16. Marshall to Eisenhower, Ref No-R1573.

17. *Armor in the Invasion of North Africa*, 64.

18. *Armor in the Invasion of North Africa*, 21–24.

19. *Armor in the Invasion of North Africa*, 62.

20. Reed and Duvall, 141.

21. US Navy, *Combat Narratives*, 13; Hewitt, *Memoirs*, 151; *Armor in the Invasion of North Africa*, 30. However, although the Armor School number regarding transports available is different, the order of magnitude of the fleet's growth is representative.

22. Karig, 177.

23. US Navy, *Combat Narratives*, 6; Lohse and Middaugh, 13; Howe, 61; Hewitt, *Memoirs*, 157; Wing at War Series, no. 6, *The AAF in Northwest Africa: An Account of the Twelfth Air Force in the Northwest Africa Landings and The Battle of Tunisia* (Washington, DC: Center for Air Force History, 1992, Reprint), 9; *Armor in the Invasion of North Africa*, 21–22.

24. Morison, 2:267; Hewitt, *Memoirs*, 148; Wings at War Series, no. 6, 11; *Armor in the Invasion of North Africa*, 29.

25. Howe, 40–41, 45, 117–118; Karig, 175, 201; Morison, 2:51; AEF Report, 4; Hewitt, *Memoirs*, 147.

26. Karig, 178; US Navy, *Combat Narratives*, 13; Hewitt, *Memoirs*, 157; Armor in the Invasion of North Africa, 61.

27. Morison, 2:116; US Navy, *Combat Narratives*, 14; Lohse and Middaugh, 39; *Armor in the Invasion of North Africa*, 111.

28. Rick Atkinson, *An Army at Dawn: The War in North Africa, 1942–1943* (New

York: Henry Holt and Co., 2002), 38; Karig, 179–180; US Navy, *Combat Narratives*, 14; Hewitt, *Memoirs*, 147, 160; *Armor in the Invasion of North Africa*, 121.

29. Morison, 2:49; Atkinson, *An Army at Dawn*, 104–105; AEF Report, 11; Hewitt, *Memoirs*, 164; *Armor in the Invasion of North Africa*, 63.

30. Morison, 2:45–50; Atkinson, *Army at Dawn*, 105; Lohse and Middaugh, 19–20; Hewitt, *Memoirs*, 164.

31. Morison, 2:50; US Navy, *Combat Narratives*, 18.

32. *Armor in the Invasion of North Africa*, 63; Atkinson, *An Army at Dawn*, 69; Carter and Duvall, 136, 162.

33. US Navy, *Combat Narratives*, 34; *Armor in the Invasion of North Africa*, 67, 110.

34. *Armor in the Invasion of North Africa*, 110, 112; Morison, 2:117; Karig, 192–195; Atkinson, *An Army at Dawn*, 143.

35. Morison, 2:116–118.

36. *Armor in the Invasion of North Africa*, 119.

37. Lewis, 51.

38. Morison, 2:117; Howe, 155; Atkinson, *An Army at Dawn*, 144; Hewitt, *Memoirs*, 171; *Armor in the Invasion of North Africa*, 119–120.

39. AEF Report, 12.

40. *FM 31-5*, 16.

41. *Armor in the Invasion of North Africa*, 123; Howe, 153; Lucian K. Truscott, *Command Missions: A Personal Story* (New York: E. Dutton and Co., 1954), 91; Karig, 191–193; Hewitt, *Memoirs*, 151; Porch, 350. Messages were also transmitted from USS *Texas* at 0630 that morning.

42. Howe, 153–155; Morison, 2:121–122; Truscott, 91, 96–97; Atkinson, *An Army at Dawn*, 111; Hewitt, *Memoirs*, 167; *Armor in the Invasion of North Africa*, 123; SoS Report of Operations, 2–3.

43. US Navy, *Combat Narratives*, 39.

44. Howe, 155; Morison, 2:122, 126; Karig, 192–196; Carter and Duvall, 162–163; US Navy, *Combat Narratives*, 39; Hewitt, *Memoirs*, 167–168; Symonds, 87.

45. Morison, 2:123; Karig, 195; US Navy, *Combat Narratives*, 41; Lohse and Middaugh, 42; Wings at War Series, no. 6, 10; *Armor in the Invasion of North Africa*, 127.

46. Howe, 159; Truscott, 112; US Navy, *Combat Narratives*, 39; *Armor in the Invasion of North Africa*, 122, 127; SoS Report of Operations, 18.

47. Howe, 157; Truscott, 95; Wilson A. Heefner, *Dogface Soldier: The Life of Lucian K. Truscott* (Columbia: University of Missouri Press, 2010), 65–66; Headquarters, Seventh Infantry, Brief Resume of the Action of RLG-7, Commanding General, Western Task Force, Lessons Learned from Operation TORCH, 10, CARL Digital Library, Call Number N12155.

48. Brief Resume of the Action of RLG-7, 8–10; Howe, 158; Morison, 2:123–124; Truscott, 95; *Armor in the Invasion of North Africa*, 126.

49. Brief Resume of the Action of RLG-7, 10; Morison, 2:127; Truscott, 109, 113; Atkinson, *An Army at Dawn*, 109; Lohse and Middaugh, 41; Hewitt, *Memoirs*, 171; SoS Report of Operations, 18.

50. Howe, 160; Heefner, 65–66; *Armor in the Invasion of North Africa*, 126.

51. Karig, 195–196; Atkinson, *An Army at Dawn*, 145; Heefner, 66; Lohse and Middaugh, 43; *Armor in the Invasion of North Africa*, 126; SoS Report of Operations, 17.

52. Howe, 156–157; Heefner, 66; Lohse and Middaugh, 43.

53. *Armor in the Invasion of North Africa*, 127–128.

54. Bass, 7.

55. *Armor in the Invasion of North Africa*, 128.

56. Howe, 160–161, 169; Truscott, 117; Heefner, 66; Carter and Duvall, 163–164; Brief Resume of the Action of RLG-7, 9; *Armor in the Invasion of North Africa*, 123; SoS Report of Operations, 18.

57. Morison, 2:123; Symonds, 91.

58. US Navy, *Combat Narratives*, 46; *Armor in the Invasion of North Africa*, 130; War Department, Services of Supply, Lessons Learned from Recent Amphibious Operations in North Africa, February 12, 1943, Annex G-1, CARL Digital Library, Call Number N6023.

59. Morison, 2:128; AEF Report, 12; US Navy, *Combat Narratives*, 43–44.

60. Howe, 167; Morison, 2:132; Truscott, 119–120; Karig, 200.

61. US Navy, *Combat Narratives*, 45; *Armor in the Invasion of North Africa*, 121.

62. Morison, 2:130; Karig, 198; Atkinson, *An Army at Dawn*, 146–148; Heefner, 67; US Navy, *Combat Narratives*, 42; Wing at War Series, no. 6, 11; SoS Report of Operations, 18.

63. Howe, 165, 169; Morison, 2:130–131; Truscott, 120; Karig, 199; Atkinson, *An Army at Dawn*, 141; Carter and Duvall, 165; US Navy, *Combat Narratives*, 43; Lohse and Middaugh, 11, 39; Hewitt, *Memoirs*, 147; *Armor in the Invasion of North Africa*, 61, 121, 133.

64. Morison, 2:131; Howe, 169; US Navy, *Combat Narratives*, 46; Hewitt, *Memoirs*, 147.

65. Howe, 169; Morison, 2:131; Carter and Duvall, 166.

66. Truscott, 120–123; Heefner, 67; US Navy, *Combat Narratives*, 45; *Armor in the Invasion of North Africa*, 134; Howe, 170; Morison, 2:133.

67. Lohse and Middaugh, 13; Morison, 2:55; Howe, 121; *Armor in the Invasion of North Africa*, 66.

68. Morison, 2:56–57; Karig, 201–202; Howe, 117–118; US Navy, *Combat Narratives*, 55–57; Lohse and Middaugh, 29; *Armor in the Invasion of North Africa*, 57, 66–67.

69. US Navy, *Combat Narratives*, 55.

70. US Navy, *Combat Narratives*, 57; *Armor in the Invasion of North Africa*, 67.

71. Brief Resume of the Action of RLG-7; Morison, 2:58–59; Karig, 202–203; Howe, 123–124; *Armor in the Invasion of North Africa*, 57, 67.

72. Brief Resume of the Action of RLG-7, 2; As referenced in Morison, 2:61; *Armor in the Invasion of North Africa*, 67–70; SoS Report of Operations, 3.

73. Morison, 2:60; Howe, 124; US Navy, *Combat Narratives*, 57.

74. Report of Commanding General 3rd ID to General Patton as referenced in Morison, 2:60.

75. *Armor in the Invasion of North Africa*, 70; Howe, 124.

76. Morison, 2:60–61.

77. Brief Resume of the Action of RLG-7, 10; Morison, 2:61; Howe, 124–125.

78. US Navy, *Combat Narratives*, 57.

79. Howe, 125; Morison, 2:73.

80. Howe, 125; Lohse and Middaugh, 30–31; Brief Resume of the Action of

RLG-7, 9; *Armor in the Invasion of North Africa*, 70, 74; War Department, Services of Supply, Lessons Learned, Annex G; SoS Report of Operations, 4.

81. Brief Resume of the Action of RLG-7, 2; Morison, 2:60–62; Howe, 125; Carter and Duvall, 170; Atkinson, *An Army at Dawn*, 109; Lohse and Middaugh, 31.

82. Howe, 125; Morison, 2:64; *Armor in the Invasion of North Africa*, 71.

83. SoS Report of Operations, 4; Brief Resume of the Action of RLG-7, 8–9; Morison, 2:64; Lowe, 125. The two references do not match in the number of destroyed craft.

84. Lowe, 125–126.

85. Carter and Duvall, 170; Morison, 2:79. Another account by the US Navy has the percentage up to a 64 percent loss rate.

86. Carter and Duvall, 170; Porch, 352.

87. Strahan, 3.

88. Strahan, 2, 188.

89. Strahan, 2.

90. Morison, 2:57, 63; Lowe, 125–126; Oral Interview with Carl Gatin, National World War II Museum, On Line Archive, www.ww2online.org/view/carl-gatlin #fighting-in-casablanca.

91. Lowe, 125; *Armor in the Invasion of North Africa*, 72.

92. Morison, 2:82–83; Porch, 352.

93. Atkinson, *An Army at Dawn*, 136.

94. *Armor in the Invasion of North Africa*, 71; Morison, 2:64–65.

95. Howe, 127; US Navy, *Combat Narratives*, 57; *Armor in the Invasion of North Africa*, 71; SoS Report of Operations, 4.

96. Morison, 2:75; Karig, 203; Howe, 130; US Navy, *Combat Narratives*, 57–58.

97. Morison, 2:75.

98. Brief Resume of the Action of RLG-7, 10; Howe, 130; Lohse and Middaugh, 33; *Armor in the Invasion of North Africa*, 72.

99. *Armor in the Invasion of North Africa*, 71; Howe, 127; Atkinson, *An Army at Dawn*, 137.

100. Howe, 128; Lohse and Middaugh, 28.

101. Howe, 128–129; SoS Report of Operations, 7.

102. Morison, 2:99; Howe, 134.

103. Morison, 2:110–111; 133–134; Porch, 352; Hewitt, *Memoirs*, 172–173; Wings at War Series, no. 6, 10.

104. Lowe, 131; Lohse and Middaugh, 34; Hewitt, *Memoirs*, 173. Hewitt reports Patton was delayed only by three hours.

105. *Armor in the Invasion of North Africa*, 73.

106. Brief Resume of the Action of RLG-7, 10; Morison, 2:81; *Armor in the Invasion of North Africa*, 74.

107. Atkinson, *An Army at Dawn*, 136; Porch, 352.

108. "Lighterage" is a generic term for vessels specifically designed for ship-to-shore movement. Hewitt, *Memoirs*, 148; *Armor in the Invasion of North Africa*, 87.

109. Howe, 97–102; Morison, 2:135–138; Karig, 184–185; Carter and Duvall, 175; US Navy, *Combat Narratives*, 46; *Armor in the Invasion of North Africa*, 88.

110. Howe, 100–101; Morison, 2:137–138; Karig, 185; Carter and Duvall, 176; US Navy, *Combat Narratives*, 49; Lohse and Middaugh, 21.

111. Headquarters, 1st Infantry Division, 301-03: After Action Report Against Enemy, 4 Sept–10 Nov, dated 5 Dec 1942, 3, Collection Historical Records First Infantry Division, RRMRC Digital Archive (hereafter referred to as 1st ID REPORT).

112. War Department, Lessons Learned from Recent Amphibious Operations, 1, Annex F-1; 1st Infantry Division, Subject: TORCH OPERATION REPORT, 5, CARL Digital Archive, Call Number N6193.

113. Howe, 103; Morison, 2:142–143; US Navy, *Combat Narratives*, 48.

114. Howe, 102–104; Morison, 2:142; US Navy, *Combat Narratives*, 48; *Armor in the Invasion of North Africa*, 96.

115. Karig, 185; *Armor in the Invasion of North Africa*, 89; SoS Report of Operations, 14.

116. Karig, 187; US Navy, *Combat Narratives*, 49.

117. Howe, 105, 145–146; Karig, 186–187; Carter and Duvall, 176; US Navy, *Combat Narratives*, 49–50; Lohse and Middaugh, 25; Wings at War Series, no. 6, 11; *Armor in the Invasion of North Africa*, 93.

118. Howe, 104–105; Karig, 188.

119. Lohse and Middaugh, 25; *Armor in the Invasion of North Africa*, 98.

120. Howe, 105; Morison, 2:148; Karig, 188; Carter and Duvall, 176; US Navy, *Combat Narratives*, 50–51.

121. *Armor in the Invasion of North Africa*, 102–103.

122. Karig, 190; US Navy, *Combat Narratives*, 54.

123. Morison, 2:151–152; Karig, 189; Carter and Duvall, 182; US Navy, *Combat Narratives*, 51–52.

124. Morison, 2:152; Karig, 189; US Navy, *Combat Narratives*, 52; *Armor in the Invasion of North Africa*, 101–102; SoS Report of Operations, 14.

125. Carter and Duvall, 174–175.

126. Carter and Duvall, 187; Karig, 210; US Navy, *Combat Narratives*, 62, 64; Heavey, 47. (However, the United Kingdom was short some twenty-five crews that were filled by American personnel.); Daniel, *Landings*, 6.

127. Headquarters, 1st Infantry Division, Subject: TORCH OPERATION, November 24, 1942, 1, CARL Digital Archive, No Call Number Assigned; 301 INF (16) Co, 1st Bn 1 Aug 1942–15 June 1945; Heavey, 47; US Navy, *Combat Narratives*, 62, 64 Morison, 2:223; Daniel, *Landings*, 4; Karig, 210–212; AEF Report, 9; National World War 2 Museum On line Archive Interview with Theodore Skinner, www.ww2online.org/view/theodore-skinner#combat-tour-in-north-africa.

128. Daniel, *Landings*, 5.

129. 301 INF (16), 1.

130. Heavey, 29; Morison, 2:223.

131. Heavey, 31.

132. Howe, 62.

133. Daniel, *Landings*, 4, 8; AEF Report, 14; 1st Infantry Division, Subject: TORCH OPERATION, 2.

134. Morison, 2:223; Howe, 192–205; Atkinson, *An Army at Dawn*, 78–79; Daniels, *Landings*, 6, 8.

135. Headquarters, 1st Infantry Division, Field Order No. 1, 11 October 1942, Annex 8, CARL Digital Archive, Call Number N11291; Headquarters 1st Infantry

Division, Subject: TORCH OPERATION REPORT, November 24, 1942, CARL Digital Archive, No Call Number Assigned; Daniel, *Landings*, 8.

136. The two cutters *Walney* and *Hartland* were originally American-built vessels provided to the Royal Navy under Lend-Lease.

137. Karig, 216; Symonds, 88; Daniel, *Landings*, 8.

138. Atkinson, *An Army at Dawn*, 88.

139. Wings at War Series, no. 6, 17.

140. AEF Report, 13; Atkinson, *An Army at Dawn*, 91; Wings at War Series, no. 6, 16–17; Daniel, *Landings*, 8; Assistant Chief of the Air Staff Intelligence, Report by Colonel William Bentley on Paratroop Operations in North Africa, March 17, 1943, CARL Digital Archive, Call Number N3047.

141. Karig, 211, 216–217; US Navy, *Combat Narratives*, 63; Howe, 193.

142. Daniel, *Landings*, 7; AEF Report, 7, 13.

143. Howe, 194.

144. Heavey, 47–48; Karig, 213–214; US Navy, *Combat Narratives*, 63; Howe, 195; Morison, 2:236.

145. Heavey, 47.

146. US Navy *Combat Narratives*, 69.

147. Daniel, *Landings*, 8; Oral Interview with Theodore Skinner.

148. Morison, 2:267; Hewitt, *Memoirs*, 143; Harrison, 61–62.

149. Heavey, 49; Howe, 196–198; Morison, 2:236; War Department, Services of Supply, Lessons Learned, Annex F-1.

150. Howe, 199; Morison, 2:235.

151. 1st Infantry Division, Subject: TORCH OPERATION REPORT, 2.

152. Howe, 199.

153. Daniels, *Landings*, 6, 9; Lohse and Middaugh, 48.

154. 301 INF (16), 1; Heavey, 49; Carter and Duvall, 188–189; Karig, 213–214; Howe, 205–206; Atkinson, *An Army at Dawn*, 79–80; Daniels, *Landings*, 10; 1st Infantry Division, Subject: TORCH OPERATION, 2.

155. 1st Infantry Division, Subject: TORCH OPERATION REPORT, 2; Howe, 206; AEF Report, 13.

156. Heavey, 50; Karig, 217; Atkinson, *An Army at Dawn*, 85.

157. Heavey, 51; US Army, *Engineer School Special Text ST 25-1*, 66.

158. Carter and Duvall, 189.

159. Carter and Duvall, 200.

160. US Navy, *Combat Narratives*, 70; Howe, 230; Karig, 218–219.

161. US Navy, *Combat Narratives* 71; Howe, 234; Morison, 2:190. AEF Report, 9.

162. Carter and Duvall, 184; Howe, 230, 234–235, 236–237; Morison, 2:190–191; AEF Report, 7, 15.

163. Howe, 241; AEF Report, 9.

164. Howe, 241–244.

165. Carter and Duvall, 183–184; Morison, 2:193; AEF Report, 11; Ruppenthal, *Logistical Support of the Armies*, 330; Howe, 62; War Department, Services of Supply, Lessons Learned, Annex D.

166. Eastern Assault Force, United States Army, Lessons from Operation TORCH, 26 December, 1942, 2, CARL Digital Archive Call Number N6193; Howe, 62.

167. Eastern Assault Force Lessons, 2; Porch, 350–351; Howe, 237–138; Morison, 2:200–201; War Department, Services of Supply, Lessons Learned, Annex G.

168. War Department, Headquarters, Services of Supply, Lessons Learned from Recent Amphibious Operations in North Africa, Annex G-1, CARL Digital Archive, Call Number N6023; Eastern Assault Force Lessons, 7; Howe, 244–246, 247; Morison, 2:202.

169. Morison, 2:202.

170. Eastern Assault Force Lessons, 6–7; Brief Resume of the Action of RLG-7, 9; Morison, 2:203; War Department, Services of Supply, Lessons Learned, Annex F-1.

171. Eastern Assault Force Lessons, 6–7; Morison, 2:193.

172. Howe, 236–237; Morison, 2:204.

173. Morison, 2:205.

174. Morison, 2:206.

175. Karig, 219; Morison, 2:204.

176. Porch, 351; Howe, 251; AEF Report, 16; Symonds, 94.

177. Howe, 244; Karig, 223; Morison, 2:209.

Chapter 3. Training as Soon as Possible: FAITC and LANCRAB, Spring 1943

1. Allied Force Headquarters, Commander-in-Chief's Dispatch, Sicilian Campaign, 1943, 24, CARL Digital Archive, Call Number 15457 (hereafter referred to as AFH Dispatch), 31; Porch, 415, 368; Carlo D'Este, *Bitter Victory: The Battle for Sicily* (New York: E. P. Dutton, 1988), 34–35.

2. Albert Garland and Howard McGraw Smyth, *US Army in War II, Mediterranean Theater of Operations: Sicily and the Surrender of Italy* (Washington, DC: Center for Army History, 2002), 8; Porch, 417.

3. Garland and McGraw, 10; D'Este, *Bitter Victory*, 34, 36–39; AFH Dispatch, 4; Yung, 47.

4. Garland and McGraw, 17; Porch, 417; AFH Dispatch, 31.

5. AEF AAR, 10.

6. AEF AAR, 12.

7. Headquarters, Seventh Infantry, Brief Resume of the Action of RLG-7, Commanding General, Western Task Force, Lessons Learned from Operation TORCH, 1; AEF AAR, 10.

8. Commander Amphibious Force, Atlantic Fleet, Correspondence to Commander-in-Chief US Fleet, Subject: TORCH Operation, Comments and Recommendations, December 22, 1942, 2. CARLA Call Number N6108 (hereafter referred to as AFAF, CAR).

9. Allied Force Headquarters, Staff Memorandum, 7: Lessons of Operation Torch, 19 January 1943, 4, CARL Digital Archive, Call Number N6024, 36 (hereafter referred to as Staff Memorandum, 7).

10. Samuel Eliot Morison, *History of the United States Navy Operations in World War II, Volume 9: Sicily—Salerno—Anzio, January 1943–June 1944* (Boston: Little, Brown and Company, 1954), 21; United States Naval Administration in World War

II, Action Report-Western Naval Task Force, The Sicilian Campaign: Operation "Husky" July–August, 1943, 86, CARL Digital Active, Call Number N6884 (hereafter referred to as Action Report-Western Naval Task Force); Yung, 39; Edwards, 23.

11. Headquarters, Seventh Infantry, Brief Resume of the Action of RLG-7, Commanding General, Western Task Force, Lessons Learned from Operation TORCH, 3, 5; AFAF, CAR, 4, 6; Staff Memorandum, 7, 55, 36; *Armor in the Invasion of North Africa*, 143.

12. Staff Memorandum, 7, 4, 13.

13. AFAF, CAR, 9–10; Staff Memorandum, 7, 28.

14. Staff Memorandum, 7, 12.

15. AFAC, CAR, First Conclusions on Amphibious Aspects of Operation TORCH, dated January 9, 1943, 1; Eastern Assault Force, Lessons Learned, 4.

16. Reports by Observers on Current Operations in North Africa, February 12, 1943, Annex D, CARL Digital Archive, Call Number N6023; Headquarters, Seventh Infantry, Brief Resume of the Action of RLG-7, Commanding General, Western Task Force, Lessons Learned from Operation TORCH, 5; 1st ID AAR, 2, CARL Digital Archive, Call Number N12177, 8; Staff Memorandum, 7, 21, 27, 28, 29, 51, 53, 62; *Armor in the Invasion of North Africa*, 146.

17. AFAF, CAR, 25; US Atlantic Fleet, Summary of First Conclusions, 1; Ruppenthal, 331; *Armor in the Invasion of North Africa*, 144.

18. Staff Memorandum, 7, 29, 30, 61, 62; SoS Report of Operations, 32.

19. Staff Memorandum, 7, 26, 28, 62, 28, 51, 52, 60; SoS Report of Operations, 26.

20. Staff Memorandum, 7, 29.

21. AFAF, CAR, 13; SoS Report of Operations, 26; Reports by Observers on Current Operations in North Africa, Annex G-2.

22. AFAF, CAR, 15; Eastern Assault Force, Lessons Learned, 3.

23. Commanding General, Western Task Force, Lessons Learned from Operation TORCH, 8; Staff Memorandum, 7, 3, 6, 7, 26. *Armor in the Invasion of North Africa*, 145 Eastern Assault Force, Lessons Learned, 3. LCM-Landing Craft Medium; LCV-Landing Craft Vehicle; LCP-Landing Craft Personnel.

24. Staff Memorandum, 7; Heavey, 54; Eastern Assault Force Lessons Learned, 3.

25. Headquarters, Seventh Infantry, Brief Resume of the Action of RLG-7, Commanding General, Western Task Force, Lessons Learned from Operation TORCH, 6–7; 1st ID AAR: *Armor in the Invasion of North Africa*, 75, 145.

26. AFAF, CAR, 25.

27. Staff Memorandum, 7, 3, 19, 22, 27, 36; Reports by Observers on Current Operations in North Africa, Annex C-1.

28. Reports by Observers on Current Operations in North Africa, Annex C-2; *Armor in the Invasion of North Africa*, 75; Headquarters, Seventh Infantry, Brief Resume of the Action of RLG-7, Commanding General, Western Task Force, Lessons Learned from Operation TORCH, 6; Seventh Army, Report of Operations of the United States Seventh Army in the Sicily Campaign, 10 July–17 August 1943, a-8, CARL Digital Archive, Call Number Special 940.514273 U56ro; Morison, 9:80; SoS Report of Operations, 27. The rest of the troops personal items and gear remained afloat and landed at a later time.

29. Staff Memorandum, 7, 3, 6, 11, 21, 23, 51, 55, 65, 66; US Atlantic Fleet, Summary

of First Conclusions, 1; *Armor in the Invasion of North Africa*, 144; Commanding General, Western Task Force, Lessons Learned from Operation TORCH, 8; 1st Infantry Division, Subject: TORCH OPERATION REPORT, 5.

30. The one-third rule states that one-third of planning time should be consumed by higher staff, leaving two-thirds of the remaining planning time for subordinate units to act accordingly. Staff Memorandum, 7, 4, 19, 26, 63.

31. Staff Memorandum, 7, 26, 51, 65; 1st Infantry Division, Subject: TORCH OPERATION REPORT, 5.

32. Allied Force Headquarters, Subject: Signal Communications of Operation X, 16 February 1943, 2, CARL Digital Archive Call Number 46038c; 1st Infantry Division, Subject: TORCH OPERATION REPORT, 5; Digest of Report.

33. Signal Communications of Operation X, 7; Eastern Assault Force, Lessons Learned, 3; Reports by Observers on Current Operations in North Africa, Annex H.

34. AFAF, CAR, 16, 18; Staff Memorandum, 7, 20, 29, 31.

35. Signal Communications of Operation X, 15.

36. AFAF, 16; Staff Memorandum, 21.

37. AFAF, 18.

38. AFAF, 19; Staff Memorandum, 7, 3, 15.

39. Fifth Army History, *Part 1: From Activation to the Fall of Naples*. Registered Copy 338, 2, CARL Digital Archive, Call Number N2783A; Martin Blumenthal, *Mark Clark: The Last of the Great World War II Commanders* (New York: Gongdon and Weed, 1984), 112–113, 115.

40. Fifth Army History, pt. 1, 5.

41. Fifth Army History, pt. 1, 6; Heavey, 56; Ruppenthal, 331; Hewitt, *Memoirs*, 192.

42. Blumenthal, 118; Hewitt, *Memoirs*, 191, 195.

43. Seventh Army, Report of Operations, a-6; Historical Record, Operations Second Armored Division, Sicily, April 22 to July 25, 1943, 1, CARL Digital Archive, Call Number N2146.32–3.

44. Hewitt, *Memoirs*, 192.

45. Hewitt, *Memoirs*, 195–196; Edwards, 23.

46. Carter and Duvall, 214.

47. Headquarters Fifth Army Invasion Training Center, Training Doctrine, May 20, 1943, 4, CARL Digital Archive, Call Number N6429; US Atlantic Fleet, Summary of First Conclusions, 4; Staff Memorandum, 7, 10.

48. Fifth Army History, Part 1, 6; US Atlantic Fleet, Summary of First Conclusions, 1; Blumenthal, 118.

49. Fifth Army Invasion Training Center Doctrine, 7–17; Fifth Army History, pt. 1, 6; *Armor in the Invasion of North Africa*, 144.

50. Fifth Army Invasion Training Center Doctrine, Annex 3-Logistics.

51. Fifth Army History, Part 1, 6; 3rd Infantry Division, Report of Operations, 10 September 1943, Section 1 Operations, 1, CARL Digital Archive, No Call Number Assigned; Historical Record, Second Armored Division, 1.

52. Fifth Army History, Part 1, 8, 13; National World War 2 Museum On Line Archives, Oral interview with Roy D. Goad, www.ww2online.org/view/roy-goad #invasion-at-salerno.

53. Fifth Army History, pt. 1, 9.

54. Fifth Army History, pt. 1, 11.

55. Fifth Army History, pt. 1, 6, 13.

56. Daniel, *Landings*, 13.

57. Daniel, *Landings*, 13.

58. Flunking out of West Point and with an indifference to academic endeavors and discipline, de la Mesa was known by the nom de guerre as "Terrible Terry."

59. Action Report, Western Naval Task Force, 31; 3rd Infantry Division, Report of Operations, 2–3; C.O.H.Q. Bulletin No Y/1-Notes on the Planning and Amphibious Assault Phase of the Sicilian Campaign, by a Military Observer, October 1943, 6, CARL Digital Archive, Call Number N6530.1; AFH Dispatch, 17; Heavey, 57; von Der Osten, 66; Daniels, 13, According to this reference the 1st Division landings fell under the title CONQUERER.

60. Action Report, Western Naval Task Force, 31.

61. Daniel, *Landings*, 13–14; Truscott, 207; Seventh Army in the Sicily Campaign, a-4; Morison, 9:31; After Action Report, Western Naval Task Force, 31.

62. Bradley and Blair, 174.

63. Historical Record-Operations of US Second Armored Division (Kool Force), 5 August 1943, 1, CARL Digital Archive Call Number N11274.1; Report of Operations, 3rd Infantry Division, 3.

64. Fifth Army Invasion Training Center Doctrine, Annex 1 to Logistical Plan, 1–10; After Action Report, Western Naval Task Force, 31.

65. Action Report, Western Naval Task Force, 31. The overall Naval Component Commander was Sir Admiral Andrew B. Cunningham, with Hewitt's counterpart, Sir Admiral Bertram Ramsey, commanding the Eastern Naval Task Force.

66. AFH Dispatch, 20, 25; Report of Operations, 3rd Infantry Division, 3.

67. Action Report, Western Naval Task Force, 54.

68. 3rd Infantry Division, Report of Operations, 5; Heavey, 55, 62; Action Report, Western Naval Task Force, 27, 65; Carter and Duvall, 213; Report of Seventh Army Operations, a-10.

69. Bradley and Blair, 173.

70. Reports by Observers on Current Operations in North Africa, Annex F-1; Whitmarsh, 43.

71. Naval Institute Press, *US Naval Vessels, 1943* (Annapolis, MD, Naval Institute Press, 1943); Naval Institute Press, *Allied Landing Craft of World War Two* (Annapolis, MD: Naval Institute Press), 65; Hewitt, *Memoirs*, 184, 191; US Naval History and Heritage Command (NHHC) H-021-2, "Operation Husky, the Invasion of Sicily, and Operation Avalanche, the Invasion of Italy, September 2018," www.history.navy.mil/about-us/leadership/director/directors-corner/h-grams/h-gram-021/h-021-2.html.

72. Naval Institute Press, *Allied Landing Craft of World War Two*, 65.

73. Action Western Naval Task Force, 51; Naval Institute Press, *US Naval Vessels, 1943*.

74. *Jane's Fighting Ships of World War II* (New York: Jane's Publishing Company, 1989), 304; Karig, 166; Symonds, 152; Naval Institute Press, *Allied Landing Craft of World War Two*, 65; Whitmarsh, 43–44.

75. Erine Pyle, "Life on an LST," *New York Times*, March 4, 1944, http://www
.navsource.org/archives/10/16/16idx.htm.

76. *Allied Landing Craft of World War Two*, 34; Naval Institute Press, *US Naval
Vessels, 1943*; Whitmarsh, 30–35.

77. Naval Institute Press, *Allied Landing Craft of World War Two*, 34; Whitmarsh, 30–35.

78. Naval Institute Press, *Allied Landing Craft of World War Two*, 27; Naval Institute Press, *US Naval Vessels, 1943*; Whitmarsh, 30–35.

79. Naval Institute Press, *Allied Landing Craft of World War Two*, 30.

80. *Jane's*, 304–305; Karig, 166; Whitmarsh, 30–35.

81. C.O.H.Q. Bulletin No Y/1, 4; Historical Record, Operations Second Armored Division, 5.

82. Morison, 9:29; Carter and Duvall, 214.

83. Garland and Smyth, 103; Morison, 2:266, 268, 270, 273; Karig, 224, 233;
Carter and Duvall, 214; Hewitt, *Memoirs*, 191.

84. Morison, 2:271; C.O.H.Q. Bulletin No Y/1, 5.

85. Lewis Combs, "Innovation of Amphibious Warfare," in *The Military Engineer*, February 1944, 36, no. 220, 46; Morison, 2:31; Heavey, 57; Hewitt, *Memoirs*,
201; von Der Osten, 71.

86. Action Report, Western Naval Task Force, 51; Whitmarsh, 44.

87. Carter and Duvall, 213, 224; Morison, 2:252, 273; AFH Dispatch, 17.

88. Morison, 9:32; von Der Osten, 60.

89. Karig, 226.

90. Carter and Duvall, 227.

91. NHHC, *FTP-211 Ship to Shore Movement*, January 1943, www.history.navy
.mil/research/library/online-reading-room/title-list-alphabetically/s/ship-to-sho
re-movement0.html#general.

92. Action Report, Western Naval Task Force, 16.

93. C.O.H.Q. Bulletin No Y/1, 3; Report of Operations, 3rd Infantry Division
in Sicily Operation, 1, CARL Digital Archive; Christopher Rein, *The North African Air Campaign: The US Army Air Forces from El Alamein to Salerno* (Lawrence:
University Press of Kansas, 2012), 148.

Chapter 4. "Can't Get the Air Force to Do a Goddam Thing": Operation
Husky, July 1943

1. Reports by Observers on Current Operations in North Africa, Annex A;
D'Este, *Bitter Victory*, 72.

2. Garland and McGraw, 55–57; D'Este, *Bitter Victory*, 76.

3. Vice Admiral H. K. Hewitt, Action Report Western Naval Task Force, The
Sicilian Campaign: Operation "HUSKY," July–August 1943, 1, CARL Digital Archive, Call Number N6884.

4. Headquarters Seventh Army, Report of Operations of the United States
Seventh Army in the Sicilian Operation, 10 July–17 August 1943, APO #750, 1 October, 1943, b-4, CARL Digital Archive, Call Number Special 940514273U56ro.

Morison, 9:95; Porch, 423; Carlo D'Este, *Patton: A Genius for War* (New York: Harper, 1996), 506; Garland and Smyth, 136; Hewitt, *Memoirs*, 199.

5. Seventh Army in the Sicily Campaign, a-4, a-6; C.O.H.Q. Bulletin No Y/1, 5.

6. John Greham and Martin Mace (Ed), *Despatches from the Front: The War in Italy, 1943–1944* (South Yorkshire, UK: Pen and Sword, 2014), 10; After Action Report, Western Naval Task Force, 23.

7. 82nd Airborne Division, Sicily and Italy, Section 1-Division Report, 5 CARL Digital Archive, Call Number N11960; After Action Report, Western Naval Task Force, 23.

8. Bloomenthal, 121; D'Este, *Bitter Victory*, 193; Garland and Smyth, 78–79.

9. Garland and Smyth, 81; Porch, 423–424; D'Este *Bitter Victory*, 207; Morison, 9:47–48.

10. Garland and Smyth, 79; Porch, 424–425; D'Este, *Bitter Victory*, 193; Morison, 9:48–49; Ossad, 126–127.

11. D'Este, *Bitter Victory*, 198–199; Garland and Smyth, 80.

12. C.O.H.Q. Bulletin No Y/1-Notes, 2, 7; D'Este, *Bitter Victory*, 166–167, 171, 175; Porch, 420–421; Garland and Smyth, 106; Third Infantry Division, Report of Operations, Sicilian Operation, 10 September, 1943, CARL Digital Archive No Call Number Assigned; USNHHC, H-021-2; Heefner, 105; Report of Operations, Seventh Army in the Sicily Campaign, C-5.

13. Wilson A Heefner, *Dogface Soldier: The Life of General Lucian K. Truscott* (Columbia: University of Missouri Press, 2010), 105.

14. Wesley Frank Craven and James Lea Cate, *The Army Air Forces in World War II, Volume 2: Europe, Torch to Pointblank* (Chicago: University of Chicago Press, 1949), 450; D'Este, *Bitter Victory*, 162; CARL; Alan F. Wilt, "Allied Cooperation in Sicily and Italy 1943–1945," in Benjamin Franklin Cooling, ed., *Case Studies in the Development of Close Air Support* (Washington, DC: Office of Air Force History, 1990), 200.

15. Garland and Smyth, 106; Wilt, "Allied Cooperation in Sicily and Italy 1943–1945," 200.

16. Craven and Cate, 2:484.

17. USAF Warrior Studies, *Condensed Analysis of the Ninth Air Force in the European Theater of Operations* (Washington, DC: Office of Air Force History, 1984), 7. Rein, 23, 33; Ian Gooderson, *Air Power at the Battlefront: Allied Close Air Support in Europe, 1943–1945* (London: Frank Cass, 1998), 51.

18. FM-100-20, *Command and Employment of Air Power (1943)*, 8, www.ibiblio.org/hyperwar/USA/ref/FM/FM100-20/index.html#c2s3, 8; War Office/RAF Air Staff, *Army Air Ops Pamphlet #1*, "General Principles and Organization 1944" as reference in Benjamin Franklin Cooling (Ed), "The Battle for France," by W. A. Jacobs in *Case Studies in Close Air Support* (Washington, DC: Office of Air Force History, 1990), 251.

19. Combat Studies Institute No. 6, Larger Units: Theater Army—Army Group—Field Army (Fort Leavenworth, KS: Combined Army Center, 1985), 2–21, CARL; Wilt, "Allied Cooperation in Sicily and Italy 1943–1945," 199–200.

20. Craven and Cate, 2:451.

21. Garland and Smyth, 106.

22. Julian William Cunnings and Gwendolyn Kay Cummings, *Grasshopper Pilot: A Memoir* (Kent, OH: Kent State University Press, 2005) 31; Hewitt, *Memoirs*, 201; Heefner, 104.

23. Craven and Cate, 2:450; D'Este, *Bitter Victory*, 166–167; Rein, 144.

24. Rein, 145.

25. Action Report, Western Naval Task Force, 17.

26. E. W. MacMillan, "Fighter Control and Aircraft Warning in Amphibious Operations," AAF School of Applied Tactics, AAF Tactical Center, Orlando FL, January 1945, 5–7, CARL Digital Archive Call Number N5269.40; Craven and Cate, 2:450–451; Wilt, "Allied Cooperation in Sicily and Italy 1943–1945," 199.

27. Jacobs in *Case Studies in Close Air Support*, 255.

28. Army Service Forces, Office of the Chief Signal Officer, JEIA Rpt. No. 5796, "The Adequacy of the Tactical Air Communications System, Mediterranean Theater of Operations," 31 October 1944, File No SPSOI 370.2, 5–6, CARL Digital Archive, Call Number N3631 (hereafter referred to as Tac Air Comms in the MTO).

29. Alan F. Wilt, "Allied Cooperation in Sicily and Italy 1943–1945," 199.

30. MacMillan, "Fighter Control and Aircraft Warning in Amphibious Operations," 9, 18.

31. D'Este, *Bitter Victory*, 163–164; D'Este, *Patton: A Genius for War*, 505.

32. Rein, 147.

33. After Action Report, Western Naval Task Force, 18; Report of Operations, Seventh Army in the Sicily Campaign, C-6.

34. MacMillan, "Fighter Control and Aircraft Warning in Amphibious Operations," 22.

35. Rein, 147–148.

36. Morison, 9:22–23; D'Este, *Bitter Victory*, 172; D'Este, *Patton: A Genius for War*, 505.

37. After Action Report, Western Naval Task Force, 44.

38. Joseph Edwin Brown, "Deception and the Mediterranean Campaigns of 1943–1944," Study Project, Army War College submission, 1986, 86, https://apps.dtic.mil/sti/citations/ADA168052.

39. Report of Operations, Seventh Army in the Sicily Campaign, C-6.

40. Frank James Price, *Troy Middleton: A Biography* (Baton Rouge: Louisiana State University, 1974), 147.

41. Captain W. V. Ledley, "Naval Fire Support in Sicily," in *Field Artillery Journal*, December 1943, US Field Artillery Association, 896.

42. After Action Report, Western Naval Task Force, 79.

43. After Action Report, Western Naval Task Force, 83.

44. 3rd Infantry Division, Report of Operations, 7; AFH Dispatch, 24, 25; Action Report, Western Naval Task Force, 36, 83–84.

45. After Action Report, Western Naval Task Force, 26, 39; Morison, 9:75.

46. Truscott, 210; Heefner, 110–111; Garland and Smyth, 123, 125; Morison, 9:75–78; Action Report, Western Naval Task Force, 6, 39, 45; C.O.H.Q. Bulletin No Y/1, 21–22.

47. 3rd Infantry Division, Report of Operations, 8.

48. Garland and Smyth, 126–129; Morison, 9:81–82.

49. Action Western Naval Commander, 5; Garland and Smyth, 129–130; Morison, 9:83; 3rd Infantry Division, Report of Operations, 8–9; the USS *Buck* was assigned to support Green Beach but was redirected when the two destroyers designated to support Red Beach collided.

50. 3rd Infantry Division, Report of Operations, Forward Comments by General Truscott; Karig, 250–251; Carter and Duvall, 227; Action Report, Western Naval Task Force, 62.

51. Truscott, 210, 213; Garland and Smyth, 131; Morison, 9:89.

52. D'Este, *Bitter Victory*, 260; Morison, 9:80.

53. Frank Blazich, "Bridging the Gap from Ship to Shore," *Naval History* 35, no. 4 (August 2021), www.usni.org/magazines/naval-history-magazine/2021/august/bridging-gap-ship-shore; Morison, 9:105–111; Combs, 44.

54. Blazich; Morison, 9:105–111; Combs, 46.

55. Garland and Smyth, 131; Morison, 9:90.

56. Blazich; Combs, 46.

57. 3rd Infantry Division, Report of Operations, 9.

58. Morison, 9:84–86; Action Report, Western Naval Task Force, 4, 5, 97.

59. 3rd Infantry Division, Report of Operations, 9; Garland and Smyth, 133; Morison, 9:87.

60. 3rd Infantry Division, Report of Operations, 10; C.O.H.Q. Bulletin No Y/1, 25; Seventh Army in the Sicily Campaign, b-4.

61. Morison, 9:88; Action Report, Western Naval Task Force, 78.

62. Action Report, Western Naval Task Force, 4, 5.

63. Action Report, Western Naval Task Force, 4; Garland and Smyth, 133; D'Este, *Bitter Victory*, 261; Heefner, 111; Truscott, 214; 3rd Infantry Division, Report of Operations, 11.

64. Morison, 9:92–96, 98; Garland and Smyth, 135–136; After Action Report, Western Naval Task Force, 38.

65. Report of Operations of the United States Seventh Army in the Sicilian Operation, b-4; Craven and Cate, 2:449; Rein, 150–151; Ossad, 129; USNHHC, H-021-2; 82nd Airborne Division, Division Report, 6, CARL Digital Archive Call Number N11960.

66. Action Report, Western Naval Task Force, 40; Allied Force Headquarters Memorandum for the Commander-in-Chief, Subject Sicilian Campaign, 26 August 1943, 4, CARL Digital Archive.

67. Rein, 150–151; Porch, 426; D'Este, *Bitter Victory*, 238–242; Rick Atkinson, *Day of Battle: The War in Sicily and Italy, 1943–1944* (New York: Henry Holt and Co., 2007), 78; Craven and Cate, 2:449–450.

68. Action Report, Western Naval Task Force, 3–4; D'Este, *Bitter Victory*, 275; Morison, 9:94, 97; Garland and Smyth, 136–137; Atkinson, *Day of Battle*, 79; Report of Operations, 3rd Infantry Division, 8.

69. D'Este, *Bitter Victory*, 275; Morison, 9:97; Garland and Smyth, 138–139.

70. Action Report, Western Naval Task Force, 46; Morison, 98–99; Daniel, *Landings*, 14–15.

71. Morison, 9:99–100; Garland and Smyth, 139; Daniel, *Landings*, 15; 301 Inf (16), 4.

72. See www.USSMaddox.org.

73. Action Report, Western Naval Task Force, 40; D'Este, *Bitter Victory*, 275; Morison, 9:102; C.O.H.Q. Bulletin No Y/1 Notes, 7; AFH Dispatch, 26.

74. Report of Operations of the United States Seventh Army in the Sicilian Operation, b-4, b-6; AFH Dispatch, 26.

75. Action Report, Western Naval Task Force, 5; Morison, 9:103; Daniel, *Landings*, 16; 301 Inf (16), 4; Garland and Smyth, 151; D'Este, *Bitter Victory*, 284.

76. Garland and Smyth, 152.

77. Report of Operations of the United States Seventh Army in the Sicilian Operation, b-4; Morison, 9:103–104; Garland and Smyth, 152, 162; D'Este, *Bitter Victory*, 288.

78. Garland and Smyth, 154; D'Este, *Bitter Victory*, 286.

79. Action Report, Western Naval Task Force, 59; Report of Operations, Seventh Army in the Sicily Campaign, C-8.

80. Garland and Smyth, 158–159; Operations, US Second Armored Division, 5.

81. Action Report, Western Naval Task Force, 40; Atkinson, *Day of Battle*, 86; Allied Force Headquarters Memorandum for the Commander-in-Chief, Subject Sicilian Campaign, 26 August 1943, 6, CARL Digital Archive.

82. Notes on Operation Husky, 28 July; Action Report, Western Naval Task Force, 49, 55, 56.

83. Morison, 9:107; Atkinson, *Day of Battle*, 100.

84. Note 25, Morison, 9:107; C.O.H.Q. Bulletin No Y/1, 27; Historical Record, Operations Second Armored Division, April 22–July 25 1943, 5; Atkinson, *Day of Battle*, 80; Action Report, Western Naval Task Force, 54.

85. AFH Dispatch, 25.

86. Report of Operations of the United States Seventh Army in the Sicilian Operation, b-4; Morison, 112; Action Report, Western Naval Task Force, 8; Bradley and Blair, 183; Garland and Smyth 164–165.

87. Garland and Smyth, 169–170; Morison, 9:112; D'Este, *Patton*, 507; Ossad, 131.

88. Garland and Smyth 170; Morison, 9:113–116.

89. Action Report, Western Naval Task Force, 1, 8, 86. D'Este, *Bitter Victory* 298–299; Garland and Smyth, 170–171, 187–188; Atkinson, *Day of Battle*, 102–103; Daniel, *Landings*, 18; C.O.H.Q. Bulletin No Y/1, 23; Historical Record, Operations Second Armored Division, 5; Heavy, 59; Morison, 9:118; AFH Dispatch, 27; D'Este, *Patton*, 509.

90. Garland and Smyth, 171; Historical Record, Operations, Second Armored Division, 5; Ledley, "Naval Fire Support in Sicily," 896; Ossad 131; USNHHC, H-021-2; Greham and Mace, 39; Allied Force Headquarters Memorandum for the Commander-in-Chief, Subject Sicilian Campaign, 26 August 1943, 2, CARL Digital Archive.

91. Action Report, Western Naval Task Force, 86; Morison, 117.

92. Action Report, Western Naval Task Force, 1.

93. Action Report, Western Naval Task Force, 87.

94. Garland and Smyth, 175; D'Este, *Bitter Victory*, 307; Craven and Cate, 2:453.

95. Garland and Smyth, 177; Rein, 152; USNHHC, H-021-2.

96. 82nd Airborne Divion, Division Report, 5 CARL: N11960.

97. Report of Operations of the United States Seventh Army in the Sicilian Operation, b-6; Garland and Smyth, 181–182, D'Este, *Bitter Victory*, 308; Craven

and Cate, 2:454; Ossad, 130; USNHHC, H-021-2; 82nd Airborne Divion, Division Report, 8, CARL: N11960.

98. Commander-in-Chief's Dispatch, 23, CARLA; Craven and Cate, 2:455.

99. Garland and Smyth, 184; Morison, 9:120–121; Bradley and Blair, 175, 178, 183–184; Seventh Army in the Sicily Campaign, b-6; Porch, 426; Atkinson, *Day of Battle*, 109; Rein, 152.

100. Daniel, *Landings*, 17; Garland and Smyth, 154; 301 Inf (16), 5; Action Report, Western Naval Task Force, 9.

101. Morison, 9:123–124; D'Este, *Bitter Victory*, 277.

102. Price, 148; Ossad, 128.

103. After Action Report, Western Naval Task Force, 38–39.

104. Garland and Smyth, 139–142; Morison, 129–130; Action Report, Western Naval Task Force, 23, 38.

105. Action Report-Western Naval Task Force, 41.

106. Morison, 9:106, 128–130; Garland and Smyth 161; Action Report, Western Naval Task Force, 33, 35, 40; AFH Dispatch, 24.

107. Morison, 9:131.

108. Morison, 9:129–130; Garland and Smyth, 142–143, 161; Action Report, Western Naval Task Force, 40; Atkinson, *Day of Battle*, 86; Allied Force Headquarters Memorandum for the Commander-in-Chief, Subject Sicilian Campaign, 26 August 1943, 1–2, CARL Digital Archive, No Call Number Assigned.

109. Garland and Smyth, 154.

110. Morison, 9:137; Garland and Smyth, 139, 144; Atkinson, *Day of Battle*, 86.

111. Atkinson, *Day of Battle*, 86.

112. Morison, 9:138; Garland and Smyth, 146, 161.

113. Morison, 9:140; Action Report, Western Naval Task Force, 55.

114. Action Report, Western Naval Task Force, 40; Atkinson, *Day of Battle*, 86; Allied Force Headquarters Memorandum for the Commander-in-Chief, Subject Sicilian Campaign, 26 August 1943, 7.

115. Morison, 9:139, 140; Garland and Smyth, 161; Action Report, Western Naval Task Force, 41, 54.

116. Morison, 9:140; Omar Bradley, *A Soldier's Story* (New York: Henry Holt, 1951), 129–130.

117. Action Report, Western Naval Task Force, 5; Morison, 9:139–140; Price, 149.

118. Action Report, Western Naval Task Force, 56; Report of Operations, Seventh Army in the Sicily Campaign, C-1 to C-2, C-6.

119. Action Report, Western Naval Task Force, 56.

120. Allied Force Headquarters Memorandum for the Commander-in-Chief, Subject Sicilian Campaign, 26 August 1943.

121. Garland and Smyth, 161.

122. Morison, 9:144–146; Garland and Smyth, 161.

123. Wilt, "Allied Cooperation in Sicily and Italy 1943–1945," 202.

124. Action Report, Western Naval Task Force, 60.

125. Notes on Operation HUSKY, 28 July 1943.

126. Engineer Amphibian Command, Tentative Training Guide No 7, The Organization of the Far Shore, CARL Digital Archive, Call Number N15536.

127. Action Report, Western Naval Task Force, 40; Atkinson, *Day of Battle*, 86; Allied Force Headquarters Memorandum for the Commander-in-Chief, Subject Sicilian Campaign, 26 August 1943, 4.

128. Ruppenthal, 334.

Chapter 5. As Much as Could Be Expected: Salerno, September 1943

1. Commander Western Naval Task Force, *The Italian Campaign: Western Naval Task Force Action Report of The Salerno Landings: September–October 1943*, 5, CARL Digital Archive, Call Number N5339 (hereafter referred to as CWNTF Action Report Salerno).

2. Garland and Smyth, 524; Porch, 485–486; Martin Blumenson, *The United States Army in World War II, Mediterranean Theater of Operations: Salerno to Cassino* (Washington, DC: US Government Printing Office, 1993), 4; Fifth Army History, pt. 1, 23.

3. Fifth Army History, pt. 1, 20; Fifth Army, *Engineer History: Mediterranean History*, 1:4, CARL Digital Archive, Call Number N1154A; Carlo D'Este, *Fatal Decision: Anzio and the Battle for Rome* (New York: HarperCollins, 1986), 38; Heefner, 126.

4. Center of Military History (CMH), *Salerno* (Washington, DC: US Government Printing Office, 1989 (reprint), 4; Morison, 9:247, 255; Western Naval Task Force Operational Plan No. 7–43, Short Title "AVON/W1," August 14, 1942, 2–4, Annex A, CARL Digital Library, Call Number N6809; Fifth Army History, pt. 1, 27.

5. Morison, 9:255; AVON/W1, Annex A, 32 and Appendix I; Blumenson, *Salerno to Cassino*, 78–79; Fifth Army, *Engineer History*, 1:4; Porch, 499; Greham and Mace, 82, 104.

6. Price, 165; Porch, 494; D'Este, *Fatal Decision*, 37; CWNTF Action Report Salerno, 137.

7. CMH, *Salerno*, 8–9; Morison, 9:255; Morison, 258; AVON/W1, Annex L; Blumenson, *Salerno to Cassino*, 54; Fifth Army, *Engineer History*, 1: 21, 26; Karig, 265; CWNTF Action Report Salerno, 158.

8. CWNTF Action Report Salerno, 158.

9. Kent Hewitt, "The Allied Navies at Salerno: Operation Avalanche—September 1943," *Proceedings*, September 1953, Volume 79/9/607, US Naval Institute Press; D'Este, *Bitter Victory*, 276.

10. Blumenson, *Salerno to Cassino*, 85–86; Fifth Army History, pt. 1, 29; Porch, 495; D'Este, *Fatal Decision*, 37–38.

11. AVON/W1, Change 1; CMH, *Salerno*, 7–8; Porch, 491–492; Blumenson, *Salerno to Cassino*, 157; Hewitt, "Allied Navies at Salerno"; Fifth Army History, pt. 1, 18, 25; Karig, 259; Edwards, 26; Gutierrez, 74.

12. Center of Military History (CMH), *Salerno: American Operations from the Beaches to the Volturno, 9 September–6 October 1943* (Washington, DC: US Government Printing Office, 1990), 9; Fifth Army History, pt. 1, 13; Kent Hewitt, "Allied Navies at Salerno."

13. CWNTF Action Report Salerno, 92.

14. Hewitt, "Allied Navies at Salerno"; Morison, 9:269; CWNTF Action Report Salerno, 93–96.

15. Morison, 9:250–251; AVON/W1, Annex I; Karig, 261; US Navy Heritage and History Command (USNHHC), "Operation Husky, the Invasion of Sicily, and Operation Avalanche, the Invasion of Italy," H-021-2, www.history.navy.mil/ab out-us/leadership/director/directors-corner/h-grams/h-gram-021/h-021-2.html; Fifth Army History, pt. 1, 19, 27; Fifth Army, *Engineer History*, 1:6; Karig, 261; Edwards, 26; CWNTF Action Report Salerno, 7–8, 12, 118.

16. The two large fleet carriers replaced five smaller escort carriers that provided air support until 12 September and then withdrew for refueling. Craven and Cate, *The Army Air Forces in World War II*, 2:497; Morison, 9:251; Karig, 260; USNHHC, H-021-2: Wilt, 203.

17. AVON/W1, Annex A. Blumenson, *Salerno to Cassino*, 54; Matthew St. Clair, "Air Support of the Allied Landings in Sicily, Salerno, and Anzio," in *Joint Forces Quarterly*, October 2006, Issue 39, 103.

18. CMH, *Salerno*, 13. Morison, 9:252; A US Navy accounts claim there were no losses during the inbound journey. US Naval History and Heritage Command (USNHHC), "The US Navy and the Landings at Salerno Italy," www.history .navy.mil/browse-by-topic/wars-conflicts-and-operations/world-war-ii/1943/sale rno-landings/landings-at-salerno-italy.html; Craven and Cate, 2:520; Karig, 260; CWNTF Action Report Salerno, 8.

19. On this point the official histories disagree. The navy source claims it was to maintain the element of surprise. Army sources claim it was about concern over troop safety and destruction of infrastructure that might prove useful to Allied forces once ashore. Morison, 9:249, 261; AVON/W1, Annex B, Appendix 1; Blumenson, *Salerno to Cassino*, 56; Eric Morris, *Salerno: A Military Fiasco* (New York: Stein and Day Publishers, 1983), 43. The official Army history claims that Admiral Hall had list of 173 targets; USNHHC, "H-021-2: Operation Husky, the Invasion of Sicily and Operation Avalanche, The Invasion of Italy," www.history .navy.mil/about-us/leadership/director/directors-corner/h-grams/h-gram-021/h-021-2.html; Edwards, 26; D'Este, *Fatal Decision*, 38; CWNTF Action Report, 142.

20. Blumenson, *Salerno to Cassino*, 56.

21. Craven and Cate, 2:494, 504, 509, 517; CMH, *Salerno*, 12; Hewitt, "Allied Navies at Salerno"; Fifth Army History, pt. 1, 26.

22. Fifth Army, *Engineer History*, 1:12; Karig, 262, Gutierrez, 98.

23. AVON/W1, Change 1para (d) 88 (5), Annex A; Craven and Cate, 2:498; Blumenson, *Salerno to Cassino*, 167; Morison, 9:250; St. Clair, 103; CWNTF Action Report Salerno, 196.

24. Rein, 184.

25. Wilt, 202.

26. St. Clair, 104; CWNTF Action Report Salerno, 196.

27. MacMillan, "Fighter Control and Aircraft Warning in Amphibious Operations," 10, 14; CWNTF Action Report Salerno, 103, 196, 200.

28. Craven and Cate, 2:494, 526; Morison, 9:250; Mark Clark, *Calculated Risk* (New York: Harper and Brothers 1950), 185; USNHHC, H-021-2; Wilt, "Allied Cooperation in Sicily and Italy 1943–1945," 202.

29. MacMillan, "Fighter Control and Aircraft Warning in Amphibious Operations," 27.

30. Craven and Cate, 2:499; CWNTF Action Report Salerno, 202.

31. CWNTF Action Report Salerno, 202.

32. Wilt, 203.

33. Wilt, 203; CWNTF Action Report Salerno, 196.

34. Craven and Cate, 2:523.

35. St. Clair, 104–105.

36. Blumenson, *Salerno to Cassino*, 69; Morison, 9:260–261; Edwards, 26; CWNTF Action Report Salerno, 91–92.

37. Morison, 9:239; Fifth Army History, 1:23, 30; Fifth Army, *Engineer History*, 1:7; Porch, 469; Blumenson, *Mark Clark*, 133.

38. Morison, 9:252–253; Porch, 496; Hewitt, "Allied Navies at Salerno"; Garland and Smith, 509; Morris, 128. Fifth Army History, 1:30; Karig, 267; von Der Osten, 96; CWNTF Action Report Salerno, 91.

39. Blumenson, *Salerno to Cassino*, 78, 86; Ian Blackwell, *Fifth Army in Italy, 1943–1945: A Coalition at War* (South Yorkshire, UK: Pen and Sword, 2012), 141.

40. Blumenson, *Salerno to Cassino*, 69, 86; Fifth Army History, pt. 1, 23, 28.

41. Craven and Cate, 2:511.

42. CMH, *Salerno*, 15–16; Porch, 495; Morison, 249, 260; Lloyd Clark, *Anzio: Italy and the Battle for Rome—1944* (New York: Atlantic Monthly Press, 2006), 22–23; Blumenson, 79, 86.

43. Hewitt, "Allied Navies at Salerno"; CHM, Salerno, 17; Blumenson, *Salerno to Cassino*, 73; Morison, 9:258, 261; Eric Morris, 43; USNHHC, H-021-2; CWNTF Action Report Salerno, 103.

44. Blumenson, *Salerno to Cassino*, 73; Morris, 42; CWNTF Action Report Salerno, 138, 141–142.

45. CWNTF Action Report Salerno, 11, 148.

46. CMH, *Salerno*, 17; Blumenson, *Salerno to Cassino*, 91; National World War 2 Museum On Line Archives, Oral History interview with Charles Coolidge, www.ww2online.org/view/charles-coolidge#monte-cassino-and-anzio; USNHHC, On Line Archive, *Savannah IV CL 42*, www.history.navy.mil/research/histories/ship-histories/danfs/s/savannah-iv.html; Hewitt, "Allied Navies at Salerno"; Morison, 9:259; Karig, 261; USNHHC, H-021-2; Fifth Army History, pt. 1, 31; Fifth Army, *Engineer History*, 1:7; CWNTF Action Report, 141, 148.

47. CMH, *Salerno*, 18–19; Morison, 9:258; Blumenson, *Salerno to Cassino*, 74–74; Fifth Army History, pt. 1, 27, 28.

48. Blumenson, *Salerno to Cassino*, 74; Atkinson, *Day of Battle*, 204.

49. CWNTF Action Report Salerno.

50. Morris, 42.

51. US NHHC, H-021-2; Morison, 9:261; Blumenson, *Salerno to Cassino*, 76; Karig, 261; CWNTF Action Report Salerno, 12.

52. Morison, 9:259–261; Blumenson, *Salerno to Cassino*, 76; Craven and Cate, 2:520–521; Fifth Army History, pt. 1, 31; Karig, 261; CWNTF Action Report Salerno, 141.

53. Blumenson, *Salerno to Cassino*, 77.

54. Morison, 9:263–264; Blumenson, 77; Karig, 261–262; Morris, 90; Fifth Army

History, pt. 1, 32; Fifth Army, *Engineer History*, 1:12; Atkinson, *Day of Battle*, 204; D'Este, *Fatal Decision*, 39.

55. CWNTF Action Report Salerno, 147, 150–151.

56. Blumenson, *Salerno to Cassino*, 77–79; CMH, *Salerno*, 23; Karig, 262; Morris, 90, 93; USNHHC, H-021-2; Fifth Army History, pt. 1, 27; von Der Osten, 86; Gutierrez, 86, 87, 93.

57. Morris, 91–92; Fifth Army History, pt. 1, 32, Atkinson, *Day of Battle*, 207; CWNTF Action Report Salerno, 12–13, 14.

58. Blumenson, *Salerno to Cassino*, 77; Morison, 92; Clark, 188.

59. Morris, 92.

60. CMH, *Salerno*, 19; Morison, 9:264; Morris, 131; CWNTF Action Report Salerno, 99, 141, 152.

61. CMH, *Salerno*, 27; Craven and Cate, 2:494; Morris, 48; CWNTF Action Report Salerno, 200.

62. National World War 2 Museum On Line Archives, Oral interview with Roy D. Goad, www.ww2online.org/view/roy-goad#invasion-at-salerno; Hewitt, "Allied Navies at Salerno"; CMH, *Salerno*, 27; Karig, 262.

63. Karig, 266; Edwards, 26; von Der Osten, 95.

64. Alfred Price, *Luftwaffe Handbook* (New York: Charles Scribner and Sons, 1977), 53; Blumenson, *Salerno to Cassino*, 90, 107, 148; Hewitt, "Allied Navies at Salerno"; Rein, 186; Karig, 266; USNHHC, H-021-02; Fifth Army History, pt. 1, 37; Fifth Army, *Engineer History*, 1:12; Morison, 9:283; Rein, 186.

65. CWNTF Action Report Salerno, 169–170.

66. CMH, *Salerno*, 25; Blumenson, *Salerno to Cassino*, 84; Morison, 91; Fifth Army History, pt. 1, 32; Fifth Army, *Engineer History*, 1:12.

67. Blumenson, *Salerno to Cassino*, 75; Karig, 262; Clark, 188; Fifth Army History, pt. 1, 32; Fifth Army, *Engineer History*, 1:12; Blumenson, *Clark*, 134.

68. Blumenson, *Salerno to Cassino*, 80; Clark, 188; Fifth Army History, pt. 1, 32; Fifth Army, *Engineer History*, 1:12; CWNTF Action Report, 142.

69. CWNTF Action Report Salerno, 110.

70. CMH, *Salerno*, 21–23; Blumenson, 80; Karig, 262; Morris, 143.

71. Blumenson, *Salerno to Cassino*, 92; Fifth Army History, pt. 1, 33; Atkinson, *Day of Battle*, 207; Porch, 498; Gutierrez, 86, 90.

72. Blumenson, *Salerno to Cassino*, 80; CMH, *Salerno*, 27.

73. Blumenson, *Salerno to Cassino*, 81; Morison, 92. However, times regarding the arrival of armor ashore differ by account.

74. Blumenson, *Salerno to Cassino*, 81, 89; CMH, *Salerno*, 33.

75. Blumenson, *Salerno to Cassino*, 84; CMH, *Salerno*, 26.

76. Morison, 9:267; USNHHC, CL-42; Fifth Army History, pt. 1, 33; Atkinson, *Day of Battle*, 207.

77. USNHHC, H-021-2; Morison, 9:267.

78. Morison, 9:266; Karig, 263; Fifth Army History, pt. 1, 33.

79. Morison, 9:269. Fifth Army History, pt. 1, 33–34; CWNTF Action Report Salerno, 14, 151, 152.

80. Fifth Army, *Engineer History*, 1:19; CWNTF Action Report Salerno, 98.

81. Morris, 93; Fifth Army, *Engineer History*, 1:12.

82. Morison, 9:264; CMH, *Salerno*, 26–27; CWNTF Action Report Salerno, 114.

83. Morison, 9:264.

84. Blumenson, 80; von Der Osten, 86–87.

85. von Der Osten, 89.

86. Morison, 9:264; Clark, 190.

87. Hewitt, "Allied Navies at Salerno"; Edwards, 26.

88. Morison, 9:264; CWNTF Action Report, 151.

89. CMH, *Salerno*, 24.

90. CMH, *Salerno*, 25–26; Clark, 190; Fifth Army, *Engineer History*, 1:12; Atkinson, *Day of Battle*, 207; CWNTF Action Report, 151.

91. CWNTF Action Report Salerno, 14, 141.

92. Clark, 188. Blumenson, *Salerno to Cassino*, note 16 on page 83; CMH, *Salerno*, 19; Fifth Army History, pt. 1, 32; Fifth Army, *Engineer History*, 1:7; Craven and Cate, 2:521.

93. Fifth Army History, pt. 1, 33; Fifth Army, *Engineer History*, 1:12; Atkinson, *Day of Battle*, 205; CWNTF Action Report, 148–149.

94. CMH, *Salerno*, 23–24; Hewitt, "Allied Navies at Salerno"; Blumenson, *Salerno to Cassino*, 81–82.

95. Morison, 9:261–265; CMH, *Salerno*, 22; CWNTF Action Report Salerno, 150.

96. Morison, 128.

97. USNHHC, H-021-02.

98. CMH, *Salerno*, 23.

99. Morison, 9:267; Hewitt, "Allied Navies at Salerno."

100. Morison, 9:265; Hewitt, "Allied Navies at Salerno"; Craven and Cate, 2:521; Morris, 89.

101. CMH, *Salerno*, 31; CWNTF Action Report Salerno, 150; CWNTF Action Report, 149.

102. CWNTF Action Report Salerno, 2, 14–17, 150–151, 179.

103. Hewitt, "Allied Navies at Salerno"; CMH, *Salerno*, 23, 26; Fifth Army, *Engineer History*, 1:7; Gutierrez, 88.

104. CWNTF Action Report Salerno, 149.

105. Karig, 262; CMH, *Salerno*, 23.

106. CMH, *Salerno*, 24; CWNTF Action Report, 149.

107. CWNTF Action Report Salerno, 151.

108. Blumenson, *Salerno to Cassino*, 87; Morison, 9:269; Clark, 191; Hewitt, "Allied Navies at Salerno"; Porch, 499.

109. Fifth Army, *Engineer History*, 1:10.

110. Morison, 9:269; USNHHC, "CL-42, USS Savannah."

111. CWNTF Action Report Salerno, 142.

112. Blumenson, *Salerno to Cassino*, 92. Fifth Army History, 34.

113. CMH, *Salerno*, 36; Blumenson, *Salerno to Cassino*, 90, 92; Atkinson, *Day of Battle*, 207.

114. Clark, 191.

115. Fifth Army History, pt. 1, 35; Proch, 500; Blumenson, *Salerno to Cassino*, 118; Karig, 269–270; CMH, *Salerno*, 53–54; CWNTF Action Report Salerno, 8.

116. USAF Historical Studies: No. 74 *Airborne Missions in the Mediterranean 1942–1945* (Maxwell AFB, AL: USAF Historical Division, 1955), 65. Fifth Army

History, pt. 1, 38; Blumenson, *Salerno to Cassino*, 118; Price, 164–165; Karig, 270; Blumenson, *Clark*, 134.

117. Price, 165.

118. CMH, *Salerno*, 67; Fifth Army History, pt. 1, 35, 39; Blumenson, *Salerno to Cassino*, 129–130; Morison, 9:280, 286–287; Fifth Army, *Engineer History*, 1:7; CWNTF Action Report Salerno, 2.

119. 82nd Airborne Divion, Division Report, 49, CARL: N11960; Heefner, 128.

120. USAF Historical Studies: No 74, 61; Blumenson, *Salerno to Cassino*, 126–130; Morison, 9:291; Craven and Cate, 2:531; Rein, 187; D'Este, *Fatal Decision*, 41; 82nd Airborne Divion, Division Report, 49, CARL: N11960.

121. USAF Historical Studies: No 74, 61; Morison, 9:291.

122. USAF Historical Studies: No 74, 65–69; Craven and Cate, 2:533; Morison, 9:291–292; 82nd Airborne Divion, Division Report, 49, CARL: N11960.

123. MacMillan, "Fighter Control and Aircraft Warning in Amphibious Operations," 19–20.

124. MacMillan, "Fighter Control and Aircraft Warning in Amphibious Operations," 20.

125. Craven and Cate, 2:534–535; CMH, *Salerno*, 74.

126. Karig, 270; Craven and Cate, 2:530–531; Morison, 9:292.

127. Morison, 9:292.

128. CMH, *Salerno*, 72–74; Blumenson, *Salerno to Cassino*, 120, 130; Porch, 501; Morison, 9:280, 294; Price, 167; D'Este, *Fatal Decision*, 41; CWNTF Action Report Salerno, 3.

129. Morison, 9:286, 293; Blumenson, *Clark*, 137; Gutierrez, 107.

130. Hewitt, "Allied Navies at Salerno"; Blumenson, *Salerno to Cassino*, 124; Porch, 501; Morison, 9:290, 293; Price, 165; Blumenson, *Clark*, 137; Gutierrez, 107–108.

131. USNHHC, "US Navy Landings at Salerno"; Morison, 9:290.

132. Blumenson, *Salerno to Cassino*, 125.

133. Blumenson, *Salerno to Cassino*, 124–125; Morison, 9:294; Gutierrez, 108.

134. Blumenson, *Clark*, 138; D'Este, *Fatal Decision*, 41.

135. Craven and Cate, 2:499.

136. Craven and Cate, 2:499.

137. Morison, 9:269; CWNTF Action Report Salerno, 97.

138. CWNTF Action Report Salerno, 142, 231.

139. Edwards, 26.

Chapter 6. The Anzio Highway: Central Italy, January 1944

1. Blumenson, *Salerno to Cassino*, 150.

2. Blumenson, *Salerno to Cassino*, 151; Blumenson, *Clark*, 141.

3. Gutierrez, 109.

4. Blumenson, *Salerno to Cassino*, 152; Blumenson, *Clark*, 141; Heefner, 130.

5. GMDS, A Study of German Operation at Anzio Beach Head, 22 January 44–31 May 44, Combined British, Canadian, and American Staff, April 1946, 5, CARL Digital Archive, Call Number N14023; Center for Military History, *Anzio*,

Pub 72-19 (Washington, DC: US Government Printing Office), 3; Center for Military History, *Anzio Beach Head, 22 January–25 May 1944, Publication 100-10* (Washington, DC: Center for Military History, 1990), 2; Wilt, 204.

6. Report by the Supreme Allied Commander Mediterranean to the Combined Chiefs of Staff on the Italian Campaign, 8 January 1944 to 10 May 1944, 1, CARL Digital Archive Call Number 940.5421 A436; Center for Military History, *Anzio, Pub 72-19*, 4.

7. Jon B. Mikolashek, *General Mark Clark, Commander of America's Fifth Army in World War II and Liberator of Rome* (Havertown, PA: Casemate Publishing, 2013), 74.

8. Atkinson, *Day of Battle*, 255, 314.

9. Report by the Supreme Allied Commander Mediterranean, 4; Robert Coakley and Richard M Leighton, *US Army in World War II, The War Department: Logistics and Strategy, 1943–1945* (Washington, DC: US Government Printing Office, 1989), 231; Blumenson, *Clark*, 159.

10. Morison, 9:326.

11. Report by the Supreme Allied Commander, 6.

12. Report by the Supreme Allied Commander Mediterranean, 2; Coakley and Leighton, *The War Department 1943–1945*, 232.

13. Atkinson, *Day of Battle*, 242; Coakley and Leighton, *The War Department 1943–1945*, 224; Gutierrez, 114.

14. Report by the Supreme Allied Commander Mediterranean, 1; CMH, *Anzio Beach Head*, 2; Morison, 9:318; Blumenson, 145.

15. Wesley Frank Craven and James Lea Cate, *The Army Air Forces in World War II, Volume 3: Europe, Argument to VE Day* (Chicago: University of Chicago Press, 1951), 336; CMH, *Anzio, Pub 72-19*, 4; Fifth Army, *Fifth Army History, Part 4: Cassino and Anzio* (N.p.: Bibliogov, 2013 [Florence: L'Impronta Press, 1944]), 10; Report by the Supreme Allied Commander Mediterranean, 1; Blumenson, *Clark*, 170.

16. Atkinson, *Day of Battle*, 327.

17. Fifth Army History, pt. 4, 11; Report by the Supreme Allied Commander Mediterranean, 2; Morison, 9:317; Coakley and Leighton, *Logistics and Strategy*, 232; Blumenson, *Clark*, 159.

18. Report by the Supreme Allied Commander Mediterranean, 4; Morison, 9:326.

19. Fifth Army History, pt. 4, 11–18; Coakley and Leighton, *Logistics and Strategy*, 232; Martin Blumenson, *Anzio: The Gamble That Failed* (New York: J. B. Lippencott, 1963), 51–52; Morison, 9:327; Blumenson, *Clark*, 160; Report by the Supreme Allied Commander, 8; Carlo D'Este, *Fatal Decision*, 76–77, 96–97.

20. Fifth Army History, pt. 4, p12; Report by the Supreme Allied Commander Mediterranean, 2.

21. Fifth Army History, pt. 4, 13; Report by the Supreme Allied Commander Mediterranean, 3.

22. Blumenson, *Salerno to Cassino*, 357; Blumenson, *Anzio: The Gamble That Failed*, 72; Report by the Supreme Allied Commander Mediterranean, 12.

23. Fifth Army, *Engineer History*, 1:sec. 4; Report by the Supreme Allied Commander, 3.

24. CMH, *Anzio, Pub 72-19*, 5; Fifth Army History, pt. 4, 12; Report by the Supreme Allied Commander Mediterranean, 3; CMH, *Anzio Beach Head*, 3, 4; Morison, 9:317; Blumenson, *Clark*, 173.

25. Blumenson, *Salerno to Cassino*, 353; CMH, *Anzio Beach Head*, 3, 5; Fifth Army History, pt. 4, 13, 21; Report by the Supreme Allied Commander Mediterranean, 3; US Navy History and Heritage Command (USNHHC), "Operation Shingle: Landing at Anzio, Italy, 22 January 1944," www.history.navy.mil /content/his tory/nhhc/browse-by-topic/wars-conflicts-and-operations/world-war-ii/1944 /anzio.html; The Infantry School, Fort Benning Georgia, Advanced Infantry Officers Course 1947–1948, Captain Frank W. Keating, "The Operations of the Fifth Army in the Establishment of the Beachhead at Anzio-Nettuno, South of Rome, 22 January–24 May 1944 (Anzio Campaign)," CARL Digital Archive, No Call Number Assigned.

26. Fifth Army History, pt. 4, 12–13, 19; Report by the Supreme Allied Commander Mediterranean, 13; CMH, *Anzio Beach Head*, 7–8; Morison, 9:340.

27. Greham and Mace, 152.

28. Report by the Supreme Allied Commander Mediterranean, 13.

29. Fifth Army History, pt. 4, 19; CMH, *Anzio Beach Head*, 8, 107; Report by the Supreme Allied Commander Mediterranean, 11, 13; Heefner, 148–149.

30. Morison, 9:327–328; USNHHC, Operation Shingle; Report by the Supreme Allied Commander Mediterranean, 20; D'Este, *Fatal Decision*, 100.

31. Morison, 9:342, 347; CMH, *Anzio Beach Head*, 17, 107; Karig, 282.

32. Karig, 283; Blumenson, *Anzio: The Gamble That Failed*, 166–167.

33. CMH, *Anzio Beach Head*, 107; Clark, 303; Report by the Supreme Allied Commander Mediterranean, 18, 20.

34. Blumenson, *Anzio: The Gamble That Failed*, 166–167.

35. Report by the Supreme Allied Commander Mediterranean, 3.

36. Fifth Army, *Engineer History*, 1:sec. 4, 86.

37. Fifth Army History, pt. 4, 19–20.

38. Report by the Supreme Allied Commander Mediterranean, 3; CMH, *Anzio Beach Head*, 5; Morison, 9:329.

39. Craven and Cate, 3:337; Morison, 9:326; Blumenson, *Clark*, 162–163; Wilt, 205.

40. Report by the Supreme Allied Commander Mediterranean, 14.

41. Blumenson, *Salerno to Cassino*, 354, 356; CMH, *Anzio Beach Head*, 3; Morison, vol. 9 330; Blumenson, *Clark*, 171, 173; Report by the Supreme Allied Commander Mediterranean, 14; D'Este, *Fatal Decision*, 111–112; Greham and Mace, 152; Heefner, 149.

42. Morison, 9:336.

43. D'Este, *Fatal Decision*, 109.

44. Report by the Supreme Allied Commander, 5.

45. Morison, 9:325.

46. D'Este, *Fatal Decision*, 99.

47. Report by the Supreme Allied Commander Mediterranean, 9; D'Este, *Fatal Decision*, 98–101.

48. Porch, 528; Blumenson, *Anzio: The Gamble That Failed*, 60–61; Morison, 9:328; Blumenson, *Salerno to Cassino*, 354–356; Blumenson, *Clark*, 172.

49. Blumenson, *Salerno to Cassino*, 355–356; Blumenson, *Clark*, 171–172; Porch, 528; Blumenson, *Anzio: The Gamble That Failed*, 60–61; Morison, 9:328; D'Este, *Fatal Decision*, 107.

50. Martin Blumenson, "General Lucas at Anzio," in Kent Roberts Greenfield, ed., *Command Decisions* (Washington, DC: Center for Military History, 1990), 327, as referenced in Porch, 538.

51. Porch, 535; Morison, 9:352; Robert Katz, *The Battle for Rome: The Germans, The Allies, The Partisans, and the Pope: September 1943–June 1944* (New York: Simon and Schuster, 2003), 152.

52. Craven and Cate, 3:339–342; St. Clair, 105; CMH, *Anzio Beach Head*, 8–9; Morison, 9:331; GMDS, A Study of German Operation at Anzio Beach Head, 10; D'Este, *Fatal Decision*, 121–122.

53. Fifth Army History, pt. 4, 60; Morison, 9:332; Report by the Supreme Allied Commander Mediterranean, 15; D'Este, *Fatal Decision*, 107.

54. Blumenson, *Salerno to Cassino*, 355; USNHHC, Operation Shingle; Morison, 9:332; D'Este, *Fatal Decision*, 108.

55. Blumenson, *Salerno to Cassino*, 355.

56. Morison, 9:332; CMH, *Anzio Beach Head*, 11; Blumenson, *Anzio: The Gamble That Failed*, 63.

57. Heefner, 151.

58. Heefner, 151–152.

59. D'Este, *Fatal Decision*, 109; Heefner, 151–152.

60. Heefner, 152.

61. Report by the Supreme Allied Commander Mediterranean, 13.

62. Keating, "The Operations of the Fifth Army in the Establishment of the Beachhead at Anzio-Nettuno," 6; Morison, 9:329; Fifth Army, *Engineer History*, 1:81.

63. Craven and Cate, 3:339–342; Report by the Supreme Allied Commander Mediterranean, 15; Greham and Mace, 151.

64. Fifth Army History, pt. 4, 18–19, 68; CMH, *Anzio Beach Head*, 9; Morison, 9:329.

65. Blumenson, *Salerno to Cassino*, 305–306; Morison, vol. 9. 333; Blumenson, *Clark*, 167–168; Report by the Supreme Allied Commander Mediterranean, 16, 18.

66. Blumenson, *Salerno to Cassino*, 305; Porch, 528; Morison, 9:330.

67. Report by the Supreme Allied Commander Mediterranean, 19; Harrison, 169.

68. Alex Zmuda, *Memories of Monte Cassino and the Rapido River Crossing, One Year of Burzen Komando, 1637, The Winter 550 kilometer March and Finally 3 Months of Hell at Rogansee*, Self Published Manuscript, January 31, 1995. National World War II Museum Archives.

69. Blumenson, *Salerno to Cassino*, 318–319; CMH, *Anzio Beach Head*, 13; Blumenson, *Anzio: The Gamble That Failed*, 80; Report by the Supreme Allied Commander Mediterranean, 16; D'Este, *Fatal Decision*, 83.

70. CMH, *Anzio, Pub 72-19*, 8; Craven and Cate, 3:346; Blumenson, *Salerno to Cassino*, 306; CMH, *Anzio Beach Head*, 13; GMDS, A Study of German Operation at Anzio Beach Head, 9; Blumenson, *Clark*, 165, 167–168; Blumenson, *Anzio: The Gamble That Failed*, 81.

71. GMDS, A Study of German Operation at Anzio Beach Head, 8; Blumenson, *Anzio: The Gamble That Failed*, 70; D'Este, *Fatal Decision*, 129.

72. CMH, *Anzio Beach Head*, 10–11; GMDS, A Study of German Operation at Anzio Beach Head, 7–8, 11–12; Blumenson, *Salerno to Cassino*, 361.

73. Report by the Supreme Allied Commander Mediterranean, 3; CMH, *Anzio Beach Head*, 13; Fifth Army History, pt. 4, 61; Morison, 9:333; Blumenson, *Salerno to Cassino*, 357.

74. Report by the Supreme Allied Commander Mediterranean, 13.

75. Morison, 9:337–338; CMH, *Anzio Beach Head*, 14; Blumenson, *Anzio: The Gamble That Failed*, 73; General Subjects Section, Academic Department, The Infantry School, Fort Benning GA, Advanced Infantry Officer's Course 1948–1949, Captain Van T, Barfoot, "The Operation of the Third Platoon Company 'L,' 157th Infantry in the Battle of Anzio," CARL Digital Archive, No Call Number Assigned; Blumenson, *Clark*, 172; Fifth Army, *Engineer History*, 1:85.

76. Keating, "The Operations of the Fifth Army in the Establishment of the Beachhead at Anzio-Nettuno," 6; Blumenson, *Anzio: The Gamble That Failed*, 72.

77. CMH, *Anzio Beach Head*, 9; Blumenson, *Anzio: The Gamble That Failed*, 63; Fifth Army History, pt. 4, 21; Keating, "The Operations of the Fifth Army in the Establishment of the Beachhead at Anzio-Nettuno"; Morison, 6; Blumenson, *Salerno to Cassino*, 358.

78. GMDS, A Study of German Operation at Anzio Beach Head, 10; Morison, 9:338; CMH, *Anzio Beach Head*, 14–17; Fifth Army History, pt. 4, 62–63; Blumenson, *Salerno to Cassino*, 358; Karig, 281; Heefner, 151.

79. Fifth Army, *Engineer History*, 1:81; Karig, 282; Report by the Supreme Allied Commander Mediterranean, 17; D'Este, *Fatal Decision*, 120.

80. Keating, "The Operations of the Fifth Army in the Establishment of the Beachhead at Anzio-Nettuno," 6; Blumenson, *Anzio: The Gamble That Failed*, 75; Report by the Supreme Allied Commander Mediterranean, 17; D'Este, *Fatal Decision*, 120.

81. Karig, 282.

82. Blumenson, *Salerno to Cassino*, 358; Blumenson, *Anzio: The Gamble That Failed*, 74; Report by the Supreme Allied Commander Mediterranean, 17; Heefner, 153.

83. Morison, 9:340–341; CMH, *Anzio Beach Head*, 14–15; Fifth Army History, pt. 4, 21, 62–63; Keating, "The Operations of the Fifth Army in the Establishment of the Beachhead at Anzio-Nettuno"; Morison, 6.

84. Morison, 9:342; Fifth Army, *Engineer History*, 1:86.

85. Morison, 9:341.

86. USNHHC, Operation Shingle; *Fifth Army History*, pt. 4, 64–65; Morison, 9:345–346; Blumenson, *Salerno to Cassino*, 358–359; Report by the Supreme Allied Commander Mediterranean, 21; D'Este, *Fatal Decision*, 122.

87. Morison, 9:351.

88. Fifth Army History, pt. 4, 63; Morison, 9:343.

89. Bass, 20.

90. Morison, 9:342; Fifth Army, *Engineer History*, 1:sec. 4.

91. Morison, 9:342–343; Blumenson, *Anzio: The Gamble That Failed*, 76; Blumenson, *Salerno to Cassino*, 360.

92. Morison, 9:343.

93. Blumenson, *Salerno to Cassino*, 386; Blumenson, *Clark*, 173.

94. Fifth Army History, pt. 4, 65; Morison, 9:343; Keating, "The Operations of the Fifth Army in the Establishment of the Beachhead at Anzio-Nettuno," 7; Blumenson, *Salerno to Cassino*, 359; Fifth Army, *Engineer History*, 1:85; Report by the Supreme Allied Commander Mediterranean, 18.

95. Fifth Army History, pt. 4, 64–65, 71; CMH. *Anzio Beach Head*, 24, 111; Fifth Army, *Engineer History*, 1:sec. 4; D'Este, *Fatal Decision*, 123.

96. CMH, *Anzio Beach Head*, 111.

97. Morison, 9:349.

98. Morison, 9:347.

99. Report by the Supreme Allied Commander Mediterranean, 20.

100. Morison, 9:349; Fifth Army, *Engineer History*, 1:85.

101. CMH, *Anzio Beach Head*, 24; Morison, 9:350.

102. Barfoot, "The Operation of the Third Platoon Company 'L'"; Morison, 9:356.

CMH, *Anzio Beach Head*, 25.

103. CMH, *Anzio Beach Head*, 110.

104. Fifth Army History, pt. 4, 65; CMH, *Anzio Beach Head*, 18; Keating, "The Operations of the Fifth Army in the Establishment of the Beachhead at Anzio-Nettuna," 7; Blumenson, *Salerno to Cassino*, 359; Report by the Supreme Allied Commander Mediterranean, 13.

105. Blumenson, *Salerno to Cassino*, 363; GMDS, A Study of German Operation at Anzio Beach Head, 11; Blumenson, *Clark*, 170.

106. Blumenson, *Salerno to Cassino*, 361; Blumenson, *Anzio*, 82; Report by the Supreme Allied Commander Mediterranean, 18, 20.

107. CMH, *Anzio Beach Head*, 20; Morison, 9:347; Blumenson, *Salerno to Cassino*, 361.

108. Blumenson, *Salerno to Cassino*, 363; Wilt, 205; Heefner, 153.

109. Blumenson, *Salerno to Cassino*, 386; Morison, 9:351–352.

110. Blumenson, *Salerno to Cassino*, 386; Blumenson, *Clark*, 172; Gutierrez, 194.

111. Morison, 9:352; Gutierrez, 195.

112. Morison, 9:344.

113. GMDS, A Study of German Operation at Anzio Beach Head, 11; Porch, 535–536; CMH, *Anzio Beach Head*, 20–21; Morison, 9:344; Fifth Army History, pt. 4, 68; Blumenson, *Salerno to Cassino*, 363; Katz, 161; Report by the Supreme Allied Commander Mediterranean, 21.

114. Fifth Army History, pt. 4, 67, 69; CMH, *Anzio Beach Head*, 22–24; Morison, 9:347.

115. CMH, *Anzio Beach Head*, 24; Barfoot, "The Operation of the Third Platoon Company 'L'"; Keating, "The Operations of the Fifth Army in the Establishment of the Beachhead at Anzio-Nettuna," 8.

116. Fifth Army History, pt. 4, 68.

117. CMH, *Anzio Beach Head*, 24; Morison, 9:344, 355; Fifth Army History, pt. 4, 72.

118. Wilt, 203.

119. Craven and Cate, 3:352; CMH, *Anzio Beach Head*, 26; Fifth Army History, pt. 4, 72.

120. XII ASC was renamed VII Tactical Air Command in April 1944.

121. Wilt, 206.

122. Wilt, 206.

123. Wilt, 206.

124. Wilt, 207.

125. St. Clair, 106; Ian F. Wilt, "Allied Cooperation in Sicily and Italy 1943–1945," 206.

126. Tac Air Comms in the MTO, 5–6.

127. Tac Air Comms in the MTO, 6.

128. Porch, 536, CMH, *Anzio Beach Head*, 20, 24; Barfoot, "The Operation of the Third Platoon Company 'L'"; Advanced Officers Class #1, Major Jewitt A. Dix, Military Monograph: "The 81st Reconnaissance Battalion at Anzio Beach,12 April 1948," CARL Digital Library, No Call Number Assigned; Keating, "The Operations of the Fifth Army in the Establishment of the Beachhead at Anzio-Nettuno," 8; Morison, 9:356; Report by the Supreme Allied Commander Mediterranean, 21.

129. Porch, 538; CMH, *Anzio Beach Head*, 113.

130. Porch, 537.

131. Dix, "The 81st Reconnaissance Battalion at Anzio Beach"; Fifth Army History, pt. 4, 71; Fifth Army, *Engineer History*, 1:85.

132. Fifth Army History, pt. 4, 71, 73.

133. Blumenson, *Salerno to Cassino*, 390; CMH, *Anzio Beach Head*, 27–28; Fifth Army History, pt. 4, 73; Report by the Supreme Allied Commander Mediterranean, 21.

134. CMH, *Anzio Beach Head*, 27; Porch, 536–537; Fifth Army History, pt. 4, 69, 71, 73; Keating, "The Operations of the Fifth Army in the Establishment of the Beachhead at Anzio-Nettuno," 7.

135. Keating, "The Operations of the Fifth Army in the Establishment of the Beachhead at Anzio-Nettuno," 9; Morison, 9:358; CMH, *Anzio Beach Head*, 30.

136. CMH, *Anzio Beach Head*, 28–30; Fifth Army History, pt. 4, 76; Morison, 9:358, Clark, 296; Heefner, 156.

137. Fifth Army History, pt. 4, 78; CMH, *Anzio Beach Head*, 42; Report by the Supreme Allied Commander Mediterranean, 22.

138. Morison, 9:363–364; CMH, *Anzio Beach Head*, 67–68.

139. CMH, *Anzio Beach Head*, 89.

140. Heefner, 159.

141. Porch, 539; Clark, 306.

142. Carlo D'Este, *Fatal Decision*, 135.

143. Clark, 306.

144. Lucian Truscott, *Command Missions: A Personal Story* (New York: Arno Press, rpt., 1979) as referenced in Heefner, 160.

145. D'Este, *Fatal Decision*, 103.

146. Wilt, 206.

Chapter 7. The Friendly Invasion Before D-Day: Operation Overlord, 1943–1944

1. Gordon Harrison, *United States Army in World War II, The European Theater of Operations, Cross-Channel Attack* (Washington, DC: Center for Military History, 1993), Appendix A.

2. Outgoing Message, SHAEF, Jan 232300, Overlord-Anvil Papers Dec 1943-Apr 1944 Part I, Walter Bedell Smith Collection of World War II Documents, Box 21 Overlord Papers, NAID 12009137, https//www.eisenhower.og/sites/default/files /research/on-line documents/d-day/overlordpart-1.pdf, 1.

3. Gordon A. Harrison, *United States Army in World War II, The European Theater of Operations, Cross Channel Attack* (Washington, DC: Center for Army History, 1993), 19.

4. Harrison, 19–20; Roland Ruppenthal, *Logistical Support of the Armies*, 1:14.

5. United States Fleet, Headquarters of the Commander In Chief, Navy Department, Subject: Memorandum: Distribution of Naval Commander Western Task Force (CTF 122) Serial 000201 of 25 July 1944 and 1st and 2nd Ends (Subject: Report of NORMANDY INVASION), dated 15 September 1944, 5, https://apps .dtic.mil/sti/tr/pdf/ADA550844.pdf (accessed March 15, 2022; hereafter referred to as CTF 122, Subject Report of Normandy Invasion); Ruppenthal, 13.

6. Ruppenthal, 28.

7. Conference on Landing Assaults, 24 May-23 June, 1943, US Assault Training Center, ETOUSA, Forward; CARL Digital Archive Call Number N6318A (hereafter referred to as COLA.).

8. COLA, Forward.

9. COLA, G-5 Section.

10. COLAs, Review of Discussions following the address, Naval Support in landing operations by Comdr E. B. Strauss; Yung, 39, 61; Bass, 16.

11. Action Report, Western Naval Task Force (Sicilian Campaign), 44; Yung, 78, 95; United States Fleet, Amphibious Operations: Invasion of Northern France, Western Task Force, June 1944, Walter Bedell Smith Collection of World War II Documents, Box 48 Amphibious Operations of Northern France Western Task Force June 1944, Dwight D. Eisenhower Presidential Library (Online Documents), Abilene, KS, 4-1 to 4-3.

12. Frankin Kibler and C. T. Schmidt, The General Board, United States Forces, European Theater, The Control of the Build-Up of Troops in the Cross Channel Amphibious Operation "Overlord," 2. CARL Digital Library, No Call Number Assigned (hereafter referred to as BUCO); Symonds, 139; Samuel Elliot Morison, *History of United States Navy Operations in World War II, Volume 11: The Invasion of France and Germany 1944-1945* (Boston: Brown and Little and Co., 1957), 51–52; Karig, 291.

13. US Navy History and Heritage Command, *Operation Overlord: Concept to Execution, Planning the Invasion of France, 1942-1955*, www.history.navy.mil/brow se-by-topic/wars-conflicts-and-operations/world-war-ii/1944/overlord/overlord -planning.html; Max Hastings, *Overlord, D-Day and the Battle for Normandy* (New York: Simon and Schuster, 1984), 20; Edwin P. Hoyt, *The Invasion Before Normandy: The Secret Battle of Slapton Sands* (Lanham, MD: Scarborough House, 1999), 45–46, 53; Ruppenthal, 231–233; War Department, Omaha Beach Head 6 June-13 June 1944 (Washington, DC: Historical Division, 1945), 2, CARL Digital Library, No Call Number Assigned.

14. Supreme Headquarters Allied Expeditionary Force, SUBJECT: Operation OVERLORD, Annex C, 10 March 1944, CARL Digital Archive, No Call Number Assigned.

15. Martin Bowman, *USAAF Handbook, 1939-1945* (Mechanicsburg, PA:

Stackpole Books, 1997), 68; Jean Pierre Benamou, *10 Million Tons for Victory* (Bayeux, France: Orep Publications, 2014), 10.

16. Ewing, *Let's Go!*, 27.

17. Hoyt, 79; Symonds, 136.

18. Symonds, 135.

19. Hastings, 69; Hoyt, 32, 42.

20. Lectures, Joint Q Planning School, CARL Digital Archive Call Number N2773; Hastings, 34; Ruppenthal, 337; Mark Khan, *D-Day Assault, The Second World War Assault Training Exercises at Slapton Sands* (South Yorkshire, UK: Pen and Sword, 2014), 76–77.

21. Morison, 11:31–32; Symonds, 142–143.

22. CTF 122, Subject Report of Normandy Invasion (Annex A, Command Relationships and Planning), 2.

23. Ruppenthal, 338.

24. Symonds, 142–143.

25. Morison, 11:65.

26. First Army Operation Plan NEPTUNE, Annex 14, Changes and Amendments to Signal Communications Plan, 25 February 1944, 1, CARL Digital Archive, Call Number N7374-A.1; Morison, 11:52; Harrison, 190.

27. Karig, 291–292.

28. Karig, 301.

29. First Army Operation Plan NEPTUNE, Annex 13 Neptune Air Plan; Harrison, 214; Lewis, 235–237.

30. Bass, 9.

31. COLA, Colonel Paul W. Thompson, Commandant Assault Training Center ETOUSA (PROV); Ruppenthal, 342.

32. Ewing, *Let's Go!*, 23; Hastings, 34; Hoyt, 37; Ruppenthal, 340–342; Harrison, 162; Peter Caddick-Adams, *Sand and Steel: A New History of D-Day* (London: Arrow Books, 2019), 182–183; Bass, 9; Khan, 74. COLA, Address by Colonel Paul W. Thompson; Symonds, 140.

33. Ruppenthal, 342; Harrison, 162, 164; Hoyt, 40, 47; Bass, 11. The 28th Division was also trained at this location during this period but did not land in France until July 1944.

34. Bass, 11.

35. Morison, 11:58–60, 64.

36. Morison, 11:63.

37. Lewis, 72, 267, 286; Bass, 24; Oral Interview with Harold Baumgarten, WW II Archive.

38. Wes Ross, *146th Engineer Combat Battalion: Essayons*, unpublished manuscript, National World War II Archive, 8.

39. Ross, *146th Engineer Combat Battalion*, 8.

40. V Corps Operations Plan NEPTUNE, 26 March 1944, 2–3, CARL Digital Archive, Call Number N7375; Lewis, 72, 267, 286; Oral Interview with Harold Baumgarten, WW II Archive.

41. Khan, 34.

42. Khan, 62–63; Small, 9–11; Hoyt, 42, 81–82; Oral Interview with Harold Baumgarten, WW II Archive.

43. Khan, 73.

44. Caddick-Adams, 198–199; Hoyt 42; Small, 16; CTF 122, Subject Report of Normandy Invasion (Annex G-Training and Rehearsals), 1; Oral Interview with Harold Baumgarten, WWII Archive.

45. Small, 35; Hoyt, 118; Caddick-Adams, 238–240; Max Schoenfeld, "The Navies and NEPTUNE," in Theodore Wilson (ed.), *D-Day, 1944* (Lawrence: University Press of Kansas, 1993), 108; Yung, 166; CTF 122, Subject Report of Normandy Invasion (Annex G-Training and rehearsals), 1; Morison, 11:65.

46. Charles B. MacDonald, "Slapton Sands: The Cover-up That Never Was," extracted from *Army* 38, no. 6 (June 1988): 64–67, www.history.navy.mil/content /history/nhhc/research/library/online-reading-room/title-list-alphabetically/s /slapton-sands-the-cover-up-that-never-was.html; Caddick-Adams, 240.

47. Craven and Cate, 3:180.

48. CTF 122, Subject Report of Normandy Invasion (Annex B1-Intellegence), 4, 6, 8–10; Morison, 11:71.

49. COLA, Discussion following the talk by Comdr Strauss.

50. COLA, Discussion following the talk by Comdr Strauss.

51. Robert Miller, *Division Commander: A Biography of Major General Norman D. Cota* (Spartanburg, SC: The Reprint Company, 1989), 78.

52. CTF 122, Subject Report of Normandy Invasion (Annex L-Control Vessels) and (Annex M-Naval Scout Boats), 1.

53. Joseph Balkoski, *Beyond the Beach Head: 29th Infantry Division in Normandy* (Harrisburg, PA: Stackpole Books, 1989), 130.

54. CTF 122, Subject Report of Normandy Invasion (Annex T2-The Assault), 1; Ewing, *Let's Go!*, 39.

55. Hoyt, 43; COLA, Address by Commander Elliot Stauss.

56. War Department, Omaha Beach Head, 2.

57. Outgoing Message, SHAEF, Jan 232300, 2; Harrison, 167.

58. Kent Hewitt, "Planning Operation Anvil-Dragoon," in US Naval Institute *Proceedings*, July 1954, Volume 80.

59. David Eisenhower, *Eisenhower at War: 1943–1945* (New York: Vintage Books, 1986), 144–145; Theodore Wilson in *D-Day, 1944*, xiii; Harrison, 166, 168.

60. Harrison, 173; Robin Higman, "Technology at D-Day," in Wilson, 83.

61. Morison, 11:54.

62. Ruppenthal, 342–343; Hoyt, 83; CTF 122, Subject Report of Normandy Invasion (Annex O-Beach and Shore Party), 1.

63. Ruppenthal, 344.

64. CTF 122, Subject Report of Normandy Invasion, 16; Symonds, 205–206.

65. CTF 122, Subject Report of Normandy Invasion, Annex O Beach and Shore Party, 1; United States Fleet, COMMICH P-006, Amphibious Operations, Invasion of Northern France, Western Task Force, June 1944, 4–7. Eisenhower Online Archives, http://eisenhower.archives.gov/research/on_linedocuments/d-day/Rep ort_of Amphibious_Operations.pdf.

66. Ruppenthal, 224–225 Chart 6; Schoenfeld 103; Schoenfeld, 104; Ken Small, *The Forgotten Dead: The True Story of Exercise Tiger, the Disastrous Rehearsal for D-Day* (Oxford, UK: Osprey Publishing 1988), 20.

67. Khan, 86.

68. Hastings, 34; Ruppenthal, 345, 349; Hoyt, 43; Yung, 152, 158; CTF 122, Subject Report of Normandy Invasion, 16.

69. Symonds, 205.

70. Miller, *Division Commander*, 76.

71. CTF 122, Subject Report of Normandy Invasion (Training and Rehearsals), 1.

72. Ruppenthal, 449–350.

73. Ewing, *Let's Go!*, 27; BUCO, 2; CTF 122, Subject Report of Normandy Invasion (Annex S1-Assembly and Loading), 1; (Annex S3-Convoys, Routing, and Escort), 2; Karig, 306.

74. BUCO, 3; CTF 122, Subject Report of Normandy Invasion (Annex S1-Assembly and Loading), 1; Hoyt, 79–80; Karig, 290–291; Miller, *Division Commander*, 76–77.

75. Symonds, 141–142; Morison, 11:68; Bass, 23.

76. Morison, 11:68.

77. BUCO, 3; CTF 122, Subject Report of Normandy Invasion (Annex S3-Convoys, Routing, and Escort), 1; Morison, 11:67.

78. CTF 122, Subject Report of Normandy Invasion (Annex S3-Convoys, Routing, and Escort), 3.

79. CTF 122, Subject Report of the Normandy Invasion (Annex T1-The Approach), 1; Karig, 302–303.

80. US Navy History and Heritage Command, *Operation Overlord*; Harrison, 189–190; Hoyt, 50; Yung, 103; Lewis, 274; Darden, 10; COMMICH P-006, 4–7; Morison, 11:32–33; Harrison, 189; Balkoski, *Beyond the Beach*, 120.

81. Amphibious Operations: Invasion of Northern France, Western Task Force, pages 4–2 to 4–3; Schoenfeld, "The Navies and NEPTUNE,"108; Hoyt, 50; Lewis, 205; CTF 122, Subject Report of Normandy Invasion, 7; (Annex P-Surprise-D-Day and H-Hour), 2; Morison, 11:33.

82. Alfred Beck et al., *The United States Army in World War II, The Technical Services. The Corps of Engineers: The War Against Germany* (Washington, DC: Center for Military History, 1985), 319.

83. Action Report, Western Naval Task Force, 44, 118; CTF 122, Subject Report of Normandy Invasion, 7–8; COMMICH P-006, 4–3; Harrison, 188–189.

84. CTF 122, Subject Report of Normandy Invasion, 11.

85. William B. Kirkland, *Destroyers at Normandy: Naval Gunfire Support at Omaha Beach* (Washington, DC: Naval Historical Foundation, 1994), 26.

86. Morton L. Deyo, "Naval Guns at Normandy," www.history.navy.mil/research/library/online-reading-room/title-list-alphabetically/n/naval-guns-normandy.html; Lewis, 228.

87. Ewing, *Let's Go!*, 35–36; Lewis, 227; Darden, 6; Morison, 11:56; Harrison, 194; Bradley, *A Soldier's Story*, 254.

88. Operation Plan No. 2-44, Western Naval Task Force, Allied Expeditionary Force (Short Title "ONWEST TWO"), CARL Digital Archive, Call Number N7376, Appendix 1 to Annex D page 1 of 1 (hereafter referred to as ONWEST TWO); CTF 122, Subject Report of Normandy Invasion (Annex T2-The Assault), 2; V Corps Operations Plan NEPTUNE, 26 March, 1944, Annex 12, 4.

89. Lewis, 213.

90. Ewing, *Let's Go!*, 36; Morison, 11:56; CTF 122, Subject Report of Normandy Invasion (Annex I-Naval Gunfire Support), 1–3; Harrison, 194.

91. Craig Symonds, *World War II at Sea: A Global History* (Oxford: Oxford University Press, 2018), 531.

92. Joseph Balkoski, *Omaha Beach: D-Day, June 6, 1944* (Mechanicsburg, PA: Stackpole Books, 2004), 289.

93. Balkoski, *Omaha Beach: D-Day*, 208–209, 277–278; Kirkland, *Destroyers*, 30, 31, 36–37.

94. Kirkland, *Destroyers*, 33, 47.

95. Balkoski, *Omaha Beach: D-Day*, 276–277; Kirkland, *Destroyers*, 47–48.

96. Balkoski, *Omaha Beach: D-Day*, 254.

97. *Operation Neptune, The U.S. Navy on D-Day, June 6, 1944*, www.history.navy.mil/browse-by-topic/wars-conflicts-and-operations/world-war-ii/1944/overlord/operation-neptune.html; Deyo, 24–25; Symonds, 531.

98. Kirkland, *Destroyers*, 42.

99. Balkoski, *Beyond the Beach*, 134.

100. Balkoski, *Omaha Beach: D-Day*, 288–289.

101. CTF 122, Subject Report of Normandy Invasion, 12.

102. Symonds, 531; Kirkland, *Destroyers*, 47.

103. Kirkland, *Destroyers*, 44.

104. Kirkland, *Destroyers*, 54.

105. Balkoski, *Beyond the Beach*, 139; Balkoski, *Omaha Beach: D-Day*, 277.

106. ONWEST TWO, Appendix 2 to Annex D, 1–2.

107. CTF 122, Subject Report of Normandy Invasion (Annex I-Naval Gunfire Support), 1–3; Deyo, 17.

108. Deyo, 35.

109. Yung, 216–217.

110. CTF 122, Subject Report of Normandy Invasion (Annex I-Naval Gunfire Support), 6; (Annex D-Air Operations), 8; Deyo, 17.

111. First Army Operation Plan NEPTUNE Annex 21, 6; Harrison, 196–197; "Rocket Boats Lay Smoke Screen for Landings," In *Popular Mechanics*, February 1945, 28.

112. BUCO, 3.

113. Hoyt, 51; Harrison, 192; Yung, 95; Bass, 16, 32–38.

114. James R. Darden, "Operations of the 1st Division in the Landing and Establishment of the Beach Head on Omaha Beach 6–10 June 1944," Advanced Infantry Officers Course 1949–1950, The Infantry School, Fort Benning GA, 13, https://mcoecbamcoepwprd01.blob.core.usgovcloudapi.net/library/DonovanPapers/wwii/STUP2/A-F/DardenJamesR%20CPT.pdf.

115. Higman, 94; COLA, Review of the Discussion following the address "Armored Fighting Vehicles in a Landing Assault by Lt Col C. R. Kutz"; Lewis, 251.

116. First Army Operation Plan NEPTUNE, Annex 21, 6.

117. First Army Operation Plan NEPTUNE, Annex 22, 6.

118. Ewing, *Let's Go!*, 36; Hoyt, 51; Harrison, 192; Amphibious Operations: Invasion of Northern France, Western Task Force, page 4–4; Lewis, 246; CTF 122, Subject Report of Normandy Invasion, 14 (Annex C-Logistics), 5; Headquarters Army Ground Forces, *Development of DD Tanks*, 6 June 1946, CARL Digital Archive, Call Number N13700, Introduction, Appendix A; William Folkestad, *The*

View from the Turret: The 743 Tank Battalion During World War II (Shippensburg, PA: Burd Press, 2000), 3.

119. Army Ground Forces, Development of DD Tanks, Appendix C.

120. Unit Journal 471st Tank Battalion, CARL Digital Library, No Call Number Assigned; Action Against Enemy/After Action Report, 741st Tank Battalion, 19 June(?) 1944. https://8th-armored.org/8documents/AAR-741-Tank.pdf.

121. Action Against Enemy/After Action Report, 741st Tank Battalion, 1; Development of DD Tanks, Appendix C.

122. The exact number of tanks in this action varies slightly from reference to reference. Army Ground Forces, Development of DD Tanks, Appendix C; Armor in Operation Neptune (Establishment of the Normandy Beach Head), A Research Report prepared by Committee 10, Officers Advance Course, Armor School, Fort Knox, KY, May 1949, 79, CARL Digital Archive, Call Number N2146.40–3; Unit Journal 471st Tank Battalion; After Action Report, 741st, 1.

123. CTF 122, Subject Report of Normandy Invasion (Annex T2-The Assault), 2 (Annex C-Logistics), 5; Darden, 16; COMMICH P-006, 4–3; Harrison, 192; Oral Interview with Harold Baumgarten, WW II Archive.

124. Folkestad, 7; Army Ground Forces, Development of DD Tanks, Appendix C.

125. Armor in Operation Neptune, 81; Ewing, *Let's Go!*, 53–54; Balkoski, *Beyond the Beach*, 122, 129.

126. After Action Report, 747th Tank Battalion, June Thru December 1944, 1, CARL Digital Archive, No Call Number Assigned.

127. Ewing, *Let's Go!*, 36; First Army Operation Plan NEPTUNE, Annex 21, 7; DD Tanks, Annex C.

128. Fran Baker, *Hot Steel: The Story of the 58th Armored Field Artillery Battalion* (Delphi Book, 2014), 76; Kirkland *Destroyers*, 29.

129. Headquarters, 58th Armored Field Artillery Battalion, After Action Report Against the Enemy, 22 July, 1944, CARL Digital Archive, No Call Number Assigned; Baker, *Hot Steel* 76.

130. CTF 122, Subject Report of Normandy Invasion, 14 (Annex C-Logistics, 6).

131. COLA, Address by Brigadier General R. C. Candee CG, 8th Air Support Command. CARLA.

132. COLA, Address by Brigadier General R. C. Candee; Wilt, in Wilson, 147.

133. Yung, 38.

134. Harrison, 194; COLA, G-5 Section. CARLA.

135. Yung, 58.

136. CTF 122, Subject Report of Normandy Invasion, 9; (Annex D-Air Operations), 4. Kirkland, *Destroyers*, 45.

137. Walter Gaul, Report on German Air Force (Luftwaffe) and the Invasion of Normandy, 1944, www.history.navy.mil/content/history/nhhc/research/libra ry/online-reading-room/title-list-alphabetically/g/gaf-invasion-normandy.html.

138. Ground Liaison Officer School, Joint Air-Ground Action (Part 1), Call number N11134-A, 1.

139. Stephan A. Bourque, *Beyond the Beach: The Allied War Against France*

(Annapolis, MD: Naval Institute Press, 2018), 10, 71, 157. Eisenhower, *Eisenhower at War*, 187–188; Thomas Alexander Hughes, *Overlord: General Pete Quesada and the Triumph of Tactical Airpower in World War II* (New York: Free Press, 1995), 112.

140. Richard Davis, *Carl A. Spaatz and the Air War in Europe* (Washington, DC: Center for Air Force History, 1993), 401; Hughes, 16, 122; Hastings, 42.

141. Bourque, 157; Morison, 11:36; Harrison, 222–224.

142. COLA, G-2 Section, Summary. CARLA; Wilt, in Wilson, 145.

143. William W. Momyer, *Airpower in Three Wars (WWII, Korea, Vietnam)* (Maxwell AFB, AL: Air University Press, 2003), 185; Eisenhower, *Eisenhower at War*, 184; Lewis, 220–221; Morison, 11:37–38; Harrison, 217–219, 221.

144. Craven and Cate, 3:160.

145. Richard Kohn and Joseph Harahan, *Condensed Analysis of the Ninth Air Force in the European Theater of Operations* (Washington, DC: USAF Office of History, 1984), 17.

146. Davis, *Spaatz*, 410; Harrison, 225.

147. Headquarters, US Air Force, *Wings at War Series no 2, Sunday Punch in Normandy: The Tactical Use of Heavy Bombardment in the Normandy Operation* (Washington, DC: Center for Air Force History (New Imprint), 1992), 22.

148. Craven and Cate, 3:138.

149. Bourque, 15; Lewis, 232; CTF 122, Subject Report of Normandy Invasions (Annex D-Air Operations), 5; Harrison, 215.

150. War Department, Omaha Beach Head, 3.

151. *Sunday Punch in Normandy*, 7, 9; COLA, Address by Brigadier General R. C. Candee; War Department, Omaha Beach Head, 3.

152. Kohn and Harahan, 19–20.

153. Craven and Cate, 3:160; Wynn and Young, 104.

154. Momyer, 186.

155. Kohn and Harahan, 20.

156. Craven and Cate, 3:160–161.

157. AAF Evaluation Board in the European Theater of Operations, Summary Report of Air Attack Against Rail Transportation in the Battle of France, 1 June 1945, CARL Call Number N11557B, 36.

158. Ground Liaison Officer School, Joint Air-Ground Action (Part 1), 65.

159. First Army Operation Plan NEPTUNE, Revised Annex 12 Prearranged Air and Naval Bombardment Plan, 1; V Corps Operations Plan NEPTUNE, Annex 12 Fire Support Plan, 2; War Department, Omaha Beach Head, 29.

160. Harrison 196; *Sunday Punch in Normandy*, 9; Wilt, in Wilson, 139–140, 143; Yung, 189; CTF 122, Subject Report of Normandy Invasion (Annex D-Air Operations), 6.

161. Wynn and Young, 137; CTF 122, Subject Report of Normandy Invasion (Annex D-Air Operations), 1; War Department Omaha Beach Head, 29; Craven and Cate, 3:193–195.

162. Ewing, *Let's Go!*, 36: Davis, *Spaatz*, 418; Richard G. Davis, *Bombing the European Axis Powers: A Digest of the Combined Bomber Offensive, 1939–1945* (Maxwell AFB, AL: Air University Press, 2006), 357.

163. Balkoski, *Beyond the Beach*, 11–12.

164. Lewis, 205.

165. Craven and Cate, 3:192; Beck et al., 321.

166. As referenced in Bourque, 217–220, 227.

167. CTF 122, Subject Report of Normandy Invasion, 10.

168. Field Order no. 1 "Neptune," Force "B," 29th Infantry Division, 29, CARL Digital Archive, Call Number N7377-A.

169. Francois Robinard, *June–September 1944: 50 Airfields for Victory* (Bayeux, France: Heimdal Publishing, 2012), 30, 37.

170. Robinard, 3.

171. George Raynor Thompson and Dixie Harris, *United States Army in World War II, The Technical Services. The Signal Corps: The Outcome Mid-1943–1945* (Washington, DC: Center for Military History, 1991), 88.

172. Thompson and Harris, 89–90.

173. ONWEST TWO Appendix 2 to Annex D, 1–4.

174. First Army Operation Plan NEPTUNE, Annex 13, Air Plan, 25 February 1944, 4.

175. W. A. Jacobs, "The Battle for France," in *Case Studies in Close Air Support* (Washington, DC: Office of Air Force History, 1990), 251, 254. CTF 122, Subject Report of Normandy Invasion, 14 (Annex D-Air Operations), 1–3. CARLA; First Army Operation Plan NEPTUNE, Annex 13, 4,5.

176. Craven and Cate, 3:194.

177. Jacobs in *Case Studies in Close Air Support*, 255.

178. MacMillan, "Fighter Control and Aircraft Warning in Amphibious Operations," 10; Combined Operations, Fighter Direction Tenders-FDTs 13, 216, 217, www.combinedops.com/FDTs.htm#:~:text=Fighter%20Direction%20Tenders%20were%20floating,bristled%20with%20aerials%20and%20antenna; First Army Operation Plan NEPTUNE, Annex 13, 6.

179. CTF 122, Subject Report of Normandy Invasion, 14 (Annex D-Air Operations), 1–3; Jacobs in *Case Studies in Close Air Support*, 255; Operation Plane NEPTUNE, Annex 14, Signal Communications Plan, 5.

180. First Army Operation Plan NEPTUNE, Signal Communications Plan, Annex 14, 25 February 1944, 6.

181. Jacobs in *Case Studies in Close Air Support*, 251. CTF 122, Subject: Report of Normandy Invasion (Annex C-Logistics) 4 (Annex D-Air Operations), 3–5.

182. Bass, 21.

183. Army Service Forces, Army Pigeon Service Agency, Signal Corps, Subject: Operation of Signal Pigeon Company in France, 9 March 1945, Enclosure Use of Pigeons in the Invasion of France, p2, Reports Historical Folders, Office of the Chief Signal Officer, Entry Number #UD 1025, Records Pertaining to Pigeons 1918–1948, Record Group 0111, National Archives, College Park, MA. Courtesy of Dr Frank Blazich, Smithsonian Museum of American History.

184. First Army Operation Plan NEPTUNE, Signal Communications Plan, Annex 14, 25 February 1944, 22.

185. Enclosure, Use of Pigeons, 2. NARA.

186. CTF 122, Subject: Report of Normandy Invasion (Annex D-Air Operations), 11.

187. Roger Hesketh, *Fortitude: The D-Day Deception Campaign* (New York: The Overlook Press, 2000), 17.

188. Hesketh, 181–184.

189. BUCO, 2; CTF 122, Subject Report of Normandy Invasion (Annex Q-Diversions), 1; Hoyt, 72–73; Hesketh, 191.

190. CTF 122, Subject Report of Normandy Invasion (Annex Q-Diversions), 1; Morison, 11:75.

191. BUCO, 4; Ruppenthal, 298.

192. Hoyt, 41, 66; Ruppenthal, 27; COLA, G-5 Section.

193. CTF 122, Subject Report of Normandy Invasion (Annex C-Logistics), 7.

194. Benamou, 17.

195. Ruppenthal, 363; CTF 122, Subject Report of Normandy Invasion, 15.

196. CTF 122, Subject Report of Normandy Invasion (Annex U-Build-Up), 1.

197. CTF 122, Subject Report of Normandy Invasion (Annex U-Build-Up), 2.

198. CTF 122, Subject Report of Normandy Invasion, 15 and (Annex U-Build-Up), 2.

199. BUCO, 5.

200. BUCO, 5; Ruppenthal, 363–364; Morison, 11:27.

201. Ruppenthal, 363.

202. BUCO, 5–7.

203. BUCO, 11.

204. Morison, 11:25.

205. Supreme Headquarters Allied Expeditionary Force, Mulberry B: D+4 -D+147, CARL Digital Archive, Call Number N6117A/N1611B; Ruppenthal, 273, 278; Morison, 11:25–26; First Army Operation Plan NEPTUNE, Engineering Special Branch Plan, Annex 11, 25 February 1944; Higman 90; Ruppenthal, 278; Symonds, 206; Hoyt, 40.

206. First Army Operation Plan NEPTUNE, Engineering Special Branch Plan, Annex 11, 25 February 1944, 4; Morison, 11:26; Mulberry B; Ruppenthal, 275–276.

207. Ruppenthal, 278, 402–404; Mulberry B.

208. First Army Operation Plan, Annex 11, 7.

209. Ruppenthal, 402; Mulberry B; First Army Operation Plan NEPTUNE, Engineering Special Branch Plan, Annex 11, 25 February 1944, 4, Combined Army Research Library Archive; Morison, 11:25.

210. Ruppenthal, 406–411; John Keegan, *Six Armies at Normandy* (New York: Viking Press, 1982), 161–163; Max Hastings, *Overlord*, 196–197; Paul Kennedy, *Engineers of Victory: Problem Solvers who Turned the Tide in World War II* (New York: Random House, 2013), 276.

211. Morison, 11:166; Yung, 215.

212. Beck et al., 344; Ruppenthal, 412–415.

213. Ruppenthal, 412–413.

214. Beck et al., 344.

215. Ruppenthal, 413–415.

216. Beck et al., 344; Ruppenthal, 415–421.

217. Ruppenthal, 417.

218. Ruppenthal, 415–421. Eighteen ports on the Normandy coast were survey in detail as additionally offload locations.

219. CTF 122, Subject Report of Normandy Invasion, 3.

220. Karl Gerd von Rundstedt, *Report on the Allied Invasion of Normandy, 20 June 1944*, www.history.navy.mil/content/history/nhhc/research/library/online

-reading-room/title-list-alphabetically/g/german-report-on-the-allied-invasion
-of-normandy.html.

221. Rundstedt.

222. Rundstedt.

223. Kirkland, *Destroyers*, 45.

Chapter 8. Faultless on a Large Scale: Operation Anvil/Dragoon, August 1944

1. Jeffrey Clark and Robert Ross Smith, *United States Army in World War II: European Theater of Operations, Riviera to the Rhine* (Washington, DC: Center for Military History, 1993), 20; Headquarters 6th Army Group, *Final Report World War II 1 July, 1945*, 1, www.trailblazersww2.org/pdf/SixthArmyG3pdf.pdf; Office of the Assistant Chief of Air Staff, Intelligence, *Reports from Mediterranean Army Air Forces: The Army Air Forces in the Invasion of Southern France: An Interim Report* (Washington, DC: Center for Air Force History (Reprint), 1992), 3; Morison, 11:221; Craven and Cate, 3:409.

2. Robert Adleman and George Walton, *The Champaign Campaign* (Boston: Little, Brown, and Company, 1969), 63; Karig, 378; Morison, 11:221; Clark and Smith, 8; Sixth Army, Final Report, 1.

3. Morison, 11:226; Porch, 590; Clark and Smith, 19, 70; Seventh Army After Action Report, *Seventh Army in Southern France and Germany 1944–1945 in Four Phases*, 4, CARL Digital Archive Call Number N13215-A; Vice Admiral H. K. Hewitt, Invasion of Southern France: Report of Naval Commander, Western Task Force, 15 November, 1944, CARL Digital Archive Call Number N4323-1, 6.

4. Combined Chiefs of Staff Memorandum, 964-2 (CCS 964-2), Firm Recommendations with Regard to Operations ANVIL and OVERLORD, 11 January 1944, CARL Digital Archive, Call Number N13096, Enclosure A; Morison, 11:230; Hewitt, "Planning Operation Anvil-Dragoon," 12.

5. Hewitt, Invasion of Southern France, 3.

6. Eisenhower, *Eisenhower at War*, 318; Clark and Smith, 19.

7. Headquarters Twelfth Air Force, *XII Air Force Service Command in Operation Dragoon*, 1, Call Number 11609, CARL Digital Archive; *The Army Air Forces in the Invasion of Southern France: An Interim Report*, 3; Sixth Army, Final Report, 2; Seventh Army After Action Report, 2.

8. Clark and Smith, 10–11; CCS 964-2, 1; Craven and Cate, 3:411.

9. Kent Hewitt, "Planning Operation Anvil-Dragoon," 1; Center for Army History (CMH), *Southern France, Publication 73-21* (Washington, DC: US Government Printing Office), 3; *The Army Air Forces in the Invasion of Southern France*, 4; George G. Kundahl, *The Riveria at War: World War II on the Cote D'Azur* (New York: I. B. Tauris Publishing, 2017), 175–176; Eisenhower, *Eisenhower at War*, 316–317; Morison, 11:223–225; Clark and Smith, 15–18; Craven and Cate, 3:410–412.

10. Sixth Army, Final Report, 2; Clark and Smith, 15, 50, 22; CMH, *Southern France*, 5; *XII Air Force Service Command in Operation Dragoon*, 1; Seventh Army After Action Report, 15, 26; Harrison, 170–173; Hewitt, Invasion of Southern France, 3.

11. The Manhattan Project was still largely unknown, as its use was speculative

at this time. Eisenhower, *Eisenhower at War*, 315; Clark and Smith, 12; Morison, 11:230; Harrison, 168–167; Hewitt, Invasion of Southern France, 1.

12. CMH, *Southern France*, 5; Kundahl, 184; Hewitt, Invasion of Southern France, 1, 8.

13. 6th Army *Final Report*, 1; CMH, *Southern France*, 4; Hewitt, "Planning Operation Anvil-Dragoon," 2; Hewitt, Invasion of Southern France, 1, 8; Clark and Smith, 9, 21; Seventh Army After Action Report, 19, 22.

14. Hewitt, "Planning Operation Anvil-Dragoon," 3.

15. Clark and Smith, 41–42, 77.

16. Sixth Army, Final Report, 2; *Eisenhower at War*, 317; Morison, 11:229–230; CMH, *Southern France*, 5; *XII Air Force Service Command in Operation Dragoon*, 1; Craven and Cate, 3:413.

17. Eisenhower, *Eisenhower at War*, 325; Morison, 11:230; Heefner, 190; *XII Air Force Service Command in Operation Dragoon*, 1; Hewitt, "Planning Operation Anvil-Dragoon," 13; Seventh Army After Action Report, 77.

18. Craven and Cate, 3:409; Sixth Army, Final Report, 2.

19. Morison, 11:233; Clark and Smith, 24–25, 31; Seventh Army After Action Report, 14; Hewitt, Invasion of Southern France, 1.

20. Craven and Cate, 3:409; Sixth Army, Final Report, 2, 5; Heefner, 184; Seventh Army After Action Report, 3, 66; Armed Forces Staff College (AFSC), Instructional Publication, "The Invasion of Southern France, Operation Dragoon," Norfolk, VA, 1949–1950, 7, CARL Digital Archive, Call Number N15878.3; Adequacy of TacAir in the MTO, 2.

21. Hewitt, "Planning Operation Anvil-Dragoon," 3; *XII Air Force Service Command in Operation Dragoon*, 1; Karing, *The Atlantic War*, 379; Morison, 11:237; Clark and Smith, 33; Heefner, 182–184, 188; Headquarters Services of Supply, North African Theater of Operations, US Army, Operation Dragoon, 1, CARL Digital Archive Call Number N3663-A.

22. Seventh Army After Action Report, 66; Office of the Assistant Chief of Air Staff, Intelligence, *Reports from Mediterranean Army Air Forces: The Army Air Forces in the Invasion of Southern France: An Interim Report* (Washington, DC: Center for Air Force History (Reprint), 1992), 3; CMH, *Southern France*, 6; Kundahl, 185; Morison, 11:235; Clark and Smith, 21, 70; Craven and Cate, 3:412.

23. Hewitt, "Planning Operation Anvil-Dragoon," 3; Morison, 11:235; Clark and Smith, 73.

24. CMH, *Southern France*, 6; Seventh Army After Action Report, 5, 139.

25. Seventh Army After Action Report, 78; Craven and Cate, 3:414; Karig, 379; CMH, *Southern France*, 8; Morison, 11:235; Clark and Smith, 75, 78–79.

26. Smith and Clark, 79.

27. Seventh Army After Action Report, 159, 181, 189; Heefner, 185–187; Hewitt, Invasion of Southern France, 19, 20.

28. VI Corps, Field Order #1, Naples Italy, 30 July 1944, 1, CARL Digital Archive, Call Number N3632; Seventh Army After Action Report, 11, 79; Hewitt, Invasion of Southern France, 8, 23.

29. VI Corps, Field Order, #1; Smith and Clark, 79, 109; Morison, 11:259; CMH, *Southern France*, 5–6, 8; Heefner, 184, 187; *XII Air Force Service Command in Operation Dragoon*, 2; Seventh Army After Action Report, 5, 81, 160.

30. VI Corps Field Order #1, 2, 81; Clark and Smith, 79; Morison, 11:264–265; CMH, *Southern France*, 5–6, 8; Heefner, 187; *XII Air Force Service Command in Operation Dragoon*, 2; Seventh Army After Action Report, 134.

31. VI Corps, Field Order #1, 2, 82; Heefner, 187; Clark and Smith, 78; Morison, 11:267–268; CMH, *Southern France*, 5–6, 8; *XII Air Force Service Command in Operation Dragoon*, 2; Seventh Army After Action Report, 21, 135, 179–180.

32. 6th Army Final Report, 5; Seventh Army After Action Report, 21; Sixth Army, Final Report, 5; Clark and Smith, 37, 41, 73, 75–78; Morison, 11:233, 236–237; Heefner, 182; Craven and Cate, 3:414; Hewitt, "Planning Operation Anvil-Dragoon," 11.

33. Clark and Smith, 80–81.

34. Hewitt, Invasion of Southern France, 23; Heefner, 188.

35. Clark and Smith, 75.

36. *XII Air Force Service Command in Operation Dragoon*, 3; Morison, 11:248; Craven and Cate, 3:419; Seventh Army After Action Report, 85.

37. Craven and Cate, 3:414, 427, 431; Adleman and Walton, 133–134; *The Army Air Forces in the Invasion of Southern France*, 5, 16–17, 26–27, Clark and Smith, 39, 41, 45, 77; Morison, 11:248–249; CMH, *Southern France*, 9; Seventh Army After Action Report, 139.

38. Seventh Army After Action Report, 64; Heefner, 185.

39. Heefner, 185, 187; Clark and Smith, 77; Morison, 11:251; CMH, *Southern France*, 6, 9, 13; Seventh Army After Action Report, 74, 82, 132.

40. Craven and Cate, 3:414; Seventh Army After Action Report, 80, 132; *The Army Air Forces in the Invasion of Southern France*, 16; Clark and Smith, 39; Morison, 11:250–251; Clark and Smith, 77; AFSC Instructional Publication, 7–8.

41. Clark and Smith, 50; AFSC Instructional Publication, 9.

42. VI Corps Field Order #1, Appendix 1 to Annex 1 dated 22 July 1944, 1; CMH, *Southern France*, 9; Morison, 11:244; Heefner, 190; Craven and Cate, 3:425; Seventh Army After Action Report, 42–43, 45, 49.

43. Heefner, 187; Morison, 11:240–241; CMH, *Southern France*, 9; Smith and Clark, 57; Seventh Army After Action Report, 55–59, 102, 108.

44. Morison, 11:241; Hewitt, "Planning Operation Anvil-Dragoon," 12; Seventh Army After Action Report, 103.

45. Seventh Army After Action Report, 108.

46. The number of divisions assigned to 19th Army varies from source to source. Adleman and Walton, 65; Morison, 11:239–241; Breuer, 21–22; Clark and Smith, 57–59; CMH, *Southern France*, 9; Heefner, 187; Craven and Cate, 3:426; Seventh Army After Action Report, 46–47.

47. Clark and Smith, 67; CMH, *Southern France*, 9; Heefner 187; Seventh Army After Action Report, 49.

48. VI Corps Field Order #1, Appendix 1 to Annex 1, 2–5; Clark and Smith, 70, 111.

49. As referenced in Morison, 244.

50. VI Corps Field Order #1, Appendix 1 to Annex 1, 5.

51. 6th Army Final Report, 5; Morison, 11:221, 238; Clark and Smith, 78, 83; Hewitt, "Planning Operation Anvil-Dragoon," 9; Hewitt, Invasion of Southern France, 20–21.

52. Seventh Army After Action Report, 76; Clark and Smith, 82.

53. Clark and Smith, 82; Craven and Cate, 3:414; Seventh Army After Action Report, 140.

54. *XII Air Force Service Command in Operation Dragoon*, 3.

55. *The Army Air Forces in the Invasion of Southern France: An Interim Report*, 10; Morison, 11:243; Clark and Smith, 81; Seventh Army After Action Report, 83.

56. Seventh Army After Action Report, 139; Craven and Cate, 3:423–424.

57. VI Corps Field Order #1, Annex #2 Air Support, 1; CMH, *Southern France*, 12; Morison, 11:243; *XII Air Force Service Command in Operation Dragoon*, 3; Craven and Cate, 3:416, 424; Seventh Army After Action Report, 83, 140.

58. Seventh Army After Action Report, 141.

59. VI Corps Field Order #1, Annex #2 Air Support, 1–2; Morison, 11:243; *The Army Air Forces in the Invasion of Southern France: An Interim Report*, 10; Morison, 11:243; Clark and Smith, 82; *XII Air Force Service Command in Operation Dragoon*, 4; Craven and Cate, 3:415; Seventh Army After Action Report, 83, 84, 140; AFSC Instructional Publication, 9.

60. Clark and Smith, 44, 81.

61. *The Army Air Forces in the Invasion of Southern France: An Interim Report*, 17; Seventh Army After Action Report, 181.

62. MacMillan, "Fighter Control and Aircraft Warning in Amphibious Operations," 10; *The Army Air Forces in the Invasion of Southern France: An Interim Report*, 8–16; Craven and Cate, 3:430. Combined Operations, Fighter Direction Tenders-FDT 13, 216, 217.

63. MacMillan, "Fighter Control and Aircraft Warning in Amphibious Operations," 11–12.

64. Morison, 11:242.

65. Craven and Cate, 3:417; Seventh Army After Action Report, 144; Morison, 11:246.

66. Craven and Cate, 3:418.

67. *The Army Air Forces in the Invasion of Southern France: An Interim Report*, 17.

68. VI Corps Field Order #1, Annex 3, Naval Gunfire Support, 1; Hewitt, "Planning Operation Anvil-Dragoon," 11; Kent Hewitt, "Executing Operation Anvil-Dragoon," in *Proceedings*, August 1954, Volume 80/8/618.

69. Craven and Cate, 3:415; Seventh Army After Action Report, 82, 131–132 Although these two references differ on the number of daily sorties provided.

70. VI Corps Field Order #1, Annex 3, Naval Gunfire Support, 2–3.

71. Clark and Smith, 44–46; CMH, *Southern France*, 6; VI Corps Field Order #1, Annex 3, 1.

72. Seventh Army After Action Report, 64.

73. Heefner, 185; Clark and Smith, 45–46.

74. Seventh Army After Action Report, 86, 112–113; Clark and Smith, 44.

75. Hewitt, "Planning Operation Anvil-Dragoon," 7; Seventh Army After Action Report, 27, 88.

76. Seventh Army After Action Report, 87.

77. Seventh Army After Action Report, 88.

78. Craven and Cate, 413–414; Seventh Army After Action Report, 31.

79. Seventh Army After Action Report, 66, 100, 104, 122; Hewitt, Invasion of Southern France, 3–4, 23.

80. Seventh Army After Action Report, 105.

81. Hewitt, "Planning Operation Anvil-Dragoon," 8; Heefner, 188; CMH, *Southern France*, 10; Morison, 11:241; Seventh Army After Action Report, 118; AFSC Instructional Publication, 8.

82. Morison, 11:242; Seventh Army After Action Report, 117.

83. *XII Air Force Service Command in Operation Dragoon*, 2–3; Seventh Army After Action Report, 120.

84. Seventh Army After Action Report, 142; CMH, *Southern France*, 12.

85. *XII Air Force Service Command in Operation Dragoon*, 5; Morison, 11:249; Craven and Cate, 3:426; AFSC Instructional Publication, 10.

86. Morison, 11:380–381; Craven and Cate, 3:426; Hewitt, "Planning Operation Anvil-Dragoon," 10; Seventh Army After Action Report, 142.

87. AFSC Instructional Publication, 13; Hewitt, "Executing Operation Anvil-Dragoon"; Seventh Army After Action Report, 127, 136–137.

88. Hewitt, "Executing Operation Anvil-Dragoon"; Seventh Army After Action Report, 147.

89. Seventh Army After Action Report, 131; CMH, *Southern France*, 11; Morison, 11:246; Heefner, 190; Craven and Cate, 3:415; AFSC Instructional Publication, 9.

90. Hewitt, "Executing Operation Anvil-Dragoon"; Seventh Army After Action Report, 132, 159.

91. Seventh Army After Action Report, 133.

92. Craven and Cate, 3:428, CMH, Southern France, 13.

93. Seventh Army After Action Report, 144, 160; Morison, 11:382–383; Hewitt, Invasion of Southern France, 21.

94. Seventh Army After Action Report, 131, 132, 144; Morison, 11:382–383.

95. Seventh Army After Action Report, 143.

96. Morison, 11:383.

97. Morison, 11:383.

98. Craven and Cate, 3:429.

99. CMH, *Southern France*, 13–14; Seventh Army After Action Report, 146–149.

100. CMH, *Southern France*, 13–14; Seventh Army After Action Report, 150.

101. CMH, *Southern France*, 14; Clark and Smith, 109; Seventh Army After Action Report, 181.

102. AFSC Instructional Publication, 13; Hewitt, "Executing Operation Anvil-Dragoon"; Morison 11:383; Clark and Smith, 110–111; Seventh Army After Action Report, 161.

103. CMH, *Southern France*, 14; Clark and Smith, 112–114; Final Report, 6th Army Group, 3, 5; AFSC Instructional Publication, 14; Seventh Army After Action Report, 161–162, 164.

104. Seventh Army After Action Report, 185; Clark and Smith, 115–116.

105. CMH, *Southern France*, 14; Seventh Army After Action Report, 184–185; Clark and Smith, 116–117; 6th Army Final Report, 5; Hewitt, "Executing Operation Anvil Dragoon."

106. Morison, 11:384; Seventh Army After Action Report, 184–186; Clark and Smith, 117–118; AFSC Instructional Publication, 14.

107. Clark and Smith, 123.

108. CMH, *Southern France*, 14; Morison, 11:385; Clark and Smith, 118; Hewitt, "Executing Operation Anvil-Dragoon."

109. Craven and Cate, 3:429.

110. CMH, *Southern France*, 14–15; Seventh Army After Action Report, 179; Clark and Smith, 120–121, 123–124.

111. NHHC, *Operation Dragoon: The Invasion of Southern France*, 15 August 1944, www.history.navy.mil/browse-by-topic/wars-conflicts-and-operations/world-war-ii/1944/operation-dragoon.html; AFSC Instructional Publication, 14; Hewitt, "Executing Operation Anvil-Dragoon."

112. Seventh Army After Action Report, 191; Clark and Smith, 122; Craven and Cate, 3:430.

113. 6th Army Final Report, 6; Hewitt, "Executing Operation Anvil-Dragoon."

114. Seventh Army After Action Report, 193.

115. NHHC, Operation Dragoon, Clark and Smith, 122.

116. Hewitt, Invasion of Southern France, 33.

Conclusion

1. John North, *North-West Europe 1944–5: The Achievement of 21st Army Group* (London, UK: Her Majesty's Stationary Office, 1953), 212–213; US Ninth Army, Engineer Operations in the Rhine River Crossing, June 30 1945, 8, CARL Digital Archive Call Number N11660; XVI Corps Engineers, Crossing the Rhine, 24 March 1945, CARL Digital Archive Call Number N10091.4; Charles B. McDonald, *The US Army in World War II, European Theater of Operations, The Last Offensive* (Washington, DC: Center for Army History, 1993), 266–267.

2. NHHC, Oral History—World War II Rhine River Crossing (1945), Vice Admiral Alan G. Kirk, USN, www.history.navy.mil/content/history/nhhc/research/library/oral-histories/wwii/recollections-of-vice-admiral-alan-g-kirk-rhine-river-crossing-in-1945.html; Navy Department, United States Naval Forces France, Report of Rhine River Crossing by US Navy, no date posted, 2, CARL Digital Library Call Number N9312.

3. Report of Rhine River Crossing, 4–6; Craven and Cate, 3:769–770; NHHC, "Operation Plunder: Crossing the Rhine, March 1945," www.history.navy.mil/content/history/nhhc/browse-by-topic/wars-conflicts-and-operations/world-war-ii/1945/operation-plunder.html; Andrew Rawson, *The Rhine Crossing, 9th US Army and 17th US Airborne* (South Yorkshire, UK: Pen and Sword, 2006), 20–21.

4. Craven and Cate, 3:774; Engineer Operations in the Rhine River Crossing, 19.

5. Engineer Operations in the Rhine River Crossing, 19, Enclosure No. 3. Sea Mules were small, 41-foot-long tugboats that floated atop four pontoons.

6. Engineer Operations in the Rhine River Crossing, 15, 19.

7. Craven and Cate, 3:771; McDonald, 299–300; North, 214.

8. McDonald, 309.

9. McDonald, 313.

10. Craven and Cate, 3:772; McDonald, 300.

11. Craven and Cate, 3:774.

12. Report of Rhine Crossing, 5–6.

13. Combat Studies Institute, *Battlebook 19-A, Rhine River Crossing by US Third Army and Fifth Infantry Division, 22–24 March 1945* (Ft. Leavenworth, KS: Combat Studies Institute, 1984), 38; Engineer Operations in the Rhine River Crossing, 8.

14. Thompson and Harris, 91; Tac Air Comms in the MTO, 24.

15. Hewitt, Invasion of Southern France, Foreword.

16. CTF 122, Subject Report of Normandy Invasion, 3.

Bibliography

Published Primary Sources

Beck, Alfred, et al. *The United States Army in World War II, The Technical Services. The Corps of Engineers: The War Against Germany*. Washington, DC: Center of Military History, 1985.

Blumenson, Martin. *The United States Army in World War II, Mediterranean Theater of Operations: Salerno to Cassino*. Washington, DC: US Government Printing Office, 1993.

Bradley, Omar, and Clay Blair. *A General's Life: An Autobiography*. New York: Simon and Schuster, 1983.

Center for Military History. *Publication 100-11, Omaha Beachhead (6 June–13 June 1944)*. Washington, DC: US Government Printing Office, 1945 (1994 reprint).

———. *Anzio, Pub 72-19*. Washington, DC: US Government Printing Office, n.d.

———. *Southern France, Publication 73-21*. Washington, DC: US Government Printing Office, 1984.

———. *Salerno*. Washington, DC: US Government Printing Office, 1989.

———. *Anzio Beach Head, 22 January–25 May 1944, Publication 100-10*. Washington, DC: Center for Military History, 1990.

———. *Salerno: American Operations from the Beaches to the Volturno, 9 September–6 October 1943*. Washington, DC: US Government Printing Office, 1990.

Clark, Jeffery, and Robert Ross Smith. *United States Army in World War II: European Theater of Operations, Riviera to the Rhine*. Washington, DC: Center for Military History, 1993.

Clark, Mark. *Calculated Risk*. New York: Harper and Brothers, 1950.

Coakley, Robert, and Richard M. Leighton. *US Army in World War II, The War Department: Logistics and Strategy, 1943–1945*. Washington, DC: US Government Printing Office, 1989.

Coll, Blanche, Jean Keith, and Herbert Rosenthal. *The United States Army in World War II, The Technical Services. The Corps of Engineers: Troops and Equipment*. Washington, DC: Office of the Chief of Military History, Department of the Army, 1959.

Combat Studies Institute No. 6. *Larger Units: Theater Army—Army Group—Field Army*. Fort Leavenworth, KS: US Army Combined Arms Center, 1985.

Cooling, Benjamin Franklin, ed. *Case Studies in the Development of Close Air Support*. Washington, DC: Office of Air Force History, 1990.

Craven, Wesley Frank, and James Lea Cate. *The Army Air Forces in World War II, Volume 2: Europe, Torch to Pointblank*. Chicago: University of Chicago Press, 1949.

———. *The Army Air Forces in World War II, Volume 3, Europe, Argument to VE Day.* Chicago: University of Chicago Press, 1951.

Cunnings, Julian, and Gwendolyn Kay Cummings. *Grasshopper Pilot: A Memoir.* Kent, OH: Kent State University Press, 2005.

Davis, Richard. *Carl A. Spaatz and the Air War in Europe.* Washington, DC: Center for Air Force History, 1993.

———. *Bombing the European Axis Powers: A Digest of the Combined Bomber Offensive, 1939–1945.* Maxwell AFB, AL: Air University Press, 2006.

Edwards, Harry. *A Different War: Marines in Europe and North Africa.* Washington, DC: Marine Corps History Center, 1994.

Eisenhower, Dwight D. *Crusade in Europe.* Garden City, NY: Double Day and Company, 1949.

Garland, Albert, and Howard McGraw Smyth. *US Army in War II, Mediterranean Theater of Operations: Sicily and the Surrender of Italy.* Washington, DC: Center for Army History, 2002.

Greenfield, Kent Roberts, ed. *Command Decisions.* Washington, DC: Center for Army History, 1960.

Harrison, Gordon. *United States Army in World War II, The European Theater of Operations, Cross-Channel Attack.* Washington, DC: Department of the Army, Office of the Chief of Military History, 1951.

Headquarters, US Air Force. *Wings at War Series no 2, Sunday Punch in Normandy: The Tactical Use of Heavy Bombardment in the Normandy Operation.* Washington, DC: Center for Air Force History (New Imprint), 1992.

Hewitt, Kent (Evelyn Cherpak, ed.). *The Memoirs of Admiral Kent Hewitt.* Newport, RI: Naval War College Press, 2004.

Hough, Frank, Verle Ludwig, and Henry Shaw Jr. *Headquarters U.S. Marine Corps, Pearl Harbor to Guadalcanal. History of U.S. Marine Corps Operations in World War II, Volume 1.* Historical Branch, G-3 Division: US Government Printing Office.

Howe, George. *United States Army in World War II, The Mediterranean Theater of Operations, Northwest Africa: Seizing the Initiative in the West.* Washington, DC: Center of Military History, 1993.

Kohn, Richard, and Joseph P. Harahan. *Condensed Analysis of the Ninth Air Force in the European Theater of Operations.* Washington DC: Office of Air Force History, 1984.

Lohse, Alexandra, and Jon Middaugh. *US Navy Operations in World War II, Operations Torch: The American Amphibious Assault on French Morocco.* Washington, DC: Naval History and Heritage Command, 2018.

McDonald, Charles. *The US Army in World War II, European Theater of Operations, The Last Offensive.* Washington, DC: Center for Army History, 1993.

Momyer, William. *Airpower in Three Wars (WWII, Korea, Vietnam).* Maxwell AFB, AL: Air University Press, 2003.

Morison, Samuel Eliot. *History of the United States Naval Operations in World War II, Volume 2: Operations in North African Waters, October 1942–June 1943.* Boston: Little, Brown, and Company, 1975 Reprint.

———. *History of the United States Navy Operations in World War II, Volume 9:*

Sicily—Salerno—Anzio, January 1943–June 1944. Boston: Little, Brown and Company, 1954.

——. *History of United States Navy Operations in World War II, Volume II: The Invasion of France and Germany 1944–1945.* Boston: Brown and Little and Co., 1957.

Office of the Assistant Chief of Air Staff, Intelligence. *Reports from Mediterranean Army Air Forces: The Army Air Forces in the Invasion of Southern France: An Interim Report.* Washington, DC: Center for Air Force History (Reprint), 1992.

Ruppenthal, Roland. *The United States Army in World War II, The European Theater of Operations, Logistical Support of the Armies, Volume I: May 1941–September 1944.* Washington, DC: Center of Military History, 1985.

Thompson, George Raynor, and Dixie Harris. *United States Army in World War II, The Technical Services. The Signal Corps, The Outcome Mid-1943–1945.* Washington, DC: Center for Military History, 1991.

Truscott, Lucian. *Command Missions: A Personal Story.* New York: E. Dutton and Co, 1954.

USAF Historical Studies. No. 74 *Airborne Missions in the Mediterranean 1942–1945.* Maxwell AFB, AL: USAF Historical Division, 1955.

US Army. *Engineer School Special Text ST 25-1: History and Traditions of the Corps of Engineers.* Fort Belvoir, VA: The Engineer School, 1953.

US Navy. *Combat Narratives: The Landings in North Africa, November 1942.* Washington, DC: Office of Naval Intelligence, 1944.

Von Der Osten, Robert. *LST 388: A World War II Journal.* Deeds, GA: Atlanta Publishing, 2017.

War Department. *Basic Field Manual, Landing Operations on Hostile Shores.* Washington, DC: US Government Printing Office, 1942.

Published Secondary Sources

Adleman, Robert, and George Walton, *The Champaign Campaign.* Boston, MA: Little, Brown, and Company, 1969.

Amphibian Newspaper. Camp Gordon Johnston, Carrabelle, FL.

Atkinson, Rick. *An Army at Dawn: The War in North Africa, 1942–1943.* New York: Henry Holt and Co, 2002.

——. *The Day of Battle: The War in Sicily and Italy, 1943–1944.* New York: Henry Holt and Co., 2007.

Baker, Fran. *Hot Steel: The Story of the 58th Armored Field Artillery Battalion.* Delphi Books, 2014.

Balkoski, Joseph. *Beyond the Beach Head: 29th Infantry Division in Normandy.* Harrisburg, PA: Stackpole Books, 1989.

——. *Omaha Beach: D-Day, June 6, 1944.* Mechanicsburg, PA: Stackpole Books, 2004.

Bass, Richard. *The Brigades of Neptune.* Devon, UK: Devon England, 1994.

——. *Spirits of the Sand: The Story of the United States Army Assault Training Center in Northern Devon.* Brighton, UK: Menin House, 2014.

Benamou, Jean Pierre. *10 Million Tons for Victory: 1944 A Fantastic Armada*. Bayeux, France: Orep Publications, 2014.

Blackwell, Ian. *Fifth Army in Italy, 1943–1945: A Coalition at War*. South Yorkshire, UK: Pen and Sword, 2012.

Blumenson, Martin. *Anzio: The Gamble That Failed*. New York: J. B. Lippencott, 1963.

———. *Mark Clark: The Last of the Great World War II Commanders*. New York: Gongdon and Weed, 1984.

———. "General Lucas at Anzio." In Kent Roberts Greenfield, ed., *Command Decisions*. Washington, DC: Center for Military History, 1990.

Bourque, Stephan. *Beyond the Beach: The Allied War Against France*. Annapolis, MD: Naval Institute Press, 2018.

Bowman, Martin. *USAAF Handbook, 1939–1945*. Mechanicsburg, PA: Stackpole Books, 1997.

Breuer, William. *Operation Dragoon: The Allied Invasion of Southern France*. Novato, CA: Presidio Press, 1987.

Caddick-Adams, Peter. *Sand and Steel: A New History of D-Day*. London, UK: Arrow Books, 2019.

Carter, Worral Reed, and Elmer Ellsworth Duvall. *Ships, Salvage, and Sinews of War: The Story of the Fleet Logistics Afloat in the Atlantic and Mediterranean Waters During World War II*. Washington, DC: US Government Printing Office, 1954.

Clark, Lloyd. *Anzio: Italy and the Battle for Rome—1944*. New York: Atlantic Monthly Press, 2006.

Clifford, Kenneth. *Amphibious Warfare in Britain and America from 1920–1940*. Laurens, NY: Edgewood, 1983.

Cole, Merle. *Cradle of Invasion: A History of the US Naval Amphibious Training Base, Solomons, Maryland, 1942–1945*. Solomons, MD: Calvert Marine Museum, 1984.

Coles, David. "'Hell by the Sea': Florida's Camp Gordon Johnston in World War II." *Florida Historical Quarterly* 73, no. 1 (July 1994).

Combat Studies Institute. *Battlebook 19-A, Rhine River Crossing by US Third Army and Fifth Infantry Division, 22–24 March 1945*. Fort Leavenworth, KS: Combat Studies Institute, 1984.

Combs, Lewis. "Innovation of Amphibious Warfare." *Military Engineer* 36, no. 220 (February 1944).

D'Este, Carlo. *Fatal Decision: Anzio and the Battle for Rome*. New York: Harper Collins, 1986.

———. *Bitter Victory: The Battle for Sicily*. New York: E. Dutton, 1988.

———. *Patton: A Genius for War*. New York: Harper Collins, 1996.

Eisenhower, David. *Eisenhower at War: 1943–1945*. New York: Vintage Books, 1986.

Ewing, Joseph. *29 Let's Go! A History of the 29th Infantry Division in World War II*. Nashville, TN: Battery Press, 1979.

Folkestad, William. *The View from the Turret: The 743 Tank Battalion During World War II*. Shippensburg, PA: Burd Press, 2000.

Gooderson, Ian. *Air Power at the Battlefront: Allied Close Air Support in Europe, 1943–1945*. London. Frank Cass, 1998.

Greenwood, John. "The US Army and Amphibious Warfare During World War II." *Army History*, Summer 1993. PB 20-93-4 (No. 27).

Greham, John, and Martin Mace, eds. *Despatches from the Front: The War in Italy, 1943–1944*. South Yorkshire, UK: Pen and Sword, 2014.

Gutierrez, Dave. *Patriots from the Barrio: The Story of Company E, 141st Infantry Division: The Only All Mexican American Army Unit in World War II*. Yardley, PA: Westholme Publishing LLC, 2018.

Hastings, Max. *Overlord, D-Day and the Battle for Normandy*. New York: Simon and Schuster, 1984.

Heavey, William. *"Down Ramp": The Story of Army Amphibious Engineers*. Landsville, PA: Coachwhip Publications, 2010 Reprint.

Heck, Timothy, and B. A. Friedman, eds. *On Contested Shores: The Evolving Role of Amphibious Operations in the History of Warfare*. Quantico, VA: Marine Corps University Press, 2020.

Heefner, Wilson. *Dogface Soldier: The Life of Lucian K. Truscott*. Columbia: University of Missouri Press, 2010.

Hesketh, Roger. *Fortitude: The D-Day Deception Campaign*. New York: The Overlook Press, 2000.

Hewitt, Kent. "The Allied Navies at Salerno: Operation Avalanche—September 1943." *Proceedings*, September 1953, Volume 79/9/607, US Naval Institute Press.

———. "Planning Operation Anvil-Dragoon." *Proceedings* 80 (July 1954).

Hoyt, Edmund. *The Invasion Before Normandy: The Secret Battle of Slapton Sands*. Lanham, MD: Scarborough House, 1999.

Isely, Jeter, and Philip Crowl. *The U.S. Marines and Amphibious War: Its Theory and Its Practice in the Pacific*. Princeton, NJ: Princeton University Press, 1951.

Jane's Fighting Ships of World War II. New York: Jane's Publishing Company, 1989.

Karig, Walter. *Battle Report, Volume 2: The Atlantic War*. New York: Farrar and Rinehart, 1946.

Katz, Robert. *The Battle for Rome: The Germans, The Allies, The Partisans, and the Pope: September 1943–June 1944*. New York: Simon and Schuster, 2003.

Keegan, John. *Six Armies at Normandy*. New York: Viking Press, 1982.

Kennedy, Paul. *Engineers of Victory: Problem Solvers who Turned the Tide in World War II*. New York: Random House, 2013.

Khan, Mark. *D-Day Assault: The Second World War Assault Training Exercise at Slapton Sands*. South Yorkshire, UK: Pen and Sword Books, 2014.

Kirkland, William. *Destroyers at Normandy: Naval Gunfire Support at Omaha Beach*. Washington, DC: Naval Historical Foundation, 1994.

Kundahl, George. *The Riveria at War: World War II on the Cote D'Azur*. New York: I. B. Tauris Publishing, 2017.

Langsam, Walter. *Historic Documents of World War II*. New York: Van Nostrand Company, 1958.

Ledley, W. V. "Naval Fire Support in Sicily." *Field Artillery Journal*, December 1943. US Field Artillery Association.

Lewis, Adrian. *Omaha Beach: A Flawed Victory*. Chapel Hill: University of North Carolia Press, 2001.

Lorelli, John. *To Foreign Shores: US Amphibious Operations in World War II*. Annapolis, MD: Naval Institute Press 1990.

Mikolashek, Jon. *General Mark Clark, Commander of America's Fifth Army in World War II and Liberator of Rome*. Havertown, PA: Casemate Publishing, 2013.

Miller, Robert. *Division Commander: A Biography of Major General Norman D. Cota*. Spartanburg, SC: The Reprint Company, 1989.

Millett, Alan. *Semper Fidelis: The History of the United States Marine Corps*. New York: Macmillan Publishing Company, 1980.

Nasca, David. *The Emergence of American Amphibious Warfare 1898–1945*. Annapolis, MD: Naval Institute Press, 2020.

Naval Institute Press. *US Naval Vessels, 1943*. Annapolis, MD: Naval Institute Press, 1943.

———. *Allied Landing Craft of World War Two*. Annapolis, MD: Naval Institute Press, 1944.

North, John. *North-West Europe 1944–5: The Achievement of 21st Army Group*. London: Her Majesty's Stationary Office, 1953.

Ossad, Steve. *Omar Bradley Nelson: America's GI General, 1893–1981*. Columbia: University of Missouri Press, 2017.

Overy, Richard. *Why the Allies Won*. New York: W. W. Norton, 1995.

Porch, Douglas. *The Path to Victory: The Mediterranean Theater in World War II*. New York: Farrrar, Straus, and Giroux, 2004.

Price, Alfred. *Luftwaffe Handbook*. New York: Charles Scribner and Sons, 1977.

Price, Frank James. *Troy Middleton: A Biography*. Baton Rouge: Louisiana State University, 1974.

Rawson, Andrew. *The Rhine Crossing, 9th US Army and 17th US Airborne*. South Yorkshire, UK: Pen and Sword, 2006.

Rein, Christopher. *The North African Air Campaign: The US Army Air Forces from El Alamein to Salerno*. Lawrence: University Press of Kansas, 2012.

Robinard, Francois. *50 Aerodromes for the Victory, June–September 1944*. Bayeux, France: Heimdal, 2012.

"Rocket Boats Lay Smoke Screen for Landings." *Popular Mechanics*, February 1945.

Ross, Wes. *146th Engineer Combat Battalion: Essayons*. Unpublished manuscript, National World War II Museum Archive.

Rottman, Gordon. *US World War II Amphibious Tactics: Mediterranean and European Theaters*. Westminster, MD: Osprey, 2006.

Small, Ken. *The Forgotten Dead: The True Story of Exercise Tiger, the Disastrous Rehearsal for D-Day*. Oxford, UK: Osprey Publishing 1988.

St. Clair, Matthew. "Air Support of the Allied Landings in Sicily, Salerno, and Anzio." *Joint Forces Quarterly*, no. 39 (October 2006).

Strahan, Jerry. *Andrew Jackson Higgins and the Boats That Won World War II*. Baton Rouge: Louisiana State University Press, 1998.

Symonds, Craig. *Neptune: The Allied Invasion of Europe and the D-Day Landings*. New York: Oxford University Press, 2014.

———. *World War II at Sea: A Global History*. Oxford: Oxford University Press, 2018.

Weigley, Russell. *Eisenhower's Lieutenants: The Campaign of France and Germany 1944–1945*. Bloomington: Indiana University Press, 1990.

Whitmarsh, Andrew. *D-Day Landing Craft: How 4,126 Ugly an Unorthodox Allied*

Craft Made the Normandy Landings Possible. Cheltenham, UK: The History Press, 2024.

Wilson, Theodore, ed. *D-Day, 1944*. Lawrence: University Press of Kansas, 1993.

Yung, Christopher. *Gators of Neptune: Naval Amphibious Planning for the Normandy Invasion*. Annapolis, MD: Naval Institute Press, 2006.

Archival Sources

Combined Arms Research Library (CARL) Digital Archives, Fort Leavenworth, KS.

1st Infantry Division After Action Report. Call Number N12177.

3rd Infantry Division, Report of Operations, 10 September 1943, Section 1 Operations. No Call Number Assigned.

3rd Infantry Division, Report of Operations, Sicilian Operation, 10 September 1943. No Call Number Assigned.

7th Army After Action Report, *Seventh Army in Southern France and Germany 1944–1945 in Four Phases*, 4. Call Number N13215-A.

82nd Airborne Division, Sicily and Italy, Section 1-Division Report. Call Number N11960.

V Corps Operations Plan NEPTUNE, 26 March 1944. Call Number N7375.

VI Corps, Field Order #1, Naples Italy, 30 July 1944. Call Number N3632.

XVI Corps Engineers, Crossing the Rhine 24 March 1945. Call Number N10091.4.

Adjutant General, US Army letter to Commandant, Command and General Staff College, Fort Leavenworth, Kansas, Subject: Request for Background Information, RE: List of Assault Landings made during World War II, 9 December 1955. No Call Number Assigned.

After Action Report, 747th Tank Battalion, June Thru December 1944. CARL Digital Archive, No Call Number Assigned.

Allied Force Headquarters, Commander-in-Chief's Dispatch, Sicilian Campaign, 1943. CALL Number 15457.

Allied Force Headquarters Memorandum for the Commander-in-Chief, Subject Sicilian Campaign, 26 August 1943. No Call Number Assigned.

Allied Force Headquarters, Staff Memorandum 7: Lessons of Operation Torch, 19 January 1943. Call Number N6024.

Allied Force Headquarters, Subject: Signal Communications of Operation X, 16 February 1943. Call Number 46038c.

Armed Forces Staff College (AFSC), Instructional Publication. "The Invasion of Southern France, Operation Dragoon," Norfolk, VA 1949–1950. Call Number N15878.3.

Armor in Operation Neptune (Establishment of the Normandy Beach Head), A Research Report prepared by Committee 10, Officers Advance Course, Armor School, Fort Knox, KY, May 1949. Call Number N2146.40-3.

Armor School, Armor Invasion of North Africa: A Research Report, Fort Knox, KY. Call Number 2146.43.

Army Service Forces, Office of the Chief Signal Officer, JEIA Rpt. No. 5796 "The Adequacy of the Tactical Air Communications System, Mediterranean

Theater of Operations." 31 October 1944, File No SPSOI 370.2. Call Number N3631.

Assistant Chief of the Air Staff Intelligence, Report by Colonel William Bentley on Paratroop Operations in North Africa, March 17, 1943. Call Number N3047.

Assistant C/S intelligence Historical Division. US Air Force Historical Study, no. 105 (AAFRH-5), Air Phase of North African Invasion, November 1944. CARL Digital Archive. No Call Number Assigned.

Becker, Marshall. *The Amphibious Training Center, Study No. 22.* Call Number N15036A.

C.O.H.Q. Bulletin No Y/1-Notes on the Planning and Amphibious Assault Phase of the Sicilian Campaign, by a Military Observer, October 1943. Call Number N6530.1.

Combined Chiefs of Staff Memorandum 964-2 (CCS 964-2), Firm Recommendations with Regard to Operations ANVIL and OVERLORD, 11 January 1944. Call Number N13096.

Commander Amphibious Force, Atlantic Fleet, Correspondence to Commander-in-Chief US Fleet, Subject: TORCH Operation, Comments and Recommendations, December 22, 942. Call Number N6108.

Commander-in-Chief, Allied Expeditionary Force, Report on Operation Torch. Call Number N7290.2.

Commander Western Naval Task Force. *The Italian Campaign: Western Naval Task Force Action Report of The Salerno Landings: September–October 1943.* Call Number N5339.

Conference on Landing Assaults, 24 May–23 June 1943, US Assault Training Center, ETOUSA, Forward. Call Number N6318A.

Derrill Daniel, "Landings at Oran, Gela, and Omaha Beaches (An Infantry Battalion Commander's Observations)," Armed Forces Staff College, Norfolk, VA, September—January 1947–1948, Call Number N16759.

Eastern Assault Force, United States Army. Lessons from Operation TORCH, 26 December 1942. Call Number N6193.

Engineer Amphibian Command. *Engineer Amphibian Troops and Operations: Tentative Training Guide 4.* Call Number N15535.

Engineer Amphibian Command. *Tentative Training Guide No 7, Engineer Amphibian Troops, The Organization of the Far Shore.* Call Number N15536.

Field Order no. 1 "Neptune," Force "B," 29th Infantry Division. CARL Digital Archive, Call Number N7377-A.

Final Report on Landing Operations LT 3-OT 18, January 8 to January 18, 1942. Call Number R2824.

Fifth Army. *Engineering History, Volume 1.* Call Number N1154A.

Fifth Army History. *Part 1: From Activation to the Fall of Naples.* Registered Copy 338. Call Number N2783A.

First Army Operation Plan NEPTUNE, 25 February 1944. Call Number N7374-A.1.

GMDS. A Study of German Operation at Anzio Beach Head 22 January 44–31 May 44. Combined British, Canadian, and American Staff, April 1946. Call Number N14023.

Ground Liaison Officer School, Joint Air-Ground Action (Part 1), Call number N11134-A.

Headquarters, 1st Infantry Division, Field Order No. 1, 11 October 1942. Call Number N11291.

Headquarters, 1st Infantry Division, Subject: TORCH OPERATION, November 24, 1942. No Call Number Assigned.

Headquarters 5th Army Invasion Training Center. Training Doctrine, May 20, 1943. Call Number N6429.

Headquarters, 7th Army. Report of Operations of the United States Seventh Army in the Sicilian Operation, 10 July–17 August 1943, APO #750, 1 October 1943. Call Number Special 940514273U56r0.

Headquarters, 7th Infantry. Brief Resume of the Action of RLG-7, Commanding General, Western Task Force, Lessons Learned from Operation TORCH. Call Number N12155.

Headquarters, 9th Infantry Division. Notes on Training an Amphibious Division, 30 October 1942. Call Number N6148.

Headquarters, 12th Air Force. *XII Air Force Service Command in Operation Dragoon.* Call Number 11609.

Headquarters, 58th Armored Field Artillery Battalion. After Action Report Against the Enemy, 22 July 1944. No Call Number Assigned.

Headquarters Amphibious Training Command. Training Circular 10, December 17, 1942, Synopsis of Events, 38th Infantry Division Landing Exercise. Call Number N3095.

Headquarters Army Ground Forces. *Development of DD Tanks*, 6 June 1946. Call Number N13700.

Headquarters Services of Supply, North African Theater of Operations, US Army, Operation Dragoon. Call Number N3663-A.

Headquarters Services of Supply, Report of Operations in North Africa, 12 December 1942. Call Number N6186.

Hewitt, Vice Admiral H. K. Action Report Western Naval Task Force, The Sicilian Campaign: Operation "HUSKY," July–August 1943. Call Number N6884.

———. Invasion of Southern France, Report of the Naval Commander, Western Task Force, 15 November 1944. Call Number N4323-1.

Historical Record, Operation Armored Division, Sicily, April 22 to July 25, 1943. Call Number N2146.32-3.

Historical Record—Operations of US Second Armored Division (Kool Force), 5 August 1943. Call Number N11274.1.

Infantry School, Fort Benning Georgia, Advanced Infantry Officers Course 1947–1948, Captain Frank W. Keating, "The Operations of the Fifth Army in the Establishment of the Beachhead at Anzio-Nettuno, South of Rome, 22 January–24 May 1944 (Anzio Campaign)." No Call Number Assigned.

———. Advanced Infantry Officer's Course 1948–1949, Captain Van T, Barfoot, "The Operation of the Third Platoon Company 'L,' 157th Infantry in the Battle of Anzio," CARL Digital Archive. No Call Number Assigned.

———. Advanced Officers Class #1, Major Jewitt A. Dix, Military Monograph: "The 81st Reconnaissance Battalion at Anzio Beach, 12 April 1948." CARL Digital Library. No Call Number Assigned.

Joint Board. *Joint Action of the Army and Navy*. Washington, DC: US Government Printing Office, 1927. No Call Number Assigned.

Kibler, Franklin, and C. T. Schmidt. The General Board, United States Forces, European Theater, The Control of the Build-Up of Troops in the Cross Channel Amphibious Operation "Overlord." No Call Number Assigned.

Knapp, H. S. "Cooperation of the Army and Navy" US Naval War College Lecture, 1907. Call Number 355.46 K67.

Lectures, Joint Q Planning School. Call Number N2773.

MacMillan, E. W. "Fighter Control and Aircraft Warning in Amphibious Operations," AAF School of Applied Tactics, AAF Tactical Center, Orlando FL, January 1945. Call Number N5269.40.

Navy Department, United States Naval Forces France. Report of Rhine River Crossing by US Navy. Call Number N9312.

Operation Plan No. 2-44 of the Western Naval Task Force, Allied Naval Expeditionary Force ("ONWEST TWO"). Call Number N7376.

Reports by Observers on Current Operations in North Africa, February 12, 1943. Call Number N6023.

Report by the Supreme Allied Commander Mediterranean to the Combined Chiefs of Staff on the Italian Campaign, 8 January 1944 to 10 May 1944. Call Number 940.5421A436.

Seventh Army. Report of Operations of the United States Seventh Army in the Sicily Campaign, 10 July–17 August 1943. Call Number Special 940.514273 U56ro.

Supreme Headquarters Allied Expeditionary Force. Mulberry B: D+4 -D+147. Call Number N6117A/N1611B.

Supreme Headquarters Allied Expeditionary Force. SUBJECT: Operation OVERLORD, March 1944. No Call Number Assigned.

United States Naval Administration in World War II. Action Report-Western Naval Task Force, The Sicilian Campaign: Operation "Husky" July–August, 1943. Call Number N6884.

Unit Journal 471st Tank Battalion. No Call Number Assigned.

US Marine Corps. *Tentative Landing Manual, 1934*. Call Number N17315.492.

US Ninth Army. Engineer Operations in the Rhine River Crossing, June 30, 1945. Call Number N11660.

War Department, Services of Supply. Lessons Learned from Recent Amphibious Operations in North Africa, February 12, 1943. Call Number N6023.

War Department Letter to Commandant Command and General Staff School, Fort Leavenworth, Kansas, Subject: Handling Supplies Across the Beaches, 25 October 1944. Call Number N3562.

War Department. Omaha Beach Head 6 June–13 June 1944, Washington, DC: Historical Division, 1945. No Call Number Assigned.

Western Naval Task Force Operational Plan No. 7-43, Short Title "AVON/W1," August 14, 1942. Call Number N6809.

Dwight Eisenhower Presidential Museum, Abilene, KS
Box Number 21, 48

Library of Congress, Manuscripts Division, Washington, DC
Papers of Kent Hewitt, Box Number 2

National Archive, College Park, MD
Record Group 0111

National World War II Museum Digital Archive
Oral Interview, Baumgarten, Harold. www.ww2online.org/view/harold-baumgart
    en#loading-up-and-crossing-the-english-channel.
Oral Interview, Coolidge, Charles. www.ww2online.org/view/charles-coolidge
    #monte-cassino-and-anzio.
Oral Interview, Gatin, Carl. www.ww2online.org/view/carl-gatlin#fighting-in-ca
    sablanca.
Oral Interview, Goad, Roy. www.ww2online.org/view/roy-goad#invasion-at-sa
    lerno.
Oral Interview, Klimas, Irvin. www.ww2online.org/view/irvin-klimas#task-force
    -d-day.
Oral Interview, Skinner, Theodore. www.ww2online.org/view/theodore-skinner
    #combat-tour-in-north-africa.

US Naval Heritage and History Command Digital Archive
FTP-211 Ship to Shore Movement. January 1943. www.history.navy.mil/research/li
    brary/online-reading-room/title-list-alphabetically/s/ship-to-shore-moveme
    nto.html#general.
German Air Force and the Invasion of Normandy by Oberst Walter Gaul. www.his
    tory.navy.mil/content/history/nhhc/research/library/online-reading-room
    /title-list-alphabetically/g/gaf-invasion-normandy.html.
Morton L. Deyo. "Naval Guns at Normandy." www.history.navy.mil/research/lib
    rary/online-reading-room/title-list—alphabetically/n/naval-guns-normandy
    .html.
Operation Dragoon: The Invasion of Southern France. 15 August 1944. www.history
    .navy.mil/browse-by-topic/wars-conflicts-and-operations/world-war-ii/1944
    /operation-dragoon.html.
"Operation Husky, the Invasion of Sicily, and Operation Avalanche, the Invasion
    of Italy." September 2018. www.history.navy.mil/about-us/leadership/direct
    or/directors-corner/h-grams/h-gram-021/h-021-2.html.
Operation Neptune: The U.S. Navy on D-Day, June 6, 1944. www.history.navy.mil
    /browse-by-topic/wars-conflicts-and-operations/world-war-ii/1944/overlord
    /operation-neptune.html.
Operation Overlord: Concept to Execution, Planning the Invasion of France, 1942–1955.
    www.history.navy.mil/browse-by-topic/wars-conflicts-and-operations
    /world-war-ii/1944/overlord/overlord-planning.html.
"Operation Plunder: Crossing the Rhine, March 1945." www.history.navy.mil
    /content/history/nhhc/browse-by-topic/wars-conflicts-and-operations
    /world-war-ii/1945/operation-plunder.html.
"Operation Shingle: Landing at Anzio, Italy, 22 January 1944." www.history.navy

.mil/content/history/nhhc/browse-by-topic/wars-conflicts-and-operations
/world-war-ii/1944/anzio.html.

Oral History—World War II Rhine River Crossing (1945). Vice Admiral Alan
G. Kirk, USN. www.history.navy.mil/content/history/nhhc/research/libra
ry/oral-histories/wwii/recollections-of-vice-admiral-alan-g-kirk-rhine-river
-crossing-in-1945.html.

Rundstedt, Karl Gerd. *Report on the Allied Invasion of Normandy, 20 June 1944.*
www.history.navy.mil/content/history/nhhc/research/library/online
-reading-room/title-list-alphabetically/g/german-report-on-the-allied-inva-
sion-of-normandy.html.

Savannah IV CL 42. www.history.navy.mil/research/histories/ship-histories/dan
fs/s/savannah-iv.html.

US Army Corps of Engineers. Map, 1995, Florida Department of Environmental
Protection. September 2011. Carrabelle, Franklin County, FL 32322. Project
Number: IO4FLo11004. September 1996.

US Naval History and Heritage Command. United States Navy. *Fleet Training
Publication 167(FTP-167), Landing Operations Doctrine.* www.history.navy.mil
/research/library/online-reading-room/title-list-alphabetically/l/landing-op
erations-doctrine-usn-ftp-167.html#ch2-1.

"The US Navy and the Landings at Salerno Italy." www.history.navy.mil/brow
se-by-topic/wars-conflicts-and-operations/world—war-ii/1943/salerno-land
ings/landings-at-salerno-italy.html.

Electronic References

Action Against Enemy/After Action Report, 742st Tank Battalion, 19 June(?)
1944. https://8th-armored.org/8documents/AAR-741-Tank.pdf.

Blazich, Frank. "Bridging the Gap from Ship to Shore." *Haval History* 35, no. 4
(August 2021). www.usni.org/magazines/naval-history-magazine/2021/august
/bridging-gap-ship-shore.

Brown, Joseph Edwin. *Deception and the Mediterranean Campaigns of 1943–1944,
Study Project, Army War College submission,* 1986, 86. https://apps.dtic.mil/sti
/citations/ADA168052.

Combined Operations, Fighter Direction Tenders-FDTs. www.combinedops.com
/FDTs.htm#:~:text=Fighter%20Direction%20Tenders%20were%20floating
,bristled%20with%20aerials%20and%20antenna.

Correspondence, Marshall to Eisenhower, Ref No-R1573, Directive to the Commander in Chief Allied Expeditionary Force from the Combined Chiefs
of Staff, 5 October 1942. National Archives and Records Administration
(NARA), as referenced at: https://liberationtrilogy.com/books/army-at
-dawn/historical-documents/slideshow/.

Darden, James. "Operations of the 1st Division in the Landing and Establishment
of the Beach Head on Omaha Beach 6–10 June 1944," Advanced Infantry Officers Course 1949–1950, The Infantry School, Fort Benning, GA. https://
mcoecbamcoepwprdo1.blob.core.usgovcloudapi.net/library/DonovanPapers
/wwii/STUP2/A-F/DardenJamesR%20CPT.pdf.

DD-627. www.hazegray.org/danfs/destroy/dd627txt.htm.

Department of Defense. *Joint Publication 3-02, Amphibious Operations*. www.jcs.mil /Portals/36/Documents/Doctrine/pubs/jp302/pdf?ver=CbqCq6-mhWVNjs XKkqZRwA%3d%3d2019.

Department of the Navy. *Fleet Training Publication 167, Landing Operations Doctrine*, 1938. www.history.navy.mil/research/library/online-reading-room/ti tle-list-alphabetically/l/landing-operations-doctrine-usn-ftp-167.html#ch1-5.

FM-100-20, Command and Employment of Air Power (1943). www.ibiblio.org/hyper war/USA/ref/FM/FM100-20/index.html#c2s3.

Headquarters, 1st Infantry Division, 301-03: After Action Report Against Enemy, 4 Sept–10 Nov, dated 5 Dec 1942. Collection Historical Records First Infantry Division, RRMRC Digital Archive.

Headquarters 6th Army Group, *Final Report World War II 1 July 1945*. www.trail blazersww2.org/pdf/SixthArmyG3pdf.pdf.

MacDonald, Charles B. "Slapton Sands: The Cover-up That Never Was." Extracted from *Army* 38, no. 6 (June 1988). www.history.navy.mil/content/his tory/nhhc/research/library/online-reading-room/title-list-alphabetically/s /slapton-sands-the-cover-up-that-never-was.html.

Office of the Historian US State Department. FOREIGN RELATIONS OF THE UNITED STATES: DIPLOMATIC PAPERS, 1942, EUROPE, VOLUME III. "Memorandum of Conference Held at the White House, by Mr. Samuel H. Cross, Interpreter." https://history.state.gov/historicaldocuments/frus19 42v03/d471.

Peabody, Hitch. "Paramount Interests: Command Relationships in Amphibious Warfare," Naval War College Paper, Newport RI, 18 May 2004. https://apps .dtic.mil/sti/citations/ADA425987.

Pyle, Ernie. "Life on an LST." *New York Times*, March 4, 1944. http://www.nav source.org/archives/10/16/16idx.htm.

United States Fleet, COMMICH P-006, Amphibious Operations, Invasion of Northern France, Western Task Force, June 1944. Eisenhower Online Archives. http://eisenhower.archives.gov/research/on_linedocuments/d-day/Re port_of_Amphibious_Operations.pdf.

United States Fleet, Headquarters of the Commander in Chief, Navy Department. Subject: Memorandum: Distribution of Naval Commander Western Task Force (CTF 122) Serial 000201 of 25 July 1944 and 1st and 2nd Ends. (Subject: Report of NORMANDY INVASION), dated 15 September 1944. https://apps.dtic.mil/sti/tr/pdf/ADA550844.pdf.

US War Department, *Basic Field Manual: FM 31-5 Landing Operations on Hostile Shores* June 1941. www.ibiblio.org/hyperwar/USA/ref/FM/FM31-5/FM31-5-2 .html#s2.

USS Thompson, Index of Allied Warships during Operation Neptune. www.dday -overlord.com/en/material/warships/uss-thompson.

www.USSMaddox.org.

Index

A-36s attack aircraft, 115, 148, 155, 190

Advanced Amphibious Training Bases, 106–107

Afrika Korps, 49, 87

Air Observation Post Center, 97–98

Air Support Control Center (ASCC), 148–149, 166, 273, 278

air support parties (ASPs), 116, 278

Alban Hills, Italy, 177, 186, 192

Alexander, Sir Harold, 110, 165, 169

Algiers, 49, 79–86

Allen, Major General Terry de la Mesa, Sr., 74, 98, 123–124, 127

"Alligator" tracked vehicle, 38

amphibious assault/operations: air support in, 10, 224–225; beachhead establishment in, 10; challenges of, 16–17; collaboration regarding, 26, 271–272, 273; command relationships in, 9; components of, 272; concerns regarding, 26–27; as core competency, 6–7; critique of, 26–27; debarkation in, 9–10; development of craft for, 23 (see also specific craft); early development of, 14; embarkation in, 9–10; engineer role in, 27; as growth industry, 13; ignorance regarding, 17; inexperience with, 14; lessons regarding, 17; loading requirements for, 28; logistics and communication in, 10–11; naval surface fire support in, 9; offloading process for, 53; process of, 8–9; ship-to-shore movement in, 9–10 (see also ship-to-shore movement); shortage of landing craft for, 21–23; tactical surprise in, 117; Tentative Landing Manual (United States Marine Corps) for, 9; troop requirements for, 31; watercraft

development for, 19, 38. See also specific assaults and operations

Amphibious Assault School, 28, 272

Amphibious Force, Europe, 48

Amphibious Force Atlantic Fleet (AFAF), 27–28, 38, 40, 46, 53, 88–89, 90

Amphibious Force Pacific Fleet, 285n66

Amphibious Objective Area (AOA), 5, 51, 225, 273, 275, 278, 290n10. See also specific operations

Amphibious Training Base (Solomons Island), Maryland, 38–39

Amphibious Training Center (ATC), 1, 31, 36–37, 43–45, 46, 47, 205, 276

Amphibious Training Center (Scotland), 32, 81

Anderson, Major General Johnathan, 62

Andrews, Captain Charles, 143

antiaircraft artillery (AAA) gunners, 61, 116, 162–163

Anzio assault, 173–174. See also Operation Shingle

"Anzio Highway," 277

"Apex" drone boat, 253–254

Army Corps of Engineers, 19, 27, 32–33

Army General Cognitive Testing, 32

Army Ground Forces, 29, 31, 34, 35–36, 46

Army Rangers, 5, 6, 78, 124–125, 182, 185, 192–193, 194

Arzew Beach, Algeria, 32, 78, 98

Attack Transports (APAs), 206

Australia/New Zealand, 16–17

Axis: air attacks of, 133–134, 138; counterattacks of, 130–131; defense strategy of, 112; delaying of, 124; limitations of, 112–113; photo of, 126; political and military turmoil of, 142;

Axis (cont.)
  victory over, 87, 278. See also
  Germany/German forces; specific
  operations

B-24 bomber aircraft, 115, 264
battlefield air interdiction (BAI), 3, 113, 271
Baumgarten, Harold, 1–2, 198
Bayerlain, General Fritz, 228
Beach Control Board, 258
beachhead establishment, 10, 276–277. See
  also specific operations
beachmasters, duties of, 30
beach party, 30, 90, 100, 136–137, 277
Bennet, Rear Admiral Andrew, 95
Biddle, General William, 16
Biological Survey Agency, 19
Biscari, Sicily, 112, 132
Bizerte, Tunisia, 106–107
Blackstone (Western Task Force), 53,
  54–55, 69–70, 71, 72
Battalion Landing Team (BLT), 27, 66, 67
BLT 1-30, 65
BLT 23-0, 65, 66, 67
Board of Construction and Repair (BCR), 20
Braddy, Lieutenant Commander Robert
  E., Jr., 70–71
Bradley, Lieutenant General Omar, 44,
  98–99, 100–101, 111, 135, 203, 216
Brainard, Rear Admiral Noland, 27
Brann, General Donald, 173
Brereton, Lieutenant General Lewis, 203
Brushwood (Western Task Force), 53–54,
  55, 62, 65, 66–67, 68
Build Up Control (BUCO), 237–238
Burroughs, Admiral H. M., 51
Butcher, Captain Harry, 65

C-47 cargo aircraft, 75, 76, 124, 130–131,
  162, 260–261, 276
Caffey, Colonel B. F., 82
Camp Bradford (Little Creek, Virginia), 42
Camp Carrabelle, Florida, 36–37, 43–44, 47
Camp Edwards, Massachusetts, 36, 40,
  42–43
Candee, Brigadier General A. C., 224–225
Casablanca, Morocco, 49, 53, 62, 87
Casablanca Conference, 88, 198
Castiglione, Sicily, 79, 84

Catania, Sicily, 110–111
Cent Force (Husky), 111, 112, 132–137
Central Task Force (CTF), 32, 49, 73–79,
  81–82, 133, 221, 233, 235, 237. See also
  Operation Torch
Churchill, Sir Winston, 16, 23, 24, 50, 87,
  171, 173, 178, 245
cipher procedures, 93–94
Civitavecchia, Italy, 180
Clark, Lieutenant General Mark,
  94, 146, 160, 163–164, 165, 180, 185,
  187–188, 194
Close Air Support (CAS), 113, 116, 137,
  149, 197, 271
Collins, Major General Lawton, 203
Combined Control Center, 278
Combined Task Force 122 (CTF 122), 6
Comiso, Sicily, 112, 132
Commander Landing Force (CLF), 9, 18,
  50–51, 273
Commander of the Amphibious Task
  Force (CATF), 9, 18–19, 50–51,
  257–258, 264–265, 273
communication: for air support, 148–149;
  in amphibious assault, 10–11; confusion
  regarding, 42; delays in, 93–94;
  development of, 42; education for,
  278; improvements to, 278; networks
  for, 278; in Operation Overlord, 20,
  231–233, 234; in Operation Shingle, 190,
  191–192; pigeon, 233; success in, 89
Conference on Landing Assaults 1943,
  200–201, 204
Conolly, Rear Admiral Richard, 95, 105, 119
Cooke, Rear Admiral Charles, 216
Corsica, 256
Cota, Major General Norman, 208
coxswains: at Advanced Amphibious
  Training Bases, 106–107; challenges of,
  91, 138–139; improvements to, 274–275;
  in Operation Avalanche, 151, 154; in
  Operation Torch, 58, 82, 84, 208;
  reduction of, 63; surf challenges of,
  60; unfamiliarity of, 108
cross-channel invasion, 21, 22, 23, 87, 88,
  226. See also specific operations
Crowl, Phillip, 12
Culebra, Island, 16, 19, 26
Cunningham, Admiral Alfred, 82

Dahlquist, Major General John, 250, 264–265
Dai-Hatsu Type 14 landing craft (Japan), 21, 22
Daniels, Josephus, 16
Darlan, Admiral Francois, 51, 84
"Dauntless" dive bomber (SBDs), 54, 61
Dawley, Major General Ernest, 145, 169, 170
D-Day. *See specific operations*
Department of the Navy, 19
Devereau, Brenda, 201–202
Devers, Lieutenant General Jacob, 194, 200, 246
Dewoitine 520, fighter aircraft, 58
Dime Force, Husky, 111, 123–132, 137–138
dive-bombing, 60–61
Dog Island, Florida, 43
Doolittle, Lieutenant General James, 203
Dornier Do 217 bombers (Germany), 155, 188–189
Dual Drive (DD) tanks, 222–223
DUKW ("Duck") 37; benefits of, 274; challenges regarding, 127–128; on D-Day, 158; in Operation Anvil/Dragoon, 253–254; in Operation Avalanche, 156, 157, 158; in Operation Husky, 123, 127–128, 138; in Operation Shingle, 179, 182, 185, 189; photo of, 39, 189; testing of, 38

Eagles, Major General William, 250
Eaker, Lieutenant General Ira, 255
Eastern Task Force (ETF), 49, 79–86, 88, 110, 133. *See also* Operation Torch
8th Air Force, USAAF, 226, 227, 230, 275
Eighth Army (Britain), 110–111, 112, 141, 143, 177
Eighth Fleet, 96, 247
82nd Airborne (AB) Division, 98, 112, 126–127, 145, 167, 233
Eisenhower, General Dwight D.: on amphibious craft building, 23; on amphibious training, 46; in England, 198–199; on Ernest Dawley, 169, 170; on French friendship, 52; on landing craft losses, 22–23, 65; leadership decisions of, 110; on Operation Anvil/Dragoon, 244–245; on Operation Husky, 128, 138; on Operation

Overlord, 209, 226; on Operation Torch, 49, 82, 88; as Supreme Allied Commander, 199, 226, 245, 275; on training, 82, 88, 99
Ellis, Major Earl "Pete," 17–18
embarkation, 70, 83, 90, 91–92, 145–146, 175, 285n69. *See also specific operations*
Engineer Amphibian Command, 29, 30–31, 33, 37–38, 139, 276
engineers, 27, 31, 78, 108
Engineer Special Brigade (ESB), 31, 135, 210–211, 276
England. *See* Great Britain
Eureka (boat), development of, 19, 20–21
European Theater of Operations (ETO), 8, 11, 19, 32, 276
European Theater of Operations, United States Army (ETOUSA), 200, 204
Evinrude Motors, 33
Exercise Beaver, 211
Exercise Copy Book, 98–99
Exercise Cowpuncher, 145
Exercise Muskrat, 211–212
Exercise Tiger, 206–207

Fedhala, Morocco, 62, 68, 91–92
Field Manual 31-5, Landing Operations on Hostile Shores (FM 31-5), 24, 25–26, 28–30, 107–108, 200
Field Manual 100-20, Command and Employment of Air Power's, 115, 117, 179, 225, 275
15th Panzergrenadier Division (Germany), 112, 144, 161, 186
15th Regimental Combat Team (RCT), 119, 121, 122
Fifth Army (United States), 94–95, 145, 175, 190
Fifth Army Invasion Training Center (FAITC), 95, 96–97, 98, 99, 100, 259, 272–273, 274–275
5th Engineer Amphibian Brigade (EAB), 31, 211
fighter control units (FCUs), 115–116, 273, 278
Fighter Direction Tenders (FDTs), 232, 256
First Airborne Task Force (FABTF), 251–252, 260, 262

1st Armored Division (AD), 27, 74, 76–77, 145, 186
First Army (United States), 268–269
1st Engineer Special Brigade (EAB), 31, 74, 78, 90, 211
1st Fallschirmjäger Division (Germany), 181–182, 193
1st Infantry Division (ID), 26, 27, 34–35, 74, 98, 111–112, 123–124, 130, 205, 212, 242
1st Naval Beach Battalion (NBB), 182, 186
First Special Service Force (Sitka), 252, 263
504th Parachute Infantry Regiment (PIR), 124, 130, 131, 162, 174, 183, 187
509th Parachute Infantry, 74, 75, 174, 183
Fleet Training Publication 167 (FTP-167), 18, 107
FLEX (fleet exercises), 18, 20–21
Force 343, 110
Force 545, 110
Forrestal, 261
45th Infantry Division (ID) (United States): in Copy Book exercise, 98; movement into Italy by, 143; in Operation Anvil/Dragoon, 250, 259, 262, 265; in Operation Avalanche, 145, 162; in Operation Husky, 112, 132, 137; in Operation Shingle, 186; photo of, 133; training of, 43, 99
forward air controllers (FACs), 149, 166
4th Infantry Division (ID), 205, 242
France: air threat of, 73; American cooperation with, 52; attacks on, in Operation Torch, 66–67, 73; failures of, 16–17; fighter aircraft of, 68; fleet losses of, 67; Legionnaires of, 71–72; in Operation Torch, 51–52, 58, 81; at Oran, 74, 76; political discussions of, 84; as staging base, 17; United States Army at, 8. See also specific operations
Fredendall, Major General Lloyd R., 49, 73
Free French divisions, 246, 248, 251
French Expeditionary Corps, 177, 180
French Forces of the Interior (FFI), 246–247

Gallipoli Campaign, 16–17, 18
Gaulle, Charles de, 51
Gavin, Colonel James, 123–124
Gela, Sicily, 123–132

Germany/German forces: attacks on, 4, 6; bombardment of, 228–230; deception effort against, 143; defensive lines of, 170; early-morning attacks of, 189; forces of, 254; Germany First strategy and, 21; Gustav Line of, 170, 172, 177, 180, 181–182, 195; impotence of, 253; left hook strategy against, 172–173; at Ludendorff Bridge, 269; Operation Achse of, 141; in Operation Anvil/Dragoon, 264; in Operation Avalanche, 147–148, 154; in Operation Shingle, 192; in poor man's war, 150; regression of, 279; reinforcement of, 181–182; sabotage by, 172; threat of, 155; waning of, 245, 267; Winter Line of, 170. See also Axis
Gerow, Major General Leonard, 203
Goal Post (Western Task Force), 53, 54, 55, 56, 57, 65
Göring Division. See Hermann Göring Division (Germany)
Grandcamp Port, Normandy, 240–241
Great Britain: concerns of, 50; cross-channel invasion plans concerns of, 23; curriculum development of, 36; failures of, 16–17; Mediterranean strategy of, 23, 46, 50, 87, 141, 171; at Oran, 76–77; planning effort in, 93; shipping concerns of, 87; Soft Underbelly strategy of, 110; as staging base, 17; Terminal operation of, 81; US presence in, 200, 201–203, 204; watercraft development of, 19. See also specific operations
Great White Fleet (US), 15
Ground Control Intercepts-Landing Ship Tanks (GCI-LSTs), 116, 232, 273
Gunther, General Alfred, 178
Gustav Line, 177, 180, 181–182, 195
Guzzoni, General Alfredo, 112

Hall, Admiral J. L., 95, 160
Hall, Rear Admiral John, 124, 203
Handy, Major General Thomas, 42
Harmon, Major General Ernest, 69, 72, 145
Harrison, Captain Willard, 131
Harvard University, 33
Haywood, Commandant Charles, 16

Helensburgh, Scotland, 74
Hermann Göring Division (Germany), 112, 117, 127, 145, 162, 165, 182, 186, 188, 194
Hewitt, Rear Admiral Kent: concerns of, 41; on coxswains, 138–139; on doctrine, 107–108; with Eighth Fleet (Amphibious Force Northwest African Waters), 96; on element of surprise, 56; on *FM 100-20*, 117; leadership of, 27–29, 38, 41, 42–43, 95–96, 272; legacy of, 272; on lessons learned, 279; in Operation Anvil/Dragoon, 247–248, 254–255, 259–260, 266–267; in Operation Avalanche, 145, 157, 161, 163–164, 165, 167; in Operation Husky, 116, 117, 118, 127, 128, 130, 136–137; in Operation Torch, 51, 54, 67; on personnel support, 41–42; photo of, 29, 146; on port facilities, 100; as practitioner, 28–29; praise for, 89; on pre-assault bombardment, 89; on training, 68, 99, 139
Higgins, Andrew, 19–21
Higgins Boat, 19
Higgins Industries, 38, 65–66
Higgins Institute, 33
HMS *Alynbank*, 75
HMS *Capertown*, 236
HMS *Ceres*, 236
HMS *Ulster Queen*, 183, 188
House, Major General Edwin J., 148, 166, 173–174
Hughes-Hallett, Commodore John, 238

II Corps (United States), 94, 111, 177, 180
Imperial General Staff (British), 88
Insigny Port, Normandy, 240–241
Isely, Peter, 12
Italy, 7, 112–113, 141, 142–143, 149–150, 170–171. *See also specific locations*

Japan, 15–16, 21
"Joint Action of the Army and Navy," Naval War College Lecture, 24–26
Joint Air-Ground Action Ground Liaison Officer School, 226, 230
Joint Army and Navy Board, 15
Joint Chiefs of Staff, 25–26, 27, 33, 46

Joint US Strategic Committee, 33
Joss Force, Husky, 111, 119–123
Junkers Ju 88 bomber, 125, 147, 188–189

Kasba, French Citadel, 89
Keating, Brigadier General Frank, 36
Kesselring, Field Marshal Albert, 112, 149, 180–181
King, Admiral Ernest J., 38–39, 46, 210
King-Marshall agreement, 46
Kirk, Admiral Alan G., 203, 216, 273
Kirk, Rear Admiral Adam, 132, 133, 135, 137
Klimas, Irvin, 5, 6
Knapp, H. S., 15
Kriegsmarine, 253
Krulak, Captain Victor, 21, 283n30
Krulak, Charles, 283n30
Krupp K5E railway canon (Anzio Annie), 192

L-4 Grasshopper aircraft, 97, 114–115, 121
L-5 Sentinel aircraft, 191
Lake Pontchartrain, Louisiana, 20, 21, 38
Landing Boat Development Board (United States Navy), 20
landing craft, 56–57, 65–66, 68, 95, 96, 107, 224. *See also specific operations; specific types*
Landing Craft and Bases Northwest African Waters (LANCRAB), 95; LANCRAB UK, 203
Landing Craft Assault (LCA) vessel, 1, 3, 175
Landing Craft Flak (LCF), 221
Landing Craft Group Unit, 105
Landing Craft Gun LCG(L)), 221
Landing Craft Infantry (LCI), 101, 103–104, 105, 274. *See also specific operations*
Landing Craft Mechanized (LCMs), 65–66, 213, 268, 269, 271
Landing Craft Personnel (LCP), 40, 65, 86, 91
Landing Craft Personnel (Ramp) (LCP(R)), 21, 91
Landing Craft Personnel Large (LCPL), 65
Landing Craft Support (Medium (LCS)), 221

Landing Craft Tank (LCT), 101, 103, 107, 274, 277. *See also specific operations*

Landing Craft Vehicle (LCV), 91

Landing Craft Vehicle Personnel (LCVP), 21, 65, 101, 104, 269, 271. *See also specific operations*

Landing Ship Tank (LST): benefits of, 274; characteristics of, 101–103; construction of, 23; embarkation from, 107; function of, 101–103; innovations of, 101; in logistics, 277; overview of, 24, 101–103; photo of, 25, 121, 129, 136, 184, 260; pontoon bridges and, 120; retainment of, 173; runnels and, 106; shallow-water tankers and, 77; shortfall of, 252–253, 260. *See also specific operations*

Lattre de Tassigny, General Jean de, 251

Laycock, Captain, John N., 120

Leadership and Battle Training Center, 97

Legionnaires (France), 71–72

Lejeune, Lieutenant General John A., 17

Lewis, Rear Admiral Spencer, 250, 264–265

Licata, Sicily, 111, 112, 119

Little Creek, Virginia, 38, 41, 53

Lobnitz Pier, 238–239

logistics and communication, 10–11, 139, 277–278. *See also* communication

Lowry, Rear Admiral Frank C., 173–174, 185–186, 250, 260

Lucas, Major General John P., 34, 170, 178, 185, 187–188, 192–194

Ludendorff Bridge, 268–269

Luftwaffe. *See* Germany/German forces

Lyme Bay, England, 205–207

MacArthur, General Douglas, 12, 171–172

Mackenson, General Friedrich, 192

Manitowoc Shipbuilding Company, 33

Mark IV tank (Germany), 127, 157

Mark VI tank (Germany), 127

Marrakech, Morocco, 73

Marseilles, France, 244, 248

Marshall, General George C., 22, 46, 50, 52, 88, 210, 246

Marshall-King agreement, 91

Marvin, Colonel George, 186

Mathinet, Maurice, 62

Maudlin, Bill, 135

McNair, Lieutenant General Leslie, 46

Mediterranean Allied Air Force (MAAF), 178, 179, 183, 255, 256

Mediterranean Theater of Operations (MTO), 8, 11, 50, 104–105, 113. *See also specific operations*

Middleton, Major General Troy, 112, 135, 162

Miller, Donald, 12

Millet, Allen, 12

minefields (naval), 151–152, 167, 182–183

Molotov, Vyacheslav, 50

Monte Sole, Sicily, 120, 121

Montgomery, Field Marshal Bernard, 111, 203

Moon, Admiral Don, 203

Morison, Admiral Samuel Eliot, 28, 116, 177–178, 266

Morocco, 49, 73

Morris, Captain Robert, 186

Movement Control, in Operation Overlord, 237–238

Mulberrys, artificial harbor, 239–240, 277

Mussolini, Benito, 87, 110, 141

Naples, Italy, 142, 172

Naval Operating Base (NOB), 33, 38, 73, 96

Naval Scout Boat School, 208

naval surface fire support (NSFS), 5, 9, 57, 60, 89, 127, 273–274. *See also specific operations*

Naval War College, 15

Navy Bureau of Ships, 65–66

Nimitz, Fleet Admiral Chester, 12, 171–172

Nineteenth Army (German), 254

9th Air Force, 201, 227, 228, 230, 232, 269, 271

9th Armored Division (AD), 269

Ninth Army (US), 268, 269, 270

9th Infantry Division (ID), 28, 53, 55, 79, 81

Ninth Tactical Air Force, 207

Noce, General Daniel, 204

Nogues, General Charles, 72

Normandy Beach: assessment of, 279; concerns regarding, 50; EAB operations at, 32; land, air, and sea domains of, 6; landing on, 1; photo of, 25; tidal variations of, 214–215, 216–217. *See also* Operation Overlord

North Africa, 7, 49–50. *See also* Operation Torch
North African Tactical Air Force, 114
Northwest African Air Forces (NWAAF), 108, 113, 114, 115, 147, 166

O'Daniel, Brigadier General John, 95, 160–161, 174, 250
Office of the Director of Training Centers (Fifth Army), 94–95
Oliver, Admiral G. N., 163–164
Omaha Beach. *See* Operation Overlord
101st Airborne Division, 232, 233
116th Infantry Regiment, 3, 205, 219, 230
141st Regimental Combat Team (RCT), 152, 158–159
142nd Regimental Combat Team (RCT), 152, 154, 157, 160
143rd Regimental Combat Team (RCT), 156, 157, 160
168th Regimental Combat Team (RCT), 79, 81, 82, 83
Onslow, North Carolina, 26, 74
Operation Achse, 141, 149
Operation Anvil. *See* Operation Dragoon (Operation Anvil)
Operation Avalanche: air support for, 144–145, 148, 150, 155, 166, 225; antiaircraft artillery (AAA) control in, 162–163; antiaircraft weapons in, 156; assault waves of, 152, 154, 158–159; Avellino drops in, 162–163; beachhead establishment in, 168, 276–277; Blue Beach in, 152, 153, 158–160; convoys for, 146–147; Cowpuncher exercise in, 145; deception effort in, 143; defense plan of, 150–151; EAB operations at, 32; evacuation discussion in, 164–165; German defense in, 154, 155, 158–159, 160, 161–162, 165–166, 168; Green Beach in, 152, 155–157; H-Hour for, 146; H-Hour of, 151; Landing Craft Infantry (LCI) in, 151; Landing Craft Vehicle Personnel (LCVP) in, 151, 152, 154, 156; Landing Ship Tank (LST) in, 151, 158, 160; landings in, 147, 153, 154–155, 156–157; littoral operations in, 143; loading challenges of, 146, 167; logistics support for, 235; losses in, 155, 158, 161; map of, 153, 164; minefields in,

151–152, 154, 167; obstacles of, 151–152; overview of, 143–144; photo of, 159; planning for, 141, 143, 147, 149; Red Beach in, 152, 154, 156, 157, 160–161; reinstatement of, 178; review of, 165–168; route to, 146–147; scout crews in, 152; shaping the battle in, 147; ship-to-shore movement in, 154, 167; success in, 165; surf conditions in, 161; tanks in, 151; testing at, 43; training for, 145; Yellow Beach in, 152, 153, 158–159, 160, 161
Operation Barbarossa, 49–50
Operation Barclay, 117, 118
Operation Baytown, 141, 143
Operation Bodyguard, 233–234
Operation Bolero, 32, 199
Operation Diadem, 194
Operation Dragoon (Operation Anvil): airborne forces in, 251–252, 256, 260–261, 263; aircraft missions of, 276; amphibious assault in, 265; Blue Line in, 249–250, 252; bombardment in, 255, 262–263, 264; Camel Force in, 250–251; CATF/CLF relationships in, 273; convoys in, 258–259, 262; course of action map for, 249; D-Day of, 247; domains of, 257–258; exercises of, 260; fire support and transportation area overlays for, 257; German threat in, 253, 264, 265; H-Hour of, 250–251, 254, 263; invasion force ships for, 261; invasions of, 11; as joint/combined operation, 247; Landing Craft Tank (LCT) in, 263, 264; Landing Ship Tank (LST) in, 261–262; lessons from, 266–267; littoral obstacles in, 253–254; losses in, 266; merchant shipping in, 277; naval surface fire support (NSFS) in, 257, 260; origin of, 244; paratroopers in, 251–252; photo of, 259, 260; planning for, 209–210, 245–246, 247–248; pre-H-Hour period of, 252, 254, 262–263; Red Beach in, 251, 264; shore fire control networks in, 257; sites for, 249–250; strategy of, 248; supplies for, 258–259; surface attack in, 250; training for, 259–261; weaponry stock for, 256; weather conditions for, 262, 263–264

Operation Fortitude, 118, 234
Operation Husky: airborne troops
in, 111; aircraft availability for, 114;
aircraft beneficial to, 97; air plan for,
115; amphibious vessel function in,
102; Axis defense strategy in, 112, 125,
131; Bailey's Beach in, 132, 134, 135,
137; beachhead establishment in, 120,
276–277; beach party challenges in,
136–137; benefits of, 88; Blue Beach
in, 119, 122, 124, 125, 127, 135, 137;
causeway usage in, 120; Cent Force in,
132–137; "Copy Book" exercise for, 98;
critique of, 116; Dime Force in, 123–132,
137–138; EAB operations at, 32; element
of surprise in, 307n19; embarkation
procedure during, 92; "Fracture" effort
in, 118; German attacks in, 127, 128–129;
German counterattack in, 134; Green
Beach in, 119, 121, 124, 125, 132, 134–135;
H-Hour of, 98, 125, 133; Italian defense
and surrender in, 121, 125–126; joint
fires in, 130; Joss Force in, 119–123;
L-4 aircraft in, 114–115; Landing
Craft Infantry (LCI) in, 119–120,
124, 138; landing craft photo in, 106;
Landing Craft Tank (LCT) in, 119,
138; Landing Craft Vehicle Personnel
(LCVP) in, 102; landing procedures
of, 100; Landing Ship Tank (LST) in,
119, 122, 124, 127, 138; lessons from,
137–140, 165–166; logistics support for,
235; losses in, 121–122, 125, 131, 134–135;
main effort forces of, 110–111; naval
surface fire support (NSFS) in, 127;
paratrooper assault in, 117–118, 124,
140; personnel beneficial to, 97; photo
of, 106; planning for, 65, 87–88, 111;
pontoon usage in, 120, 129, 131; port
facilities limitations of, 100; POWs
in, 131; preparation for, 94–108; Red
Beach in, 119, 124, 125, 127, 132, 134;
Route 115 in, 129–130, 134; ship-to-
shore movement in, 135; strategy
in, 110–111, 112, 118, 123–124; supply
challenges in, 127–128; surf challenges
in, 119–120, 133; sustainment in, 100;
tactical level in, 118; as tutorial, 108;
weaponry challenges in, 127; weather

in, 118–119; Wood's Hole Beach in, 132,
134, 135, 137; Yellow Beach in, 119, 121,
124, 125, 127, 132, 133, 135
Operation Market Garden, 270
Operation Mincemeat, 117, 118
Operation Neptune, 201, 203, 233–234
Operation Nutmeg, 255
Operation Overlord: aerial spotting
in, 220–221; airborne operations in,
231, 233; airframes of, 275; air-ground
coordination in, 232; amphibious
assault legacy of, 198; amphibious
training sites in, 204–206; armor
delivery in, 222; assault waves in,
209; assumptions regarding, 201;
bombardment in, 226–230, 242; Build
Up Control (BUCO) in, 237–238;
combined arms mix of, 221–222, 223;
communication services in, 220,
231–233, 234; conference regarding,
200–201; cross-channel invasion
of, 200; cross-channel organization
in, 236–237; DD (Dual Drive) tanks
in, 222–223; Dog Sector in, 209, 211,
215–216, 223–224, 242; EAB operations
at, 32; Easy Red Sector in, 222–223;
embarkation in, 209, 212; exercises in,
206–207, 211–212; Fox Green Sector
in, 222–223; goal of, 200; H-Hour of,
215; landing craft in, 209, 210; Landing
Craft Infantry (LCI) in, 206, 209, 236;
landing craft shortage in, 209; Landing
Craft Tank (LCT) in, 206, 209, 213,
221, 222, 223–224, 236; Landing Craft
Vehicle Personnel (LCVP) in, 206;
Landing Ship Tank (LST) in, 206,
209, 213, 236; landings in, 213–215, 216–
217, 218–219; leadership of, 203–204;
lessons from, 241–243; liaisons of,
207; loading process for, 212; logistics
support for, 234–235, 238, 240; losses
in, 206–207, 219–220; map of, 213, 217;
merchant vessels in, 235–236; mission
statement of, 199; monograph packet
for, 208; Movement Control in, 237–
238; naval surface fire support (NSFS)
in, 6–7, 216–217, 219–220, 223–224;
object of, 199; Omaha Beach in, 203,
205, 209, 211, 214, 215–216, 219–220, 222,

241; overview of, 241–243; paratroopers in, 233; phases of, 217; planning for, 171; port locations for, 212–213, 240–241; pre-H-Hour fires of, 215–216, 225, 226–227; preparation for, 199–201, 207–208, 211–212; ship-to-shore movement for, 208, 209, 240; Shore Fire Control Parties (SFCPs) in, 220, 231–232; Shuttle Control in, 236; success of, 7; synthetic harbor in, 238–240; traffic loggerheads in, 212; training for, 201, 202–203; Transportation Plan in, 227, 228–230; Utah Beach in, 203, 205, 209, 211, 222, 241

Operation Plunder, 269

Operation Pointblank (Combined Bomber Offensive), 199–200, 226

Operation Richard, 188

Operation Roundup, 21, 30, 38, 50, 85, 87

Operation Shingle: air component of, 178, 189–190, 196–197, 275; asset use in, 196; beach analysis in, 174–175; beachhead establishment in, 187–188; challenges of, 183; communication in, 190, 191–192; debarkation in, 186; fleet composition of, 174; German defense in, 181, 194; German offensive in, 193–194; Green Beach in, 182, 183; H-Hour of, 180, 182; Horsefly missions in, 190; Landing Craft Infantry (LCI) in, 185; Landing Craft Tank (LCT) in, 182, 183, 185; Landing Craft Vehicle Personnel (LCVP) in, 175, 183; Landing Ship Tank (LST) in, 175–176, 182, 183, 185; landings in, 176; left-hook strategy in, 194; lessons from, 197; loading changes in, 196; logistics support for, 235; losses in, 181, 185, 194; minesweepers in, 182–183; Operation Husky as compared to, 140; in Operation Overlord, 225; oversight to, 182; overview of, 173–174; photo of, 184; Pineapple missions in, 190; planned assault for, 174, 177–178, 180; radio-controlled bombs of, 188–189; Red Beach in, 175, 182, 183; Rover Joe missions in, 191; sea as maneuver space in, 196; Spitfires in, 189; statistics regarding, 185; success of, 185; surf conditions in, 186; weather in, 186; Web Foot exercise in, 179; X-Ray Beach in, 186; X-Ray Force in, 175; Yellow Beach in, 175, 182, 186

Operation Slapstick, 141, 143

Operation Sledgehammer, 21, 30, 50

Operations Plan 712 *Advance Base Operations in Micronesia (OP-712)*, 17–18

Operation Torch: airpower advantages in, 275; Amphibious Objective Areas of, 51; Amphibious Training Base for, 39; amphibious training for, 52–53; Apple Beach movement in, 79, 81, 84; area of operations of, 71; batter up code for, 57–58; beach conditions during, 59–60, 65, 77–78; beachhead establishment in, 276–277; beach strategy of, 62; Beer Beach movement in, 79, 81, 82, 83–84; Blue Beach movement in, 58–59, 69–70, 71–72; capsizing in, 65; Central Task Force (CTF) in, 32, 49, 73–79, 81–82, 133, 221, 233, 235, 237; Charlie Beach movement in, 79, 81, 82; Commander Landing Force in, 50–51; Commander of the Amphibious Task Force in, 50–51; command structure for, 50–51; dead space hitting in, 61; debarkation failures of, 63–64, 70, 86, 92; delays in, 56, 64, 88; dive-bombing in, 60–61; Eastern Task Force (ETF) in, 49, 79–86, 88, 110, 133; element of surprise in, 56, 64; embarkation challenges of, 70; failures of, 66; fleet for, 54; French fighter aircraft in, 68; Green Beach movement in, 57–58, 59, 70–71, 71–72; H-Hour of, 56, 62, 64, 77, 82, 88; improvements following, 78–79; landing craft in, 65, 66, 68; as learning evolution, 50; lessons from, 85–86, 94, 108; loading sequence of, 63; logistics support for, 235; losses of, 60, 66, 83–84, 86, 275; naval surface fire support (NSFS) in, 56, 72; origin of, 49; overview of, 85–86; photo of, 63, 69, 83; planning for, 40, 49, 69, 75; purpose of, 50; Red Beach movement in, 58, 68, 69–70, 71–72; report regarding, 85; reviews of, 88; scheme of maneuver of, 80; scouts for, 62; ship

Operation Torch (*cont.*)
  path of, 54; ship-to-shore movement
  in, 57, 58, 62–63, 86; Shore Fire
  Control Parties (SFCPs) of, 55–56;
  shore party in, 77; surf conditions
  during, 59–60, 66; Terminal operation
  in, 81; testing at, 43; training
  complaints regarding, 99; truck
  offloads in, 83; U-Boats (Germany)
  and, 51; V formation in, 56–57; Vichy
  attacks in, 58, 59, 66–67; Vichy French
  loyalties and, 51–52; Villain operation
  in, 75; watercraft movement in, 61–62
  (*see also specific crafts*); weather for, 54,
  75; Western Naval Task Force for, 28;
  Western Task Force (WTF) for, 49,
  53–73; X Green Beach movement in,
  76; X-Ray Beach movement in, 73–74,
  76–77; X White Beach movement in,
  76; Yellow Beach movement in, 58;
  Yorker Beach movement in, 73–74,
  77–78; Zebra Beach movement in,
  73–74, 76, 78. *See also* Western Task
  Force (WTF)
Operation Varsity, 269–270
Oran, Algeria, 74–75, 76–77, 78, 96
Ost (East) German troops, 254
Ottoman Empire, 17

P-38 fighter aircraft, 115, 148, 155
P-40 fighter aircraft, 62, 63
P-47 fighter aicraft, 3, 4–5, 255
P-51 fighter aircraft, 149
Pacific theater, assault requirements
  of, 12
Paestum, Italy, 142–143
paratroopers, 117–118, 124, 140, 233,
  251–252, 270
Parks, Brigadier General Floyd, 35
Patch, Lieutenant General Alexander,
  246, 248, 261, 263, 265
Patton, General George: on the Air
  Force, 117; concerns of, 272; delay of,
  67; on the French, 52; on landings,
  69; letter to, 41, 43; on the Navy,
  53; on Operation Avalanche, 168; in
  Operation Husky, 130; in Operation
  Torch, 28, 49; in Operation Varsity,
  271; photo of, 69

Petain, Marshal Philippe, 51, 52, 84
Philippine, Islands, 7, 14
Piano Lupo, Sicily, 125, 126–127
pigeons, 233
Ponte Olivo, Sicily, 112, 123, 131
pontoons, 120, 129, 131
Port Blondin, Morocco, 66–67
Port Lyautey airfield, Morocco, 55, 57, 62
Provisional Troop Air Carrier Division, 260
Psychological Warfare Bureau, 52
Pyle, Ernie, 102

Quartermaster "Q" School (London),
  202, 273
Quebec Conference, 173, 198

radio, development of, 278. *See also*
  specific radios
Ramsay, Admiral Bertram, 203
Reggio Calabria, Italy, 141
Rhine River, Germany, 268, 270
Ridgeway, Major General Mathew, 130,
  162, 169–170
Riviera, French, 248–249
Rogers, Rear Admiral Bertram, 250
Rome, Italy, 196, 259
Rommel, Field Marshal Erwin, 49, 226–227
Roosevelt, Brigadier General, Theodore, 15
Roosevelt, Franklin D., 23, 50, 87, 247,
  271–272
Rover Joe (air missions), 149, 191
Royal Air Force (RAF), 113
Royal Naval Air Service, (RNAS), 273
Royal Navy, 8, 74
runnels, 106
Russian Caucasus Front, 16
Ryder, Major General Charles, 49, 79

Safi, Morocco, 69–70, 71, 72–73
Salerno, Italy, 32, 43, 142, 159, 172. *See also*
  Operation Avalanche
Sampson, Admiral William, 14
Saville, Brigadier General Gordon P.,
  247, 261, 263
Saving Private Ryan (film), 2, 8
Scoglitti, Sicily, 112, 117–118, 133
Scott, General Winfield, 14
SCR radios, 93, 184–185, 191–192, 220,
  224, 232, 278

2nd Armored Division (AD), 55, 99
2nd Battalion Landing Team (BLT), 59, 60–61, 74
Second Tactical Air Force, 207
Services of Supply Branch (Army), 31, 34, 85, 201
751st Tank Battalion, 174, 183
Seventh Army, 108, 111, 112, 116, 135–136, 247, 251, 257, 258, 266
79th Infantry Division (ID), 269, 270
Shafter, General William, 14
ship-to-shore movement: in amphibious assault, 9–10; amphibious truck for, 38; capabilities of, 274; conditions of, 56; deficiencies of, 86; development of, 40–41, 274; FLEX 5 and, 20–21; improvements to, 277; lessons regarding, 17; network challenges of, 93; in Operation Avalanche, 154, 167; in Operation Husky, 135; in Operation Overlord, 209, 240; in Operation Torch, 57, 58, 62–63, 86; planning for, 1; report of, 90–91; requirements of, 56; Transportation Quartermaster for, 90
Ship to Shore Movement (US Navy), 107
Shook, Hal, 2–5
Shore Fire Control Parties (SFCPs), 55–56, 220, 231–232
shore party, 29–31, 40–41, 77, 90, 277
Shore Party School, 40–41
shore regiments, elements of, 99–100
shore-to-shore movement, 31, 34, 40, 46, 105
Shuttle Control, in Operation Overlord, 236
Sicily, 7, 32, 43, 65, 87–88, 99–100, 105–106, 108–109, 111, 112. *See also* Operation Husky
Sidi Bel Abbès, Algeria, 97–98
Sidi Ferruch, Algeria, 83
Signal School, amphibious, 41–42
16th Infantry Regiment, 124, 126–127
16th Panzer Division, 150, 151, 155–156, 168
16th Regimental Combat Team (RCT), 205, 222
Slapton Sands, United Kingdom, 205–207, 211, 214
Smith, General Holland M., 20, 27, 39
Solomons Island, Maryland, 38–39, 53
Soviet Union, 22, 49–50, 246

Spaatz, Lieutenant General Carl "Tooey," 204, 226
Spitfires (fighter aircraft), 149, 189, 190
SS *Contessa*, 54, 55, 61–62
Stalin, Joseph, 50
Stark, Admiral Harold, 203
Supreme Allied Command, 198
Swensen, Lieutenant Colonel Edwin, 81

Task Force 34 US Atlantic Fleet, 51, 53
Task Force 80, 145
Task Force 80.4, 118, 166
Task Force 81, 96, 124, 145, 183–184
Task Force 81.8, 151–152, 167
Task Force 83, 96
Task Force 84, 96, 250
Task Force 85, 96, 132, 250
Task Force 86, 119
Task Force 87, 250
Task Force 122.5, 268
Task Force 141, 110
Task Force 163, 247–248
Task Force Omaha, 203, 205, 213, 217–218, 231
Task Force Utah, 203, 205, 211, 218, 231
Task Force X-Ray, 124, 125
Task Group 80.4, 118
Task Group 81.8, 151–152
Task Group 124.7, 5
TBY radios, 93
Tedder, Sir Arthur, 113
Tentative Landing Manual (United States Marine Corps), 9, 18, 31–32
3rd Infantry Division (ID): joint amphibious assault of, 26; in Operation Anvil/Dragoon, 250, 251, 259, 261–262, 263, 265; in Operation Husky, 119; in Operation Shingle, 174, 185, 188, 192–193, 194; in Operation Torch, 62; structure of, 285n66; training of, 34–35, 53, 98; vessel challenges of, 105
3rd Panzergrenadier Division (Germany), 144–145, 187
Third Army (US), 268, 271
30th Infantry Division (ID), 194, 269, 270
30th Regimental Combat Team (RCT), 119, 122–123
34th Infantry Division (ID), 27, 79, 81, 97, 98, 145

36th Infantry Division (ID): exercises of, 43–44; Gustav Line assault by, 180; instructions for, 97; mountain fighting of, 170–171; movement into Italy by, 143; in Operation Anvil/Dragoon, 250–251, 252, 259, 262, 263, 265; in Operation Avalanche, 145, 147, 153, 161; in Operation Shingle, 181; training of, 98

39th Regimental Combat Team (RCT), 81–82

Toffey, Lieutenant Colonel, John, Jr., 58

TBF (torpedo bomber), 54

Torre di Paestum, Italy, 155–156, 157

training/amphibious training: at British Amphibious Training Center (Scotland), 81–82; challenges of, 39–40; critique of, 34–35; curriculum development for, 35–36; deaths in, 1–2; development of, 48; elements of, 43, 74, 96–97; equipment during, 92; for field grade officers, 97; international, 48; landing craft, 95; mission and objectives for, 37; as navy responsibility, 46; phases of, 36; poop sheets of, 35–36; requirements for, 210; schools for, 41; for shore party, 40–41; for staff officers, 97; for subordinate units, 93. See also specific operations

Transportation Quartermaster, 41, 90, 99, 145–146

Trident Conference, 141

Troubridge, Thomas, 51, 73

Truscott, Brigadier General Lucian: on air forces, 113; leadership of, 57; legacy of, 272; in Operation Anvil/ Dragoon, 248–249, 252, 257–258, 261, 263, 265; in Operation Avalanche, 168; in Operation Husky, 111, 122; in Operation Shingle, 185, 194; in Operation Torch, 55–56, 58–59, 60, 62; restrictions of, 89; at Web Foot exercise, 179–180

26th Panzer Division, 161, 194

26th Regimental Combat Team (1st ID), 77–78

29th Infantry Division (ID), 205, 212, 231, 242

29th Panzer Division, 161, 181–182, 187, 188

Two-Ocean Navy Act, 23

U-Boats (Germany), 51, 87

United Kingdom. See Great Britain

United States: dominance of, 14; importance of, on global stage, 16; industrial capacity of, 24; Japanese competition with, 15–16; planning locations for, 93; war authority of, 266. See also specific operations

United States Army: amphibious operations of, 7–8, 34, 271–272; assault techniques of, 118; collaboration with Navy and, 271–272, 273; critique of, 26–27; cross-channel invasion proposal of, 34; curriculum development of, 35–36; division of labor of, 33; element of surprise of, 56; improvement benefits to, 279; job classifications of, 33; Landing Operations Doctrine of, 24; Navy cooperation with, 96; Navy rivalry with, 24–25; in shore-to-shore movement, 34; support for, 8; training for, 33, 35; weaponry developments in, 24

United States Army Air Forces (USAAF): critique of, 116–117; defensive air missions of, 273; improvement benefits to, 279; mission of, 5; in Operation Avalanche, 167; in Operation Husky, 114; in Operation Overlord, 225, 226–228, 230; in Operation Varsity, 271; role of, 273, 275; schism in, 113; support from, 276

United States Coast Guard, 8, 19, 33, 36

United States Marine Corps: advanced base concept of, 17; amphibious assault doctrine of, 9; amphibious assault interest of, 17; assault techniques of, 118; attack preferences of, 56; in Central Pacific, 33–34; concerns regarding, 16; critique of, 26–27; curriculum development of, 36; division of labor of, 33; FLEX (fleet exercises) of, 18; Landing Operations Doctrine (FTP-167) of, 18; purpose of, 24; size limitations of, 33; success of,

7; support for, 56; *Tentative Landing Manual* of, 9, 18; training of, 35; watercraft development for, 20

United States Navy: amphibious operations of, 271–272; amphibious training and command by, 27–28; Army cooperation with, 96; Army rivalry with, 24–25; campaign requirements of, 15; collaboration with Army and, 271–272, 273; critique of, 26–27; cross-channel invasion proposal of, 34; Gator Navy in, 53, 271–272; importance of, 15; improvement benefits to, 279; Landing Boat Development Board of, 20; *Ship to Shore Movement* of, 107; in shore-to-shore movement, 34; support from, 8

USS *Ancon*, 115, 148, 155, 162, 203

USS *Arkansas*, 218

USS *Augusta*, 67, 203

USS *Baldwin*, 218, 219

USS *Barnegat*, 62

USS *Bayfield*, 203

USS *Bernadou*, 70, 72

USS *Biscayne*, 184

USS *Boise*, 125, 128, 163

USS *Brooklyn*, 63, 120, 122, 183, 188

USS *Buck*, 120, 122–123

USS *Carmick*, 218–219

USS *Catoctin*, 247–248, 256

USS *Charles Carroll*, 65

USS *Chenango*, 62, 63

USS *Cole*, 70

USS *Dallas*, 61–62

USS *Dorthea Dix*, 70

USS *Doyle*, 218

USS *Eberle*, 57–58

USS *Emmons*, 218

USS *Endicott*, 261

USS *Frankfort*, 218, 219

USS *Harding*, 218, 219

USS *Harris*, 70

USS *Henry T. Allen*, 60

USS *Jeffers*, 125

USS *Joseph T. Dickman*, 65

USS *Knight*, 143

USS *Lakehurst*, 72

USS *Leonard Wood*, 64, 65

USS *LST-386*, 115, 157

USS *Ludlow*, 67, 160

USS *Maddox*, 125

USS *May*, 183

USS *Mayo*, 183

USS *McCook*, 218–219

USS *Monrovia*, 115

USS *Murphy*, 66–67

USS *Nevada*, 218, 232

USS *Philadelphia*, 156, 163

USS *Plunkett*, 183

USS *Ranger*, 54, 58

USS *Robert Rowan*, 131

USS *Samuel Chase*, 96, 130

USS *Sangamon*, 58, 60–61

USS *Santee*, 73

USS *Savannah*, 59, 125, 128, 155, 156–157

USS *Sentinel*, 121–122

USS *Shubrick*, 126

USS *Shulrick*, 125

USS *Texas*, 6, 218, 219

USS *Thomas Jefferson*, 64, 65

USS *Thompson*, 5–6, 7, 218

USS *Titania*, 72

USS *Tulagi*, 263

USS *Tuscaloosa*, 218

USS *Wilkes*, 67

Utah Beach. *See* Operation Overlord

Ventotene Island, Italy, 143

Vera Cruz, Mexico, 14

very high frequency (VHF) radios, 90, 191

VI Corps (United States): as Kodak Force, 250; in Operation Anvil/Dragoon, 248, 252, 265–266; in Operation Avalanche, 143, 145, 161–162, 164, 168; in Operation Shingle, 179, 185, 187, 188, 190, 192, 193, 194

Visual Forward Direction Post, 232

von Rundstedt, Field Marshal Gerhard, 228, 242

von Vietinghoff, Colonel General Heinrich, 144, 163

Walker, Major General Fred, 145, 147

War Department (United States), 19

Web Foot exercise, 179–180

Wehrmacht. *See* Germany/German forces

Wesel, Germany, 269
Western Naval Task Force, 28, 107, 111, 143, 261
Western Task Force (WTF): area of operations of, 71; Blackstone of, 53, 54–55, 69–70, 72; Brushwood of, 53–54, 55, 62, 65, 66–67, 68; capsizing in, 65; debarkation challenges of, 70; dive-bombing and, 60–61; establishment of, 110; Fifth Army from, 94; Goal Post of, 53, 54, 55, 56, 57, 65; Green Beach movement in, 57–58; invasion plans of, 55; lack of training of, 88; landing craft losses of, 60; for Operation Torch, 49; overview of, 53–73; photo of, 129; reviews of, 88; in Safi, 69–70; Shore Fire Control Parties (SFCPs) of, 55–56; structure of, 110; sub task forces of, 53–54; Task Force 34 US Atlantic Fleet and, 53; travel path of, 55

Wiese, General Friedrich, 254
Wilbur, Brigadier General William H., 95
Wilkes, Rear Admiral John, 203
Wilson, Sir Henry Maitland "Jumbo," 171, 246
Winchell, Walter, 44
World War I, 10, 16, 52
Wurzburg radars (Germany), 6
Wygand, General Maxime, 51

X Corps (Britain), 143, 177, 180
XII Air Support Command (ASC), 94, 114, 116
XII Tactical Air Command (TAC), 189, 247, 255–256
XVIII Airborne Corps, 269–270